GW00459068

The *Islamic* Challenge in Europe

The *Islamic* Challenge in Europe

Raphael Israeli

Transaction Publishers
New Brunswick (U.S.A.) and London (U.K.)

Copyright © 2008 by Transaction Publishers, New Brunswick, New Jersey.

All rights reserved under International and Pan-American Copyright Conventions. No part of this book may be reproduced or transmitted in any form or by any means, electronic or mechanical, including photocopy, recording, or any information storage and retrieval system, without prior permission in writing from the publisher. All inquiries should be addressed to Transaction Publishers, Rutgers—The State University of New Jersey, 35 Berrue Circle, Piscataway, New Jersey 08854-8042. www.transactionpub.com

This book is printed on acid-free paper that meets the American National Standard for Permanence of Paper for Printed Library Materials.

Library of Congress Catalog Number: 2008012407
ISBN: 978-1-4128-0750-0
Printed in the United States of America

Library of Congress Cataloging-in-Publication Data

Israeli, Raphael.
    The Islamic challenge in Europe / Raphael Israeli.
        p. cm.
    Includes bibliographical references and index.
    ISBN 978-1-4128-0750-0 (alk. paper)
    1. Muslims—Europe. 2. Europe—Ethnic relations. I. Title.

D1056.2.M87I87 2008
305.6'97094—dc22

                                                            2008012407

To Hava Lazarus-Yafeh
The Person, the Scholar, the Colleague, the Friend
In Memoriam

Contents

Acknowledgments

The present volume concentrates on various regions of the European continent: BENELUX, Scandinavia, Southern and Central Europe and the Balkans, where Muslim presence has barely begun to be noticed and where adjustments can still spare those comparatively smaller nations the aches and pains that the main centers of Muslim immigration into Europe have experienced. It purposely left out the three great countries of the continent (Britain, France, and Germany), where Muslim populations have grown so large that they have already altered forever the social structures of those countries.

Apart from the customary tribute that I pay to my home institution—The Harry Truman Research Institute for the Promotion of Peace at the Hebrew University in Jerusalem, for the help, the inspiration and the facilities that made this work possible, I am indebted here to Professor Irving Horowitz of Rutgers University, NJ, whose sound advice guided me through the final edition of this book. I remain responsible alone, however, for the errors and misinterpretations that may have befallen the text.

Jerusalem, Summer 2008

Introduction: Some Preliminary Reflections

This volume is a sequel to this author's *Islamikaze*[1] where this very term was first coined and the ideological and organizational setting was laid out for the 11 September 2001 events and their aftermath. Since then, mainly due to the extraordinary security measures adopted by the United States, which were much maligned by those whose acts of terror had caused the tightening of security in the first place, not one more significant terrorist event has occurred on U.S. soil, at least for now. Conversely, European allies of the United States, including some of those who reneged on their alliance and elected to cut deals with the terrorists, have become the immediate and repetitive victims thereof. But this volume will not deal with the already well-established and deeply entrenched Islam in the Big Three of Europe (Britain, France, and Germany) where its demographic impact amounting to millions (three, six, and three million respectively) has irretrievably altered the social and political make-up of those countries. Islam in those countries has been massively dealt with in other works and monographs, and it will be referred to occasionally only as a matter of comparison with other concentrations of Islam in Europe. Here we shall be concerned with the lesser agglomerations of Islam in clusters of European countries, such as Southern and Central Europe, BENELUX, Scandinavia and the Balkans where Muslim communities, though proportionately high (3 to 6% of the total population), do not amount nevertheless as yet to the many millions that render them critical masses likely to dramatically turn around the politics, the internal security and the domestic welfare, of those countries. Islam had penetrated Europe and the West since the Middle Ages, first during the invasion by the Arabs in the eighth century from the south, when they conquered Spain, Portugal and half of France, before they retreated after the Charles Martel victory in 732 near Poitiers/Tours, and the eight centuries of Muslim rule in Andalusia that ended with their final retreat from Granada in 1492 under the relentless advance of the Spanish *reconquista*. The second invasion by the Ottomans from the East, led to the fall of Constantinople into their hands and went as far as the gates of Vienna before it was arrested and thwarted in 1683. Ultimately, the break up of the Ottoman Empire during World War I put an end to that long occupation, the residues of which can still be seen in today's Bosnia, Albania, Kosovo, and Macedonia. The current third penetration is done by immigration, and the demographic inundation of Europe, together with a campaign of *da'wa* (religious propaganda) to help spread Islam, aided by a terrorist wave trying to intimidate the West.

1

International terrorism has not been limited to the confines of the "Islamist" struggle against the West in the international arena, but has expanded into the domestic scene of Islamic countries where local "Islamist" oppositions aspire to seize power from current illegitimate rulers supported by the West. This is the genesis of the Bali, Casablanca, Istanbul, Sinai, Amman, Ryad and Jedda acts of terror that were primarily directed against visiting aliens after 11 September, in order to destroy the economic base tourism had with some of those hated regimes. More ominously, many a homegrown "Islamist," who was allowed to sow lethal propaganda in Western democracies where he had initially sought asylum from oppression in his land of origin, has used his familiarity with his adoptive land to turn it into his object of terror. This is the background for 11 September and then the Madrid (March 2004) and London (July 2005) horrors.

For too long had the world accepted the Palestinian hijackings of the 1970s and 1980s as a "natural" calamity which initiated this era of international terrorism. Instead of fighting against them and uprooting them, Western governments and passengers accepted with staggering docility to be stripped at airports and searched, to have their otherwise sacrosanct privacy encroached upon and trampled upon in public, to pay ever- increasing air fares in order to cover security costs, and to repeat the mantra that a "solution to the Palestinian conflict will resolve the problem." America has reversed itself and resolved to fight only after the events of 11 September 2001. Madrid elected to yield to the terrorists' demands. London "changed the rules" only after it was rocked by a series of attacks on its public transportation. Other countries have yet to follow.

The public debate was turned on its head after the van Gogh murder in the Netherlands in 2004 and then the anti-Denmark outburst of Muslim rage in the Cartoon Affair of early 2006. Previously, far from recognizing that the fight against terrorism in Iraq, Afghanistan and worldwide was launched by the United States as a defensive measure after it was attacked on its home territory, America's detractors in Europe and the Muslim world claimed, on the contrary, that it was the American offensive moves in those countries which prompted terrorism, exactly as it was Israel's "injustices" towards the Palestinians that had triggered terrorism in the first place. Cause and effect were reversed. So, instead of joining the United States in its universal struggle against terrorism, and thus also rid themselves of its menace, they blamed the violence on American and Israeli policies, thus unwittingly becoming its unwilling accomplices and its unsuspecting next victims. However, the Cartoon Affair of early 2006 has dramatically demonstrated that the general Muslim wrath against the West and Israel had just been compressed for years due to the measures taken by Muslim governments who were afraid of American retribution. It is also likely that the wrath was contained when Muslims were confident that their presence in the West constituted a critical mass, numerous enough to instill fear of potential civil disorder in the European governments. The fear from American retribution, which was brought to bear in Afghanistan and Iraq, may have been somewhat mitigated by America's proven constraint to absorb the atrocious behavior of Syria, Saudi Arabia, Iran, and Egypt just like during the havoc of the 1973 oil price rise. In that regard one might say that the Arabs are constantly testing the limits of what America will tolerate, but they are also aware that America turns a blind eye to misdemeanors in order to secure the uninterrupted oil flow. Thus America (and other Western countries for that matter) are seen to favor totalitarian rulers in the Middle East, fearful of the regimes that may replace them—the "devil they know" approach. No American President wishes to be responsible for creating another Iran, after the ignominious behavior of Carter *vis-à-vis* the Shah.

The waves of recriminations of the Muslim world against the West and Israel, have also been expressed in the rise of Muslim parties in Turkey, Egypt, Jordan, and the Palestinian Authority. The unbridled desire of the Iranians to go nuclear, and the thug-like rhetoric of its President Ahmadinejad against Western values and the Jews in general, to the point of denying the *Shoah* in blatant terms, are indications of the spreading anti-Western antagonism in the world of Islam. The zeal in the Islamic world is directed not only against Israel and the West, but aims primarily to sweep out of power their own Western-allied regimes which are regarded as American stooges. As the major Egyptian paper, *al-Ahram,* put it, "religious identity has replaced nationalist ideology,"[2] and that applies not only in Muslim countries but also amidst Muslim minorities throughout their diasporas. This means that Muslim terrorism will continue to rise in both Europe and the Muslim world, hence the relevance of the present volume as a follow up to the saga of 11 September and its aftermath. One has to realize, nevertheless, the distortions of the basic contours of Islam, by both scholars and politicians, who wish to depict a more benign and less menacing picture of the Islamic rise than it is in fact. This is done through two distinctions that have become conventional wisdom among both critics and proponents of Islam. One is the artificial bifurcation between the so-called "Islamists" or radicals, i.e., the minority "bad guys" who spoil the lot by their violent deeds, lend a bad reputation to the majority of their coreligionists and wage war against the West and Israel ; and the majority itself, which is arguably "peace-loving" and shunning violence and has no quarrel with West. The other artificial, and equally spurious, distinction wants us to believe that Judeophobia, which is an attenuated sort of anti-Semitism, posing as anti-Zionist and anti-Israel, has nothing to do with anti-Semitism. While Islam as a whole carries no traces of anti-Semitism, they want us to believe, its present anti-Jewish manifestations are no more than a much less lethal and vastly less threatening Judeophobia. It is clear that these "scientific" distinctions, though pursued by some scholars of reputation, and may have some empirical merit to them, have much more to do with political correctness and with a degree of sheepish *dhimmi*-like submissiveness, or fear of being accused of racism, than with historical reality.

It is unconvincing that the Muslims are merely anti-Israel and anti-Zionist and not anti-Semitic, when Jews in the Diaspora are habitually attacked for no reason whatsoever today apart from the fact that they are Jews. They were historically mistreated, beaten, massacred or forced to convert until compelled to leave the lands of Islam and migrate to either Israel or Europe. French Jews, British Jews, or Belgian Jews are all citizens of the countries in which they live, and cannot influence the policies of the Israeli government even if they wished to do so. To attack them is undeniably an expression of the innate anti-Semitism in Islamic thinking. The equivalent in Jewish attitudes would be for Jews to attack their Muslim fellow-citizens in European countries every time an Arab or a Muslim country defames, vilifies, or demonizes (or indeed physically attacks) Jews in the media, school curricula, or subjects them to economic boycotts individually or collectively, all of which happen on a sustained daily basis. But that would be a case of Islamophobia, and the fact that it does not happen often proves firstly that Islamophobia, at least on the part of Jews, is a figment of the Muslims' imagination (bandied about precisely to combat the very notion of their pervasive anti-Semitism); and secondly that Jews, at least in the Diaspora, can distinguish between right and wrong, and have never lost their sense of justice and civilized behavior despite the relentless provocations of Muslims, not only radicals, against them. When part-time processes of liberalization are adopted, like in Algeria, Jordan, Egypt, and lately Palestine, namely when people are given the opportunity to express themselves freely, it is invariably political Islam that gains votes, and since it is popular vote, it cannot be said to represent "radicals," exactly as it cannot be claimed that the more than 60% of the Palestinians who voted for Hamas are all "Islamists."

If, as some claim, there were a certain percentage of Muslims who are "radical," "fundamentalist" or simply "Islamists," while the majority is Muslim of the good brand, which politicians like Bush and Blair plainly call "peace-loving," then how come that we see vast crowds, which seem to represent the local majorities, in every place where Muslims burst out in violence, be it in Cairo, Gaza, Pakistan, Tehran, Kabul or during the Cartoon Affair? What happens to those supposedly peace-loving majorities if the violent crowds do not represent them? And when Muslim columnists, including Western-educated and degree-holders, write in the mainstream journals of the Muslim world, including in "moderate" and "pro-Western" countries, genocidal wishes against Jews and Israel, virulent recriminations against the West, and expressions of joy after 11 September or every time a bus or a restaurant blow up in the West with dozens of victims, are those representative of "radicals" or of "Islamists," or of "judeophobic" individuals who stay clear from blatant anti-Semitism? Then, where is the difference between peace-loving Muslims and "Islamists"? So, while there are theological differences of nuance between Sunnites and Shi'ites, and within the Sunnites between the four Schools of law (*madhahib*), for instance between the puritanical Wahhabis of the Hanbali cult and the more lenient Hanifites on matters of *Shari'a* law, there appears to be commonality, if not unanimity among them with regard to Jihad wars. The denigration of the Jews and the contempt and hostility towards the West are also universal, because they all draw from the same medieval Abu Yussuf and Ibn Taymiyya and the more modern Hassan al-Banna, Sayyid Qut'b, or Mawdudi. Understandably, not every Muslim would observe the strictest prescriptions of those scholars to the letter, but at the same time no sweeping doctrinal authoritative alternative to them has emerged to challenge them, let alone replace them.

Those referred to as "Islamists" call and regard themselves simply as plain Muslims, who are perhaps more zealous than others and wish to fulfill Muslim goals here and now. But are they so distinguishable from other Muslims that they deserve to be treated as if they were different Muslims or as if they had invented a different version of Islam? All religious Muslims venerate the great masters of radical Islam like Hasan al-Banna, Sayyid Qut'b, Mawdudi, and Qaradawi, even if they are not categorized as "radical." The latter relate to the masses of common Muslims the way activists or militants in a political party refer to the rank and file of sympathizers who only vote when the day comes, but are not involved in any day-to-day politics. But we do not distinguish between "radical" and "common" party members. Yes, they differ, in both cases, as far as the degree of commitment, activity and observance are concerned, but we cannot set them apart ideologically, and they continue to belong to the same core of belief and conviction. For if there were a "liberal" or "moderate" tendency in Islam, it would be evinced, first of all, by theologians of Islam who would stand up courageously and battle against the ideas and theses of the "Islamists." However, while truly moderate and daring individuals of Muslim descent (and sometimes conviction) do exist, principally in the safety of the West, we cannot discern any significant trend of moderation and "peace-loving" inclination which rallies behind it masses of Muslims. So, what is erroneously dubbed "moderate" or non-Islamist Islam, is actually the silent majority who is, unfortunately, more likely than not to follow the outbursts of jubilation when the Jews or Israel are harmed, to watch bluntly anti-Semitic series on popular television which depict Israelis (and Americans for that matter) as blood-drinkers, world-conspirers and children-killers, and to absorb genocidal statements by their leaders and clerics avidly and reiterate their belief in the same nonsensical slogans and conspiracy theories that are circulated in their media. One year after the events of 11 September 2001 Dan Rather of *CBS News* undertook a worldwide survey of Muslim (not Islamist) reactions to those horrific events. From a sample of eight Muslim countries, between Morocco and Pakistan, where he polled the literate population in remote villages in each one of those countries, the overwhelming majority of the populace, which was not "radical," spelled out their conviction that the horror was "of course" perpetrated by the Jews, the Mossad, and such delusive fairy tales.

Did the Palestinians suddenly become "Islamists" when the radical Hamas won elections among them? No, they remained as Muslim as they were before the elections. They erupted into unabashed joy when 11 September happened, much to Arafat's embarrassment who sent his security forces to disband those "radical" children to avoid further disgrace. Why did they do that? Because they were indoctrinated by their school textbooks, which assured them the imminent victory of Islam against the "corrupt and tyrannical" West. They burst forth in jubilation when Israeli and Western families are shown torn into pieces, and they re-enacted harrowing scenes of explosions against Israel, showing cardboard buses or restaurants burning and limbs of children flying around, with huge crowds of children, passers-by, shopkeepers, students, and policemen clapping hands and rejoicing. Even their universities and school plays staged such reen-actments. Could all those be "Islamists"? No, not in their eyes. Israelis and the West are perceived as the enemies of Islam (not of Islamists). Therefore one should rejoice at their defeat, and because they are not defeated often enough for the Muslims' taste, no Muslim can skip the delight of replaying that defeat and savoring it in slow motion. Another question is why are America and Israel particularly targeted and their national flags usually accompany each other, when a Muslim frenzy of burning and destroying blows up in any part of the globe. The answer is two-fold: first both of those countries stand out as the consummate representatives of strength, modernity, prosperity and success, something which only brings out the impotence and backwardness of the Islamic world. That is the source of "humiliation" that Muslims reiterate so often and so intensely, for only the existence of that successful world permits Muslims to grasp what they missed, and they get humiliated by the hopelessness of lagging behind. Secondly, their dream to remedy the situation by creating a *Pax Islamica* to encompass the entire universe has been scuttled principally by Israel in its immediate vicinity and by America worldwide, for the United States is the only power able and willing to stand up to them and obstruct their goal of establishing a world caliph-ate. That double frustration has been shared by Muslims in general, regardless of whether one categorizes them as "Islamists" or otherwise.

After 11 September a talk show was held by *al-Jazeerah* network (repre-senting what is known as "moderate" and "peace-loving" Islam) where the question was posed to the panelists and the viewers about whether Bin Laden was a terrorist or a hero. The only moderate panelist, a Tunisian, was mocked and humiliated by his co-panelists and the moderator of the show for daring to dissent from the otherwise unanimous opinion which crowned Bin Laden as a national hero. Viewers who called or e-mailed from the entire Islamic world, were almost unanimous in the same consensus. That was not a poll among "Islamists," but among the rank-and-file of Muslims, most of whom were supposedly the educated owners of personal computers. Yet, their reaction was "Islamist" in substance. So, where is the distinction? Yes, there are Islamikaze activists who are ready to blow themselves up for the cause of Islam in the process of killing Westerners and Jews. But they are only a handful, who are recruited, trained, financed, indoctrinated, and dispatched by a vast infrastructure of Muslim states, organizations and individuals, and surrounded by the sympathy and admiration of the vast masses of the Muslim public and the mainstream press in countries that are clients of the United States or signed peace with Israel. Who is then an "Islamist" among all those layers of activists and supporters, and who is the "moderate" and "peace-loving"?

In the United States and Europe, it was found that several Muslim intellectuals, leaders and clerics, who gained favor with the authorities and access to the highest echelons of power, for their supposed "moderation" and their openness to "dialogue," were later arrested for their illicit fundraising for Muslim terrorist organizations, for incitement to terrorism or for suppressing women's rights; did they suddenly turn from "moderate" to "radical"? No, they were the same Muslims who were perceived previously as moderate when they acted or refrained from acting in a certain way, who became "Islamists" when they were caught red-handed engaging in subversive acts. In both instances they acted as Muslims in the name of Islam; it is Western and westernized Muslim scholars who attached to them those epithets which they themselves never recognized. Similarly, clerics and other Muslims who dub the Jews "descendants of pigs and monkeys," basing themselves on a Qur'anic passage, or cite the *Hadith* which claims that on the Day of Judgment Jews will hide behind rocks and trees, but the latter will acquire the magic power of denouncing them and inviting the Muslims to come and kill them, are not exactly setting themselves apart from Islamists by being less anti-Semitic and merely "Judeophobic." All Muslims who cite those passages, and they do regularly and perennially, are making blunt anti-Semitic and genocidal statements against the Jews, and no amount of rhetorical maneuvering can mitigate that fact.

It seems that the fictional distinction that is drawn between Islam and "Islamists," which is usually made either by Western scholars and politicians or by Muslim moderates who live in the West, emanates more from an instinct of self-defense and survival than from a sober observation of reality. In Muslim countries themselves it is often hard to tell who is who, inasmuch as Palestinian, Saudi, Egyptian, and Pakistani clerics, who belong to the "moderate" establishment, often issue *fatwa*s and deliver sermons that are every bit as "extremist" as the "radical" ones. Even imported or home grown Muslim clerics in the West do not make any effort to distinguish or to distance themselves from "Islamists," because they themselves cannot tell the difference. Western scholars and politicians, who want to cater to Islam, for electoral or other worldly perks, on the one hand, but cannot deny the rage of their own people against violent Islam, on the other hand, find shelter in that distinction which allows them to claim that the Islam they support or defend is "moderate," while the violence that their people condemn emanates solely from the "extremist Islamists." At the same time politicians and scholars critical of Islam need that distinction to shelter themselves from accusations of "racism," as if multi-cultural and multi-racial Islam were a "race," or from anti-Muslim bias and hatred. Muslim scholars and public figures who live in the West resort to that distinction in order to avoid a blanket condemnation of Islam of which they are part, and to escape suspicions by their coreligionists that they "sold-out" to the West or that they committed an act of "treason" against their culture and religion. Many of them find it more expedient to claim that they are "secular Muslims," a notion that is unacceptable to Islam in all its nuances, and some of them convert to Christianity in order to feel free to lash out at their previous religion, though they know that they are handily offset by the much larger numbers of Westerners who convert to Islam.

The fact is that throughout the Muslim world, the legitimacy of Israel is challenged, the Holocaust is denied systematically, as evidenced by the popularity there of such Holocaust deniers as Robert Faurisson, Roger Garaudy, or David Irving, by the prohibition of *Schindler's List* on their screens and the violent declarations of the Iranian President on both scores. This is a common denominator of most Muslims, nothing differentiates between "radicals" and "moderates" there, exactly as anti-Jewish stereotypes, be they anti-Semitic or "Judeophobic" are current among them all, with few exceptions. That is the reason why we find them contradicting themselves on the Sho'ah, denying it on the one hand and wishing Hitler had brought his annihilation plan to completion on the other; urging a "scholarly, free and objective" research of the Holocaust, in order to prove that it never was. Similarly, the belief in and the spread of the *Protocols of the Elders of Zion,* the Blood Libel, the poisoning of wells by Jews, the conspiracy theories where Jews star, are recurring themes in Palestinian (not only Hamas) as well as mainstream Egyptian, Jordanian, Saudi, Pakistani and others' writings, systems of beliefs and propaganda. Genocidal threats against the Jews abound not only in bin Laden's statements and in Ahmadinejad's delusions, but also in columns of Egyptian, Saudi, Palestinian and other newspapers of the respectable mainstream. Is this Judeophobia of the "moderates" or plain anti-Semitism of the "Islamists"? Words have significance, and it is imperative to streamline our vocabulary, otherwise we are under the permanent threat of losing our ability to express what we mean or to comprehend what we are told.

Matters are further complicated and made less comprehensible to Western minds by the paranoia and conspiracy theories that are very widespread in the Muslim world, among "Islamists" and others alike, whether Muslims are modern and Western-educated or traditionalist and obscurantist. Those theories that are rampant even among Muslims living in the West would insist that world leaders who support Israel are Jewish (like Presidents Reagan and Bush). That the UN of all places, is the mastermind of the Jews who utilize it as the tool for their world dominion, and that the major violent acts that shook the world, like the world wars, the world revolutions and 11 September, are all the fruit of Jewish imagination and execution. Their minds are so permeated with these nonsensical theories that they become impervious to logical, rational debate that is open to argument, discussion and to conviction. Therefore, the difficulty of dealing with Muslim minds consists not only of removing the mountains of pure delusion that choke their free thinking, but also of persuading them that the very attempt to counter-argue those futilities is not necessarily part of the world conspiracy that is being woven against them. It is possible to explain their imaginary picture of the world by their need to project on their enemies the analytical shortcomings that bewitch them, but it is impossible to move them out of the illusory scenarios that they have constructed around themselves and then they cling to them with a tenacity that defies and contradicts Western standards of perception and conduct. The result is that even when Muslims initiate and launch an act of violence, they accuse the West of it and dub it, or what led to it, as an act of aggression of which they are the victims and which warrants their retaliation.

As long as the Muslim anti-Western and anti-Semitic discourse was internal, little attention was paid to it in the outside world. But since the end of the Afghanistan War (1979-89) which also signaled the end of the Cold War and the return of the *Mujahideen* to their Muslim home countries, tremendous energies were released by the *Afghanis* (i.e, the foreign battle-hardened graduates of the war in Afghanistan) which were channeled both domestically ("Islamist" activity in Algeria, Saudi Arabia, Sudan, Lebanon, Egypt, Jordan, Pakistan, and Taliban Afghanistan), and internationally to wage a worldwide Jihad, led by bin Laden's al-Qa'ida, but carried out simultaneously on Arab, American, African, Asian and European soil. The rising prices of oil afforded some oil-producing Muslim countries and their rulers the possibility to finance the spread of Islam of the puritanical and violent brand in the West and to absorb some of the unemployed *Afghani Mujahideen*, while the others were turned loose and ended up in the battle fields of Iraq, Lebanon, Bosnia, Chechnya and Palestine, or became mercenaries of violence in America and Europe. The Danish Cartoon Affair proved a golden opportunity for Muslim regimes who began to feel the heat of terrorism breathing down their necks, to redirect the rage and fury of the masses outwardly against the West and Israel, regardless of whether we define them as radicals or moderates, anti-Semitic or Judeophobic, for Western institutions were attacked in Libya, Egypt, Palestine, Syria and Lebanon, and the boycott of Danish products was launched by Saudi Arabia and other Gulf states which are usually considered "moderate" and "pro-Western."

When one examines the spread of Islam into Europe one must take stock of all those considerations, and come to the conclusion that it is not enough to account for Muslim immigration into the Old Continent and its transformation in those lands, but also go into the dialectic between European countermeasures after the major acts of terror that occurred there and the Muslim worldview which regards those defensive measures as aggression, persecution, racism, discrimination against the ever-docile and always "poor," helpless, innocent and "victimized" Muslim who had just come to seek work. When Britain or Germany idolize multiculturalism as a way to "enrich" European culture, and they celebrate the fake "difference" between moderate Islam of the mainstream and the violent few, the Muslims regard that by and large, as an attempt to dilute Islam in order to dominate and eliminate it. Only their unrestricted and violent activity against local Jews in Europe, and in favor of recognition of their own mores and norms, such as wearing the veil, forcing marriage on their women or pursuing "honor killings," would be acceptable as a fair and civil behavior of the host countries towards them. In other words, not satisfied with full equality of opportunity, freedom of speech and of religious cult, Muslims demand special privileges for themselves, like the prerogative to train terrorists or incite violence against other fellow-citizens, because in their skewed view of democratic society, only too much freedom and *laissez-faire*, even at the detriment of the host state and society, is enough freedom for them. When they burn down a Jewish synagogue in Berlin or Paris, they expect their adopted countries to accept that as a matter of course, and they are often aided in that belief by the local extreme-left or extreme-right, or church organizations that boost Muslim demands due to their common anti-Semitism or in order to appear as "progressive" multiculturalists.

Enough books have been written, with specialized monographs of events country by country, that analyze the future that awaits Europe and the West; attempt to detect the motivations of the terrorists or the suffering of their victims; the anatomy of major attacks like 11 September, Madrid 2004, or London's 7/7; the socioeconomic dislocations of the immigrants which are supposedly at the base of the growing wave of terror which threatens to submerge all Europe; or else the self-satisfied delusions of Western governments who elect to sink in their illusory "multiculturalism" instead of taking stringent measures to rescue their societies and preserve their patrimonies. But all this remains theoretical and incomprehensible to many Western minds which are not accustomed to thinking in apocalyptic terms, or to imagining the unimaginable, before the next disaster strikes. For this reason, this book will rather concretize threats by describing them in their harrowing details, depict the dangers by illustrating them through personal stories that were, and exemplify the impending disaster, if nothing is done to stem it. Western governments, whose most cherished goal is to be re-elected next time around, still tend to act as firemen who rush to extinguish fires and provide immediate satisfaction to their prospective voters, and avoid long-term solutions of fire-prevention that are most costly both financially and electorally. Unless national Churchills emerge, who would sacrifice short term interests and instill long-term blood and sweat struggles to face Muslim world terrorism, an assortment of petty and myopic Chamberlains will continue to govern our chanceries and lead us from bad to worse.

Notes

1.   R. Israeli, *Islamikaze: Manifestations of Islamic Martyrology,* Frank Cass, London, 2003.
2.   *Al-Ahram Weekly,* "Beyond the Vacuum," 13-16 April 2006.

1

The Influx of Muslims into Europe: Britain, France, and Germany

Europe was stunned, like the rest of the world, by the horrors of 11 September, and European delegations and leaders poured into Washington D.C. to present their condolences and sympathies to the United States. But as soon as the United States began to react to terrorism by fighting it actively, first in Afghanistan and then in Iraq, it would have found itself almost lonely on the scene if it were not for the devoted loyalty of Tony Blair, who harnessed the resources of his country to that battle. Quite the contrary, many Europeans elected their bilateral deals with Saddam's Iraq over the eradication of its regime, and instead of instilling into their citizenry the need to stand up to the new barbarians, they behaved like the spoiled "soft" states who have lost the will to stand up for their values and future. One ought to remember that the rich and powerful Empires of Rome, Persia, Byzantium and China, who were dipped in their self-contentment, had much to lose because they had grown fat and lazy, and were unwilling to fight anymore, lost the battles to the Vandals, the Arabs, the Turks and the Mongols (and then the Manchus), respectively, because the latter had nothing to lose, looked with contempt upon life, but coveted the wealth of their neighbors and concluded that it behoove them to inherit it, rather than abandon it in the hands of the declining and spoiled empires they attacked and destroyed.

In 2007 terms, the Muslim world, which consists of some 57 Muslim-majority countries spanning the two continents of Asia and Africa, comprises about 1.5 billion Believers, making it after Christianity the second-largest faith. Islam spread since its inception, as did other faiths, by conquest, by missionary work or by expanding trade from the core-areas of Islam in the Middle East to the Far East and the Coasts of Africa. While it was extending its rule into others' territories it necessarily came into armed conflict with the prevailing cultures, like the Zoroastrians of Iran, the Berbers in North Africa, the Hindus of the Indian Sub-continent, or the Jews and the many Christian denominations of the Middle East and Europe. But since the arrest of the Muslim Ottomans at the gates of Vienna by the Europeans in the late seventeenth century, and the defeat of the Muslim Moghuls in India by the British in the nineteenth century, a reversal in the fortunes of Islam has unfolded. Thenceforth, Islamic might would be in the descent and the European and Western power on the ascent. As Islamdom withdrew, independent Judeo-Christian and Hindu nations emerged in the Balkans, in India and in the Levant, and the remaining Islamic world was colonized by Europe, until its re-emergence as independent nation-states after the world wars.

Colonization had its long-term effects nonetheless, inasmuch as moderniza-tion, both in thought and in effect, has set in and began gnawing at the monopoly of Islam in those societies. As a result, the elites of those emerging new nations took to Western culture and learned the languages, the mores, the civilizations, the institutions and the thought of their occupiers and remained tied to them long after their emancipation from their rule. So, after attaining independence, many formerly colonized populations moved to the metropolis of their previous occupiers and established Muslim communities there. Some of the new com-ers were more at home in the ambience of their newly adopted cultures than in their original homes where they had become alienated, others went in search of better economic opportunities, still others came for study periods or to seek political asylum, but then were reluctant to relinquish the freedom, prosperity and tranquility of the West and to return to the poverty, oppression, and turmoil of their own countries. Compared to the immense populations of their original homelands, these were tiny trickles of privileged individuals or families who were intent on adapting to their new environments, adopting their new coun-tries and cultures as their own and taking the necessary steps to merge into the host-cultures of their choice. Their limited numbers on the one hand, and their dispersion among the general alien population on the other, was a built-in guar-antee that in no time they would integrate into the mainstream and assimilate completely. Or so they thought.

But the rapid economic growth of Europe in the aftermath of World War II, due to both the reconstruction of the ravages of the war and the economic and technological revolutions that those societies underwent, coupled with the very slow pace of reproduction of European populations, which did not replace the human losses of war, and where both men and women were seeking careers rather than raising families, brought about an acute shortage of manpower. Previ-ous colonies, where manpower was available which required relatively limited cultural adaptation, became the never-drying-up limitless sources for unqualified laborers, who little by little at first, and then in droves, would lavishly replenish the slacking pool of workers in Europe. Needless to say that vast countries like the United States, Canada and Australia, which had been founded as immigrant societies in the first place, would also absorb much of this massive immigration from Muslim countries to the West. This growing movement of populations now came to encompass not only adventurers and seekers of new economic op-portunities, but also increasing numbers of "political refugees," some of whom were genuine asylum seekers from the oppressions of their regimes at home, but many of them learned to abuse the generosity, concern for human rights and openness of the West, to run away from "justice" in their own countries or to use their countries of asylum as launching pads for political struggle against their home regimes. Eventually, some of the latter would turn against their adoptive countries and launch terrorist campaigns against them.

These new immigrants, who for the most part gained local citizenship after the requisite period of residency which varies from one country to another, no sooner had they raised their status from temporary immigrants to permanent residents or full-fledged citizens, than they began to list their impact on their adoptive countries in different areas:

1. Under the humanitarian heading of "family reunion," they secured immigration rights for many of their relatives back home, thus markedly increasing their numbers; for many of the radical Muslims, this has become a sort of "soft Jihad" to encourage Muslim immigration into their new adoptive countries in order to increase their influence through sheer numbers;

2. Due to their social and religious needs, they constructed Muslim communities in certain localities throughout Europe, where their numbers created local majorities that no running candidate for elections could ignore; the growth of the communities required the construction of mosques and Muslim cultural centers, part of which were and remain innocent houses of prayer, but others grew into secret lodges of subversion and under-cover nests for incitement and recruitment of radical youth;

3. Muslim communities, side-by-side with their irreproachable cultural activities, soon also engaged in illicit avenues of civil disobedience and criminal activities, and sometimes in radical incitement against the state; as a result, prisons in Europe are saturated with Muslim inmates out of proportion to their rate numbers in the general population;

4. Muslim communities have imported the Middle Eastern conflict into their host countries, with the attending acts of violence and an unbridled anti-Semitic campaign against local Jewish communities which had otherwise lived peacefully for many centuries;

5. Muslim individuals, and some of their leaders, make no secret of their intent to change Europe to their tune, not to adapt to it. They demand, and in some cases achieve, in the name of multi-ethnicism and multi-culturalism, their own school systems, in their own native languages, financed by the host state and in the long run to its own detriment.

6. European countries have adopted multiculturalism, and increasingly multilingualism, not as the implementation of the chosen social ideal of cross-fertilizing different cultural groups by allowing them to enrich each other, but as an imposed reality whereby they have abdicated their role to absorb the new comers and integrate them into the existing systems, and instead let the immigrants dictate their own visions of "integration," which means in effect separatism, secession, or an eventual takeover when demography had run its course.

These are the topics that will be discussed below in the coming chapters. Suffice it to tackle now the problem of demography which is the most pressing. Generally speaking, the billion and a half Muslims of the world are distributed into three major blocks: about one third in the Middle East and Africa, with the Arabs constituting over half of them, another 150 million in Turkey and Iran (75 million each) and the rest in black Africa, particularly in Nigeria and the Horn of Africa. The other third encompasses the Indian subcontinent with its three major components of Pakistan, India, and Bangladesh with about 150 million each, and smaller Muslim populations in Afghanistan and Central Asia. The rest is concentrated in East and South-east Asia, with about half of it in Indonesia, the largest Muslim country, Malaysia, and Muslim minorities in Thailand, Burma, and the Philippines, and the Muslims of Russia and China (about 25 million in each). The inroads of Islam into the Western societies of Europe, the United States, and Australia are a quite new phenomenon, as indicated above, and as their numbers increase, either via immigration (legal or illegal) or by natural growth, their sheer rate in the general population and their awakening to their Muslim identity discourage their integration and give rise to the problems they encounter in their European experience. There are already areas of France, Belgium and the Netherlands, and also Germany and Britain, where Muslim children constitute the majority of the school population, a situation that is pregnant with disaffection and can potentially lead to unrest and terror.

While the demographic trends in Europe seem irreversible, in view of the European population's reluctance to perpetuate itself, on the one hand, and its pressing needs for manpower to replace its lost, aging and retiring segments of society on the other, it seems that a reassessment of the immigration policies is in the offing with regard to asylum seekers who do not necessarily respond to the labor needs of the host countries. Europe began rethinking its "safe haven" status also following Ayaan Hirsi Ali's departure from Dutch politics (see below) played off fears about "bogus" asylum seekers. In Vienna, for example, tourists on the *Ringstrasse* were sighting a "strange" and unusual sight and exclaiming: "Did you see that one girl—so young! And wearing a veil, they will form a separate culture." That sentiment is no longer isolated. Earlier in May 2006, Austria's Interior Minister Liese Prokop announced that 45% of Muslim immigrants were "unintegratable," and suggested that those people should "choose another country."

In the Netherlands, one of Europe's most integrated Somali refugees and a critic of radical Islam, Ayaan Hirsi Ali, resigned her seat in parliament in the wake of criticism that she faked details on her asylum application to the Netherlands in 1992. And France's lower house of parliament (*l'Assemblee Nationale*) passed a strict new immigration law, now awaiting Senate approval. Indeed, recent rumblings from the top echelons of governments across Europe suggest that the continent is rethinking its once-vaunted status as a haven for refugees as it becomes more suspicious that many immigrants are coming to exploit its social benefits and democratic principles. "The trend today in Europe is more and more to try to control immigration flow," says Philippe De Bruycker, founder of the Odysseus Network, an academic consortium on immigration and asylum in Europe. "At the same time we still say we want to respect the right of asylum and the possibility of applying for asylum. But of course along the way we create obstacles for asylum seekers," he acknowledges a day after Ms. Prokop made her controversial statement on 15 May 2006.

Ms. Hirsi Ali, who was elected to parliament in The Hague in 2003, was informed by her own political party that her Dutch citizenship was in question. Immigration Minister Rita Verdonk, a former prison warden with a tough stance on immigration, said "the preliminary assumption must be that - in line with case law of the Dutch Supreme Court—[Hirsi Ali] is considered not to have obtained Dutch nationality." At issue were several inconsistencies in Hirsi Ali's application for asylum in 1992. She gave a false name and age, and said she was fleeing from Somalia's civil war, not from a forced marriage. Though she had publicly admitted in 2002 to the deception, a recent TV documentary heightened public scrutiny of the controversial parliamentarian, who had been under 24-hour protection from death threats since the murder of Theo van Gogh, the director of a film she wrote. Hirsi Ali's case was seen as particularly ironic. But it also highlights the dramatic change in Europe since the turn of this century and millennium.[1]

In the years following the World War II, chagrined United States and Europe vowed to follow the Geneva Conventions and create safe havens for refugees. Yet such lofty ideals were hard to uphold after massive influxes of workers in the 1960s and early 1970s were halted during an economic downturn. Those immigrant populations—often Muslims from North Africa and the Middle East—were swollen with family reunification, yet often remained economically and socially distinct from the societies that they had adopted. The image of the immigrant began to change, and distinctions between those who came for work and those who came for safety began to blur. Now, says Jean-Pierre Cassarino, a researcher at the European-Mediterranean Consortium for Applied Research on International Migration, "asylum seekers are viewed as potential cheaters." Today tensions between immigrants and native Europeans appear to be increasing. The perception that an ever increasing number of newcomers—who neither speak the language of their adopted country nor accept its cultural mores—are changing the culture, has increased support for ideas once only advanced by far-right political parties. "France, Austria, and the Netherlands all have had very significant electoral success of the far-right parties," says Michael Collyer, a research fellow in European migration policy at the University of Sussex. He points to France's success of a strict new immigration law proposed by Interior Minister Nicolas Sarkozy, later elected as France's President in May 2007. Mr. Sarkozy's proposal would institutionalize "selective" immigration, giving an advantage to privileged immigrants of better economic and education status that are more "integratable." It would also change the rights of family reunification for workers already in the country; speed up the expulsion of undocumented (another politically correct euphemism for illegal infiltrators, recently adopted by the United States too with regard to its Mexican population influx) immigrants who are discovered or whose applications for asylum are rejected; lengthen the amount of time it takes to apply for permanent residency status for married couples; and toughen visa requirements. Most controversial, Sarkozy announced deportations for undocumented immigrant school children. "We speak of the need to fight immigration but we don't have a clear position on whether we need immigrants," says Mr. De Bruycker, noting the precipitous dip in population growth in European Union countries in the last half century. He adds that a series of recent incidents have affected the image of immigrants in the European mind: the murder of a Jewish man—Ilan Halimi—on the outskirts of Paris in Spring, 2006 for example, by a band of (Muslim) immigrant youths; or the murder of a Malian woman and a Flemish child in Antwerp in May 2006 by the son of a founder of Belgium's most far-right party. "In Europe, we are still unable to accept that we are a continent of immigration," says De Bruycker.[2]

The basic datum when one considers demographic growth in the Islamic world is that, beyond its expansion into new areas, such as Western democracies, it has sustained a consistent internal growth of 3% for many years that is a doubling of the total population every generation of 25 years. This means that with this break-neck pace of birthrate on the one hand, that is due to tradition, to prohibitions on birth control and to the general trend in the developing world where the rich get richer and the poor more children, and the decreasing mortality due to health improvements on the other, there is a virtual population explosion in the Islamic world. Countries like Iran, Turkey, Egypt, which boasted in the 1980s populations of 35-40 million each, have doubled it since, not to speak of Indonesia, Pakistan, India and Bangladesh, where the Muslim populations that were already high in the 1980s, attaining 100 million in Indonesia and the 70-80 million mark for the rest, have also doubled since. Smaller-sized countries like Saudi Arabia, Syria, Morocco, and Algeria have also doubled their populations (from 10-15 to 20-30 million), and the Palestinians of the West Bank and Gaza (from 1.6 to 3.2 million). This trend does not seem to relent, so that in general, the three-quarter billion Muslim population of the 1980s has soared during this period to one billion and-half, that is 25% of the world population of an estimated six billion. Moreover, since most of this population is young, the rapid demographic growth in those countries will continue apace as the innumerable populations of children come of age.

Caution must be added nonetheless insofar as demographic statistics in those countries are not always reliable, but there is little doubt that the trends are clear. Moreover, while European statistics on incoming Muslim legal immigrants can be counted on, the countless illegal migrants tend to baffle the arithmetic and leave many data of this massive human movement in the dark.

The lack of statistics in the Muslim countries of emigration, for either the legal or the illegal migrants to the West, further complicates the calculations that demographers have attempted thus far. One thing is certain: the immense surpluses of Muslim manpower, for the most part un-educated and unskilled, if they do not find outlets into the rich Gulf States, which usually elect trained Arab workers in their education system and their bureaucracy, sneak their way into Western democracies, either as "political refugees," and as welcome manpower for manual jobs that Europeans are reluctant to do, or as illegal migrants who could easily slip through the porous European borders. When Europe changed the rules and began to tighten its control of the borders following the major terrorist attacks of Madrid and London in 2004-2005, the large 30 million-strong Muslim population of Europe was already difficult to supervise due to the lax and liberal freedom of movement of Europeans across the entire expanse of the Union. Another source of demographic growth of the Muslim population in the West is domestic proselytization, which though not massive at this point, produces some of the most devout and radical Muslims, like the Black Muslims of America, and potential recruits for terrorism, like Richard Reid in the United Kingdom. In France alone, it is estimated that in the decade between 1995 and 2005, some 50,000 Christian French have converted into Islam.

These figures amount in their aggregate to a Muslim population of about 6% in the European Union today, with countries like France reaching the 10% mark (six out of 60 million of the total), while in other countries to something less than that (7% in the Netherlands and Belgium (one out of 15 million and 0.7 out of 10 million, respectively), in Scandinavia 5% or less (in Sweden 0.5 out of close to 10 million; in Denmark 0.2 out of five million, and in Norway and Finland even less). In the large-population countries such as Germany, Britain, Italy and Spain, though Muslims can be counted in the millions, they are diluted among the massive preponderant Christian environment and do not transcend a few percentage points. However, Muslim visibility and public prominence seem out of proportion to their real numbers for a number of reasons:

1. They are usually concentrated in the large cities and clustered together in certain neighborhoods, which in the eyes of the members of the host culture seem as having slipped out of their own jurisdiction. In many areas of Paris, Marseille, Malmo, Berlin, etc., local Europeans feel as strangers (in French "*depayses*") in their own countries;

2. Due to the background of the unskilled immigrants, who are usually uneducated, they feel alienated inasmuch as many of them preserve their languages and mores, are different in dress, food and way of life, and they build up a high degree of frustration which occasionally explodes in violent demonstrations.

3. Alienation, poverty, and frustration often lead many of the youth among the immigrant Muslim population to crime. In all European countries which absorbed Muslim immigrants, statistics exist, that are not often

publicized for fear of "bigotry" or "racism," telling the sad story of Muslim prison inmates out of proportion to their rate in the population. That often drives the host countries to frustration and self-pitying when they realize that their generosity and openness in welcoming the immigrants and supporting their training and welfare, often turned into a permanent burden on the state instead of a relief of its manpower shortage;

4.   Muslim alienation has tended not only to lead them to build their own enclaves within their host societies, where even the forces of order sometimes do not dare to enter, but it makes them insensitive to the general host population, something which in turn boosts the Europeans' reluctance to absorb them into their culture. For example, mosques, which call for prayer at odd hours, may turn the previously quiet neighborhoods into areas of friction. Or when naturalized Muslims demand, in the name of their new citizenship, that the cross that garnishes the national flags of their host countries be eliminated because it hurts their feelings, their shelter societies are stunned by what seems to them as a presumptuous demand.

5.   The phenomenon of growing numbers of converts into Islam in major European countries such as France and Britain (50,000 in each in the past decade), some of whom became famous (like Cat Stevens who became Yusuf Islam) or infamous (i.e, Richard Reid), though it contributes only marginally to demography, plays a growing role in the visibility of the Muslim community.

6.   From time to time, scandals like forced marriages of young Muslim women in Europe, or their murder to protect the "honor" of the family, the Rushdie affair of the 1990s, acts of terror and violent demonstrations like in the Danish Cartoon Affair of 2005-2006, all tend to raise the profile of Islam in Europe and make it seem particularly menacing.

On the other hand, several factors militate against an even faster rise of Muslim communitarian identity and demographic growth in Europe, as discussed in Amitai Etzioni's seminal work:[3]

1.   The large numbers of Muslims who have assimilated over the past generation or two in their European environment, especially among the young who have been absorbed by the local educational systems, have grown ignorant of their original cultures and languages, and are more interested in developing peaceful and successful careers than in spreading Islam or responding to its call. Those Muslims, whose rate among their community is hard to ascertain, would not be likely to stand to be counted as Muslims, and may intermarry with the local folks and ultimately assimilate.

2.   Precisely due to the ascendance of militant Islam in Europe and the West in general, with the attending violence that sometimes accompanies its assertion of its identity and its manifestation of disaffection

and discontent, more assimilated and quiet Muslims who are reluctant to be identified with their radical kin, distance themselves from them and elect to melt unnoticed into the general population;

3. Unlike the radical militants who do not hide their intent to Islamize European societies, by peaceful means of conversion if possible, and recruiting for terrorist operations, if necessary, the non-observant Muslims on the contrary seem to have reconciled to the idea of integrating into their adoptive societies and state their intentions to maintain peace and to mind their own business. While the radicals would rather establish their own Muslim political parties, non-observant Muslims indicate their will to adapt via affiliation to the existing political system.

As long as Islam lived within the traditional boundaries of Islamdom, its tensions and frictions with the West remained outside the domain of the Western public, except for politicians, diplomats, merchants and military men who had to deal with it. Misunderstood, shunned, demonized as it may have been in the eyes of Europeans, it was remote and lay beyond the horizon. Similarly, when Muslim visitors arrived to the West since the turn of the twentieth century, for study or business, they were for the most part respectful, even admirers, of its culture and modernity, they adopted a low-profile demeanor of a student who wished to learn and a self-effacing attitude of awe towards everything Western which was deemed superior. But with the rise of fundamentalist Islam in the past few decades, and the increase of Muslim immigration into the West which brought them into permanent contact with Western societies, Muslims learned to face up to their host societies and even to confront them in debate. Their gathered self-confidence and self-assertion taught them that they could debate the West, without being arrested, humiliated or even imprisoned or executed, as in their home countries. For the Europeans, the clash of civilizations which took place from time immemorial on the borders of Christendom moved into their own heartland and they were unprepared to face it, on the psychological and the societal levels. Convinced that their open and democratic societies would prevail and entice the new immigrants to abandoning their roots and identity, they were shocked to discover that over the years, far from bridging the gap that yawned between them and their un-integrated immigrants, it had on the contrary widened, and the differences grew into clashes, the complaints into demands, the debates into explosions of violence. So much so, that once the westerners realized that they were obliterating their traditionally homogeneous societies in favor of multicultural, multiethnic and multireligious (and at times even multilingual) ones, the social contract which held them together previously began dissipating, much to the chagrin of local nationalist parties and to the frustration of the rest.

The explosion of the Cartoon Affair throughout the world in early 2006 does not make matters easier for the Europeans, who see their goodwill and hospitality towards Muslims "rewarded" by violent demonstrations around the globe, as if cartoons of the Prophet, insensitive as they may have been, could be a real reason for this eruption of outrage against the West, and not a simple and direct occasion or pretext to air the Muslim general anger and frustration with the West. This will not facilitate the adherence of Turkey into the European Union either, primarily for demographic reasons. For, if the opponents of Turkey within the Union were thus far reluctant to let her in due to the Islamic Party that took the helm of power there since 2002, now they realize that the so-called "Islamic fundamentalism" almost invariably translates into discord and trouble for Europe, and bringing Turkey in would mean not only freedom of movement of Turkish labor and nationals throughout Europe, but also spreading the message of Islam, and not necessarily only of the benevolent kind, into all corners of the continent. The numbers are staggering: with some 6-7% Muslims today (over 30 out of over 450 million), frictions are already difficult. How much more so when the 75 million nation would join, raising the rate of Muslims to 20% (100 out of over 500 million). The rapid growth of the Muslim population on the one hand, and the shrinkage of the European family unit on the other, would mean that in the next generation Europe may become half Muslim. If that is the will of the Europeans, then there is no faster or more efficient way to achieve that goal than admitting Turkey; but if they are concerned to preserve their Christian heritage and European culture, their technological advancement and modern style of life, Islamization of their societies is not the most hopeful avenue to pursue. Already second thoughts about Turkey have begun to take root in the European Union. Britain, the most ardent proponent of Turkish integration into the system, has itself agreed to suspend the talks between the parties, when it realized that Turkish oppression of the Kurds continues unabated, that women are still discriminated against in Turkish society and that Turkish school textbooks contain thousands of cases of racism and human rights abuses, notably negative portrayals of Greeks, Jews, Kurds, and Armenians.[4]

Demography has a long-term effect on the chances of co-existence in countries where Muslims are in the minority, because of the built-in contradiction between the requirement of Muslims to live under Islamic rule, since only there the Law of Allah can be brought to bear, and the grim necessity for many Muslims to escape from the persecutions of their Muslim regimes in order to seek refuge in the West. Believers who live in non-Muslim lands must either regard their stay there as temporary, and in the meantime do their best to live their Muslim life undisturbed, or return to the Abode of Islam as soon as they can, or try to turn their country of residence into a Muslim one by seizing power in it. For this reason, the existence of Muslim minorities under non-Islamic rule has always alternately pursued these trajectories and driven the Muslim guest culture into a state of mind varying from a quietist acceptance of a permanent minority status to violent rebellion. The response of the Muslim minority depends in no small measure on the perceived threat posed to it by the majority host culture. Whenever co-existence with it seems feasible, as was the case with Muslim minorities in the West before the rise of fundamentalism among them, they could always say that as long that they could perform the obligations of their faith without inhibition, they could consider themselves as living within enclaves of the Abode of Islam, a state of affairs they could bear indefinitely. But as soon as perceived oppression made their lives as Muslims untenable, and they diagnosed their position in consequence as dwellers of the Abode of War, they were set on a collision course with their hosts, and conflict ensued.

To this rather simplistic scheme one ought to introduce three more variables: first, the general Muslim environment, which when rising and embracing the road of militancy can draw behind it Muslim minorities who are fascinated by its power which compensates for their feelings of oppression, underprivileged status and hopelessness in tackling the requirements of modern life. Then, the demographic data of the minority come into play, to wit, the larger the minority, to the point of constituting local majorities in certain areas, the more it feels self-confident to challenge the majority. Indeed, in areas where large concentrations of Muslims are clustered together, they feel strong enough to advance demands and to resort to violence or to threaten the use of violence if their demands are not fulfilled. Thirdly, the nature of the regime under which they live plays its part. Namely, if the regime is oppressive as in their own countries of origin, they would be less inclined to rebel, knowing what their punishment would entail; but under the liberal democratic rule of the West, it is easier for them to act to undermine it and paradoxically seek its destruction although, or because, it gives them more leeway. This is the case with Muslims in the liberal democracies of Europe.

Majority-minority relations in general are by nature dynamic and their fortunes usually hinge on the infringements upon the uneasy balance between the two parts of the equation. When the minority becomes or is perceived as a demographic, economic or political menace to the majority, for example, fears and suspicions increase, followed by oppression on the part of the majority and self-imposed isolation by the minority, ultimately leading to alienation, conflict, separation, rebellion, and secession. All the while both parties test the boundaries of co-habitation and co-existence and attempt to limit autonomy of the minority on the one hand and push it to its utmost on the other. The collision course is the result of the failure of the parties or one of them to stop on the verge of the precipice and instead their rush to trigger the violent explosion. These modalities come in cycles: material acculturation of the minority (in specch, dress, manners, mores, customs) goes a long way to condition it to become more sensitive to its environment and to the interests of the host culture. So next time it rebels it finds that it had accumulated more affinities with the majority than ever before and that its rebellion more than it states its disgust with the majority proclaims its fear lest it be engulfed by it. Following periods of assimilation into the majority, voices of renewal are raised, warning the minority that unless it revives its roots it runs the imminent danger of total disappearance. Revival—religious, ethnic, cultural, linguistic, or otherwise—breeds opposition and rejection by the majority culture, sometimes leading to violent rebellion and attempts at secession by the minority and its brutal repression, so as to remove the perceived threat that it poses to the majority, and back to square one. During this trajectory from quietism to violence, the minority people often embrace multi-identities, in periods of assimilation emphasizing the majority culture, in eras of conflict asserting their own ethno-cultural-religious-linguistic distinctiveness. Like the modalities of co-existence themselves, identities also vary, combining various components from the composite menu from which they are constantly called to choose.

These rules apply handily to Muslim minorities the world over, as their current predicament in non-Muslim lands readily illustrates. One more element is needed nonetheless to explain the mechanics of these dynamics, and that is charismatic leadership, without which the transition from quietism to rebellion is difficult, nay impossible. For if acculturation, assimilation, quietism, and a passive mood towards the majority require no leadership, just indifference and a societal *laissez-faire*, the traumatic cross-over to rebellion, violence and upheaval which require risk-taking and a revolutionary spirit, depend much on a political or religious leader who commands authority and attracts followers. In the case of Muslim minorities the actor is more likely to be religious or to combine religion and politics due to the inextricability of the sacred and the profane, the holy and the secular in Islamic political tradition. A distinction is called for nevertheless between the activity of religious actors in Islamic-majority countries and Muslim-minority ones. If we take it for granted that a certain convergence of events is what provides the religious actor with the opportunity to act, it goes also without saying that in situations of Muslim-minority existence the field of friction between the Muslim guest-culture and the majority host culture is usually wider and thornier than in homogeneous Muslim countries. For, granted that within Muslim entities too there are wide-open possibilities for conflict, as strife abounds on behalf of the Muslim majority towards non-Muslim minorities (Sudan, Iran, Nigeria, etc.), or between different Muslim sects and factions (Afghanistan, Pakistan, the Gulf States, Iraq, Egypt, and the like), the situation is different when Muslim minorities are concerned. The reason is that within Muslim-majority states it is the official government who conducts the repression against other factions or minorities, and while the oppressed (e.g., the *Gama'at* or the Muslim Brothers in Egypt, Syria, and Jordan) usually produce charismatic leaders who lead the resistance as religious actors, the latter seldom challenge the state legitimacy. All they wish is to remove the regime, alter its policies, or gain a share of power within the state apparatus. However, since Muslims are required to live in Islamic lands, their presence under non-Islamic rule poses insoluble problems which end in crisis and unrest. Under such convergence of events, where the plight of the Muslim minority is identified as "religious," only recognized religious actors who arise to meet the challenge are capable of dealing with it for the most part.

There was a time when Muslim minorities were quite limited in numbers and scope of dispersion, usually as a result of interaction with the colonial powers who encouraged a certain amount of "natives" to tread their cultural ways in their own metropolitan centers, and some of them intermarried and stayed. However, the large waves of Muslim immigrants since the mid-twentieth century to the Americas, Australia and Europe, and more so the opening labor markets in the West to Muslim "Guest-workers," coupled with important movements of conversion to Islam as a result of intense Muslim *da'wa* (mission), has dramatically increased the numbers of Muslim migrants to those countries. Moreover, the "Guests" have come to regard themselves as permanent residents with all attending privileges of citizenship and social benefits. In an interesting twist, not only don't they regard any longer their presence outside the realm of Islam as temporary, embarrassing and calling for justification, but with the birth in place of the second and third generations, who grow to learn the languages, cultures and ways of their new habitats, the process of their acculturation into their new homelands has accelerated. As long as their rate in the general populations of their new countries was negligible, and the socio-political environment was liberal (like in the United States, Canada, Australia, Israel, and Europe), then social pluralism and individual freedom of worship were advocated by the Muslim minorities. Under oppressive regimes like the Soviet or the Chinese, the Muslims were quick to adopt material acculturation into their host society, with all the trappings of language, dress, education, and participation in the elites and social customs. The core of the faith was kept almost intact however, with the Muslim calendar, festivals, dietary laws, worship, and places of prayer preserved to the extent possible. This was easier in areas where Muslim minorities were more sizeable and commanded the critical mass necessary to entertain communal life, and much more difficult when the Muslim population was so sparse as to render any public display of Muslim identity impractical.

These situations of rebellious guest cultures, which no longer accept their minority status, can give rise to violence that is aimed either at secession or various forms of autonomy, or grows into an irredentist claim when the minority dwells in adjacent proximity/territorial continuity to their mother-country where the main bulk of their people is located (the Kurds in Turkey, Iran, Iraq and Syria, the Hungarians of Transylvania and Voivodina, the Sudeten Germans and the Arabs of Israel, the Turkic-Muslim population of Eastern Turkestan). Such claims, which may be bolstered especially when the minority becomes too sizeable to govern, or grows into a local majority in its area of residence, gain currency when the demographic growth of the minority is so much faster than that of the host culture as to arouse hopes of a "democratic" takeover by the one-man one-vote device that worked in Zimbabwe and South Africa. In other words, minorities of this sort, be they national or religious, do not seek to merge through integration as in Brazil and create a race-less society where no value is given to creed or original culture, but to dominate through victory and enslavement of the others when the numbers so allow. In these situations religious actors find a fertile ground to act, by advocating demographic growth in their communities, denigrating the majority culture so as to discourage acculturation into it, creating an atmosphere of separateness and strife, inventing irredentist claims and mobilizing their community to obey them in the pursuance of those ambitions.

When Muslim minorities become frustrated by the unworkability of a pluralistic society, like in Cyprus, the Philippines, Israel, China, and more and more within European countries, they become antagonistic to their host society. So much more so, when they perceive the majority as having transgressed the limits of previous coexistence and encroached upon their freedom of worship or conduct. In such cases, they use Western vocabulary (freedom, tolerance, democracy, human rights) to impress upon their hosts that while they wish to play by the rules of their adoptive countries, it is the latter that violate them. In more extreme cases, like with some Muslim fundamentalist leaders (religious actors *par excellence)* in London, they claim that they came to Europe in order to change it, not to be reshaped by it, or they reject Western attitudes lock, stock, and barrel (like the banning of the veil in French schools). This sets the Muslim minority, especially the fundamentalist elements in its midst, on the collision course with the host authorities. Militant elements among this disaffected minority may seek political or cultural autonomy (the London Muslim "Parliament," or various national or international Muslim Associations, or organizations of Imams and mosque leaders, or the Heads of the Arab Local councils in Israel, or the demand for autonomy and for an "Arab" or "Muslim" university and other separate institutions). In India Muslims had conquered the land and subjugated Hinduism, but when Muslim power was eroded by the British, Islam sought and achieved separation from the Hindus for the most part, rather than submit to the democratic rule of modern India that would have allowed the Hindus to exercise political domination over the Muslims. When the majority of Indian Muslims established their own state (Pakistan), their *'ulama* spoke of the reinstitution of the *Shari'a* as their state law. There was no alternative to this arrangement if one bears in mind the fact that Islam is incompatible with other political ideologies. Maulana Mawdoodi, the prominent Indian Muslim modernist has put it this way: "To be a Muslim and adopt a non-Muslim viewpoint is only meaningless. "Muslim nationalist" and "Muslim Communist" are contradictory terms as "Communist Fascist" and "chaste prostitute."[5]

Thus, as orthodox Muslims see it, and much more so the fundamentalists among them, Islam is an either-or affair. Either Islamic law and institutions are given full expression and dominate state life or, failing that, if the state is non-Islamic, Muslims should try to reverse the situation or leave. In practice, however, things are not so clear-cut. As long as an appearance of peace and accommodation can be maintained, the minority Muslim community, although entertaining a vague hope for the fulfillment of its political aspirations at some future time, can contain the discrepancy between dream and reality, and the tension between the two can go unresolved. But if persecution of the minority is intensified, for example in non-democratic countries, to the point where no real Muslim life can be ensured, and when a practical opportunity arises, the minority Muslims are likely to seize it and proclaim either a separate Muslim entity or a Muslim state regardless of whether the Muslim population is a majority or a minority in the territory in question. For an Islamic state can encompass either. Muslims have experienced both a Muslim majority under non-Islamic rule as in Christian Valencia where Muslims outnumbered the Christians four to one,[6] or the modern Muslim colonies under Christian rule, and a Muslim minority rule in Hindu-majority India and the Umayyad Muslim rule over a Christian-majority state in the Iberian Peninsula. It is Muslim rule, then, that defines the borders of the Abode of Islam, not Muslim majorities or minorities. In recent years the enhanced stature of Islam has led the Muslim center to take a keener and deeper interest in the minorities on its periphery. This renewed interest has been manifested in the resolutions of the Islamic Conferences which have been bringing under one roof delegates from some 57 Muslim-majority countries representing some 1.5 billion Believers. More interest has been taken by remote Muslim communities in participating in the Pilgrimage to Mecca, where two million people from all nationalities share their fellowship with their brothers and enhance the identity of the universal *umma*. These are the building blocks of Muslim-minority discontent and rebellion, which in our days may lead to what is termed "terrorism."

Despite the initial naïve days of Muslim immigration into Europe, when it was a matter of course to assume that Muslim minorities would integrate painlessly into the much more prosperous nations where they made their new homes, difficulties began to emerge from the outset, which were dismissed as pangs of acculturation. But as the years elapsed, the Muslim communities grew, and their Muslim radicalism came to the surface, the illusion of integration began to fade, substituted for by the equally illusory vision of multicultural societies, which made cultural concessions to the immigrants in order to accommodate them and make them partners of the system, not its clients. But that too, far from satisfying the Muslims of Europe, whose growing numbers gave them the necessary self-confidence to defy the system and even start acting against it, only further increased the sense of alienation in their midst from their host countries. The Europeans, in turn, sensing that their liberalism had turned against them, began to try to back-pedal, but it was too late, and the collision course became inevitable. A survey done in Europe and published in April 2006, found that the degree of anti-Muslim bias was "dangerously high" among the Europeans, and "can lead to a vicious circle of isolation and radicalization of the immigrant youth," not willing to admit that they were already dragged into that vicious circle and that by abstaining from pronouncing the word "Muslim," substituting for it instead "immigrant youth," "suburb youth," "immigrant population" or "unemployed youth," they were simply hiding their heads in the sand. Beate Winkler, the Head of the European Monitoring Center on Racism and Xenophobia, told 100 European imams convened in Vienna to discuss integration of their communities into Europe, that European countries had enough laws to foster integration, but they were not well implemented, and real issues are often avoided. The Europeans attending the conference agreed that attitudes towards Islam had hardened since 11 September and the subsequent Madrid and Amsterdam attacks. Winkler suggested that Europe could help further by supporting mosque construction, providing time for religious broadcast and assuring proper education of imams and Islamic religious teachers. On the other hand, she demanded that work be actively conducted against Muslim extremism, honor killings, forced marriages, spousal abuse and self-imposed isolation in order to help solve issues arising from *halal* butchering or the wearing of headscarves.[7]

Sometimes, the hysterical fear from Muslim immigration can cause individual harm to innocent Muslim families which have nothing to do with violence or subversion, but these are the unavoidable ricochets when one attempts to chop down the existing wild growth of illegal immigration. A case in point was cited in the *Washington Post* recently.[8] Eight-year-old Andrianina Ralison of Bourg-La-Reine, France is described by his teacher as one of the top achievers in her class. This boy from Madagascar is also an illegal immigrant. And under the tough new immigration laws, Andrianina—along with hundreds of other schoolchildren and their parents across France—was scheduled to be deported to his native country the day after school ended on 4 July 2006. "Why don't they want us here?" Holiarisoa Ralison, 31, said her son asked the day she received the deportation order. All across Western Europe, this kind of argument is raised by people fearful of losing their national identity and anxious over struggling economies, while seeking new ways to stem explosive growth in immigrant populations. For now, the political consensus in France is to crack down, and since fall 2005—as part of tougher new policies—authorities began pulling immigrant children out of school to be deported with their families. But many teachers, classmates, and parents rebelled. Teachers at a school in central France hid students from police, even at the risk of being fined thousands of Euros for helping illegal immigrants. Other schools went on strike to protest the sudden evictions. Students and teachers staged street demonstrations. Local town halls run by Socialist officials who oppose the government's increasingly hard-line approach supported many of the families in their legal appeals to remain in the country. Interior Minister (now President) Nicolas Sarkozy, architect of the new assault on illegal immigration, relented and declared a temporary amnesty for families with children in school and agreed not to deport them until the end of the school year of 2005/2006. "Kids, teachers and parents are angry with the situation," said Richard Moyon, founder of the Education without Borders Network, an association of teachers that organizes protests as part of its efforts to assist youngsters threatened with deportation. "One of the roles of a teacher is to teach kids the ideals of the republic—freedom and equality. How can teachers explain what freedom and equality are when you've got in front of your eyes this kind of example of children seeing their friends deported?"[9] But these good-hearted people forget that one of the principles of the Republic is also to abide by the law, hence the imperative of seizing those who have infiltrated illegally and deporting them. Otherwise, the entire idea of border control and of legal migration would collapse.

Following pressure from Moyon's group and sympathetic politicians, the French Interior Ministry issued new guidelines to the local governing authorities that decide whether to grant residency papers to illegal immigrants. Families may be given more favorable consideration if their children have spent at least a year in French schools, were born in France or arrived at a young age and speak French fluently. The guidelines are advisory only; local authorities are not required to use them. The French government estimates that illegal immigrants number between 200,000 and 400,000. Officials suggest that at least 50,000 of those are children; advocacy groups say the number of children could total 100,000. In the past few years, French authorities have stepped up raids on city streets and at subway stations in immigrant neighborhoods, pressured employers to stop hiring illegal workers and rejected larger numbers of applications from illegal immigrants seeking visas. Deportations have increased by nearly 70%, from 11,692 in 2003 to 19,489 in 2005, according to the Interior Ministry. Even with the new guidelines the fate of the Ralison family remains uncertain. Holiarisoa Ralison, was nabbed on 18 April in a police raid at a train station that is a 15-minute walk from the building where she lives. After two hours in the local jail, she was handed a letter and released. "It said I had to be taken to the border," said the mother of two. "I started to cry. I felt like I'd been stabbed, that this was the end for my family if we had to go back to this poor country." She appealed the decision and appeared before a judge a few days later. "The judge asked if I had anything to say for myself," she recounted. "I said, 'We became outlaws to have better futures for our kids—not to hurt anybody.'" She lost the appeal. In contrast to the United States, where many illegal immigrants slip through porous southwestern borders, or Spain, where thousands of desperate African immigrants have arrived on leaky boats, most immigrants arrive in France on tourist visas. Like the Ralisons, many were born in former French colonies in the Middle East and Africa where cultural and linguistic ties with France remain. While the United States vigorously screens tourist visas from applicants in developing nations, France historically has been lenient in granting them to citizens of impoverished former colonies.[10]

But then France had to pay for its leniency, at the expense of the immigrants who for a while entertained the illusion of being integrated in the culture of their choice, only to see themselves rejected and deported. Nirina Ralison, had arrived at Charles de Gaulle International Airport in Paris from Madagascar in the spring of 2002 with a visa for a three-month internship at a French pharmaceutical laboratory, sponsored by his employer in Madagascar. He never started the internship. Instead, he found a job as a deliveryman and lived in a cramped apartment with six other men. A year later, he'd saved enough money to fly his wife, Holiarisoa, to France. She left their five-year-old son and two-year-old daughter with her stepmother in Madagascar. Eighteen month later, in December 2004, the couple brought their children to France on tourist visas. They enrolled their son, Andrianina, and later their daughter, Raitrosoa, in local French schools. The French government does not require schoolchildren to have legal residency papers. Holiarisoa found jobs baby-sitting and cleaning houses. Both parents—who spoke French—took precautions common among illegal immigrants. They always paid for subway and train tickets, never trying to sneak through gates, even when money was short. Nirina worked for multiple employers, in part so he wouldn't be spotted by authorities in the same places or driving the same routes. "Even without papers, life here is 10 times better than in Madagascar," said Holiarisoa, sitting in the living room of the family's small apartment, where mother, father and two children share the same bedroom—adults on a lower bunk bed, children in the upper. In Madagascar, Holiarisoa was an office administrator for a construction company, making about $66 a month. Her husband made about $75 a month working in a pharmaceutical lab. In France, she said, she earns about $875 a month baby-sitting and cleaning houses while her husband brings home about $1,125 a month from his multiple jobs. But the greatest motivation, she said, was for the children. At home, most youngsters dropped out of school by the time they were 10 or 11 years old, she said. Now the family lives in daily fear of deportation. "Every time we hear a car stop, we think it's the police coming to get us," she said. "We don't sleep at night. If my husband is late from work, I start panicking."[11] Even though it is not clear from this report whether this family is Muslim or otherwise, its case is worth citing because it tells the story of almost every illegal immigrant family, most of which are Muslim, as one individual who sneaked in brings in his nuclear and then his extended family, making the demography such a scarecrow for the Europeans.

A warning by former head of the Israeli Mossad, Ephraim Halevy, that "by mid-century major cities in Germany and Russia will have a Muslim majority" did not add much comfort to the frightened Europeans, not so much owing to the credibility of the speaker as to the authority and reputation of his previous job. Indeed, the former Mossad Director said during a meeting of the Board of Trustees of the Technion in Haifa that in his estimation by the middle of the century major cities in Germany will have a Muslim majority and so will many member districts of the Russian Federation. Halevy spoke of the Islamic terror, saying it is "the main problem of the world today." "We are in the middle of World War III, and I see no end to it," he said. Halevy said that he had spoken recently with a Russian official who disagreed with his prediction regarding the growing Muslim population in Europe. The former head of the Mossad also addressed the issue of Hamas, which can be interpreted as an encouragement to the European security establishment in battling its own Muslim terrorists, saying it is "a young movement, consisting of only 19-year-olds, and it is a ruthless enemy of Israel. The success of the Israeli defense establishment in fighting this organization is immense."[12] He implied then that while the immigration and growth of the Muslim populations in Europe was unstoppable, to the point of becoming local majorities as years wear on, their terrorist threat was manageable and controllable. But while Europeans are certainly concerned about their safety and about the inability of their governments to protect them in their own lands from Muslim terrorism in the short run, they are much more worried about what will become of their nations, countries, cultures and religions in the long run, should the waves of immigration, and their rate of population growth not subside. All the more so since there is lately a tendency of the old *jihadists* who had left Europe to go to Iraq and other battlefields, to return to their European bases. So, while the Saudis are planning a fence with their Iraqi border to keep out any returning *jihadis*, the Europeans will have them back thanks to their "human rights" pieties, with all the dire consequences involved.

According to a report of AFP, the returnees are highly motivated, battle-hardened, mobile—and therefore, dangerous. And the return of Europe's *jihadists* from Iraq is giving the Continent's intelligence services nightmares. As far back as October 2005, Iraqi Interior Minister Bayan Jabr warned that intercepted correspondence between Abu Musab Zarqawi, the leader of al-Qa'ida in Iraq, and other figures in the movement had revealed a decision to send large numbers of Islamist volunteers back to their countries of origin to wage holy war. Mr. Jabr said several hundred militant fighters had left for home by fall 2005. Baltazar Garzon, a Spanish judge who has led inquiries into al-Qa'ida in Spain, said in an interview that there were indications that large numbers of veterans of the Iraqi *jihad* were returning to Europe. "I cannot say how many cases we are talking about, but it is a question of logic. Up until now, inquiries were focused on volunteers traveling to Iraq. Now we are beginning to get indications that they have begun to return," he said. "Infrastructures are being put in place to accommodate them," added the judge, who spoke from the French city of Lyon, where he was attending an Interpol meeting. In the past several years, hundreds of *jihadist* volunteers from almost every country in Europe have traveled to Iraq, via Syria, Egypt, Turkey, or Iran. Once there, they have been more or less integrated into the anti-U.S. resistance, often to commit Islamikaze "suicide" attacks. In 2005, the prestigious International Institute for Strategic Studies in London estimated the number of foreign volunteers in Iraq to be at least 1,000. On 11 May 2006 the head of France's domestic-security service, Pierre de Bousquet, indicated that about 15 young French people, obviously Muslim, remained in and around Iraq. At least nine have been killed there. Foreign volunteers "have become a bit of a nuisance there and are being urged to return to Europe to pursue *jihad* there. We have seen a few examples," he said. Claude Moniquet, director of the

Brussels-based European Strategic Intelligence and Security Center, estimates that there are "several hundred" former fighters from Iraq in Western Europe and says they are "potentially very dangerous." "Given the high motivation and the youth of these Iraqi volunteers, the risk that they will start to commit terrorist acts on European soil is very real," he said. "It is pretty much impossible to organize the surveillance of several hundred people across Europe," he said. "Effective surveillance of one person requires an absolute minimum of 12 to 15 officers. Multiply that by several hundred, and you need thousands. And even then, we're talking about a makeshift operation."[13] This is what gives the Europeans good reasons to be wary of their Muslims.

Under the heading of "Europe's Debate on Immigration is dysfunctional," *the Economist* had some scathing criticism to make.[14] It asserted that America is not the only country wrestling with immigration. As the Senate was passing its version of an immigration bill, Spain was calling on the European Union to help it stem a flood of migrants from West Africa to the Canary Islands. The EU sent patrol boats and aircraft to the seas which thousands have crossed (and where hundreds have died) in the hope of getting into Europe. Britain and France are reforming their immigration laws. Britain and Italy are fretting over the deportation of immigrant criminals. Six countries favor European "integration contracts"—tests of would-be citizens' knowledge of their host countries as a pre-condition for getting passports. But if both sides of the Atlantic are experiencing similar upheavals, there is a big difference between their debates. Americans are letting it all hang out. Tumultuous demonstrations clog the streets. Politicians, lobbyists and interest groups clog the talk shows. In Europe, debate does not grip countries in the same way. After second-generation immigrants staged their suburban car-flagrations in France in late 2005, the Prime Minister weirdly downplayed the riots' significance. Questions about the impact of immigration merge into issues such as asylum, and even Islamist terror. Debate exists, but it is distorted and submerged. "The big difference in the way Europeans and Americans look at immigration," argues Kathleen Newland of the Migration Policy Institute in Washington, D.C., "springs from the fact that America protects its welfare system from immigrants but leaves its labor markets open, while the EU protects its labor markets and leaves its welfare system open." Immigrants to Europe are welcomed with welfare benefits but cannot get jobs (their unemployment rate is far higher than average). America makes it easy even for illegal immigrants to get jobs but stops even legal ones claiming means-tested welfare benefits or subsidized housing. The result is that in America political debate centers on illegal immigration, and there is no sense that legal immigrants impose burdens on others. This obviously emanates from the fact that America is basically made out of immigrants, while Europe has a homogeneous culture and tradition which has now to stand the test of absorbing strangers into its midst. Therefore in Europe, even legal immigrants are often seen as sponging on others through welfare receipts; and the fact that some have taken jobs, which would not otherwise be done so cheaply is forgotten. In Europe, says Danny Sriskandarajah of Britain's Institute for Public Policy Research, it is harder to talk about immigration as an economic issue. Instead, all migrants are caught in a web of suspicion. Politically, the debate is different, too. In America, immigration is a mainstream issue, and splits both parties, Republicans especially. Not so in Europe. With few exceptions, the parties most willing to raise immigration as a political issue lie outside the mainstream—notably (though not only) far-right parties such as France's National Front and the Danish People's Party. The Netherlands is an exception: there, the politics of immigration entered the mainstream after two critics of multiculturalism were murdered. Britain is a partial exception, too. Labour and Conservatives have espoused the cause of immigration control. But for the most part, big parties of center-left and center-right have not made deep reform of immigration a high priority.[15]

Because immigration has been the preserve of the fringe, Europe's debate about it is bedeviled with accusations of racism (which does exist). Naturally, this harms those who want to impose controls: they are tainted by association. But paradoxically, it does not help those who back immigration and benefit from it either (such as employers of immigrant labor). Europe has no equivalent to the alliance of Senators John McCain and Ted Kennedy (usually political foes) who sponsored the Senate bill. Without a space in the political center for friends of immigration, public fears of immigration go unaddressed and unalloyed. And on the other side, there is less political representation of immigrants in European countries. Hardly any of the 36,000 mayors in France are immigrants; none of the parliamentary deputies from mainland France are (in contrast, America has two dozen congressmen with Latino backgrounds). Europe's response to the issue was bound to be more complex than America's. Europe's black economy is large: that makes it that much harder for migrants to integrate through normal (legal) employment channels. Europeans harbor fears of globalization and immigrants are the most visible sign of that process: that makes it harder for beneficiaries to argue that immigration is essential to Europe's economic health (over the past five years, nearly half the new doctors and nurses employed by Britain's National Health Service qualified abroad). Nearly every government accepts that there need to be European, as well as national, immigration policies now that most internal EU border controls have been swept away. But nobody agrees on what those should be, and meanwhile governments are rewriting their own national policies, so policy is less coherent than a generation ago. Lastly, none of the usual engines of integration work well in Europe: churches, the military, jobs, schools. Secular Europeans barely comprehend devout Muslims. With some exceptions, the armed forces are not an avenue of advancement. And a recent OECD report showed that more than a third of second-generation immigrant children who had their education in European countries failed to reach a basic benchmark in mathematics (America was no better on this score).Over the next quarter-century, European countries will face huge pressure to import more immigrant workers to mitigate demographic decline (immigrants can make only a dent in the problem, but that's a different matter). They will not be able to take them in unless there is public support for immigration. Gregory Maniatis, a migration adviser to several European governments, says Europe needs the equivalent of America's civil-rights movement for its own immigrants. At the moment, there is little sign of the continent taking the issue that seriously.[16]

Alarming analyses, that have the virtue of offering a new, more realistic perspective, by knowledgeable and concerned personalities in Europe in the face of the mounting immigration, must be heeded too. They are not written by "Islamophobes," but by strategists and demographers who envision a dark future for Europe should the present trends continue. Some make outlandish suggestions, but they also consider the device of multiculturalism, which has become the new fetish in Europe, as the means that has allowed Islam to come back to Europe and to keep its separate identity, instead of integrating into existing cultures. So, rather than speaking about pluralism, which would have allowed various groups from different backgrounds to rally around a social contract made out of common core values, in order to maintain a shared state and societal entity, multiculturalism has encouraged Muslim and other immi- grants to stick to their separate cultures, languages, religions etc. and to demand that their own values, which are often contradictory with the host culture, gain equal footing and equal time (In the Netherlands this was dubbed the "pillars of Dutch society"). This process by nature brings about disintegration of society, and gives rise to frictions and competition between the various groups for the state resources, instead of rallying them together for the common good. The result is that groups like Muslims, who wish to live by their standards, demand special privileges in maintaining their customs, language, religious training and even habits that run counter to European tradition, like forced marriages, honor killings and the like. Thus, even while policymakers are still grappling with how to assimilate immigrants, these analyses suggest that "assimilation was becoming redundant," in other words that the problem of assimilation has come and gone before politicians have even acknowledged its existence. For example, when the question of volatile young men who fail to find a vocation (or a wife!) keeps appearing again and again in much of the European media, it is not made any easier by the Muslim penchant for polygamy, whereby some men grab more than their fair share of women.

As long ago as the 1970s, one used to read about males from the Gulf going in search of wives in Pakistan, India and Bangladesh, because of a scarcity in their home countries (which therefore prohibitively raised the bride price for local women amongst the underclasses). Now, these problems are inflicted on European cultures and societies. One of Britain's most senior military strategists has warned that Western civilization faces a threat on a par with the barbarian invasions that destroyed the Roman Empire. In an apocalyptic vision of security dangers, Rear Admiral Chris Parry said future migrations would be comparable to the Goths and Vandals while North African "Barbary" pirates could be attacking yachts and beaches in the Mediterranean within 10 years. Europe, including Britain, could be undermined by large immigrant groups with little allegiance to their host countries—a "reverse colonization" as Parry described it. These groups would stay connected to their homelands by the Internet and cheap flights. The idea of assimilation was becoming redundant, he said. The warnings by Parry of what could threaten Britain over the next 30 years were delivered to senior officers and industry experts at a conference in June 2006. Parry, head of the Development, Concepts and Doctrine Centre at the Ministry of Defence, is charged with identifying the greatest challenges that will frame national security policy in the future. If a security breakdown occurred, he said, it was likely to be brought on by environmental destruction and a population boom, coupled with technology and radical Islam. The result for Britain and Europe, Parry warned, could be "like the fifth century Roman empire facing the Goths and the Vandals." Parry pointed to the mass migration which disaster in the Third World could unleash. "The diaspora issue is one of my biggest current concerns," he said. "Globalization makes assimilation seem redundant and old-fashioned ... [the process] acts as a sort of reverse colonisation, where groups of people are self-contained, going back and forth between their countries, exploiting sophisticated networks and using instant communication on phones and the Internet." Third World instability would lick at the edges of the West as pirates attacked holidaymakers from fast boats. "At some time in the next 10 years it may not be safe to sail a yacht between Gibraltar and Malta," said the admiral. Parry, an Oxford graduate, is not claiming all the threats will come to fruition. He is warning, however, of what is likely to happen if dangers are not addressed by politicians. He foresees wholesale moves by the armed forces to robots, drones, nanotechnology, lasers, microwave weapons, space-based systems and even "customized" nuclear and neutron bombs. Lord Boyce, the former Chief of the Defence Staff, welcomed Parry's analysis. "Bringing it together in this way shows we have some very serious challenges ahead," he said. "The real problem is getting them taken seriously at the top of the government."[17]

The paradigm of ancient Rome has been a subject of serious public discussion lately in the context of immigration policy. Boris Johnson, the British Conservative MP and journalist, produced a book and television series drawing parallels between the European Union and the Roman Empire. Terry Jones, the former Monty Python star, has spoken up for the barbarians' technological and social achievements in a television series and has written: "We actually owe far more to the so-called 'barbarians' than we do to the men in togas." Parry identified the most dangerous flashpoints by overlaying maps showing the regions most threatened by factors such as agricultural decline, booming youth populations, water shortages, rising sea levels and (radical) Islam. He predicts that as flood or starvation strikes, the most dangerous zones will be Africa, particularly the northern half; most of the Middle East and Central Asia as far as northern

China; a strip from Nepal to Indonesia; and perhaps eastern China. He pinpoints 2012 to 2018 as the time when the current global power structure is likely to crumble. Rising nations such as China, India, Brazil, and Iran will challenge America's sole superpower status. This will come as "irregular activity" such as terrorism, organized crime and "white companies" of mercenaries burgeon in lawless areas. The effects will be magnified as borders become more porous and some areas sink beyond effective government control. Parry expects the world population to grow to about 8.4 billion in 2035, compared with 6.4 billion today. By then some 68% of the population will be urban, with some giant metropolises becoming ungovernable.

In an effort to control population growth, some countries may be tempted to copy China's "one child" policy. This, with the widespread preference for male children, could lead to a ratio of boys to girls of as much as 150 to 100 in some countries. This will produce dangerous surpluses of young men with few economic prospects and no female company. "When you combine the lower prospects for communal life with macho youth and economic deprivation you tend to get trouble, typified by gangs and organized criminal activity," said Parry. "When one thinks of 20,000 so-called *jihadists* currently fly-papered in Iraq, one shudders to think where they might go next." The competition for resources, Parry argues, may lead to a return to "industrial warfare" as countries with large and growing male populations mobilize armies, even including cavalry, while acquiring high-technology weaponry from the West. The subsequent mass population movements, Parry asserts, could lead to the "Rome scenario." The Western Roman Empire collapsed in the fourth and fifth centuries as groups such as Ostrogoths, Visigoths, Suevi, Huns and Vandals surged over its borders. The process culminated in the sack of Rome in 455 by Geiseric the Lame, king of the Alans and Vandals, in an invasion from North Africa. Parry estimated there were already more than 70 diasporas in Britain. In the future, he believes, large groups that become established in Britain and Europe after mass migration may develop "communities of interest" with unstable or anti-western regions. Any technological advantage developed to deal with the threats was unlikely to last. "I don't think we can win in cyberspace—it's like the weather—but we need to have a raincoat and an umbrella to deal with the effects," said Parry. Some of the consequences would be beyond human imagination to tackle.[18]

Other researchers and thinkers believe that the demographic drowning of Europe by and in Islam, if the cooptation of Turkey came to pass, might oblige the Continent to "adapt its societies to Islam." One of them is Franck Fregosi, a specialist on the place of Islam in Europe at the Law and Religion Research Center at Strasbourg's Robert Schuman University. An expert in contemporary Islam in France and Europe, Fregosi is studying the processes of Islam's institutionalization, organization, and handling in a European context. He also is looking at the multiple forms of religious authority and the Islamic authorities in France and analyses present relations between Islam and European society. There is currently a vigorous debate in the Netherlands, Germany and France about Muslim integration. Is there truly a European uneasiness about Islam, or even a general European obsession with Islam, asks columnist Philippe Jacques?[19] This stems largely from al-Qa'ida attacks and the "9/11 effect." The manifestations of this obsession are different in the various European countries. Each focuses on one particular aspect of Islam: France has been unsettled by the ban on Muslim girls wearing the *hijab* in secular state schools. The Netherlands was rocked by the murder of filmmaker Theo van Gogh who produced a film criticizing Islam and was to make a documentary on Pim Fortuyn who slated imams and their homophobic sermons. In Italy supporters of the xenophobic "Northern League" group sprayed pig urine onto ground set aside for the construction of mosques. These reprehensible incidents represent in the opinion of the writer a drift towards an outrageous radical version of Islam and also an unacceptable reaction to it . In fact a representation of Muslims in Europe cannot be reduced to just a few cases such as Theo van Gogh's assassination. The question stands: "Can we really talk today of a European Islam?" Demographically speaking, European Islam is a reality. European Muslims have strong roots in Europe because not all of them are first-generation immigrants. Many living in Europe today were actually born within European borders. Yet their identity also stems from the history peculiar to each country. German Muslims are of Turkish origin while French Muslims mostly have roots in North Africa. Many British Muslims hail originally from the Indian subcontinent. These communities define themselves partly by their differing countries of origin. For example, Turkish Muslims living in Germany see themselves as a separate community without substantial ties binding them to French North African Muslims. These European Muslims are demanding, and their demands are heeded by thoughtful Europeans, not to be relegated to second-class citizens, he believes.[20]

Young French girls suspended from a state school in Alsace for wearing their *hijab* had no qualms about going to be educated in Belgium. They belonged to a Turkish radical Muslim group which is actually largely based in Germany. Thanks to such Islamic links, European Muslims cross European borders a great deal and in this sense are ahead of other Europeans. Nevertheless, we cannot really talk of a European Muslim community, nor even of a national Muslim community in each member of the European Union . In reality it is made up of small fiefdoms which all compete to attract members from the Muslim population. In France, for instance, large Muslim federations do not unite a large majority of the faithful despite the existence now of the French Muslim Council. In several French cities there are many different mosques, each with its own small separate community. Spanish Muslim communities have similarly failed to establish enough common ground to draw up a religious education program. The various authorities are certainly not "all singing from the same hymn sheet." Some writers and observers contend that this religion is pluralistic in its practice and theoretical interpretations and should remain so, for there is always a risk of standardization. Must these Muslim communities adapt to fit into Europe, asks an author? Not necessarily, for the question, indeed the challenge, is not so much one of adapting Islam to European society but of adapting European society to Islam, thus fulfilling the dream, indeed the demand of Muslim leaders like Abu-Hamza in Britain. The rationale is that discriminatory attitudes against the Muslim community increase Muslim frustration and harden the resolve of certain groups who turn to radicalism. The challenge for Europeans then, is to create a framework in which Muslims may be integrated into society as fairly as possible. Most European states use public money to fund religious groups, yet Islamic groups very rarely actually receive such money. Therefore he contends that European mentalities and bureaucracies need to change. In Belgium, for example, Muslim groups cannot receive public funds because the authorities do not acknowledge them as representative bodies. Only after completely succumbing to Islam and accepting the notion of altering European culture in order to accommodate the Muslims who want to take over and control it, would the author ask whether Islam is compatible with European humanist values. The concept of "values" is a complex one, contends the author. We need to ask ourselves what "values" this question presumes. Christianity has long defined itself in opposition to Islam. Yet Islam and Islamic culture have deeply affected European history. The famous Islamic architecture in Andalusia remains as a testament to this. At one stage most of the Spanish population in certain parts of the country was Muslim and parts of the Balkan region still are. This area was at one time part of the Ottoman Empire, the "sick man of Europe" at the beginning of the twentieth century. Today we need to look beyond this binary division of history and the systematic opposition of Islamic and Christian Europe. By this more comprehensive yardstick, Turkey's entry into the European Union is hardly outrageous. Its accession to the EU would simply represent for Muslims a slightly more important place for Turkish Islam within Europe.[21] This *dhimmi*-like attitude towards Islam will certainly facilitate not only its penetration into Europe but also the Islamization of the Continent, much to the chagrin of strategists like Parry.

Representatives in Britain of the Baha'is, Buddhists, Jains, Zoroastrians, Hindus, Sikhs, Muslims and Jews recited prayers, read passages extolling tolerance and ceremonially laid copies of their scriptures on a table at the center of the tent in London to celebrate tolerance. President Clinton, Archbishop Desmond Tutu, the U2 singer Bono and the President of the World Jewish Congress sent messages saluting the center's use of religion to underpin dialogue and replace conflict with understanding. It only remained to clarify what Muslims meant by dialogue and tolerance. Richard Chartres, the Bishop of London, who has been the driving force behind the rebuilding of St Ethelburga's, noted that the three Abrahamic religions of Christianity, Judaism and Islam began in desert tents. Sir Jonathan Sacks, the Chief Rabbi, spoke of the significance of the tabernacle—a form of tent—in the Old Testament. This tent, paid for by an anonymous benefactor, is able to withstand the London rain and will be pitched permanently in one of the world's most densely populated cities. Prince Charles told the faith leaders: "We are all trying to explain the nature of mystery and, in a sense, it is almost impossible to explain. If only we could understand each other's groping to understand the mystery, not try to overdo the way in which we decide that we know everything, we might, perhaps, reduce the level of conflict and violence and misunderstanding."[22] The problem is that dialogue has been treated in the West as if it were a real policy, whereas it is in fact a non-policy, designed only to fill an awkward vacuum and to make royal princes and legislators feel virtuous for "doing something." But while Europeans have regularly entered a "dialogue" in good faith, fully intending to find common ground with their unruly Muslim interlocutors—for the Muslims, "dialogue" means something else entirely. For them, it signifies the submission of a lesser culture and religion to their own superior one. They hope to inspire in the Europeans a "Damascene conversion" to an Islamic view of the world. Anything short of that is regarded by them as an abject "failure of dialogue," and a signal to resort to threats of violence or acts of terrorism. They are well practiced at both, while the Europeans have literally become pushovers at this stage in their history. They don't believe anything is worth fighting over. Nor do they have a stomach for a fight of unlimited duration. They would rather capitulate than investigate in depth the meaning of tolerance, understanding, dialogue, and peace to the "Islamists." The problem today lies in the juxtaposition of a resurgent Islam on the one hand, and a self-deprecating Europe on the other, unsure of itself, its values or even what it stands for. Its people have made a virtue of instant self-gratification, and therefore invest next to nothing in the future—hence they have stopped having children. Their preferred way of life amounts to a "credit card culture." They want everything, and they want it instantly. Never mind that their governments no longer raise sufficient funds from taxation to cover exorbitant welfare entitlements, or that a bleak financial future awaits tomorrow's pensioners. In short, Europe has become a disgrace to its own heritage in sharp reversal of its fortunes when at the turn of the twentieth century the Muslim Ottoman Empire was considered the "sick man of Europe," and was therefore no match for a confident West. Defense Secretary Donald Rumsfeld was onto something apart from the obvious when he distinguished between "old" and "new" Europe—except that in their eagerness to grab some (necessarily short-term) economic benefits after emerging from Soviet control, the headlong rush of "new" Europe to join the European Union will inevitably contaminate them with the prevalent Western disease.

There is another drawback to this constant resort to "dialogue." It lulls the Western populations into believing that their governments are doing something constructive to avert violence or threats of violence in their future. In reality, nothing could be further from the truth, for this non-policy simply serves to embolden and concomitantly empower those Muslims whom the government has chosen to act as intermediaries with the wider Muslim community. Invariably, the government has chosen these Muslims largely because they are the activists (or "militants," "fundamentalists" in another parlance) and therefore prominent, while the government comforts itself with the injudicious belief that these figures represent "moderate" Islam. However, these Muslims have been living in Europe long enough to have learnt to tailor their vocabulary precisely according to whom they are facing across the table. They speak the language of peace, reconciliation and goodwill to Westerners, and reserve their true thoughts and beliefs for fellow Muslims. In other words, they have learnt to "work the system," admirably so. In effect, these "moderate" Muslim leaders are gradually extracting one concession after another from Western policymakers, rendering "dialogue" a one-way street. They enter each session with the full intention of testing the limits of the concessions they may extract, and it is a rare government minister who would risk disappointing them—or else the headlines in the papers the following day would be sure to inflame the Muslim community. Herein lies the value of the worldwide Muslim penchant for overreacting to every perceived slight, real or imagined, by demonstrating loudly and violently their "rage." Temperament comes into play here too, for unlike other peoples who experience anger or humiliation, Muslims are either unable or unwilling to contain those sentiments. One has only to recall the Arafat-orchestrated "Days of rage" in the early days of the *Intifadah* against Israel to understand that, in sharp contrast to Westerners, Muslims make a fetish of celebrating their anger. Such an uncontrolled behavior is unthinkable in the West, not because of lack of provocation, particularly since 11 September. Funerals too are manipulated to vent wrath and fury, emotion, general mayhem and impromptu rifle shooting. The total and shameless lack of dignity, even at what should be a somber occasion, is jarring to Western eyes. Bodies are held aloft and bounced along the route, in a manner that would be regarded as disrespectful to the deceased in other cultures. Bodies have been known to fall off the stretcher amid the *melee*, as was recorded for posterity in the case of Iran's Ayatollah Khomeini.

A much more sober view of interfaith discourse with the Muslims was offered by the Danes, both the royal house and the press. Under the heading "The Muslims have all Europeans just where they want them—prostrating themselves in the name of 'dialogue'," the *Copenhagen Post Online* addressed this issue. It contended that "the clash of civilizations is currently on hold," in the two separate conferences that sought to mend fences damaged by the tornado of the Mohammed Cartoon crisis, following the calls for "dialogue and understanding" that rang out when the storm raged at its highest in January 2006. With the winds subsiding, the two separate conferences were held in Copenhagen and the United Arab Emirates in mid-May 2006 which sought to put those calls into action. The Copenhagen conference, entitled "The Thoughts and Personality of the Prophet Mohammed," brought Muslim and Christian religious leaders together on a Sunday at the Danish Institute for International Studies. The day marked both Easter and the anniversary of the Prophet Mohammed's birthday, providing an opportunity to find common ground between the two faiths, according to organizers from the Islamic Cultural Center. Imam Ali, chairman of the Center, said that "Islam in Denmark is a new phenomenon. Because of the caricatures, "we think it is important to hold a conference to introduce the Prophet in a proper way." Iran's ambassador to Denmark, Ahmad Danialy, making his first public appearance in Denmark since being recalled by the Iranian Foreign Ministry in January 2006, addressed the gathering and noted that the crisis had "hurt the feelings of the Muslim world and caused a great deal of concern. Now after the lapse of this period of unpleasant and bitter experience, I am very pleased to witness a beautiful and jovial gathering of the erudite and learned here in Copenhagen.... The conference is a step in the right direction for improving relations. The truth of the matter is that the world needs to direct new attention to one fundamental principle and that is: Respect for the sanctity of religions in all places and at all political, cultural and social levels...."[23]

It is unthinkable that this glib Ambassador was not aware of how his President treated the Jews and Israel or how his clerics deprecated day in day out Christianity and other faiths, or how Palestinian and other Muslims burned down Jewish synagogues in the West Bank and in European cities. But if the purpose of the conference was "to introduce the Prophet (the Muslim one, not all the rest), the proper way," then why should we expect any care or concern for any faith except the Islamic one? The conference in the United Arab Emirates, organized by the Tabah Foundation, brought 60 young people from Denmark and the Arab world together under the banner "The Search for Mutual Understanding," namely that the Danes should learn to respect Islam, never mind their own beliefs and culture. The delegates discussed a range of issues the cartoon crisis revealed as sore points between religious Muslims and secular Western culture, such as freedom of expression and the role the media can play in hindering or facilitating global understanding. The four-day conference held in Abu Dhabi "exceeded the expectations of Jeppe Bruus Christensen," chairman of the Danish Youth Council, who naively, unfoundedly and prematurely declared: "I don't think we should underestimate how important this is in the Arab world. It has gathered a great deal of attention," but he did not know that it was interpreted throughout the Arab world as a desperate attempt by Denmark to apologize for its "horrible" deed, as a capitulation to Muslim demands which did not earn it any credit, but only scorn and contempt. He felt the two groups managed to "understand" each other and "accepted" mutual criticism, but he failed to comprehend that the Muslim goal was to assert its victory, not compromise, because its system cannot recognize that it can be at fault, unlike other (lesser) faiths. Thus, his feeling that the whole exercise "has been very constructive and positive" and that "we have been able to agree upon common values, such as having the right to criticize each other," would have been in vain had he read the Arab reports of the conference. Other participants from Denmark and the Mid-East were more sober and realistic when they merely agreed that the conference "underscored the need for bridging the gaps that the conflict had revealed," and that "We have to accept that there are areas where we remain distant from each other." Moreover, to illustrate the depth of that gap, some Muslims continued to consider Denmark, one of the most open, tolerant and hospitable countries of the world, to be "a racist and closed country."[24]

Much closer to the reality was the evaluation by some Danish participants who heard their country being deprecated while it could be the model of tolerance for the entire Islamic world, when they said that "we have to acknowledge that that's the way it's going to be for some time." The conference also gave young Muslims the chance to meet their Danish counterparts and test the images presented by the media in their countries. "It's been very important for me to obtain the human aspect. To meet people and hear their opinion instead of seeing it in the media," said a 19-year-old Egyptian who admitted that preconceived notions, such as that "Danes hate us," were difficult to reject, but the conference's people-to-people approach helped (in what? If the gaps remained as wide and the preconceived notions remained unshakable?). On the other hand, another Arab youth from Saudi Arabia, where Danish goods were initially boycotted, said that he was surprised in a positive way about the Danish young people, for "They were much more open and understanding about our culture than I had expected." But was he about theirs in the same way? He acknowledged that while dialogue and respect had been established at the conference, transferring the experience to his home country could prove difficult. He explained: "We'll be challenged when we come back to our countries, because some people have different attitudes. They use a different approach than dialogue, but we still need to work to spread the message that it is possible to live in this world together."[25] One wishes he were right.

The Danish Queen, Margrethe, more reflective than the British Royal House, stated that Islam poses a challenge both globally and locally, and the challenge should be taken seriously. In her biography based on interviews between the Queen and the book's author, journalist Annelise Bistrup, the Queen affirmed that "There is something impressive about people, whose existence is immersed in religion from dawn to dusk, from the cradle to the grave … but it is a challenge, which we need to take seriously. We have admittedly ignored it for too long. Because we are tolerant and a little lazy. I don't find it easy at all. Nor especially pleasant," she said. Unlike other royals and politicians who make gratuitous declarations just to please their Muslim citizens or to placate their wrath, Queen Margrethe has studied Islam through her archaeological pursuits, and says she does not feel entirely unprepared to enter the debate. "There is something fascinating about people who go to such lengths to surrender themselves to a religion. But there is also something frightening about the all-encompassing side of Islam," she said. She courageously added that "The challenge must be met, at the risk of getting some less flattering labels attached, for there are some things we should not meet with tolerance. When we are tolerant, we should be careful to note whether it stems from convenience or conviction." Queen Margrethe said we might stand at crossroads, and that crossroads often only reveal themselves after we have crossed them. She warned that, "one doesn't always turn out to have taken the right road. But we have at least realized that we cannot let ourselves be shooed off by things that frighten us. We cannot compromise our notions of justice and legitimacy." Queen Margrethe said her interviews with her biographer Bistrup brought up forgotten memories that could be worthwhile for others, especially young people, to hear.[26]

London is also the site where the legal manipulations of the Islamists have been hitherto tolerated, something that will inevitably affect the world struggle against terrorism and its Muslim financing as viewed from Britain's best and closest ally in the United States. Judge Richard Casey of Manhattan's Southern District Court has handed down a decision against Rachel Ehrenfeld, an American citizen and director of the American Center for Democracy. Ehrenfeld has written extensively about the Saudi fifth column in the United States that uses its oil wealth to invade American colleges, circulate materials in secondary schools reflecting Wahhabist ideology, and provided lucrative incentives to officials in the State Department and politicians in Washington to promote Saudi interests. Her 2003 book, *Funding Evil: How Terrorism is Financed and How to Stop It*, among other things, revealed connections between Saudi billionaire Sheikh Khalid Salim bin Mahfouz and his sons, and al-Qa'ida funding. Despite the fact that he lives in Saudi Arabia, and that Ehrenfeld's book was published in the United States and not even on sale in Great Britain, the Sheikh decided to become what is known as a "libel tourist" and sued Ehrenfeld in the United Kingdom—notoriously plaintiff friendly—for defamation and libel. Had Mahfouz filed in the United States he would have had to prove that the book misstated the facts and was written in malice, a standard he could not have met. Moreover, he would have been subject to a discovery process that would reveal more than the Saudi billionaire wanted the world to know, especially since he'd already been under the microscope for bank fraud and money laundering in a failed Muslim bank he financed, and for which he was forced to make restitution. The Saudi billionaire is ranked the 210th richest man in the world, and his sons are already named as defendant in the United States by several of the families whose relatives died on 11 September, because of their links to funding al-Qa'ida terrorists who struck that fateful day.

The pretext for filing in a British court was that 26 copies of Ehrenfeld's book which made it into the hands of British citizens who ordered the book via Amazon.com. A Justice in the United Kingdom decided a default judgment against Ehrenfeld, and ordered her to pay the Saudi more than $200,000 in damages plus court costs, and barred her book in the United Kingdom. The judgment rendered by the British court can only be enforced in the United States by legal action. When Ehrenfeld filed in the Southern district court in Manhattan to block the collection process, she knew that more than money was at stake. As her attorney stated to the Court: "The freedom to ferret out and publish facts without fear of expensive lawsuits and huge judgments in foreign countries whose defamation laws negate a commitment to freedom of expression and public discourse, is pregnant and antithetical and contrary to our fundamental policy." But Judge Casey ignored Ehrenfeld's plea for her First Amendment rights, and decided that he had no jurisdiction over the case. Ehrenfeld is filing an appeal and faces a daunting challenge of raising enough money to support a case that she believes will help determine whether or not American writers will be able to continue to expose America's enemies.[27]

This state of affairs allowed British converts to Islam to take up the vocation of notorious Muslim preachers Abu-Hamza and Bakri with foreign financing, thus lending to Islamism the aura of a "native" religion, no longer introduced by foreigners into Britain, but followed by Britons and thus completely legitimate. Indeed, a British Muslim convert has emerged as successor to Omar Bakri as the leader of a radical group that wants Britain ruled by Islamic law. *The Times* has obtained transcripts of Omar Brooks, now known as Abu Izzadeen, preaching holy war (*Jihad*) and discussing killing Tony Blair in a recent sermon in London. Abu Izzadeen had previously described the 7 July bombings as "completely praiseworthy" and organized demonstrations in support of the 11 September hijackers. His organization, the Saved Sect, of which he became head, was formed from the remnants of the disbanded Muslim extremist group *al-Muhajirun*, which the Government intended to proscribe. However, it is not on the Home Office's list of 40 banned terrorist organizations, and a spokeswoman refused to comment on whether it could be outlawed. The Crown Prosecution Service has not ruled out charges against Abu Izzadeen, which may include solicitation to murder and withholding information about acts of terrorism. Abu Izzadeen, 31, was born into a Christian family of Jamaican origin, in Hackney, East London, and was known as Trevor to some acquaintances. He converted to Islam at the age of 17 and is believed to have been involved with Bakri at Finsbury Park mosque in the late 1990s. Before he was fully radicalized, Abu Izzadeen trained and worked as an electrician. He eventually chose a new name, which means "Might of the Faith" in Arabic, and immersed himself in his new religion. He married and now lives in Leyton, East London, with his wife and three young children. Vitriolic lectures for his website were recorded—until recently—by Bakri, who is now in exile in Lebanon. But Abu Izzadeen himself has started preaching sermons and posting them on the website, suggesting that he has taken over as *emir* of the Saved Sect. He is one of a generation of young British-born radical converts to step into the shoes of notorious clerics such as Bakri, Abu Qatada and Abu Hamza al-Masri. Abu Hamza is in jail and Abu Qatada is being held without charge under anti-terrorism laws. The Saved Sect, also known as the Saviour Sect, rejects democracy and wants Britain to adopt *Shari'a*, or Islamic law. It believes that it is the only group representing the true Islamic path, but has links with another *al-Muhajirun* (the Immigrants) successor, *al-Ghuraba'* (the Strangers), whose leader was arrested during extremist protests against the publication of cartoons depicting the Prophet Muhammad in early 2006.[28]

In lectures given at a London location, Abu Izzadeen said that a war was being fought to make Islamic law "completely dominant" in Britain, and that "all Jews and Christians are going to hell fire." He also praised Mullah Omar, the Taliban leader, saying: "This man is a winner." His lectures, entitled "The Christian Crusades," describe conflict in the Middle East and Britain as a present-day crusade. Abu Izzadeen said:

> There is a war here [in Britain]. Maybe you don't have weapons, but there are arrests against the Muslim community, there is brutality by the police. It is a form of war against the Muslims here as well…. If I said to you we're going to conquer Rome, or if I said to you, we're going to kill George Bush and we're going to kill Tony Blair, you would say to me: 'Which come first bro?'(…) Muslims do not "need to stand by the British flag…. There is without doubt a war taking place between the Muslims and the non-Muslims … you must take part in the struggle…. Tony Blair is a *taghoot* [believer of false religions]. The British forces in Iraq and Afghanistan, the police in the UK, they are all fighting for the sake of *taghoot*.[29]

When Mr. Blair announced after the London bombings that he would ban "the successor organization of *al-Muhajirun*, the group praised the 11 September terrorists, describing them as the "Magnificent 19." Legislation tightening the Terrorism Act came into force some months later, when it became illegal to glorify or incite terrorism. A Home Office spokeswoman said: "The list of proscribed organizations is kept under constant review. The Terrorism Act 2006 widens the criteria of proscription to include those groups which glorify terrorism. All possible candidates for proscription will be considered against these criteria. The Saved Sect website also carried a statement from Abu Musab al-Zarqawi, the commander of al-Qa'ida in Iraq. On the BBC program *Newsnight* in 2005, Abu Izzadeen said that the July 7 bombings would make people "wake up and smell the coffee." He added that he would never denounce "suicide bombings," "even if my own family was to suffer, because we always stand with the Muslims regardless of the consequences," and elaborated on his sect's program:

> We can envisage that, if alive in the United Kingdom today, Jesus would undoubtedly have supported *jihad* in Afghanistan and Iraq, as opposed to the capitalist-driven U.S.-led alliance … and would also have been no doubt interned under the Home Secretary Mr. Clarke's new terrorism laws, thereby languishing in Belmarsh Prison…. The call of moderate and apostate "Muslims" [of the Muslim Council of Britain] upon the Metropolitan Police to take action and arrest the 'extremists' behind the peaceful protests in central London (against the cartoons of Prophet Muhammad) was indeed a call of apostasy and betrayal. They have repeatedly called for the arrest and deportation of a vast number of Islamic activists, including scholars such as Sheikh Abu Hamza, Sheikh Faisal, and Sheikh Abu Qatada—may Allah assist them and release them from captivity…. Since the majority of Muslims living in the West are on the brink of committing apostasy (e.g. by voting for man-made law and allying with the disbelievers), it is important for us to identify the ways in which they

are leaving the fold of Islam and tackle these problems directly.... If we look to the reality of the so-called mosques in Britain today, hardly any are built by Muslims ... therefore, they cannot be considered to be mosques. These halls have become places of corruption, calling Muslims to vote, inviting *kuffar* (non-Muslim) MPs and prime ministers, as well as lying about Allah, His Messenger and the religion of Islam. It is even considered to be a form of heresy to call these places Houses of Allah.... Sodomy, bestiality and incest are all crimes that are acceptable in un-Islamic societies. Recently the British government legalized homosexual marriages. It was not enough that they allowed homosexuals to practice their vile filth openly, but they felt the need to take a step further into the pits of humanity.[30]

All this causes much less outrage in Britain than if it occurred in Muslim lands, which execute their citizens for homosexuality and apostasy in their own countries. A comparative story on two converts in Britain, who then became more fanatic than the most extremist Muslims, was reported by the *Times*.[31] One of them, David Copeland, a neo-Nazi whose ideas were said to be the inspiration for the man who let off a nail bomb in Central London in 1999, has converted to an extremist form of Islam. Another, David Myatt, a founder of the hardline British National Socialist Movement (NSM) who has been jailed for racist attacks, has changed his name to Abdul Aziz ibn Myatt. Copeland, who is serving six life sentences after three people died in his Soho bomb attacks, was a member of the NSM. Myatt is reportedly the author of a fascist terrorist handbook and a former leader of the violent far-right group Combat 18. But now he subscribes to radical Islamist views. In an Internet essay entitled "From Neo-Nazi to Muslim," Myatt asks:

How was it that I, a Westerner with a history of over 25 years of political involvement in extreme right-wing organizations, a former leader of the political wing of the neo-Nazi group Combat 18, came to be standing outside a mosque with a sincere desire to go inside and convert to Islam? These were the people who I had been fighting on the streets, I had sworn at and had used violence against—indeed, one of my terms of imprisonment was a result of me leading a gang of skinheads in a fight against "Pakis." [I support] the killing of any Muslim who breaks his oath of loyalty to Islam, and the setting up of a Muslim superstate. I had been staunchly opposed to non-white immigration into Britain and twice jailed for violence in pursuit of my political aims, spent several decades of my life fighting for what I regarded as my people, my race and my nation, and endured two terms of imprisonment arising out of my political activities... But the pure authentic Islam of the revival, which recognizes practical *jihad* (holy war) as a duty, is the only force that is capable of fighting and destroying the dishonor, the arrogance, the materialism of the West.... For the West, nothing is sacred, except perhaps Zionists, Zionism, the hoax of the so-called Holocaust, and the idols which the West and its lackeys worship, or pretend to worship, such as democracy. They want, and demand, that we abandon the purity of authentic Islam and either bow down before them and their idols, or accept the tame, secularized, so-called Islam which they and their apostate lackeys have created. This may well be a long war, of decades or more —and we Muslims have to plan accordingly. We must affirm practical *jihad*— to take part in the fight to free our lands from the *kuffar* (Unbelievers). *Jihad* is our duty.[32]

Myatt, who briefly became a monk after his second spell in prison, said that he became a Muslim while working long hours alone on a farm. He grew up in Africa, moved to Britain in 1967 and spent time living in Worcestershire. In July 2000 *Searchlight*, the anti-fascist magazine, described him as "the most ideologically-driven Nazi in Britain, preaching race war and terrorism." He issued a statement in response to the Soho nail bombings saying: "Neither myself nor anyone else connected to the NSM can be held responsible for these bombs in any way. That responsibility lies with the person who constructed them, planted them and caused them to explode. Only that person, and God, know the motive behind the attacks." Myatt said that "all bombs are terrible and barbaric, whether detonated by lone bombers, Western governments in Iraq or Zionists in Palestine..." The NSM considered the creation of a revolutionary situation in this country as necessary since it wished to build an entirely new society, based upon personal honor, and believed this could only be done by destroying the dishonorable and corrupt society of the present. However, the NSM neither preached, nor sought to incite, what is called "racial hatred." Instead, it strove to propagate the warrior values of honor, loyalty and duty, and make the British people aware of, and come to value, their ancestral warrior culture and warrior heritage." Myatt also said that he had given up hope of a breakthrough by the far Right and believed that Muslims were the best hope for combating Zionism and the West. Echoing the current reality in Britain and elsewhere in Europe, where prisons have become fertile grounds for converts to Islam, Myatt appealed to other dysfunctional people like himself to rally to his new religion:

> There will not be an uprising, a revolution, in any Western nation, by nationalists, racial nationalists, or National Socialists—because these people lack the desire, the motivation, the ethos, to do this and because they do not have the support of even a large minority of their own folk.... If these nationalists, or some of them, desire to aid us, to help us ... they can do the right thing, the honorable thing, and convert, revert to Islam—accepting the superiority of Islam over and above each and every way of the West."[33]

Despite these voices that were quite widespread in Britain before 7 July struck, few were ready for the attacks, at the same time that there was awareness in wide circles that it might happen. Take this account, for example, which makes the point that British authorities were slow to recognize the growing threat of terrorism by angry British Muslims before the deadly bombings in London of 7 July, though there is no evidence that the attack could have been prevented, according to the report issued in May, 2006. "If more resources had been in place sooner, the chances of preventing the July attacks could have increased," stated the report by Parliament's Intelligence and Security Committee. Acknowledging that its determinations were reached "largely in hindsight," the committee also concluded that no matter how extensive the government's anti-terrorism efforts, "it seems highly unlikely that it will be possible to stop all attacks." The parliamentary report on the deadliest attack in Britain since

World War II, and a separate report issued by the Home Office, concluded that two of the July 7 bombers probably had contact with al-Qa'ida during visits to Pakistan in 2003 and from late 2004 into early 2005. But they said there is no solid evidence to suggest that al-Qa'ida directly planned or directed the London attacks, in which 52 commuters were killed on three subway trains and a bus. The bombers, all young British Muslims who mixed chemicals for their crude bombs in a bathtub, were likely inspired by al-Qa'ida but acted on their own, motivated by "fierce antagonism to perceived injustices by the West against Muslims," the Home Office report stated. The long-awaited reports seemed unlikely to end speculation about the 7 July attack and a failed attack on July 21, in which five men are charged with getting onto London subways and a bus with bombs that failed to explode. Although British officials for years had warned of the likelihood of an attack by Islamic extremists, many Britons were shocked to learn that three of the four 7 July bombers were British-born. Had the authorities and the public heeded the press reports and interviews by Bakri and Abu-Hamza, they would have certainly not been surprised. David Davis, the Shadow Home Secretary of the opposition Conservative Party, said the reports "raised more questions than answers" about what he called "a major failure of our intelligence services" to pick up earlier on the home-grown extremist threat. But he too was wrong, because the information was there, it was simply not taken seriously. He also questioned the reports' independence from Prime Minister Tony Blair's government and security services, which, despite being the focus of key aspects of the probes, provided much of the information used to compile the reports. "It is the government's view, not an independent view," Davis said in the House of Commons.[34]

As if all this incriminating evidence of the brewing Islamic subversion in Britain and elsewhere was not sufficient to stop terrorism before it erupted, it was accompanied by the distancing of Europe, except for Britain, from the furious American reprisals after 11 September, which indicated to the Islamists that they can pursue their anti-Western activities in the heart of the West almost undisturbed. For, granted that 11 September traumatized the entire West, which began to awaken to the new dangers Islam posed to its security, yet the sense of urgency and immediacy of the issues was late in coming. Until 11 September, the Islamic world was considered friendly to the West, and the essentially Islamic struggles taking place in Bosnia, Kosovo, Palestine, Kashmir or the Philippines, were regarded as so remote, incomprehensible and irrelevant to Western culture that few bothered to look those names up in world atlases, let alone deepen their knowledge about them. But as of 11 September, not only did these names begin to resound clearly in the minds of ordinary people in the West who had been unaware of them, but many rushed to read the Qur'an and works about Islam, or to visit Islamic centers in the West in a quest to comprehend what makes that faith tick; and it is believed that more than a few even asked to join the ranks of the Believers. So, in a small measure, the "Islam Rush" was due not to an "invading" foreign Islam that one needed to know and understand, but to the shocking realization that the "enemy" emerged from within. After all, the 19 Islamikaze who committed the Twin Tower horror, were asylum seekers in the United States who were educated there or in Europe, became acquainted with Western openness and democracy and were expected to demonstrate loyalty to their countries of refuge. The fact that they did not and that their common denominator was their Islamic faith, took the Americans, as well as the Europeans, by surprise, especially due to the Saudi and Egyptian identity of the perpetrators, and made them feel that a fifth column was growing in their midst, especially when it turned out that their operators, in this case al-Qa'ida, had organized, financed, indoctrinated and dispatched them from the outside.

In Western Europe, Australia, and Canada—the main targets of legal and illegal immigration from Muslim countries—the first thoughts of putting strictures on those immigrants began to rise, as these countries realized that some Muslim immigrants did not move to the Western democracies just to improve their lot, or to work and provide for their families who stayed behind, but that an entire scheme lay behind their move which would revolutionize the status of entire Muslim communities in the United States and Europe: from being asylum seekers, political refugees and foreign workers, to becoming a real social and security liability. For, while many of them are grateful for their new home and go about their business, the political and religious activists among them pressure the others to take a stand on current affairs of concern to all Muslims, encourage them to demonstrate, even violently, against their own new countries and in favor of their original ones, and strive to increase their numbers and make a dent on local demography and politics. The difficulty of distinguishing the activists apart from the others makes all of them suspicious in the eye of the unsuspecting citizens of the host countries, who while for the most part escaping the label of "racism" by not voicing in public their concern and fear of Islam, would venture to complain privately, as they begin to feel like strangers in certain neighborhoods of their country, where even police do not dare to enter and impose order and safety. Every wave of new immigrants, legal or illegal, is aided by the previous one, which under the humanitarian excuse of "family reunion" brings entire clans in their wake. If they constituted negligible minorities, no one would be overly concerned about their impact, political or cultural on their host countries, but as their great numbers alter the median age of the general population due to their high proportion of children, their demographic "threat" becomes apparent in the long haul.

Had these minorities aspired to assimilate into their host societies and just become French, Swedes or Spaniards, peacefully and individually following their cult of Islam as a personal endeavor, no one would even notice. But as the Muslim communities grow larger they also grow more vociferous and violent for the most part, and no longer happy to be absorbed into their societies as individuals. Instead they begin to claim group rights and to justify their often-violent behavior by their right to differ from the overwhelming majority. Many minorities had been absorbed by these countries over the centuries, especially the immigration-oriented among them, such as Canada, the United States and Australia, but seldom has a minority clung to its original roots in an effort to force the host majority to yield to its will. For example, the Poles, Irish, Germans, Japanese and Jews who flocked to the United States or Australia, have willingly and wholeheartedly hoisted their new national colors, sung "America the Beautiful" and "God Save the Queen" and participated in the fighting forces of their adoptive countries in times or war. Now, Arab youth in France (as in Israel), like other Muslims in other European countries, refuse to sing the anthems of their adoptive countries and demand that their ethnic and religious heritage be recognized in their school curricula, even if it contradicts the local national ethos, and think that they have the right to rip apart the national consensus and the basic values that hold the country together. Again, were it not for Muslim spokesmen who proclaim their blueprint for infiltrating Western societies in order to subvert them from within and take them over, one would have tended to believe that these manifestations of recalcitrance among Muslim youth in Europe were merely pangs of assimilation and demonstrations of passing displeasure with their lower living standards or with the prevailing discrimination against them.

Worst of all are the violent methods which these groups are often seen resorting to, beyond the expected levels in any migrant and less affluent society. In Western Europe the native populations are terrified by the high rate of crime which is linked, according to statistics, with the immigrant Muslim population. There are recurrent, and increasingly also public, complaints by Europeans in this regard, who no longer fear being branded "racists" if they share their thoughts with others, once the level of risk to their national identity has grown so perceptible and pressing. Many of them are dismayed by the changing character of their cities and towns, where Muslim immigrants live, bring their religious rituals to the public square and alter for ever the cultural ambience that the local population had been accustomed to. Many Europeans now shun the use of public transportation in certain areas and at certain hours. Entire urban areas have brought the Muslim market place into Western cities, with the attending voices, sights and smells, much to the disgust of many, though also to the delight of some who would still laud cultural diversity if it were not for the accompanying atmosphere of violence and fear; the ugly sights of vandalism and littering in the heart of European cities previously famous for their neatness and public order; noises emanating from public squabbles or from shrieking *muezzin* calls for prayer from mosques in otherwise tranquil neighborhoods; the Muslims who squat for their Friday prayer in front of the most Italian of Christian churches in the heart of Florence and other cities; security forces that dare not enter certain Muslim neighborhoods for fear of battling violent criminals and drug dealers; and, most importantly, the oppression that many feel from their inability to air their concerns in public for fear of being seen as bigots or politically incorrect.

Right-wing political parties in these countries have learned to tap these concerns and to strengthen themselves politically, because they dare to voice in public what liberals and left-wingers consider taboo. And so, paradoxically, the liberal and socialist parties, who are lenient towards immigration and have thus increased their constituencies when the newcomers were naturalized and began voting, now find themselves impoverished when their original European constituents turn their backs on them. This has happened in France, the Netherlands, Australia and Italy, and is likely to spread into Germany and the United Kingdom if they do not tighten their restrictions on immigration into their respective territories. In the meantime, those who have immigrated- including Muslim radicals who admit in public their aspirations to subvert their benefactor states, have no qualms about milking the generous welfare systems that have absorbed them, or of using the tax payers' money, which was earned by the hard work of the local populations, to cultivate a whole subculture of parasitic dependence on state allowances which build up hatred against their naïve and well-meaning hosts. Thus, rapid breeding—in order for their community to grow demographically and strengthen its electoral influence, so as to allow it to demand more funds and allocations—has become a way for these immigrants to exert political pressure and achieve political goals. The children they have are taken care of by the host states, as is their housing, education, healthcare, unemployment benefits, pensions and minimum wages, which free them from work to sustain their unpublicized goals, such as sabotage and terrorism, building up caches of weapons, increasing Muslim proselytization, and demonstrating, at times violently for their fellow Arabs and Muslims around the world.

Muslim diasporas in the West, having acquired political power through sheer numbers, have also been attempting to dislodge from their advantageous positions the older and more established, though far less numerous, Jewish communities. By doing so they wish to eliminate the "Jewish influence" on the local governments and thereby shift the traditional political sympathies of the West from Israel to the Arabs. This is the reason why Islamic protests in Western societies almost invariably go hand in hand with anti-Semitic eruptions of violence and rampage. Again, this would seem an acceptable and legitimate way of political lobbying current in any open and liberal political system, except that Muslim populations do not, for the most part, fulfill the two conditions that go hand in hand with political protest: they do not act for the interest of their host countries rather than against it; nor do they refrain from violence and the breaking of the law. For the Muslim immigrants do not seem to have internalized and digested these restrictions and values at the same pace that they have mastered the list of benefits they can extract from their countries of shelter. On the first count, many naturalized Muslims—for example some of the perpetrators of 11 September and then the London attacks of July 2005—did not hesitate to act against their hosts who have showered them with benefits; and many other Muslims, who have sought shelter in Europe, Canada and Australia, devote their time not to assimilating into the new environment by implementing its rules, but cultivating their separate identities and building enclaves of Islam in their host countries and to their detriment. For example, far from accepting their countries' Middle Eastern policies, or their anti-terrorist struggles, they protest against them, often violently.

The second count of using violence, which is usually shunned in Western societies, raises even more concern because it ultimately hurts public order and the core of their value systems. Since the outbreak of the Palestinian al-Aqsa Intifadah in late 2000, thousands of violent demonstrations by Muslim immigrant populations have unfolded from Montreal to Sydney, from São Paolo to Durban (South Africa), from Oslo to Rome (apart from the usual anti-Israel and anti-Jewish demonstrations that have exploded throughout the Arab and Muslim world). Anti-Israeli demonstrations are certainly legitimate, but when they involve bouts of rage, the burning down of foreign Embassies and flags, and the pelting of rocks against houses of prayer, sometimes ending up in the murder of innocent civilians; or when effigies of American and Israeli leaders-who are often personal friends, and certainly political allies of the local leaders, are burnt and abuses hurled at them, this is the limit that the rule of law, of which the Muslim immigrants seem to be unaware or oblivious, cannot permit. Indeed, few local westerners participate in these acts of violence and rampage, and conversely no Jews have responded by committing the same acts against Western or Muslim countries with which the host society maintains relations. What is more, although Jewish communities worldwide have rallied around Israel, they have done so with dignity and full respect for the law, and have not allowed harm to be committed against their country of citizenship, or against the violent crowds of Muslims and their supporters.

The most distressing aspects of these outbursts of violence have been that Western countries have been turned, by their Muslim communities, into violent arenas where the Middle Eastern conflict has been exported and replayed. Not content with attacking American and Israeli symbols in most Western capitals and large cities, those hooligans who terrorize the downtown areas of their countries of residence, turned to cruel and brutal onslaughts on the local Jewish communities in France, Britain, Germany, Belgium and others, thus signaling to the world that Jews and Israel were to be equated and that anti-Semitism meant also anti-Zionism or pure and simple anti-Israeli outbursts. The worst hit were the Jewish communities of those countries where hundreds of Jewish synagogues, cemeteries, schools and other institutions were torched or otherwise desecrated, Jewish adults were attacked on their way to and from prayer, and children on their way to and from school; all that under the open eye of the local police who apparently did not dare to intervene forcefully for fear from the politically correct politicians on the eve of elections. One can only imagine what would have happened if a mosque or a church were likewise burned, or non-Jewish worshippers or children attacked and harmed. Other places too have experienced the full extent of this pogrom which in many Jewish circles was reminiscent of the infamous *Kristallnacht* of 1938. In most, though not all cases, these horrific anti-Semitic attacks were orchestrated by the Muslim communities of Europe, at times in conjunction with local inveterate anti-Semites.

The outcome of all this is that the Muslim communities in the Western democracies in general and in Europe in particular, have shown that they can act in unison to undermine public order, to pose a real threat to national security, and to harm their fellow citizens, Jewish and otherwise; this means that they can organize and demonstrate in the same fashion in their host countries wherever they judge an issue important enough to them, or when the local authorities are too lenient or reluctant to confront them. Polls organized in the United States after 11 September found that Americans overwhelmingly tied Islam and Muslims to those horrific events; 68% of them approved of randomly stopping people who might fit the profile of suspected terrorists; 83% of Americans favored stricter controls on Muslims entering the country; 58% wanted tighter controls on Muslims traveling on planes and trains; 35% of New Yorkers favored establishing internment camps for individuals who the authorities identified as sympathetic to terrorist causes; and 31% of all Americans favored detention camps for the Arab Americans as a way of preventing terrorist attacks in the United States.[35] This means that the threatened populations found themselves ahead of their authorities, who were more cautious in drastically limiting civil rights, and they were prepared to a great extent to replay the unfortunate experience of the internment of the Japanese-Americans in World War II. It was to be expected then that if and when more major acts of terror unfolded in the West, the latter would find itself compelled to curtail civil liberties and take radical measures against the Muslim minorities in its midst. Only in this "light" did the very moderate measures taken by Israel against its demonstratively hostile Muslim minority, which had come under scathing criticism from the pre-11 September world, look incredibly generous and even bordering at times with criminal neglect.

So, after 11 September we could observe two contradictory trends in the West: on the one hand Muslim minorities decried their "persecution and humiliation" for being lumped together with the terrorists of 11 September; but on the other hand, they themselves and other Muslims who were stunned by the outcome of those events, defied their countries of refuge and some of them began boasting of those feats and threatening a takeover of their host societies. The Arab- French of North African origin, including the second and third generation of *beur,* as they call themselves, who were seemingly totally assimilated Frenchmen, whistled in contempt when they heard the *Marseillaise* sung or saw the French colors hoisted in international football matches. They began to congregate around Muslim fundamentalist leaders and to adhere to all sorts of shady Muslim organizations, some of which operated under the cover of "charitable" institutions, mostly financed by Saudi Arabia or by violent groups bent on underground activity, to collect weapons for rainy days and to train their fellow Muslims for acts of terrorism. The same trends were identifiable on the morning of 11 September in the rest of Europe: England, France, Germany, Benelux and the Balkans.[36] It is significant that a columnist for the *Wall Street Journal* (European edition), Jonathan Stevenson, had to remind his readers after 11 September that as the subversive statements of Sheikh al-Bakri and his likes went ignored and unpunished in the United Kingdom, 11 out of the 19 Islamikaze hijackers had stayed in Britain a few months prior to that day of horror, and emphasized that Abu Hamza who acted from his Finsbury Park Mosque and was wanted in the Yemen for terrorism, had called for Jihad against Western Infidels, but his call remained ignored by the authorities. He gave a detailed account of several of the hijackers, of their training and shelter in Britain; and, as British law did not permit their extradition, they were permitted to thrive instead of closing the ring around them and amending legislation to allow their preventive arrest and expulsion. They indeed continued to raise funds, to purchase property, to publish their propaganda and to escape scrutiny. He confirmed that since the 1970s Britain had concentrated on the terrorist threat of the IRA and, thinking it could wean the Sinn Fein from terrorism by allowing them full expression of their agenda, and believing it could carry this non-confrontational policy over to al-Qa'ida and other Islamic groups who subscribe to its grand strategy. But he concluded that since negotiable objectives did not fit that strategy, and since Bin Laden simply wanted to "debilitate the U.S. and its allies through violence," those counter-terrorism measures would not work. Only after 11 September did London wake up and outlaw 21 terrorist front organizations—16 of them Islamic—but it still remained, all the same, a staging and logistics center for al-Qa'ida. Over 100 British Muslims had joined the Taliban in Afghanistan, and at least 55 British Muslims had received military training at terrorist bases in Afghanistan since 1996.[37]

The United States adopted stiff measures of screening its Muslim population or Muslim immigrants to the country, and other supervisory measures to curtail prospective terrorist activities. But the squeamish, hesitant and disunited Europeans, in spite of their being, paradoxically, part of the European "Union," not only did not follow immediately in U.S. footsteps, but were quick to disparage American "hysteria" and castigate Washington for its "disproportionate" reactions. In their June 2002 Conference in Spain, where they discussed clamping down on Muslim illegal immigration with a view to blocking entrance to fundamentalist elements, their disunity was rather disappointing. But it was also becoming clear that the emergency measures adopted by the United States, Britain and Israel, could not be sustained in the long run, because not only were they untenable in terms of civil liberties, but they also demanded a long-term state of alert that could wear out innocent civilians who must pay the collective price for their leaders' incompetence, irresponsibility and lack of foresight and courage in tackling a dangerous situation that had been in the making for years but which they chose not to confront. Hence the need to draw up a new policy, not a stop-gap, of re-educating the public; re-organizing state institutions to deal with the enemy from within, but without imposing new immigration limitations; surveillance of potentially subversive groups; repatriation to their countries of origin of inciters and promoters of violence; new legal systems to deal firmly and swiftly with subversive elements; constantly testing the allegiance of trouble makers to their host countries; and evincing resoluteness in battling the terrorists and their supporters and assistants in Western Europe. However, while President Bush had singled out the candidates for Western retaliation, like the countries of the "axis of Evil," Europeans sought to avoid confrontation, hoping to continue to buy the "goodwill" of terrorist organizations by allowing them to operate on their soil with impunity.

These soft policies were bound to fail, however, because unlike the "carrot and stick" policy of the United States, which rewarded allies and came down harshly on terrorists and their supporters, European governments naively thought that not using the stick was the biggest carrot they could offer, not realizing that the terrified public in the cities, towns and neighborhoods of their countries had understood that the permissive policies of the past, which had allowed hundreds of thousands of potential terrorists to flock in unchecked, could no longer be pursued. They began to clamor for security in their homes and environment, that their cities be re-Westernized, and that the grounds lost to the hordes of terrorists, by domestic oversight and blind "liberalism," or by oblivious "multiculturalism," which have hitherto served the purposes of politicians to whom the immigrants felt obligated on election day, must be reclaimed. The public in Western Europe, Canada, and Australia has indeed rewarded its tougher politicians who have spoken out against unbridled immigration, by electing right-wing parties and wiping out socialists, and this trend seems to have taken hold and forced some politicians to change course, while a rear-guard of them and their dependents, like Cherie Blair and Jack Straw, was still expressing "compassion for the bombers" and "understanding" their "despair."[38] Just imagine that should everyone who felt in despair in this world be shown compassion for mass-murdering others, and the world population would rapidly diminish. Bernard Lewis, the great luminary of Middle Eastern studies wrote back in the 1990s about the quandary of modern Islam, where "traditional dignity and courtesy towards others turned into an explosive mixture of rage and hatred," impelling it to "espouse kidnapping and assassination and try to find in the life of their Prophet, approval and indeed precedent for such an action."[39] Now, the most urgent question has become how to tame that rage, which prompts Muslim groups to blow up restaurants and buses, Buddha statues and Churches, to desecrate others' holy sites and call them names, to kidnap people and then chop off their heads live on video, and then claim that they are the "victims" of others. This feeling was often reinforced by Western liberals, who instead of castigating terrorists urged their compatriots to "understand" them, and instead of helping to uproot them, elected to look at the "root causes" of terrorism, whatever they are, and to call upon their governments to alter their policies.

For their part, Muslims have quickly grasped that by wrapping themselves in the cloak of victimhood, they have achieved the earthly vision of nirvana. It licenses them to kill and sow mayhem wherever they go, in the certainty that they will not be held accountable for their misdeeds. It is always the fault of others, or of the occupation, the aggression, the humiliation, the political degradation, the economic deprivation, the sanctions, the "fence of apartheid," *ad nauseam,* inflicted on the "defenseless" Muslims by America, Israel, Britain, and latterly Denmark. A visitor from another planet could be forgiven for thinking that Muslims have been passive actors throughout their 1,400-year history, rather than occupiers, expansionists, founders of empires, eliminators of other nations and cultures, aggressors and conquerors. Western liberals have not done the Muslims a favor by infantilizing them to such an extent in this way. That the Muslims continue to live down to the low expectations of those who are volubly sympathetic to them, has actually had the perverse effect of arresting their development. A cursory look at the UN Arab Human Development Report, for instance, will attest to a staggering level of backwardness for a part of the Muslim world which has benefited from enormous inflows of cash from oil sales over the past decades.

In Britain, immediately after 11 September, people were gripped by fear and began to prepare for the next terrorist attack, which many thought might be in London, as it indeed was on 7 July 2005. Shops began to sell gas masks and protective suits for biological, chemical and even nuclear attacks. Iran's insistence on developing nuclear weapons, and their possession of systems of delivery to the heart of Europe, only make that fear more concrete. The authorities in London have updated the procedures for mass evacuation, at the same time that Mayor Livingstone continues to embrace the top ideologue of the Islamikaze, Sheikh Yussuf al-Qaradawi. At the same time that those responsible for the underground system prepare it to once again fill the function of mass shelter as in World War II, 7 July has demonstrated that the subway tunnels are the least safe place for Londoners who remain complacent. While Tony Blair warned against "fanatics who are totally indifferent to the sanctity of life, and have little compunction about how many people they kill,"[40] his determination turned into disarray when those feared terrorists hit on 7 July, and he described them as "criminals" and voiced his "astonishment" that homegrown Britons should commit these horrors. Criminals are people who break the law for their own gain, while the young Britons who committed the 7 July horrors did not seek gain. On the contrary, they were prepared to risk their lives for their ideas and beliefs (they were fanatics as he had appropriately dubbed them before). The writing had been on the wall since 11 September, when John Stevens, the Metropolitan Police Commissioner of London warned that his city was next in line.[41] On the face of it, Bin Laden had attained his goal: to sow panic in the

West and to force it not only to squander its resources and energies on defensive measures, but also to be passive and wait for the next strike which the Islamikaze might deliver at any time and any place of their choice. Truly, the London Police had been on terrorist alert ever since, and many more of it have been patrolling the streets more than ever before in peacetime. More security guards were posted in strategic areas such as the Stock Exchange, telephone switchboards, water pumps and electric power stations; passenger airplanes were prohibited from over-flying the center of London, and regressive emergency legislation to compel everyone in Britain to carry an ID card was proposed.

But all that was not sufficient, because terrorists look always for the soft spots in the defense system and hit wherever the alert leaves something to be desired. ID cards were proposed but not distributed to the population, entrances to subways, movie theaters, shopping malls, buses and restaurants, were left unguarded, and it is there that the terrorists stuck on 7 July. It is certainly a heavy burden to do all that, but it is not impossible. It is too late to impose all those costly safeguards after the terrorists have succeeded. Now they will wait for the relaxation of these measures to hit again. What is more important is that security experts admitted that Britain had been a safe haven for terrorist networks for too many years, due to its liberal immigration policies, the many breaches at border crossing stations, the rigorous consideration shown for individual rights, the legislation that made extradition difficult and the large Muslim population (well in excess of the stated two million, but no precise data are available). Those experts also realized that the links between Arab sheikhs and businessmen and the Home and Foreign Offices had for years allowed work permits to be liberally distributed, with the depleted police force rarely carrying out spot-checks in streets, trains and other land transport. London had also served as an international center of financial services, investment and transactions for Muslim companies and organizations, which often use straw men to launder money in the service of terrorist groups. No wonder, then that 11 of the 19 terrorists who carried out the attacks on 11 September had spent time in London before proceeding to their targets, and the fear is rife that more cells of Bin Laden might still be operating clandestinely. The British distinguish between "mouths" and "brains" in these organizations, the former being extremist propaganda groups, such as the *Muhajirun* already mentioned above, headed by al-Bakri who was copiously cited above. These groups, though under surveillance, are active in recruiting Believers and disseminating hate literature, especially against Jews and homosexuals, Israel and the United States. The "brains" are smaller, compartmentalized underground groups who keep a low profile.[42] Now the British might have to adjust their categorization and add a third group, that of active terrorists, especially after the 7 July terrorist attacks in London.

This sort of state of mind has become so widespread in Europe that many articles began to appear either bemoaning the fate of sinking Europe, or calling for its awakening. There is a view that maybe Bin Laden did the European Muslims a disservice by precipitating his attack on America. Had he waited another ten years or so, they would have been far more firmly entrenched in the institutions and society of the various countries, and may have also irreversibly infiltrated the security forces and apparatus, thus putting asleep the security services for that much longer. Then they would have been in a much more advantageous position to strike. But happened what happened, and public opinion in Europe woke up following 11 September and began to wonder about what was happening to their countries. A castigating article by George Weigel, which describes the caving in of Europe and its consequences, sums up the situation. He tells that at the height of the morning commute on March 11, 2004, when ten bombs exploded in and around four train stations in Madrid, almost 200 Spaniards were killed, and some 2,000 wounded, Spain seemed to be standing firm against terror, with demonstrators around the country wielding signs denouncing the "murderers" and "assassins." Yet things did not hold. Seventy-two hours after the bombs had strewn arms, legs, heads, and other body parts over three train stations and a marshaling yard, the Spanish government of Jose María Aznar, a staunch ally of the United States and Great Britain in Iraq, was soundly defeated in an election that the socialist opposition had long sought to turn into a referendum on Spain's role in the war on terror. A 54-page al-Qa'ida document, which came to light three months after the bombings, speculated that the Aznar government would be unable to "suffer more than two or three strikes before pulling out [of Iraq] under pressure from its own people." In the event, it was one strike and out—as it was for the Spanish troops in Iraq who were withdrawn shortly thereafter, just as the newly elected prime minister, Jose Luis Zapatero, had promised on the day after Spanish voters chose appeasement. At first the Madrid bombings seemed to aggravate public opinion against a conservative government, and that led to the installation of a leftist prime minister, who then proceeded to do many of the things that aggressively secularizing governments in Spain have tried to do in the past. In fact, however, it turned out that the events of the past two years in Spain are a microcosm of the two interrelated culture wars that beset Western Europe today. The first Culture War (A) is a war between the postmodern forces of moral relativism and the defenders of traditional moral conviction. The second "Culture War B" is the struggle to define the nature of civil society, the meaning of tolerance and pluralism, and the limits of multiculturalism in an aging Europe whose below-replacement-level fertility rates have opened the door to rapidly growing and assertive Muslim populations. The aggressors in Culture War A are radical secularists, who aim to eliminate the vestiges of Europe's Judeo-Christian culture from a post-Christian European Union by demanding same-sex marriage in the name of equality, by restricting free speech in the name of civility, and by abrogating core aspects of religious freedom in the name of tolerance. The aggressors in Culture War B are radical and jihadist Muslims who detest the West, who are determined to impose Islamic taboos on Western societies by violent protest and other forms of coercion if necessary, and who see such operations as the first stage toward the Islamification of Europe—or, in the case of what they often refer to as *al-Andalus*, the restoration of the right order of things, temporarily reversed in 1492 by Ferdinand and Isabella, when they completed the *reconquista* of Iberia and expelled the Muslims. The question Europe must face, but which much of Europe seems reluctant to face, is whether the aggressors in Culture War A have not made it exceptionally difficult for the forces of true tolerance and authentic civil society to prevail in Culture War B.[43]

What is more, 60 years after the end of World War II, the European instinct for appeasement is alive and well. French public swimming pools have been segregated by sex because of Muslim protests. "Piglet" mugs have disappeared from certain British retailers after Muslim complaints that the A.A. Milne character was offensive to Islamic sensibilities. So have Burger King chocolate ice-cream swirls, which reminded some Muslims of Arabic script from the Qur'an. Bawer reports that the British Red Cross banished Christmas trees and nativity scenes from its charity stores for fear of offending Muslims. For similar reasons, the Dutch police in the wake of the van Gogh murder destroyed a piece of Amsterdam street art that proclaimed "Thou shalt not kill"; schoolchildren were forbidden to display Dutch flags on their backpacks because immigrants might think them "provocative." The European media frequently censor themselves in matters relating to domestic Islamic radicalism and crimes committed by Muslims, and, with rare exceptions, their coverage of the war against terrorism makes the American mainstream media look balanced. When domestic problems related to Muslim immigrants do come to light, the typical European reaction, according to Bawer, is usually one of self-critique. In Malmo, Sweden, the country's third-largest city, rapes, robberies, school-burnings, "honor" killings, and anti-Semitic agitation got so out of hand that large numbers of native Swedes reportedly moved out; the government blamed Malmo's problems instead on Swedish racism, and chastised those who had wrongly conceived of integration in "two hierarchically ordered categories, a 'we' who shall integrate and a 'they' who shall be integrated." Belgium, for its part, has established a governmental Center for Equal Opportunities and Opposition to Racism (CEEOR) that recently sued a manufacturer of security garage gates whose Moroccan employees work only in the factory and are not sent out to install the gates in Belgian homes. By contrast, according to the Belgian journalist Paul Belien, whose online *"Brussels Journal"* (www.brusselsjournal.com) is an important source of information on Europe's culture wars, CEEOR declined to prosecute a Muslim who created an anti-Semitic cartoon series, on the grounds that doing so would "inflame the situation." Perhaps predictably, European Jews have frequently played the role of the canary in the mineshaft amid the trials of Islamic integration. Some time ago, a Parisian disc jockey was brutally murdered, his assailant crying "I have killed my Jew. I will go to heaven." That same night, another Muslim murdered a Jewish woman while her daughter watched, horrified. Yet at the time, as the columnist Mark Steyn has written, "no major French newspaper carried the story" of these homicides. In February 2006, the French media did report on the gruesome murder of a 23-year-old Jewish man, Ilan Halimi, who had been tortured for three weeks by an Islamist gang; his screams under torture were heard by his family during phone calls demanding ransom while, Steyn reports, "the torturers read out verses from the Qur'an." He quotes one police detective shrugging off the *jihadist* dimension of the horror by saying that it was all rather simple: "Jews equal money."[44]

These patterns of sedition and appeasement finally came to global attention in early 2006 in the Danish-cartoons jihad. The cartoons themselves, depicting Muhammad, caused little comment in Denmark or anywhere else when they were originally published months earlier in the Copenhagen daily *Jyllands-Posten*. But after Islamist Danish imams began agitating throughout the Middle East (aided by three additional and far more offensive cartoons of their own devising), an international furor erupted, with dozens of people killed by rioting Muslims in Europe, Africa, and Asia. As Henrik Bering put it in the *Weekly Standard*, "the Danes were suddenly the most hated people on earth, with their embassies under attack, their flag being burned, and their consciousness being raised by lectures on religious tolerance from Iran, Saudi Arabia, and other beacons of enlightenment." The response from Europe, in the main, was to intensify appeasement. Thus the Italian "Reforms Minister," Roberto Calderoli, was forced to resign for having worn a T-shirt featuring one of the offending cartoons—a "thoughtless action" that, Prime Minister Silvio Berlusconi deduced, had caused a riot outside the Italian consulate in Benghazi in which 11 people were killed. Newspapers that ran the cartoons were put under intense political pressure; some journalists faced criminal charges; websites were forced to close. The pan-European Carrefour supermarket chain, bowing to Islamist demands for a boycott of Danish goods, placed signs in its stores in both Arabic and English expressing "solidarity" with the "Islamic community" and noting, inelegantly if revealingly, "Carrefour don't carry Danish products." The Norwegian government forced the editor of a Christian publication to apologize publicly for printing the Danish cartoons; at his press conference, the hapless editor was surrounded by Norwegian cabinet ministers and imams. EU foreign minister Javier Solana groveled his way from one Arab nation to another, pleading that Europeans shared the "anguish" of Muslims "offended" by the Danish cartoons. Not to be outdone, the EU's justice minister, Franco Frattini, announced that the EU would establish a "media code" to encourage "prudence"—"prudence" being a synonym for "surrender," regardless of one's view of the artistic merits of, or the cultural sensitivity displayed by, the world's most notorious cartoons. For all the blindness of the politicians who in the 1930s attempted to appease totalitarian aggression, they at least thought that they were thereby preserving their way of life. Bruce Bawer (following the researcher and author Bat Ye'or) suggests that twenty-first-century Europe's appeasement of Islamists amounts to a self-inflicted *dhimmitude*: in an attempt to slow the advance of a rising Islamist tide, many of Europe's national and transnational political leaders are surrendering core aspects of sovereignty and turning Europe's native populations into second- and third-class citizens in their own countries.[45]

Notes

1.   Sarah Wildman, *The Christian Science Monitor*, 24 May 2006 http://www.csmonitor.com/2006/0524/p07s02-woeu.html
2.   *Ibid.*
3.   Amitai Etzioni, *From Empire to Community,* McMillan, NY, 2004.
4.   Anthony Browne and Suna Erdem, "Education Clash Hold Up EU Talks," *The Times,* 8 April 2006.
5.   Abu al-'Ala' al-Mawdoodi, *Nationalism in India,* Malihabad, 1948, pp. 5-11.
6.   Robert Burns, *The Crusader Kingdom of Valencia,* Harvard University Press, Cambridge, MA, 1967, p. 303
7.   *Reuters*, cited by *Haaretz,* 8 April 2006.
8.   Molly Moore, "With End of French School Year Comes Threat of Deportation" *Washington Post* - 15 June 2006
9.   *Ibid.*
10.   *Ibid*
11.   *Ibid.*
12.   Ahiya Raved,   "Ex-Mossad chief warns of Muslim European cities and of World War Three," in his address to the Board of Trustees to the Technion in Haifa, Israel, 4 June 2006. http://www.ynetnews.com/articles/0,7340,L-3258745,00.html
13.   "Jihadists' return worries Europe" *Agence France Press*, cited by *Washington Times,* 18 May 2006
14.   "Talking of immigrants: America's debate on immigration may be painful, but Europe's is dysfunctional" *Economist,* 1 June 2006.
15.   *Ibid.*
16.   *Ibid.*
17.   Peter Almond, " Beware: the new goths are coming," *The Sunday Times*—11 June 2006.
18.   *Ibid.*
19.   Philippe Jacques, "The challenge is to adapt our societies to Islam," Cafe Babel—*The European Magazine*, 16 December 2004 (Translated from the French by Veronica Newington)
20.   *Ibid.*
21.   *Ibid.*
22.   Michael Binyon, " Prince pitches for religious tolerance," *The Times,* 5 May 2006.
23.   "The clash of civilizations is currently on hold," *Copenhagen Post Online*—20 April 2006, http://www.cphpost.dk/get/95174.html
24.   *Ibid.*
25.   *Ibid.*
26.   "In a new biography, Denmark's Queen Margrethe II says should be challenged" *Copenhagen Post Online*, 14 April 2005, http://www.cphpost.dk/get/87253.html
27.   By Lee Kaplan, " Islamism's Legal Manipulations," *FrontPageMagazine.com*, 9 May 2000
28.   Nicola Woolcock and Sean O'Neill, "Once a friendly Christian, he now backs the bombers: Two faces, two converts—two Muslim extremists in Britain ," *The Times*—24 April 2006.

29. *Ibid.*
30. *Ibid.*
31. Nicola Woolcock and Dominic Kennedy, "What the neo-Nazi fanatic did next: switched to Islam, Two faces, two converts—two Muslim extremists in Britain," *The Times*, 24 April 2006.
32. *Ibid.*
33. Nicola Woolcock and Sean O'Neill, "Two faces, two converts—two Muslim extremists in Britain," *The Times*, 24 April 2006.
34. Kevin Sullivan, "British Slow to Recognize Threat of Terrorism: London Bombings Couldn't Have Been Prevented, Report Says," *Washington Post*, 11 May 2006.
35. See Daniel Pipes, "Fighting Militant Islam, without Bias," *City Journal*, Autumn 2001. http://www.city-journal.org/htm/41/fightingmilitant.html
36. For a basic survey of the Muslims in Europe, se the now outdated work of Gilles Keppel, *La Revanche de Dieu.*
37. *Wall Street Journal, Europe,* 15 November 2001. See also article by Jocelyne Cesari, in MSANews 6 June 2000 who drew a wide background of the situation of the Muslims in Western Europe.
38. *Associated Press,* cited by *Ha'aretz,* 20 June 2002.
39. Bernard Lewis, "The Roots of Muslim Rage," *Atlantic Monthly,* September 1990.
40. Sharon Sadeh, "The London Bridge is Collapsing," *Haaretz*, 30 September.
41. *Ibid.*
42. *Ibid.*
43. George Weigel, "Europe's Two Culture Wars"—*Commentary*—May 2006.
44. *Ibid.*
45. *Ibid.*

2

BENELUX Countries: From Liberalism to Wariness

Belgium and Holland are the two small and significant European countries to have faced the problem of Muslim immigrations (Luxembourg is too small to count in that regard), the former as the political and economic center of the European Union, the latter for its extraordinarily liberal laws towards immigrants which have turned sour. Undoubtedly the two heroes of the awakening to Muslim danger and the domestic struggle in those countries to contain it, are Hirsi Ali, a Somalian-Muslim woman naturalized Dutch and elected member of the Dutch Parliament, and the late director Theo van Gogh who was assassinated in the streets of Amsterdam for his film critical of Islam. Both have paid for their courage. She has been forced into hiding, and he with his life. However, their symbolic impact is immense. First, by courageously putting their lives on the line in spite of the threats against them; second, by taking their individual initiative where the authorities were helpless; third, by showing the way to other people, perhaps the silent majority who felt like them but constraints of political correctness prevented them from acting; fourth, by becoming household names and symbols of what needed to be done.

Due to her involvement in political life, Hirsi had also made news unrelated to Islam in Europe and attracted fire. For example, in September 2005, just before the Cartoon Affair broke out, she sought to have a small Christian Dutch party outlawed because it opposed homosexual marriage and abortion. But in March 2006 her voice was heard again when she demanded from Belgium to ban the country's large nationalist party "Vlaams Belang"(VB) because of its "Islamophobia." Indeed, in an interview she gave to an Antwerp newspaper, she explained why she regarded that party as dangerous:

> I would ban the VB because it hardly differs from the Hofstad Group [the *Jihadi* terrorist network in the Netherlands that killed van Gogh]. Though the VB members have not committed any violent crimes yet, they are just postponing them and waiting until they have an absolute majority. On many issues they have exactly the same opinions as the Muslim extremists: on the position of women, on the suppression of gays, on abortion. This way of thinking will lead straight to genocide.[1]

Whether Hirsi wished to redeem herself in the eyes of her Muslim community, or to warn in her straightforward style against the revival of fascism, her objections found echoes in a Europe that is now torn between politically correct conduct and a defensive instinct to show a strong hand towards Islam. For example, she was charged of denouncing a "leading conservative European party as Nazi-like" and warning was served that she "is as much of an enemy to the West as she is to traditional Islam," and therefore the "anti-Islamist conservatives who view her as their hero are deluding themselves and weakening the West." She was also accused that by opposing "religious totalitarianism" instead of just "Islamic totalitarianism," she was clearly targeting Christianity as well as Islam. In her attempt to ban Christian parties and Christian values she equated with Nazism, she actually meant Christianity no less than Islam, thereby defining herself as anti-Christian and anti-Western. This attack by Conservative Lawrence Auster, that was carried on Internet, also insinuates Hirsi's involvement with the new "perverted" film that was shown to prospective immigrants to the Netherlands. It showed footage of a gay couple kissing, which if it was shunned by the immigrants they would fail the test, and it would keep many Muslims out.

Auster then asks in mock horror: "If that country [and by inference Hirsi herself] adopts decadence and perversion as its official culture, as surely as it permits free Muslim immigration, then Hirsi plays that double role: she is both a libertarian leftist [meaning that she believes in the absolute moral freedom for perversion,] but not in ordinary political freedom for political parties that oppose perversion; and at the same time she is herself a Muslim immigrant, who despite her apostasy seeks to ban Islamophobia and thus make it impossible for the West to defend itself from Islam." The author of this attack also advanced the claim that this has become the pattern of Muslim immigrants to the West: Conservatives eagerly include in their ranks "conservative" immigrants, like Hirsi herself, who use their position among conservatives to silence other conservative opposition to the continued immigration or empowerment of their own religious or national group, and came to the conclusion that Muslims could not be counted on, whether they are moderates or apostates, to "resolve the Muslim problem," and that conservatives like him could only depend on themselves.[2]

During all the period of her single-handed courageous fight for Muslim women rights, she has lived many years in fear and exile under perpetual threats towards her life. Just like Salman Rushdie who could no longer endure the murderous *fatwa* on his life and had to immigrate to the United States to remake his life, Hirsi also came to that conclusion. Her landlords had received threats towards their lives if they continued to shelter their famous tenant. They decided to give her up. The court system gave her only four months to find another place to live and did not provide her with any assistance. For it was the Islamists who now determined the Dutch agenda, not the generous and tolerant Dutch legal system. The day of 28 April 2006 is considered to be a Dutch day of infamy, when The Hague gave its verdict in the case started by Hirsi's neighbors who sensed her presence was a security risk for them. Apparently nothing has changed since World War II, when the common folk used their police and their courts to remove people being threatened instead of protecting them. Betrayal and cowardice have become integrated in the European psyche. Disgusted and disappointed by the host country she had elected as her place of asylum, Hirsi also left for the United States, resigning her membership in the Dutch Parliament. She joins Rushdie in the land of ultimate freedom where she will not be persecuted. Her fate has been better than that of, say, Anne Frank's though. She will not be led to gas chambers but to the pampering comfort and warm welcome of America. But for Holland the same disgrace will continue to hover over the country's famous tolerance.[3]

Hirsi's story was intertwined with that of Dutch filmmaker Theo van Gogh. On 2 November 2004, van Gogh was riding his bicycle along one of Amsterdam's main streets, when a young man, later identified as Mohammed Bouyeri who was of Dutch and Moroccan descent, wearing a *galabiya* approached him and shot him eight times. As he lay bleeding on the ground, van Gogh (great-grand-son of Theo, brother of painter Vincent van Gogh,) asked the man to spare his life. Eyewitnesses related that van Gogh said to the assailant, "I'm sure we can talk about this." But Bouyeri then pulled out two butcher knives and slashed van Gogh's throat and plunged the second knife into his chest. To the knife, he attached a five-page letter in Dutch, containing a *fatwa*, or death decree. It was addressed to Ayaan Hirsi Ali, the member of the Dutch Parliament from the Liberal Party and a Muslim of Somali origin. About six months earlier, van Gogh—who was known to have made harsh comments about Muslims—made an 11-minute film called *Submission* based on a script by Hirsi Ali. In the film, five women appear, each with a story of her own. Verses from the Qur'an are inscribed on their naked bodies. Their spokeswoman, a young actress wearing a *hijab* (the Muslim head covering), prays to Allah in their name and presents their stories to Him. "Look, Allah," the heroine says. "I devoted myself to you utterly, but everything is going wrong. And still, Allah, you continue to remain silent."

Hirsi Ali immediately went underground once she learned about the van Gogh's murder. At first she was taken to her home, afterwards during the course of a few months, she moved from a Dutch Navy base to a few police stations and then to the United States. She explained:

> This was not the first time information had been received that I was going to be murdered, but in the past it was always something remote, unrealized, theoretical. It is in the realm of theory when your bodyguards tell you, "We will not drive along this street now," or "You have to travel in an armored car." But it's different when the throat of someone you worked with is slashed and he is stabbed. That is something I will never forget. And I will also not forget my terrible sense of guilt, and the sadness and guilt because Theo ignored my request not to include his name in the credits for *Submission*. He was very stubborn and told me that he did not intend to forgo the

credit. "I live in a free country," he told me, "and I will not allow people to prevent me from putting my name on my film." I couldn't stop him. I underwent a deep crisis, which is still affecting my life.[4]

Ayaan Hirsi Ali—one of the best known, most highly regarded, and most controversial politicians in Europe—was born in Mogadishu, Somalia in 1969. Her mother, who is illiterate, wanted to remove her from school, but Hirsi Ali persisted and completed her schooling. In 1992, her father was about to arrange a marriage for her with a relative who lived in Canada and whom she had never met. She was supposed to go to Germany and from there fly to Canada. But instead of marrying, she decided to get on a train from Germany to Holland, where she requested political asylum. She then held various short-term jobs, from cleaning to mail sorting, while studying Dutch, social work, and eventually political science at the University of Leiden. Between 1995 and 2001, she worked as an independent interpreter and translator for the National Migration Service. After earning her masters in political science, Hirsi Ali became a fellow at the Wiardi Beckman Foundation, a scientific institute linked to the social-democratic PvdA, the Dutch Labor Party. In November 2002 she switched to the liberal VVD party, which offered her a position in Parliament. Hirsi Ali was an assistant of the VVD parliamentary party between November 2002 and January 2003. In January 2003 she was elected to the Tweede Kamer, the House of Representatives of the Dutch Parliament. In 2004, following the murder of Theo van Gogh, Hirsi Ali became the most closely guarded politician in the history of modern Holland—a country where the justice minister used to travel to work on a bicycle until a few years ago. But the murder has not deterred her. Despite the risk, she continued to go on helping other Muslims, especially Muslim women from immigrant families, and women throughout the Muslim world. Not all of them seem to want that help.

Hirsi Ali's book *The Caged Virgin: An Emancipation Proclamation for Women and Islam*, was published in English, and there is no doubt that it will add another bit of fuel to the fire in the Muslim public discourse. In the book, Hirsi Ali turns her criticism on moderate, silent Islam. Its symbol, she says, is the father of Mohamed Atta, the leader of the plane hijackings on 11 September, 2001. Not long after the events, she writes, Atta's father appeared on television looking bewildered. He could not believe that his son, who had been a promising architecture student in Germany, was behind the attacks. His son, he stated on television, had nothing to do with it. The Jews and the CIA and others were to blame, but not his son. Moderate Islam, says Hirsi Ali, will continue to be the hostage of extremist Islam until it liberates itself from the dynamic of denial and stops imputing blame to others.[5]

Hirsi Ali's father, Hirsi Magan Isse, was one of the leaders of the resistance against the Somali despot Siad Barre and was forced to flee the country together with his family. They wandered through Saudi Arabia and Ethiopia, later settling in Kenya. Hirsi Magan, who attended universities in the United States and

Italy, did not want his two daughters, Ayaan and her younger sister, to undergo female circumcision. However, he had lived far from his family for years, and so it happened that when Ayaan was five and her father was away, her grandfather organized the circumcision for her and her sister. Today, Hirsi Ali is a strong opponent of circumcision for both men and women. She is reluctant to speak of her own experience, however:

> What happened to me has happened to 135 million girls around the world. Every day, 60,000 girls undergo castration, mutilation. My story is of no relevance at all in this context. As a representative of the Dutch people, including Dutch girls and women who are the daughters of migrants or are seeking political asylum, I do not think I should talk about the experiences I underwent, how they affected me sexually and emotionally and so forth, but on the ways to fight this custom. You have to understand that in the place I come from, Somalia, all the girls undergo female circumcision. It is a tradition dating back thousands of years. The custom can be understood only from a cultural, symbolic point of view. In terms of the symbolic value in the milieu I come from, female circumcision and ritual circumcision of males are similar traditions. My grandmother wanted me to undergo the act because she loved me, because she was concerned about me. She was afraid that I would not be able to find a husband if I did not undergo circumcision. She also believed that the clitoris would grow to vast dimensions if it was not cut in time. In the world I come from there are a great many myths about women and about female sexuality, which help reinforce the custom. In the Somali culture the act is performed because the clitoris is considered an impure organ, and also in order to preserve the girl's virginity. Unlike the Saudis, who have enough money and means to implement sexual segregation, a type of apartheid between men and women, the Somalis are poor and their young women are part of the workforce....[6]

Female circumcision was just the first stage in the indoctrination process undergone by Hirsi Ali. She encountered the systematic doctrine of extremist Islam for the first time in the mid-1980s, as a 16-year-old Nairobi high-school student. Her history teacher, Sister Aziza, took the class for an outing to the Iranian embassy and promoted a revolution. Gradually the girls started to cover themselves.... She started to wear the *hijab* and to admire the Muslim Brotherhood. Aziza started to use the "*yahud*" (Jews) word. One day she said: "You all sit up and listen." She showed the girls a magazine from Iran with pictures of dead people, piles of bodies and blood, and said: "look what the *yahud* have done to the Muslims." The pictures were Iranian propaganda. They were taken from the Iran-Iraq war, showing Iraqi soldiers killing Iranian citizens. But it wasn't shown as if the Iraqis killed those people, as if Saddam killed those people. This is what the Jews have done, and Saddam was an agent of the Jews. Sister Aziza showed how to pray: You hold your hands together, and you say: "Allah please protect us from evil, Allah please keep us healthy, Allah please take care of my mother and my father, Allah please destroy the Jews." She pursued her tale:

> We are not born as terrorists. To be able to kill yourself you have to have extreme willpower. If the entire environment, your family, your clan, your tribe, your country, is telling you that this is the straight path to Allah—and you want to become a winner,

you want to become a hero. But I did not think in those terms. I thought more in terms of being an Olympic champion. You want to enter that noble circle, to receive the gold medal from the hands of Allah, of the creator. And there is also the matter of the fear of hell. In a certain sense, to devote your life to Allah is to obtain immunity from hell. So, if you believe that life is only a transit point on the way to paradise, why go through 80 years of sin and redemption, and again sin and redemption? I think that the concept of hell in Islam is hardly understood in the West, and therefore the West is incapable of waging psychological warfare against the *shahid* idea…

For me, "*yahud*" [Jew] was not the same as human. It's the enemy. It's Satan. I remember a joke, well, it wasn't even a joke, from the time I was a very little girl. We were in Riyadh and Jedda when the oil boom started. They were trying to build an oil pump; the construction project went on forever. At last, when the project was done, they opened the top of the pump, but instead of oil, water came out. And I remember my mom saying: "See, the Jews are at it again." And I think about the three most horrible insults you could think of in my world. The insults were "*yahud*," "*shuri*" and "*hanis*." "Shuri" means a communist. "Hanis" means gay. You guys are used to laughing at it, but it's really not a laughing matter. Because it's no longer just the Saudis who think like that. These ideas are spreading throughout Islam and all over the world to people who never met Jews, who know nothing about Israelis or what Israel represents.

In 1993 I went to Antwerp with a friend. The friend said, 'We are now in the Jewish neighborhood' and pointed at an Orthodox Jew. And I lost my breath and said: "Jewish?! Is he Jewish?! Wait, where? Where?" You see, I needed to visualize this huge fantasy of evil that I had in my head. And then he showed me a few people walking around and asked, 'What exactly were you expecting?' I looked around and said, "Can you tell me, if a kid has two hands and two legs and he's walking, are there children who are Jewish as well?" And my friend responded: "Yes, there are Jewish children as well." At that moment I felt something else inside me that said it was shameful to voice what I had felt. I had to suppress that. So in 1993 I didn't talk about it again. It was in 1994, during history class, when I first saw pictures of what happened in the Second World War. I was coming from Somalia, and similar things started to happen in my country, along with Rwanda, Sudan, Liberia, Sierra Leone…. There are many things I learned at that time in history class, but the story of the Holocaust made the biggest impression on me. I went to all the Holocaust museums. I've been to Yad Vashem twice. As I understood it, the Holocaust wasn't just the story of the Jews … I don't know if this goes for everyone, but knowledge enlightened me … As a Muslim, I belong to the universal tribe. Every human individual, regardless of his beliefs, faith, sex, deserves to live and is equal. My criticism is of religion, especially Islam, and not of Muslims. Therefore, my criticism of Islam is not a rejection of Muslims. It is the idea of race that makes us destroy each other. You have to change your mind and learn to accept the other. My case is to convince fellow Muslims. I call myself Muslim not because I believe in Allah any longer, but I come out of that culture, and I want to fight to modify that culture, and create a culture of love and human rights….

Voting for Hamas is voting for terror, voting against the existence of Israel. Hamas doesn't want to recognize Israel, and yet the EU will give money to Hamas. I don't think for a moment that Hamas will spend the money on these poor people. They will use it to indoctrinate the poor people and create more terrorists. Indirectly, the EU would be financing terrorism, [using] the argument of compassion.[7]

When asked whether she was afraid to be murdered, she likened that condition to being afraid to get on a bus, and yet the fear does not prevent you from boarding the bus, going into the street, buying a pizza. You know only that you want to keep going. But yes, for weeks she can be perfectly fine, with no worries or fears. And then suddenly, something happens. She starts to look around and everyone who moves near her frightens her. And then it is gone again, it disappears. And there is a recurrent dream she has, in different variations. In the dream she feels that they are getting close to her and she wants to jump from the balcony. She runs to the balcony and there are so many men there with beards and wearing *galabiyas*, like Mohammed Bouyeri. She feels that in another moment she will die, in another moment it will all be over. But then she wakes up. This interview was held before Hirsi Ali announced her resignation from her parliamentary position following a public outcry regarding her citizenship application and the possibility that it may be revoked. Hirsi Ali announced plans to move to the United States where she will begin work with the American Enterprise Institute, a private think tank. After a decision was made by the immigration authorities to revoke her passport and citizenship because of "fraud" in the details she had submitted to gain entrance to Holland, the decision was reversed and she finally kept her passport.

On the anti-Semitic front, France as well as Belgium, Switzerland, Germany, Austria, Romania, Slovakia, Czech Republic, Lithuania and Poland all have made Holocaust denial illegal, according to the "Anti-Defamation League"—But they allow actual attacks on Jews by Muslims to continue! "When a Dutch family comes back to Holland after eight years of living in Israel, people tend to assume its members are Jewish." So says Leon Meijer, and he should know. Meijer, who completed his doctorate at the Technion in Haifa, learned that lesson the hard way when his 11-year-old daughter was told by a classmate soon after her return: "It's a pity Hitler didn't finish the job." Meijer was shocked not only by the comment, but by the discovery that the Netherlands has no laws clearly outlawing Holocaust denial. Now, six years later, there is drafted legislation, which would do just that. Under this proposal, individuals who deny or glorify genocide with the intent to hurt others could be fined or sentenced to up to a year in jail. The law would be added to current legislation prohibiting discrimination on the grounds of race and religion.

Meijer, who serves as an adviser to the Christian Union party, which sponsored the legislation, described the measure as more urgent now that "echoes" of Iranian President Mahmoud Ahmadenijad's denials of the Holocaust could be heard in Holland. "People copy these kinds of remarks," he said, also noting that the number of Holocaust survivors who can personally testify to what happened during World War II is dwindling. Though the Christian Union holds only three seats in the 150-member parliament, Meijer said that his bill enjoys a good deal of support. Even so, it would take at least six to nine months to approve. He noted that possible pitfalls include fears that the law would limit free speech, which is one reason he offered to explain why Holland—unlike its neighbors—hasn't banned Holocaust denial outright. Dutch Jewish community leader Ronny Naftaniel said the proposed law could also encounter political obstacles. Since the law isn't limited to the Holocaust but includes all genocide as defined by the International Criminal Court, objections could arise based on other conflicts, such as the current crisis in Darfur or the past experience of Armenians in Turkey. "I can imagine that there will be political difficulties, but maybe it will get through," said Naftaniel, director of the Center for Information and Documentation on Israel. Even so, he praised the initiative as "a step forward." He noted that there has been prosecution of Holocaust denial under the existing Dutch anti-discrimination laws on the basis that negation of the Holocausts insults survivors and their children. But he said that any move to codify the offense was welcome. "There are fewer and fewer survivors and even their children are not numerous anymore, and we think it's important to keep the symbol of the Holocaust complete and without debate. It should not be dependent on the survivors and their children," he said. The general climate toward Jews worsened starting in 2000, with an increase in instances of spitting, name-calling and other forms of abuse, according to Naftaniel. But he said that the attacks—none of which were violent—had leveled off in the last few years. Still, ADL associate national director Kenneth Jacobson said "any kind of effort for a Holocaust denial law is a way of dealing with the trend that's developing and to stop it in its tracks." He noted, however, that "all the polls indicate the vast majority of Europeans" are aware that the Holocaust happened.[8]

At the height of the Cartoon Affair, the Dutch Liberal Party (VVD) asked the Foreign Minister of their country, Ben Bot, to censure Javier Solana publicly for his apologetic representations of solidarity with the Muslim world. Bot said that he would do so only in a closed meeting of the EU Foreign Ministers, and intimated in a debate in Parliament that he was asked by the Danes to pursue a "hands off" policy, because they wished to calm the moods, not to escalate the affair. The Dutch remained nevertheless the least apologetic in the affair and the most insistent that European apologies had gone too far.[9] But Belgium remained obtuse in its belief that fighting "Islamophobia," even at the price of letting down its values and exposing its other minorities to Muslim harassment. In March 2006, the case of a persecuted Aramaic priest, Father Samuel, who fled his native Muslim land for the safety of Europe, found himself in the center of a controversy. He now heads a church in a Charleroi suburb, which is full to its capacity of 2,000 worshippers, in spite of the elaborate four-hour mess, and in Latin to boot. The Belgian authorities prosecute him for Islamophobia, for incitement of hatred and for racism, because of remarks he had made on TV in 2002, where he said that: "Every thoroughly Islamized Muslim child that is born in Europe is a time bomb for Western children in the future. The latter will be persecuted when they have become a minority." These are not harsher words than what was described above as the Muslim demographic threat on Europe, so the Priest, who knows

something about religious persecution at the hands of Muslims in his native Turkey, stood his ground and declared that he would be proud to go to jail for speaking his mind, and that Jesus too had stood prosecution. During his sermon in his church in March 2006, he urged his flock to follow him to court. Since he came to Belgium as a refugee in the 1970s he was assigned to the thoroughly secularized diocese of Tournai and had a clash with the Bishop who dismissed him in 2001. It was thereupon that he bought the church in Charleroi where he conducts the mess in Catholic style. His congregation members come from all over, including northern France, and it encompasses African immigrants and many young families. His sermons include attacks against secularism, but also against the "Muslim invasion of the West," and tries to share his experiences in Turkey which do not bode well for Europe's future. He warns that the Muslim invasion of Europe will cause civil war.[10]

In Claire Berlinski's judgment,[11] "Dutch passivity is something of an oxy-moron," historically speaking. In the Golden Age the Netherlands used to be a sanctuary to religious dissenters and to intellectuals like Erasmus, Spinoza and Descartes, and in today's Netherlands the value of "tolerance" continues to reign supreme. Everything is tolerated: drugs, prostitution, euthanasia, and lately also Muslim radicalism. The Dutch government has funded hundreds of mosques and Muslim clubs headed by radical clerics who are committed to destroy the European social order, including the Dutch which has given them shelter. For example, in 2003 it granted the Arab-European League, that was founded in Belgium by an avowed member of Hizbullah, Abu Jahjah, permission to open its first branch in the Netherlands. The organization already had a record of incitement and anti-Semitic attacks in Antwerp, and a statement of approval of the 11 September horrors, and Jahjah never hid his intention to implement *Shari'a* law in all Europe, or his support for the Iraqi insurgents against America. Therefore Berlinski naively wonders why in the world would the Dutch lend legitimacy to this sort of terrorist organization that is bent on the destruction of Dutch culture?, as if the Netherlands were alone in conducting what looks to us as foolish policy. But when both Pym Fortuyn, the leader of a right-wing party, and the film-maker Theo van Gogh, were murdered because they spoke openly about the Muslim immigration of which they were critical, even self-satisfied and naïve Holland was shaken out of its slumber. The age of innocence has passed as scared Parliament members live in hiding, terrorist suspects are finally deported, extremist mosques are closed down, and Islamic websites are forced out of the cyberspace. But some Dutch, like the Jewish Mayor of Amsterdam, but unlike Deputy Prime Minister Zalm continue to shun the epithet "Muslim" when they refer to immigration, to the murderous attacks on van Gogh and Fortuyn, and to the extremism the Netherlands has been struggling against. Even when a mural was hung in Rotterdam, citing the biblical prohibition "Thou shalt not kill!," the Mayor of Rotterdam ordered it removed because an Imam of a nearby mosque found it "offensive" and "racist." One wonders how the Muslims of Holland would have reacted had a similar civilized and inoffensive quotation of the Qur'an been banned from the public eye.[12]

Berlinski went on connecting between the European haplessness to deal with the Muslim threat and the harm this causes to American interests. For example she says that one in five Germans [and a much higher rate among Muslims worldwide] believes that 11 September was staged by the Pentagon. With such allies, who needs enemies? Or, put differently, the Europeans hold so critical views of America that they have finally deserved the status of its allies. Those Europeans who hold these nonsensical views, owe that to their fervent anti-Americanism, which is connected to anti-modernism and anti-Semitism and derives its motivation from nostalgia to their past glory and their projection of their failed social programs. In addition, America is free of these sentiments because it does not live the memories and the sense of guilt of Auschwitz and Dachau, and can still speak about itself without self-deprecation of self-irony. The annihilation of Kurds in Iraq, the genocide in the Sudan and the extermination of Muslims in Bosnia had left the Europeans indifferent, and it was American interference alone that put an end to those horrors. And yet, furious that they lost the moral high grounds to America, they are outraged at its successes and state in their polls that America is the second largest threat to world peace. She believes that the only way for Europe to survive its take over by Muslims is to integrate them, because they are there to stay, and the only way for the integration of these masses of Muslims is dramatic social and economic reform. She emphasizes that the bankruptcy of multiculturalism has to bring that policy to an end; that all immigrants must learn the predominant language of the country; that all funding to mosques and Islamic centers should be cut off; that all fire-breathing imams should be deported; and that the lavish social payments and job-protection must be ended.

But not all Dutch see eye to eye with these views, if one judges by the story of Rabi'a Frank (ironically, the daughter of a Jew who has the same family name of the much more tragically known Anne Frank), who converted to Islam and can see her town of Breda, on the border of the Netherlands with Belgium, only through the slits of the black veil that covers her face. While some passers-by gawked at her looks, and walked off to avoid coming close to her, she, a convert of 11 years when she married her Moroccan husband, pondered why every woman who wears a veil must be seen as oppressed, or as a potential terrorist. Sometimes she engages people, saying: "Oh, you do not have to be scared of me!" At other times she gets so annoyed that she yanks her hand under her robe as if she were holding a pistol and shouts: "Boom!" This tragic situation known to Muslim terrorist-ridden countries brings her to ask:" Why do they look at me differently? It is like staring at a handicapped person in a wheelchair. It is not polite, I am a human, even if you do not like the way I appear." But in the context of a terrorized Europe in search of its identity and future, due to the presence in its midst of a large (at least 30 million) Muslims who insist on being, behaving and demonstrating as Muslims, and sometimes wish even to force themselves on their hosts, it is easy to see that the plight of that woman is only one individual example of the deepening rift in West European societies. Many European societies have enacted, under the heading of "anti-terrorist laws," legislation intended to preserve national identity, but others regard it as Islamophobia which reflects the fears from the aftermath of the bombings in the United States and Europe. In Holland in particular, after the killing of Fortuyn and van Gogh, the 1 million Muslim population (6% of the total, but very visible and vocal), feels particularly on edge. One of the restrictive pieces of legislation under consideration, in that country that used to be the most tolerant in Europe, is to ban women from wearing face veils (*niqab*) in public, thus perhaps forcing Rabi'a Frank and her likes to renounce what she believes in or get out of her homeland with her immigrant Moroccan husband. Another much spoken about law is to ban speaking any other languages but Dutch in the streets. That sounds pretty draconian, because what would innocent Greeks or Norwegians, strolling the streets of Amsterdam as of right, speak in public if they do not master Dutch. But even if they knew, who can prevent two free people from talking any languages they deem fit?[13]

Now immigrants have to pass an exam in Dutch, in Dutch history and geography, watch a film on Dutch culture that includes two gays kissing and a topless girl walking on the beach, in order to give them the "feel" for their new society they wish to immigrate to, or to disgust them from the outset from even trying. The test is a general introduction to the Dutch way of life, including how to open a bank account. The test costs $420 each time it is taken, but the kit to prepare for it can be had for a bargain of $80. In fact the immigrants are told that they have to start all over again, and they have to understand that scenes of nudity and gay culture are part of the local experience and therefore they have to think whether they are prepared for that. Others went even further, like MP Geert Wilders, who said he was drafting a bill banning immigration to Holland for the next five years. He explained that since Dutch culture is based on Christianity, Judaism, and humanism, the Dutch should uphold it, not be embarrassed by it, because this is what they are and want to stay. Now, there is nothing totally new in these approaches, because Belgium and France have already forbidden the veils and *burqas* in public places or public schools, as in the London school district. For Rabi'a (formerly Rebecca) things are even harder than on immigrants, because not only she feels banned in her own country, but at times she is referred to as a "traitor" for having changed sides and relinquished her culture. But she insists that she is a woman and Dutch, she is also Muslim, and Muslim first, and that what seems to upset people is the idea that faith can precede nationality or culture. She had decided to wear the veil after her return from the Holy Pilgrimage to Mecca, which transformed her, but her entire venture began at age 14 when she had a crush on a 16-year-old Moroccan boy who had moved to Holland with his family. And though her parents (a

Jewish father and Catholic mother) were not agreeable, she defied them and did continue the relationship. And when Ali told her that he could not marry her unless she became Muslim (the reverse seldom if ever happens, which adds to the worries of the Dutch), because his culture (not religion, and how about hers, which was also the culture where he had immigrated by choice?) was different, she decided to read the Qur'an and she fell for it. Before that conversion, when Ali's mother knew of their intention to marry, she threatened to "break both legs" (it is not clear whether hers or his), if he went forward with his plans, but it did not occur to her that the legs of her prospective daughter in law were no less precious than hers or her son's. She left the wedding ceremony before it started, because she could not take it.[14]

Rebecca's problems only started after the wedding, because while she smiled to all Muslim women she encountered, her blond hair and blue eyes outlook did not make her any different from other Dutch girls, while she wanted to be recognized as Muslim. Then she changed her name to Rabi'a and began giving lectures about Islam. After she published an article on Islam in a local paper, a woman reader wrote to her"go back to your country," where she already was. She continued studying until she became convinced to wear both the head scarf and the face veil, and prevailed on her husband to accept, though he was initially opposed to that step, due to the negative comments he heard when they went out together. She had been simply and totally swept by the injunction that a woman who reveals her body violates the tenets of Islam. When she went on pilgrimage to Mecca with her husband and her once-estranged mother in law, she first covered her face in public, sensing that "far from being oppressed, she felt liberated." She explained "This *hijab*, this mark of piety in an act of faith, a symbol, for all the world to see," though in her native town of Breda she stands out as an oddity. Even after the supplications of her 7-year old son to take it off due to the laughing it draws from his schoolmates, she rejected the plea, because taking it off would amount to "driving a car without a seat-belt." She is a Muslim, she felt a Muslim, she had metamorphosized her identity, and nothing would change her mind despite the head-on collision with her previous culture that she is heading to.[15]

There is talk in Amsterdam, the biggest Dutch city, about introducing leg-islation that would ban unemployed women who wear a *burqa* from receiving welfare payments if it prevents them from finding a job. The issue is the latest Dutch soul-searching over its relations with its own immigrants. Multicultural Netherlands is having a serious identity crisis, these days, since the country's immigrant melting pot is feeling more like a powder keg. The latest spark in Holland's mini culture war came in April 2006 from the social affairs alderman for the city, a Muslim himself, who says women who wear *burqas* are having trouble finding jobs. His solution? Take it off or lose your benefits. Ahmed Aboutaleb has proposed introducing legislation that would allow the city to cut welfare payments to women who insist on wearing a *burqa* if it can prove the full-body covering is the reason she can't find a job. "Nobody wants to hire someone with a *burqa*," he told the Dutch women's magazine *Opzij*. "In that case, I say: off with the *burqa* and apply for work. If you don't want to do that, that's fine, but you don't get a benefit payment." Aboutaleb, a member of Amsterdam's Labor Party (PvdA) and a Dutch citizen of Moroccan descent, made the comments in response to a recent ruling by Holland's Equality Commission siding with a Muslim woman who refused to shake hands with men at work. The politician questioned whether she should be involved in education, with such rigid self-restrictions. "She has to realize that her behavior is building enormous obstacles for her in almost every situation. This woman must recognize that she is sidelining herself and that she runs the risk of being turned down for other jobs, too."

In the wake of the murder of Dutch filmmaker Theo van Gogh by an Islamic extremist in 2004, the country, once thought to be an exemplary multicultural society, began to question how well its Muslim immigrants have been integrated. Since then, the center-right government of Prime Minister Jan Peter Balkanende has introduced laws that make it harder for married immigrants to bring their partners with them to Holland and that require prospective immigrants to take tests in their homeland on their knowledge of the Dutch society and language before they can come to the Netherlands. In December 2005, the Dutch parliament in The Hague approved a law that would make it illegal to wear a *burqa* in public spaces. However, a commission is now seeking to determine whether the legislation is compatible with European human rights laws. The legislation was introduced by Geert Wilders, a conservative member of the Dutch parliament who was named on the same hit list that included Theo van Gogh and Ayaan Hirsi Ali, the makers of the film *Submission*, which is highly critical of Islam's treatment of women. Regardless of the outcome of the national law or the Amsterdam legislation, the ban would be more symbolic than anything else since there are only an estimated 50 to 100 *burqa*-wearing women among the one million Muslims living in the Netherlands. But Amsterdam sociologist Ruud Koopmans told the *Suddeutsche Zeitung* that a "ban on the *burqa* in public would be absurd. I would be surprised if the law goes through."[16]

It is therefore quite surprising that a study in the Netherlands has concluded that Islam does not conflict with Dutch values. Muslim scholars have welcomed the three-year study by the Scientific Council for Government Policy. Marzouk Abdullah Awlad, professor of Islamic Studies at the Amsterdam Free University, said: "This is indeed a step towards opening a more serious dialogue with Islam and curbing extremism irrespective of its source."[17]On the other hand, best-selling Dutch author, Leon de Winter, was questioned by *Der Spiegel,* primarily about Dutch Integration Minister, Rita Verdonk who made headlines with her demand that only Dutch should be spoken in public in the Netherlands. The interviewer wanted to know whether "let's do away with foreign languages," has become the new motto of a country that for years has served as the model of tolerance? His retort: " Ms. Verdonk was falsely quoted. You can't force people to speak Dutch. How would you be able to control it? What she did say is that it is important that all people speak Dutch. There are too many foreigners here who can't speak our language." Asked whether that was one of the reasons for unemployment among the immigrants, Winter responded: "Yes, 40% have no job. But you also have to know that 40% of the Moroccan women living in our country are illiterate. How are they supposed to be in any position to provide their children with a decent education or to explain to them how an extremely tolerant society like the Netherlands functions? All of these problems start in the living room. Too many people drop out before graduating from high school. Many want to begin their vocational training after finishing primary school—but that's too early. At that point, they don't have the same basis as the country's other youth." The interviewee then addressed what is being discussed in Holland right now, namely why does the country offer official training in Turkish and Arabic? Why doesn't the state force people to learn Dutch? He said that such proposals that would force integration, like reeducation camps for unemployed youth or language tests for people who want to immigrate to Holland, were all pretty hopeless proposals for saving a generation that has already been lost. The parents of these children were never obligated to take charge of their own destiny. The state allowed them to live in Holland and paid their rent.

He said that the problems began when the first guest workers arrived in Holland—as soon as they were let in from the third world, Holland had a guilt complex towards them and somehow saw them as "sacred victims." Then their hosts let them bring their wives and children over without having any clue that they were importing integration problems with which the Dutch had no experience. No, Holland cannot be a melting pot for its immigrants, he said, that's the United States. A social welfare state like the Netherlands can never be a country of integration. Only a country like the United States, with its weak social net, can integrate large groups of immigrants without problems. Immigrants there are forced to take two or three badly paid jobs just to survive. That would be incompatible with European moral values. But after one or two generations in the United States, these people are integrated in society. When asked about the Mayor of Amsterdam, Job Cohen's warning that unemployed immigrant youth in the city could riot as they did in Paris, he answered: "I was shocked that a politician like he, who is generally cautious in his statements, would say something like that. It's an indication that the situation is much more serious than we previously assumed. But even (in Amsterdam) you have the same causes: a lack of education and training and a lack of discipline. These youth are no longer getting any guidance and they have no idea how they are supposed to behave in society." His outlook of Islam in the Netherlands is very telling: "The mantel of Islam is often used to describe the disquiet and frustration these young man have. Much of it is a normal part of development—hormones and puberty play a natural role. That has nothing to do with religiosity. I wouldn't say that the

Netherlands has suddenly become Islamophobic. These problems also exist in other countries. The Dutch aren't afraid of Islam. We just have too little work for them and that's why many are leaving."[18]

A new center for the study of radicalism and extremism that has been established in Amsterdam, will perhaps help better understand the conduct of radical Islam, though it purports to study radicalism in general, knowing that no other faith poses such a problem to society. The Centrum voor Radicalisme en Extremisme Studies (CRES) is being hosted by the University of Amsterdam (UvA) and will bring together researchers from various universities to advance the study of religious radicalization in the Netherlands. Researcher Frank Buijs of UvA's Institute of Migration and Ethnic Studies decided there was a need for the new academic center while he was researching radicalization of Moroccan (Bouyeri, the murderer of van Gogh, is Moroccan) youth on behalf of the Ministry for Immigration and Integration. The study found 40% of the Moroccan youth in the Netherlands reject Western values and democracy. Six to seven percent are prepared to use force to defend Islam. The majority are opposed to freedom of speech for offensive statements, particularly criticism of Islam, but offenses by Muslims to other faiths seem to be more tolerated. Buijs is the first director of CRES, which will provide information to people who come into contact with radicalism as part of their work. Buijs said that the government must provide alternatives for *Salafism* (following the ancients-*aslaf)*, a contemporary movement in Sunni Islam that seeks a return to the "pure Islam" of the days of Mohammed. But Buijs did not explain why the government, who did not invent *Salafism*, should provide an anti-dote for it. Contrary to his belief that since *Salafism* is gaining ground in the Netherlands the government must do more to stimulate a more pluralistic form of Islam, any involvement by the authorities in reforming Islam by generating more varieties of it, will be construed by Muslims as unwarranted interference in their faith. Buijs and his colleagues discuss the issue in a new book *Strijders van eigen bodem—radicale en democratische moslims in Nederlan* (home-grown warriors—radical and democratic Muslims in the Netherlands).[19]

The need to study radicalism, that is Muslim radicalism, derives from the estimate among Dutch and European citizenry in general, that an Islam that is unwilling to acculturate into the host culture of Europe, will remain at odds with it. Indeed, Islam was found to be incompatible with modern Western society, according to a majority of those responding to a recent Dutch survey. Most of the people polled expressed a negative view of Islam and Muslims. The survey was released the same week that a Dutch Justice Ministry report said radical Islam had made significant inroads among the country's immigrants, posing a threat to the nation's security. Known for its *laissez-faire* social attitudes, the sharp turn in public opinion against Islam in the Netherlands has sparked a debate that has prompted criticism of Queen Beatrix and the government for allegedly abandoning Western values in the face of Muslim pressure. The poll conducted by the Dutch research firm Motivaction for the GPD newspaper chain on 2 June 2006, found that 63% of those surveyed believed Islam was incompatible with modern European life. More than a quarter of respondents said Muslim immigrants were rude, lazy, intolerant and prone to criminal behavior. They said the increase in Muslim immigration has had a negative effect on civic and social life, with almost 80% saying relations between Muslims and non-Muslims had become strained. Government-backed initiatives to acculturate Muslim immigrants had failed, respondents said, as most believed that many immigrants had walled themselves off from Western society in an attempt to create outposts of their home cultures on Dutch soil.

Some government-sponsored moves to welcome Muslims have sparked controversy. In an address to parliament on 6 June, 2006 Prime Minister Jan Peter Balkenende applauded Queen Beatrix for agreeing not to shake hands with the leaders of the Mobarak Mosque in The Hague during a state visit to commemorate the mosque's fiftieth anniversary on 2 June. Queen Beatrix agreed not to shake hands with the Muslim leaders in deference to their belief that Islam forbids men to touch women other than their wives. This move was a laudable "example of religious tolerance," the prime minister said, that would make Muslims feel more welcome. Conservative MP Geert Wilders said he was "purple" with rage at the queen's decision, calling it "*dhimmi* behavior." (A *dhimmi* is a person of the *dhimma*, an Arabic term that refers in Islamic law to the pact of surrender contracted between non-Muslims and their Muslim conquerors.) "The queen and Prime Minister Balkenende are putting Dutch norms and values in a bargain sale," Wilders said. The MP said the government, "under the pretext of tolerance, is selling out Dutch values such as equality between men and women." "We must instead make the case for Dutch norms and values," Wilders said. *The Brussels Journal* commented that Queen Beatrix's tolerance appeared only to extend to Muslims, reporting that in 1982 she refused to meet with an Orthodox Jewish group because they didn't shake hands with women. According to the justice and interior ministers, the threat of terrorism from radical Islam is "substantial." The ministers told parliament that a "rapid spread of the *Jihadist*ic ideology was underway, with a number of moderate mosques passing under the control of Islamist ideologues." Radical movements, like *Salafism,* are currently gaining influence rapidly, both on the Internet and in more and more mosques. They prefer to use the Dutch language so that more and more young Muslims are reached, with all possible radicalization risks as a result," the ministers said. The ministry report warned of possible repercussions from the upcoming release of former Dutch MP Ayaan Hirsi Ali's film *Submission 2,* which criticizes Islam for intolerance of homosexuals. The report said, "Controversial debates or artistic quotes about Islam in the Netherlands can be abused by radical Muslims abroad to agitate against the Netherlands." Citing the Muhammad cartoon controversy in Denmark, the report suggested that Muslim reaction to Hirsi Ali's film could be violent. "Not only political interests but also economic interests as well as the safety of embassies and Dutch troops abroad can be in jeopardy," the report said.[20]

The service of Dutch troops abroad, especially in what was repudiated by Muslims as anti-Islamic causes, indeed had posed an immediate danger to the country's military. Spain had summarily surrendered to them after the Madrid massacre, but Holland seemed as yet in no mood to submit, especially as it saw its Muslims celebrating the death of the troops who were killed in the service of their country. The leader of the Dutch-Belgian Arab European League (AEL) has come out in support of killing Dutch troops serving in Iraq. "I consider every death of an American, British or Dutch soldier as a victory," Dyab Abou Jahjah said in an interview with Flemish newspaper *Het Laatste Nieuws*. There were then 1,376 Dutch soldiers serving on peacekeeping duties in southern Iraq and two have been killed since the mission started in the summer of 2003. The troops were scheduled to return home in March 2005. Despite his praise for the deaths of coalition troops, Abou Jahjah said he was opposed to the beheadings of hostages in Iraq. "Beheading is ethically and religiously wrong. Muslims don't even butcher a sheep in this way," he said. What a breath of fresh air to hear that Muslim radicals entertain ethical considerations of any sort! In any case, that outspoken Lebanese-born immigrant Abou Jahjah has made fewer headlines in recent times since his political aspirations met with little success in Belgium elections. He founded the AEL in 2001 in Antwerp, Belgium. The organization—which also has a branch in the Netherlands—claims to support integration, but not assimilation of Muslim and Arab immigrants into European society. And if that aspiration is to be backed by a separate Muslim political party, then it is evident that there will be neither assimilation nor integration, but only secession and perhaps rebellion against the political system. When the foundation of the Dutch branch of the organization was announced in 2003, several Dutch politicians from mainstream parties called for it to be outlawed. The Justice Ministry had to concede there were no grounds for doing so. In April 2004 the AEL "saluted" on its website the armed resistance to the U.S.-led coalition being mounted by "the Iraqi population" in Fallujah. Meanwhile, Abou Jahjah also spoke out strongly against racism in Flanders, claiming that the Belgium region had many more racists than the one million people who voted for the extreme right-wing group Vlaams Blok. "Flanders is a right-wing bulwark in Europe," said Abou Jahjah, who recently moved from Antwerp to the Brussels' municipality Schaarbeek. "God was not generous for Flemish people when he handed out intellect,"[21] he jibed.

In the face of this brewing unrest, the complacent and easy-going Dutch had to adopt new measures to fight terrorism now, and ultimately the Muslim take-over of their country. The Dutch parliament approved new anti-terrorism measures that make it easier to arrest suspects without strong evidence and hold them longer without charge. Prosecutors will be able to approve surveillance, infiltration or wiretapping of suspects even when there is not "reasonable suspicion" that a suspect may have committed a criminal act. The new law, which goes into effect immediately, is the latest of many enacted in the Netherlands since the 11 September 2001 attacks in the United States. "Evidence a terrorist attack is being prepared" will be enough to make an arrest, the Justice Ministry said in a statement. The result is that unusual investigation methods can be used more quickly against terror, since terrorists aren't easily deterred by the threat of heavy punishments. Earlier changes have included allowing the use of evidence gathered by the secret service in criminal trials, banning membership in a terrorist group and increased penalties for terrorism-related crimes. The new law also will expand the practice of allowing spot searches by police without probable cause in "airports, industrial complexes, sports stadiums and government buildings." "Police will be able to preventatively search people, and vehicles or things without permission of a prosecutor" or judge, the ministry said. Finally, the law increases the period of time a suspect can be held without charge from three to 14 days, which is still short of the 26 days Blair obtained for Britain. "During this period, grave concerns (of a crime) are no longer required in cases where a terrorist crime is suspected; a reasonable suspicion is enough," it said. There has been little protest about the loss of civil liberties from such laws in the Netherlands, where trust in government is traditionally strong. Although Dutch prosecutors lost several high-profile cases against terrorism suspects in 2002 and 2003, they have won an equal number of important convictions under the new laws. Most notable was the conviction in March 2006 of nine Muslim men of membership in the so-called "Hofstad" terrorist network. They included homegrown radical Mohammed Bouyeri, the Amsterdam-born son of Moroccan immigrants who was earlier sentenced to life in prison for the murder of filmmaker Theo van Gogh. Other alleged members of the same group are awaiting trial on separate charges.[22]

These harsh measures did not seem to deter the terrorists, who when prepared to die as "martyrs," have little concern for trials, which would publicize their cause, even less for jails, which would help them to concoct the next plot and to train the next generation of fellow-terrorists in the comfort and congeniality of the Dutch prisons. The story of Hirshi Ali dramatizes the suffocating atmosphere in Europe, whence every critic of Islam, including Ali herself, Salman Rushdie, the Danish author of the cartoons and such scholars as Bassam Tibi, are leaving for the safer, more welcoming shores of America. If the best people leave, Europe will gradually become a cultural and economic backwater. The irony is that the loss of its human resource will negate the reason for economic migrants to try to enter Europe. But that will of course not deter the *jihadis*. An economically stagnant and backward Europe will feel like home to them. Somalia-originating and Dutch politician Ayaan Hirsi Ali has been threatened repeatedly with "execution" by Islamist extremists. She lived in an apartment with bulletproof windows, and is driven to work at the Dutch Parliament by armed guards, who vary the route to outfox would-be hit men. But an unexpected menace emerged closer to home: her own neighbors. They have fought to evict her, complaining that the presence of a well-known terrorist target in their luxury apartment tower has upset their family lives and reduced the value of their property. "Once this lady leaves, the problem is no longer there," says Ger Verhagen, a retired executive who owns a place two floors above the hunted politician. He says he has nothing personal against Ms. Hirsi Ali. But along with other residents, he wants to banish the fears stirred by the proximity of Holland's most acid—and most frequently threatened—critic of Islam. Ms. Hirsi Ali's neighbor got his wish. Three weeks after a Dutch court ordered her out of the building in response to complaints from Mr. Verhagen and other residents, she resigned from Parliament and said she would leave Holland altogether. Her decision follows a cascade of problems: angry neighbors, a government threat to revoke her citizenship and, more generally, growing public disenchantment with her denunciations of both radical Islam and more conventional Muslim doctrines. This means that a person threatened in a democratic country, far from being protected by law and by the solidarity of her fellow-citizens, is abandoned by everybody, thus vindicating the terrorists.

The travails of Ms. Hirsi Ali, raise questions about how Europe, seeking calm rather than confrontation, is grappling with the challenges posed by Islamic extremism in its midst. Ms. Hirsi Ali said the attitude of her neighbors smacks of World War II-style "appeasement." Others say they sympathize with her predicament but fault her for polarizing society with her attacks on Islamic custom as backward and incompatible with Western values. And how about her civil rights and her freedom of expression? In late April 2006 a court in The Hague (symbolically the Seat of the International Court that systematically submits to terrorists), gave Ms. Hirsi Ali four months to vacate her apartment. Her departure, the judges of travesty ruled, was necessary to protect the "human rights" of her fearful neighbors (how about hers?). The Dutch state, which owns the apartment and charges her about $1,500 a month in rent, has appealed the decision. But announcing the end of her career in Dutch politics, as is most unbefitting to a democratic state, she cited the ruling as the direct cause. "It is difficult to work as a parliamentarian if you have nowhere to live," she said.[23] Holland, the model of democracy and tolerance in Europe, has yielded to terrorist threats, as it had yielded to Nazi terrorism in the dark days of the War, when its Jews were systematically turned over to the Nazis and sent to the camps. What an illustrious record!

Before her announcement, which touched off a political firestorm, the eviction order had stirred little public outrage. On state television, a satirical talk-show host joked about it, asking a guest—the Dutch lawyer of an Islamist militant who killed filmmaker Theo van Gogh in 2004—whether Ms. Hirsi Ali would be safest living in a mosque, at Guantánamo Bay or "six feet under in a garden." The audience roared with laughter. Ms. Hirsi Ali, who gave a speech in Berlin earlier in 2006, entitled "The Right to Offend," lamented her eviction, as a triumph of self-interest over solidarity. In a trademark flash of criticism, she also evoked the debate "over what people did during the Second World War." She said caustically: "My neighbors seem to confirm the critical view that very few Dutch people were brave enough" during the Nazi occupation. Many Europeans initially rallied to President George W. Bush's "with-us-or-against-us" approach to combating extremism after the bombings in Madrid in early 2004 and the subsequent murder in Amsterdam of Mr. van Gogh, the filmmaker. Since then, however, this united front has narrowed in many parts of Europe to a populist battle against immigration. Some now see Islamist violence and the ideology that fuels it as a threat that can be tamed, or at least kept at a distance, by avoiding provocation.

On June 2006, Ali joined Vice President Dick Cheney and others in Philadelphia to honor Bernard Lewis, the British-born scholar who helped shape White House thinking about the Middle East after 9/11. She also spoke at Harvard University and the New York Public Library. When she returned to Holland, Ms. Hirsi Ali received a different reception—a stormy debate over whether she should be stripped of her Dutch citizenship and deported. The clamor followed a documentary broadcast in which she expanded upon an earlier admission that she had lied on a 1992 application for refugee status. Ms. Hirsi Ali said that the country's immigration minister, a nominal ally, had told her Monday that her passport, granted in 1997, would be annulled. Many Dutch consider her brave but disruptive and too confrontational, the way justice seekers are usually viewed as troublemakers. She had worked closely with the controversial Mr. van Gogh before his murder, writing and narrating his last film, *Submission*, which infuriated Muslims and which many non-Muslims considered gratuitously offensive. A polemic against Islamic attitudes toward women, the short film featured semi-naked actresses, with passages from the Qur'an scrawled on their bodies. She clashed with a leader of her own center-right Liberal Party, whom she branded a "reactionary," and has been pilloried by politicians on the left, who mock her fury but fear her tart tongue. Many moderate Muslims detest her; radicals want her dead. "She spits in the face of all Muslims," says Jan Schoonenboom, the head of a government-sponsored research project on Islam. He says he regrets the eviction campaign but says she's partly to blame for stirring Muslim anger. In April, his think tank, the Scientific Council for Government Policy, issued a report that, contrary to other surveys, found no fundamental clash between Islamic and Western values and condemned a "climate of confrontation and stereotypical thinking." The Council, which helps set Dutch policy, urged Holland and other European countries to reach out to Islamist groups abroad that have been involved in terrorism, such as Hamas and Hezbollah.[24] One can hardly imagine a surer way to legitimize those terrorist groups and boost their self-confidence and morale.

"They're just sticking their heads in the sand," responds Ms. Hirsi Ali, who dismisses the report as a "political pamphlet to suit the dreams of people who want to believe there is not a problem." Across Europe, dozens of people are now in hiding or under police protection because of threats from Muslim extremists, instead of the Muslims hiding; is that the lesson in democracy that Europe wishes to teach its immigrants: that the rightful and the law-abiding hide while the wild and lawless exhibit their criminal deeds and threats in public undisturbed?. Dutch police say politicians reported 121 death threats in 2005. The number in 2006 was likely be much higher. Geert Wilders, the right-wing member of parliament who also lives in a high-security apartment owned by the state, says he has received 120 menacing emails and letters since January 2006. One of the latest reads: "Oh you cursed infidel! Don't think you are safe from our mighty organization.... It is our wish to kill you by decapitation. Your infidel blood will flow freely on cursed Dutch streets!" In Germany, several researchers, journalists and members of Parliament receive police protection because of threats by radical Muslims. Hans-Peter Raddatz, an Islamic-studies expert under police protection, recently moved to the United States, adding himself to the long list of European expatriates who seek safety in the United States once their countries have failed them. Flemming Rose, the culture editor of the Danish newspaper *Jyllands-Posten*, was also mulling a move to America, at the urging of friends and security contacts, adding yet another lesson to the Muslim immigrants: they have priority in enjoying what their Western host countries have to offer over their native countrymen who are compelled to go into exile. Since Flemming set off a global storm by publishing cartoons of the Prophet Muhammad, he and the twelve Danish cartoonists who drew the caricatures are staying out of public for fear of attack. Citizens of a democracy living in fear? Unheard of.

Rose complains that Europe is going wobbly. At the height of the cartoon furor in February 2006, Danish businessmen who criticized their publication were denounced as traitors to free speech. Since then, a segment of the public, eager for a return to calm, has favored a more conciliatory approach toward Muslim anger, Mr. Rose says. "I think it is very dangerous to give in to intimidation, because it sends a signal: If you threaten enough, we will do as you please," says Mr. Rose. The United States has sometimes sent mixed signals as well. During the cartoon uproar, Washington at first denounced the drawings. As the violence grew, it stressed the importance of free speech. Determining how to respond to radical Islam "is the key culture war in Europe," Rose contends. "This will be the big issue for decades." Europe's large Muslim population has been largely ghettoized. Finding solutions, he says, involves such prickly questions as how to reform welfare systems and how best to absorb immigrants.[25]

Hirsi Ali first got police protection in 2002 and then went into hiding in November 2004, following the murder in Amsterdam of Mr. van Gogh by a second-generation Dutchman of Moroccan descent. The killer plunged into van Gogh's chest a long knife, which pinned to the corpse a rambling and venomous note addressed to Hirsi Ali. It vowed that she, too, would die. Raised as a devout Muslim, Hirsi Ali renounced her faith after arriving in Holland and now calls herself a "Muslim atheist." She says she fled to Holland to escape a forced marriage to a distant relative living in Canada. Her past, she says, allows her to understand what drives the murderous passions of those who want her dead. As a youth, she says, she supported calls by Iran's Ayatollah Khomeini for the murder of Salman Rushdie, author of *The Satanic Verses*, a novel she then judged blasphemous. Fearing for their lives after Mr. van Gogh's murder, Hirsi Ali and Wilders, her fellow legislator, shuttled between army barracks, other state installations and the homes of friends and supporters abroad. As the threats continued, the Dutch government began scouting for private properties in which to safely house them. For Hirsi Ali, it purchased a spacious apartment for more than $1.1 million. The Dutch counterterrorism agency installed bulletproof glass, alarms and other devices. Her "high-security residence" was supposed to be a secret. Mr. Verhagen, the retired businessman, says he suspected something was afoot when the apartment's previous owner announced gleefully that he'd sold his property, but said he couldn't reveal the new owner's identity.

In April 2005, Hirsi Ali moved in. She rejoiced in having a home again. "I brought furniture. I set up my desk and my computer. I started to cook again for the first time since the murder," she says. She also started work on a sequel to *Submission*, the film she'd made with Mr. van Gogh and that many blamed for his death. The new movie, which has not yet been shown, takes aim at the treatment of homosexuals in Islamic society. Hirsi Ali's new neighbors, meanwhile, started to panic. They complained about security guards blocking the elevator and harassing visitors, and about traffic snarls whenever Hirsi Ali and her security escorts entered their underground parking garage. At a meeting in April 2005 with a counterterrorism official in a hotel, they angrily criticized the government for bringing danger into their lives and demanded that independent experts review the risk of having Hirsi Ali as a neighbor. When the government refused to budge, the apartment owners hired a lawyer. A second meeting failed to resolve the standoff. The owners hired security consultants at the Dutch branch of accounting firm Ernst & Young LLP to assess whether Ms. Hirsi Ali might put them all in danger. News of Ms. Hirsi Ali's arrival spread. Dick van Tetterode, a retired doctor who lives in an adjacent building, says he worried briefly about bombs, but decided he'd probably lose only his windows. During a slow afternoon stroll outside Hirsi Ali's building, the 84-year-old doctor reflected on her predicament and on his own flight from the Nazis during World War II. A student at the time, he spent two years hiding on a Dutch farm. Two of the three people he credits with saving his life were killed by the Germans. Struggling to hold back tears, he says he regrets never thanking their children properly for their fathers' bravery. But Hirsi Ali's case is different, he says. He admires her conviction, he says, but thinks her rage at Islam belongs in the Middle East and Africa, not the Netherlands. "This is not our fight," he says. Who did what and why during World War II are still touchy questions here.

Holland deported 78% of its Jews—the highest proportion in Western Europe. Among them was Anne Frank, a Jewish girl whose hiding place in Amsterdam was betrayed by a Nazi informant.[26]

In June 2005, Ernst & Young's security advisers presented their report to Mr. Verhagen and other apartment owners. The report rated as "high" the risk in having a "high-security residence" in the building, says Mr. Verhagen. "The conclusion was clear: The government made the wrong choice," he says. Ernst & Young confirmed his account of the findings. Mr. Verhagen ordered his five grandchildren to stop visiting. "I felt unsafe in my own home," he says. Eleven of 14 apartment owners backed taking legal action to oust Ms. Hirsi Ali. The politician says she received messages from dissenting owners saying they supported her. In a suit filed in late 2005, the owners claimed that their security fears, the disruption caused by Hirsi Ali's bodyguards and the likely damage to property values violated Article 8 of the European Convention on Human Rights, which guarantees "respect for private and family life" and the home, and bars "interference by a public authority." But the plaintiffs forgot that the violation of the Convention was done by the Muslim criminals, not by Hirsi. What would happen tomorrow if neighbors of the Parliament in The Hague invoked the same Convention when Muslim groups threatened the parliament building, a scenario that is not completely imaginary? The government fought the claim, arguing that the tight security had made the building among the safest in The Hague. It also offered unspecified compensation to offset financial damage. An initial ruling in November 2005 went against the owners. Eight of the 11, determined to get rid of Hirsi Ali, pressed on. In an April 27, 2006 ruling, an appeals court rejected the argument that the risk of declining property values and the long waits for the elevator constituted a violation of human rights. But citing the murder of van Gogh and threats against Hirsi Ali, and probably sensing that they could themselves be threatened if they did not act, the judges caved in and ruled that the "more than negligibly small risk" of a terrorist attack violated the European Convention on Human Rights. Yes, there was a violation, but the violators were not spelled out; rather, the burden of the violation was unjustly put on the government, which fought tooth and nail to scuttle the eviction of Hirsi and on Hirsi herself, thus violating (by the court, following the criminals who made the threats) her right for peaceful and safe living like any other citizen.. Although it acknowledged that finding Hirsi Ali another shelter would be "unquestionably hard," it nonetheless ordered her to move out within four months.[27]

Disgusted by this sort of justice, which upheld criminals and dumped the righteous, and in despair of a democracy gone sour, which could no longer defend its citizens and catered to criminals, Hirsi decided to leave the land that had given her shelter and catapulted her to prominence. The judgment prompted disbelief in some quarters. "Put her in the middle of the Atlantic and then everyone will be safe," joked Keeps Unshod, a newspaper columnist. Others saw more ominous signs. "From a moral point of view, it stinks of cowardice," says

Johannes Hoodwink ten Cater, a professor at Amsterdam University and head of the Institute of Holocaust and Genocide Studies, a Dutch research group. An expert on Holland's treatment of Jews during the Nazi occupation, he says he has "more understanding" for people who betrayed their neighbors out of fear during wartime than for the actions of Ms. Hirsi Ali's well-off neighbors in an era of peace. Her decision to leave the country for the United States spares the Dutch government the chore of finding her a new sanctuary. She'll be gone by the court's eviction deadline. "Sad and relieved, I will pack my bags again. I will go," she said at a news conference. She says she doesn't begrudge her neighbors for their security fears, but says she suspects property prices were their main concern. This blinded them to a bigger peril, she says. "Radical Islam is not just against me. It's against them, too," she maintains. "By having me evicted, the terrorists have won. It makes the situation more dangerous for everyone." Mr. Verhagen, her neighbor, now lives in a different building in a new apartment he purchased before the ruling. His grandchildren visit again, and he's trying to sell his property in Hirsi Ali's building for more than $1.3 million. Verhagen says he's "very sad" his former neighbor decided to leave the country but doesn't regret trying to drive her out of her apartment. "I'm happy I'm out of there," he says. Where did he think she should live after he evicted her? Did he care for her rights or only for his? Did he stop for a second to reflect about the consequences of his deed? Is he sure he won't be evicted by another court order from his new place?[28]

This state of affairs where Muslims feel vindicated and watch the state institutions buckle in their favor, produces a direct radicalization of their demands and deeds. Radical Muslims are in fact rapidly gaining influence in more and more Dutch mosques, according to Justice Minister Piet Hein Donner and Home Affairs Minister Johan Remkes. In a letter to parliament, they also warned that "controversial debates" on Islam can fan radical Islam. The terrorism threat in the Netherlands is "unabatedly substantial," according to the ministers. "The rapid spread of the *Jihadistic* ideology via the virtual networks on the Internet contribute to this," they reported in their fourth Terrorism Threat Progress Report. "Radical movements, like *Salafism* (a puritan Islam), are currently gaining influence rapidly, both on the Internet and in more and more mosques. They prefer to use the Dutch language, so that more and more young Muslims are reached, with all possible radicalization risks as a result." Remkes and Donner also stated that radicalism within the army is rising. Radical Islamic networks active in the Netherlands "are currently orientating themselves more strongly internationally than previously." This is mainly "due to the situation in Iraq and Afghanistan," "The negative picture can deteriorate further because local questions, such as controversial debates on Islam, attract international attention. Such cases are grist to the mills of ultra-orthodox and radical movements such as the *Salafists*." The substantial threat is being "somewhat tempered" by a "gradually strengthening preparedness by the Islamic community to acknowledge and combat the problems of radicalization and recruitment." Various initiatives are being taken to "foster diversity in the politico-religious debate as a counterbalance to radical messages." Also, "more and more local authorities" are aware of the need to tackle radicalization in their municipality. "Not only the four big cities (Amsterdam, Rotterdam, Utrecht, and The Hague) now have a specific policy for radicalization, but smaller municipalities like Ede and Helmond have begun their own tackling of radicalization." For this, it is very important that they work together on this in a "balanced manner." In their letter, Remkes and Donner also announce that a specialized police team for terrorist arrests, the Special Interventions Service (DSI), is expected to be ready in the course of 2006. Finally, an overview is given in the letter of the state of affairs on various aspects of terrorism policy, including international cooperation. Representatives of the 20 local authorities in the Rotterdam region announced they are making a working visit to London and Toronto in October 2006, to exchange information with local authorities on early signaling of "radicalization among specific population groups," said Rotterdam police chief Aad Meijboom.[29]

A dense tug of war has remained between officials who tend to understate the dangers of Islam, and the alarmists who tend to exaggerate the threats. Even when one understands lucidly the situation, one must listen and understand the tension between the two stands, for the decisions regarding the Muslim policy of European countries will depend on the outcome of those debates, both in the Netherlands and in all of Europe. We are told that an unjustified fear of and aversion to Islam there should be far more critical of friendly countries such as the United States, Israel and Russia, according to the Scientific Council for Government Policy (WRR). That approach, which spells out appeasement and accommodation, even at the prize of bashing the United States and its allies, has been the prevailing one in the officialdom of European countries, which believes that by smoothing over the differences and pretending that they do not exist, things would work for the better. WRR researcher Jan Schoonenboom is worried about "Islam-bashing" in the debate in the Netherlands. The frequently heard statement that Islam in principle conflicts with democracy and human rights is wrong, he declares. "If you, as a Muslim in the Netherlands, keep hearing only that Islam is the equivalent of violence and that you belong to a fifth column, then you feel alien. In the debate, many big words are used without being based on facts." But one wonders: is that the real sequence of things? Is it true that the Muslims first heard they were a fifth column and were bashed before they turned to violence, or the other way round, in the Netherlands of all places, where they went on rampage and were tolerated and repeatedly exonerated by their hosts, before they were accused of wrong doings after they abused of the freedoms and hospitality accorded to them? He continued: "Look, for example, at the warnings of the Christian democrats (CDA) parliamentary leader Verhagen about the introduction of the *Shari'a*. As if we in the Netherlands would then get corporal punishment! I do not know whether it is ignorance or design on the part of Verhagen, but it does not make sense and is irresponsible." Why? Did Verhagen utter his fear from corporal punishment? No, he just suspects that *Shari'a* law may be imposed on his country, as the Muslim radicals of Europe repeatedly assure us. Schoonenboom is certainly entitled to elect the kind of law he wishes to live under, but he cannot allay the fears of his compatriots of being overtaken by another legal system not of their doing and alien to them, corporal punishment or not, or "merely" imposing forced marriages, the subjugation of women, cultivating hatred of non-Believers, engaging in *Jihad* and the like."[30]

Schoonenboom was commenting on "Dynamics in Islamic activism," a report by the WRR that was to be presented to Foreign Minister Bot. According to Schoonenboom "we should not be so spastic about the *Shari'a*." It may be that the system leads to corporal punishment in countries like Saudi Arabia and Sudan, "but under the *Shari'a* in Morocco, family law has been reformed, very much to the advantage of women's rights." The *Shari'a* for Muslims is comparable to the Ten Commandments for Christians, in the researcher's view. "It is God's plan for human nature." But according to the Commandments, man is ordered to do certain good deeds and to refrain from bad ones. The order to refrain from killing is absolute, while in the Muslim *Shari'a*, of which this researcher has no clue, enjoins its believers to launch *jihad* and kill, to enslave the Unbe-lievers and to take over the world by *da'wa* if possible, by force if necessary. The WRR researcher wipes the floor with Islam critics such as MPs Hirsi Ali, Wilders and Verhagen, law philosopher Afshin Ellian and Rotterdam politician Marco Pastors. "They often play on gut feelings in the debate, on fear of Islam and of Muslims. You also see that in the debate on the accession of Turkey to the European Union, this country is made out to be much more Islamic than it is, and Europe much more Christian that it really is." Such a total abdication of Europe's values and culture, and *dhimmi*-like submission to Muslim demands and complaints, without the advise and consent of his fellow citizens who make up their common country, is a far-reaching policy that is sure to be rejected by most Europeans, based not on their biases and "Islam-bashing," but on their bad experiences, such as Madrid, London, van Gogh and such. Schoonenboom advises "an adventurous foreign policy" for the Dutch government. "We must support the moderate Islamic powers (which are they?) much more, such as the Muslim Brotherhood in Egypt, (who are the pinnacle of Muslim radicals, so much so that the EU has declared the Hamas, their acknowledged branch, a ter-rorist organization) and Hezbollah in Lebanon (who have been stirring trouble and hatred in the Middle East), instead of secular movements without prospects in Muslim countries. We must talk to the Palestinian regime of Hamas. They are democratically elected. It is a terrorist movement, but so was Arafat's PLO. And the IRA in Ireland." Holland and the rest spoke to Arafat and the PLO when they vowed to relinquish terrorism in Oslo, then they did not. Hitler also was democratically elected, perhaps that was the reason why so many Dutch supported his regime and turned against the Jews? "On the other hand, we must be much more critical regarding our friendly countries. We must address Russia more forcefully on human rights violations in Chechnya, Israel for its decades of ignoring UN resolutions and the United States regarding Guantánamo Bay. In the Netherlands, there has practically never been a debate on the reasons for the invasion of Iraq and the Dutch support for this." (...) "We must also get rid of hypocrisy. We protest if one Christian is sentenced to death in Afghanistan, but what do we do if it is a Muslim?" Schoonenboom denies that the WRR report is naive. It is a reaction to "a real fear of dangerous developments. Do we want to go on living in a land that is plagued by fear of attacks? A cultural change is needed here. The Netherlands cannot save the world, but we can try to influence EU policy. The battle against terrorism has got out of hand, is getting the characteristics of a clash of civilizations. (...) Bush is said to be considering attacking Iran or Syria. What in God's name are we doing?"[31] This is probably, after Galloway and Livingstone in Britain, the most lopsided, cowardly and detached from the truth "analysis" of Muslims in Europe, that is bound to drag all Europe into the abyss if it were heeded.

Along these lines, Foreign Minister Ben Bot explained the advantages of the Netherlands' discussion culture to the Arab world. He was being interviewed by the Arabic station *Al Jazeera*. In front of the camera, Bot explained that things had not come to excesses in the Netherlands following the murder of filmmaker Theo van Gogh by a radical Muslim thanks to the country's dialogue. "We call that poldering; we have been doing it since the thirteenth or fourteenth century. We had to discuss and cooperate, because if the dikes were broken, we would all be the victims." The Dutch minister made a visit to Saudi Arabia and Qatar in 2006, prompted by the international "cartoon crisis." He appears to be un-impressed by critical MPs at home, such as conservative (VVD) leader Jozias van Aartsen, who considered the trip unnecessary. "In the Netherlands, there is always criticism and you never do well. If I had to take this seriously, then I could never go anywhere. I would not get to Indonesia, to Russia and to Saudi Arabia," according to Bot. Bot held "constructive talks" with his Saudi counterpart Prince Saud bin Faisal, and with King Abdullah, but he faced a tough job with the Secretary-General of the Organization of the Islamic Conference (OIC), Ekmeleddin Ihsanoglu. The Turk made a series of peppery statements after a meeting with Bot. Ihsanoglu said European countries must make laws that as well as banning *lese majeste* and holocaust denial, also ban insulting Mohammed. He warned that the anger in Muslim circles will not go away if a repeat of the cartoons is not prevented. Ihsanoglu then compared the effect of the Danish cartoons with that of the 11 September 2001 terrorist attacks in the United States and the position of Muslims with that of the Jews before the Second World War. "The comparison with 11 September does not hold water. And the comparison with the Jews is misplaced," said Bot. He also rejected Ihsanoglu's plea for a UN resolution against blasphemy and for changing Dutch or European laws to protect what is holy in Islam. "New regulations, laws or codes of conduct we are not going to set up." Bot did however add that it would be sensible if "writers, journalists, cartoonists and publishers would do some reflecting. And everyone must realize what upsets the Muslims and then accept their personal responsibility." But "it must also be no taboo to discuss the indignation among Muslims." Bot wants a debate in the Netherlands on freedom of speech and the personal responsibility of every individual. The Dutch citizen will not notice much of this; while Bot is aware of the deep indignation among Muslims in Saudi Arabia, he emphasized: "I am not mounting the pulpit in the Netherlands to talk about that."[32] In that case, where are the constructive talks he had in Saudi Arabia? He is warning precisely against accepting the Muslim *Shari'a* that his adviser has so strongly counseled him and his countrymen to do.

If such pieces of "research" and "constructive" talks across the cultural divide were bound to arouse expectations among European Muslims, as more and more ignorant and naïve well-meaning Europeans drift to their camp, their antidote became the rampaging "artists" and other sorts of outrageous trouble-makers whose sole goal is to inflame the tempers and cause an explosion, as if the Cartoons, van Gogh and Hirsi were not enough. Film director Eddy Terstall is to make a film on homosexuality among Islam leaders in the fifteenth and sixteenth centuries. The film is based on the novel *Male Harem* (*Mannenharem*) by Vinco David. David's novel is a historically based tale about male harems kept by various Islamic Mogul Emperors in India in the fifteenth and sixteenth centuries. "During the Golden Age of Islam, people's ideas on homosexuality were far more relaxed and liberal than they are today," as Terstall stated. "Right-wing imams would do well to read some books before deciding to speak out again." Terstall is a celebrated director in the Netherlands. His last film *Simon* (2004) was awarded with four Golden Calves—a Dutch version of the Oscars. Since about a year, Terstall has been toying with the idea of going into politics. The film director is a member of Labour (PvdA) and is thinking about represent-ing this party in the Lower House. David and Terstall are to work on the script together. It is unclear whether Terstall is to direct the film himself. *Sextet* and *Vox Populi*, the last two parts of his trilogy on contemporary Dutch society, will keep him busy for at least another year. Filmmaker Theo van Gogh was also involved in this trilogy before he was assassinated by a radical Muslim.[33] When strong-willed Dutchmen, from any domain of creativity, wish to make their imprint by commenting on the most divisive and sensitive issue of the Muslims in Europe, they add much to the confusion, because as against the government's tendency to calm the tempers, though they know and acknowledge the hopelessness of the situation, and the apologetic supporters who demean their threat, artists are not partisans and have no axe to grind, but their artistic one. So, anyone who is not side to the public debate will tend to be influenced by them.

A new avenue of public debate opened when the Dutch secret services AIVD (state intelligence) and MIVD (military intelligence) are investigating an un-known number of Muslims within the Dutch army, not unlike similar suspicions that were aroused among the London Metropolitan police force. The Dutch newspaper *Het Parool* reported that a growing number of Dutch soldiers sympathize with radical Islamists. The paper refers to the annual report of the MIVD, which states that it conducted a number of investigations into "alleged radicalization of military personnel" as "there are signs that indicate a possible radicalization of Muslim individuals or groups within the armed forces." The issue that arises is of capital importance for any European country: part of allocating equal opportunities to the Muslim immigrants and facilitating their integration, is to confide military jobs to them, provided there is complete confidence in their loyalty to the state, though the country is not in a state of war when that loyalty could come to the test. But if cracks show in that edifice, though they are not critical in a time of peace, then the whole concept of integration of the Muslim immigrants, and the suspicion that they might owe allegiance to other powers, emerges as a formidable obstacle to their absorption into the fiber of society and culture. During the past years the Dutch army, in order to contradict allegations of discrimination, has applied a policy of preferential recruitment among immigrant youths. The MIVD warns, however, that youths between 17 and 25 are more easily influenced by radical Islam, while the experience of Dutch troops in Afghanistan and Iraq can also lead to an enhanced radicalization.

At least ten to 20 groups of Muslim terrorists are said to be active in the Netherlands, planning assassinations of politicians and the bombing of the AIVD headquarters. General Bert Dedden, the retiring MIVD chief, said in the newspaper *De Stem* that the Ministry of Defense has started procedures to oust a radical Islamist from the army. According to Dedden about ten Dutch soldiers are known to adhere to *Salafism, Wahhabism*, or other forms of extremist Islam. These people can be a danger to Dutch national security, the general explained, because they can persuade others to become disloyal to the army or because they have access to protected buildings or grounds. "We try to prevent the disappearance of sensitive information, weapons or other material," General Dedden said. Other European countries also have growing numbers of Muslims soldiers. Last March (2006) three conscripts of the Austrian army refused to salute the Austrian flag because they said this was incompatible with their Islamic religion. It is said that one of the reasons why the French authorities did not employ the army during the November 2005 riots, despite calls to do so, was because 15% of the French armed forces are made up of Muslims. A Swiss website reported that some are concerned about the rising number of Muslim soldiers in the Swiss army. The number of Muslim citizens in Switzerland has grown from 16,000 to 310,000 during the past four decades.[34]

In Belgium, which is more sensitive to racial problems due to its centrality in Europe, the situation is not better, the rate of Muslims, mainly from North Africa, is also as high as 7-8 %, and the tension between the host and guest culture runs sky-high. More than 80,000 people marched in silence through Brussels in April, 2006 in memory of a teenager stabbed to death by two suspects of North African origin in Belgium's biggest protest in ten years, police said. Joe Van Holsbeeck, 17, was stabbed five times in the chest during the evening rush hour on 12 April when he refused to hand over his MP3 player to the men in the central railway station. On the request of Van Holsbeeck's parents, marchers did not carry any political banners but Van Holsbeeck's death triggered an uproar over crime and racial tension in Belgium. The federal prosecutor's office said, on the basis of video footage from security cameras, that two men of North African origin were suspected of carrying out the crime. Leaders of the Muslim community in Brussels said they were disturbed by the stabbing and imams called at Friday prayers for people to turn in the suspects if they knew who they were. Representatives of North African communities in the capital took part in the silent protest, officials said. Belgian Prime Minister Guy Verhofstadt said the teenager's death should not go unpunished to send a signal to society that such crimes would not be tolerated. Marchers queued up to lay a white rose or bunches of flowers as the march passed the Gare Centrale railway station. Police said it was the country's biggest demonstration since around 300,000 people took part in the so-called White March in 1996 to commemorate the victims of pedophile Marc Dutroux and to protest against the slow-moving Belgian judicial system.[35]

The half-million Belgian Muslims achieved another perk from the Belgian state in 2004, namely that it undertook to fund the wages of 245 imams, in a bid to "end discrimination against the Islamic faith." Although Islam has been recognized as an official religion in Belgium for the last 30 years, it hasn't been given the benefits of other beliefs. The federal parliament voted to grant EUR 4.83 million in 2005 to pay for imams in around 100 mosques. Under the new law, Belgian's regions must first recognize the mosques involved. Then the Justice Department will appoint the state imams on the recommendation of the Belgium Executive of Muslims—the organization which represents the 500,000 Muslims that live in Belgium. The funding is a significant financial boost for Belgium's mosques. In 2003, Islam was granted just 0.5% of the overall religious budget, with EUR 1.27 million. The Catholic Church was given 88% of the cake, almost EUR 202 million. In 2006, some churches will not receive funding for assistant curates, a decision made partly because there is a shortage of curates.[36]

Recently, the wave of anti-Semitism in Europe has been the fiercest in France. That is why reports of this sort have been focusing on that country, reporting at length on the situation of the French Jewish population. France hosts the largest Jewish and Muslim communities in Europe. But tiny Belgium, with 40,000 Jews and 500,000 Muslims has been also witnessing endless attacks on its Jewish population. The scenario taking place in Belgium exactly mirrors the one in France. The far-right/neo-Nazi fringe of the population formerly perpetrated anti-Semitic acts, but in the past few years they can be almost exclusively attributed to Muslims. For example, in just one week in 2004, six very violent anti-Semitic attacks were reported in the city of Antwerp, where a vibrant Jewish community lives. One of the attacks involved the stabbing of a sixteen-year-old teenager;

then three other young Jews were also shot at; another one was beaten and left unconscious on the pavement and so on…. One should note that Antwerp is the city where the Arab European League was founded by Abu Jajah, a Lebanese who happened to have been very involved with the Shi'a terrorist organization Hizbullah. Abu Jajah recently stated that "Antwerp is the European pillar of Zionism and that is why it has to become the Mecca of pro-Palestinian actions." His movement has also threatened Belgian Jews to stop supporting Israel or violence will fall upon them. With such a message of hate, it is not surprising that young Muslims are feeling compelled to physically attack Jews in the streets of the kingdom. Even if the official figure for anti-Semitic attacks in Belgium is around 120 annually in the past few years, it does not reflect the reality. In fact, a lot of complaints are never even filed because the victims are scared to report the violence inflicted on them. Or people just give up on going to the police. For instance Rabbi Lasker just does not report all the attacks he is the victim of anymore, because they have unfortunately become routine. In October 2001, he got attacked three times in 24 hours: once while he was walking with his wife and children and got spat on and threatened by a dozen of young Muslims; then the next day a group of about 50 Muslims attacked them with stones and hit his young daughter in the back; and finally that same day four young Muslims attacked and tried to choke him. Also more than the constant violence, there is a growing *malaise* for Belgian Jews who are afraid to live their Judaism fully and openly. Kids attending Jewish schools are frequently harassed and need to be protected by the police. The Member of Parliament and Mayor of Forest, a town in suburban Brussels, Corinne De Permentier, is appalled that two Jewish organizations had to leave her town because of the constant threats. She added that: "It is crazy that a community needs to be permanently protected by the police in a democratic country." A couple of other politicians are complaining that the Belgian government is not doing enough in terms of protection because in most of the cases, no arrests have ever been made…. Obviously, in such an environment, it is not a good time to be a Jew in Europe. That is surely why, when Elie Wiesel was in Berlin in 2004 for a conference on anti-Semitism, he was asked by close Jewish European friends a revealing new question. For the first time ever, it was not "Should we leave Europe?" but "When should we leave?"[37]

Jewish leaders have accused the European Union of covering up the true scale of anti-Semitic violence carried out by Muslim youths, reigniting a controversy over Europe's failure to confront Islamic extremism at home. A study released by the EU's Racism and Xenophobia Monitoring Center astounded experts by concluding that the wave of anti-Jewish persecution over the last two years stemmed from neo-Nazi or other racist groups. "The largest group of the perpetrators of anti-Semitic activities appears to be young, disaffected white Europeans," said a summary released to the European Parliament. "A further source of anti-Semitism in some countries was young Muslims of North African or Asian extraction. Traditionally, anti-Semitic groups on the extreme Right played a part in stirring opinion," it added. The headline findings contradict the body of the report. This says most of the 193 violent attacks on synagogues, Jewish schools, kosher shops, cemeteries and rabbis in France in 2002—up from 32 in 2001—were "ascribed to youth from neighborhoods sensitive to the Israeli-Palestinian conflict, principally of North African descent. "The percentage attributable to the extreme Right was only nine percent in 2002," it said. The report on Belgium said most of the firebomb and machine-gun attacks on Jewish targets were the result of a spillover from the Palestinian *Intifadah*. The European Jewish Congress accused the EU watchdog of twisting data from the 15 member states to suit its own ideological bias, describing the report as a catalogue of "enormous contradictions, errors and omissions." "We cannot let it be said that the majority of anti-Semitic incidents come from young, disaffected white men. This is in complete contradiction with the facts recorded by the police," it said.

The EU suppressed a report in 2003 by German academics concluding that Arab gangs were largely responsible for a sudden surge in the anti-Jewish violence, allegedly because the findings were politically unpalatable. Victor Weitzel, who wrote a large section of a far more detailed study, told *The Telegraph* that the latest findings had been "consistently massaged" by the EU watchdog to play down the role of North African youth. "The European Union seems incapable of facing up to the truth on this," he said. "Everything is being tilted to ensure nice soft conclusions." "When I told them that we need to monitor the inflammatory language being used by the Arab press in Europe, this was changed to the 'minority press'. "Honestly, it's incredible," he said. Weitzel's 48-page section—compiled with a Polish academic, Magadalena Sroda—is the fruit of months of interviews with Jewish leaders across Europe. While far-Right and traditional "Christian" forms of anti-Semitism still exist, the report homes in on a new form of "anti-Zionist Left" prejudice. This demonizes Israel and subtly leaks into prejudice against all Jews. The study describes Belgium as a country where anti-Semitism has become almost fashionable among the Left-leaning intelligentsia. But most of the report focuses on Jew-baiting by Muslim youths. It paints an alarming picture of daily life for France's 600,000 Jews, the EU's biggest community. In schools, Jewish children are beaten with impunity, and teachers dare not talk about the Holocaust for fear of provoking Muslim pupils, it said. Britain, which saw a 75% rise in incidents in 2003, was gently rebuked for hesitating to take "politically awkward" measures against Islamic radicals. "The government is very anxious not to upset the Muslim community," the report said.[38]

It has been confirmed once and again that anti-Semitism goes hand in hand with the deepening or radical Islam in Europe. One of Brussels' poorest communes, for example, is a breeding ground for Islamic extremists, according to a report by an undercover Muslim journalist. Hind Fraihi, a Flemish-Moroccan freelancer, spent two months living in Molenbeek, which has a large North African population. She posed as a sociology student. Fraihi claims to have spoken to dozens of young Muslims who have been offered arms training in Afghanistan to join Islamic extremist ranks. The Flemish newspapers *Het Nieuwsblad* and *Het Volk* published the first part of Fraihi's investigation, which is based on her observations and conversations in mosques, cultural centers and on the streets of Molenbeek-Saint-Jean. Gunther Vanpraet, the managing editor of the two newspapers, said Fraihi had wanted to see "if the rumours about an increase in the number of Muslim extremists in Belgium were true." Vanpraet said hundreds of young adults had been studying Islam for years. "They are future Muslim leaders," he said. "Alongside them is a significant group of young people who have very little hope of a normal future in our country because of their lack of training and because of the job market. This is a breeding ground for thousands of *Jihad* candidates who are ready to commit terrorist attacks and to lead the religious war against the infidels." Vanpraet said these extremists were using Belgium as a base for planning terrorism, rather than as a target. Fraihi found extremist *Jihad* writings in several Molenbeek libraries and said such documents were also in frequent circulation in the commune." The majority of the mosques which circulate these dangerous documents operate in the greatest secrecy and are difficult for the security services to infiltrate," she wrote. Extremist recruiters approach Muslim residents in the street or in mosques found Fraihi. Molenbeek mayor Philippe Moureaux and the police played down the findings in the investigation, saying the number of Muslim terrorists was small and that many were already known to the authorities and under surveillance.[39] It will not be difficult to correlate between these hot-houses of thuggery and terrorism and the rampant anti-Semitic eruptions throughout the country.

Notes

1. *Gazet van Antwerpen,* 1 February 2006.
2. Lawrence Auster@att.net, Daily report dated 17 March 2006.
3. See Judith Apter Klinghoffer, SliwaNews@aol.com, Daily report dated 4 May 2006.
4. Gitit Ginat, "Freedom fighter," www.haarez.com—18 May 2006
5. *Ibid.*
6. *Ibid.*
7. *Ibid.*
8. Hilary Leila Kriege, "Holland moves to ban Holocaust denial," *Jerusalem Post,* 10 June 2006.
9. Manfred Gerstenfeld, "The Muhammed Cartoon Controversy, Israel and the Jews: a Case Study," *Post-Holocaust and Anti-Semitism Series,* 43, 2 April 2006, by The Jerusalem Center for Public Affairs.
10. Paul Belien, "Brussels Prosecutes Aramaic Priest and Fugitive for Islamophobia," http://www.brusselsjournal.com/node/936, 27 March 2006.
11. Claire Berlinski, *Menace in Europe: Why the Continent's Crisis is America's, Too,* Interviewed about Europe, Muslim integration, instapundit.com/archives/028869.php
12. *Ibid.*

13. Molly Moore, "Dutch Convert to Islam: Veiled and Viewed as a Traitor: a Woman's experience Illustrates Europe's Struggle with its Identity," *Washington Post,* 19 March 2006.
14. *Ibid.*
15. *Ibid.*
16. "Muslims in Holland" *Spiegel Online*—21 April, 2006. http://www.spiegel.de/international/0,1518,412355,00.html
17. Bess Twiston Davies, *The Times*—22 April 2006.
18. "The Dutch Are not Afraid of Islam," Interview with Leon de Winter, *Spiegel Online*—2 February 2006. URL: http://www.spiegel.de/international/0,1518,398708,00.html
19. "Centre for extremist studies," Amsterdam , 14 June 2006. http://www.expatica.com/source/site_article.asp?subchannel_id=1&story_id=30780&name=Centre+for+extremist+studies+established
20. George Conge –"Most Dutch say Islam incompatible with Western society," *Jerusalem Post*, 19 June 2006.
21. "AEL: every Dutch soldier's death is a victory," *Expatica*—25 October 2004. http://www.expatica.com/source/site_article.asp?subchannel_id=1&story_id=13222&name=AEL%3A+every+Dutch+soldier%27s+death+is+a+victory+
22. "Dutch parliament OKs anti-terror measures," *USA Today* - 23 May 2006 http://www.usatoday.com/news/world/2006-05-23-dutch-terror_x.htm.
23. Andrew Higgins, "Taking Leave: Islamist Threats To Dutch Politician Bring Chill at Home: Ms. Hirsi Ali Quits Parliament, Plans to Resettle in U.S. after Losing Safe House," *Wall Street Journal*—17 May 2006
24. *Ibid.*
25. *Ibid.*
26. *Ibid.*
27. *Ibid.*
28. *Ibid.*
29. "Radicalisation Increases at Dutch Mosques," *NIS News Bulletin—Netherlands National News Agency ANP,* The Hague, 8 June 2006.
30. "Govt Advisors: Embrace Islam, Tackle Allies," *NIS News Bulletin—Netherlands National News Agency ANP,* The Hague, 12 April 2006.
31. *Ibid.*
32. "FM Bot Explains Dialogue Model To Muslim World," *NIS News Bulletin—Netherlands National News Agency ANP,* DOHA, 17 February 2006.
33. "'PvdA Director' To Make Film On Gay Islam Leaders," *NIS News Bulletin—Netherlands National News Agency ANP* AMSTERDAM, 22 February 2006.
34. Paul Belien, "Dutch Worry about Radical Muslims in the Military," *The Brussels Journal*, 2 May 2006
35. "Thousands march in Brussels in memory of teen," *Reuters,* 23 April 2006 http://news.yahoo.com/s/nm/20060423/wl_nm/belgium_march_dc_1
36. "State to pay imams' wages," *Expatica*—16 December 2004 http://www.expatica.com/source/site_article.asp?channel_id=3&storyid=15137
37. Olivier Guitta, "For Jews, Belgium is no better than France," *The American Thinker* 6 July 2004   http://americanthinker.com/articles.php?article_id=3655
38   Ambrose Evans-Pritchard," EU'covered up' attacks on Jews by young Muslims" *Daily Telegraph*—1 April 2004.
39   "Brussels commune fundamentalist recruiting ground' says journalist," *Expatica*—14 March 2005 http://www.expatica.com/source/site_article.asp?subchannel_id=24&story_id=17996&name=Brussels+commune+%27extremistMuslim+recruiting+ground%27

3

Spain, Italy, Central Europe —Trailing the Powers

Spain

Spain, a country geographically close to the coasts of North Africa, is the most vulnerable to illegal immigrants that wash its shores, and to claims of colonization due to its continuing grip on its enclaves of Ceuta and Melillia on Moroccan soil. The Spaniards, in fact, while spearheading the European effort, via Javier Solana, to dub the Israeli wall that is geared to keep Palestinian terrorism away as "apartheid wall," to engineer its condemnation by The Hague's International Court, and to prod Israel to evacuate "occupied territory," have themselves built a true apartheid wall around their occupied enclaves in Northern Morocco, geared to prevent North Africans from entering their own territory that is occupied by Madrid. Spain's vulnerability kept it in the forefront of the most accommodating Europeans towards Muslims, and the most critical among them towards the United States until the 11 September 2001 slaughter in New York, and particularly until the Madrid massacre on 11 March 2004. Unthinkable for a Spaniard and a European just one or two years earlier, a courageous journalist, Sebastian Vilar Rodríguez, published on Internet an article of repentance in late 2005, which is worthwhile reproducing in detail:

> I walked in the streets of Barcelona, and suddenly discovered a terrible truth: Europe died in Auschwitz. We killed 6 million Jews and replaced them with 20 million Muslims. In Auschwitz we burned a culture, thought, creativity, talent. We destroyed the chosen people, truly chosen because they produced great and wonderful people who changed the world. The contribution of these people is felt in all areas of life: science, art, international trade, and above all, as the conscience of the world. These are the people we burned. And under the pretense of tolerance, and because we wanted to prove to ourselves that we were cured of the disease of racism, we opened our gates to 20 million Muslims who brought us stupidity and ignorance, religious extremism and lack of tolerance, crime and poverty, due to an unwillingness to work and support their families with pride. They have turned our beautiful Spanish cities into the third world, drowning in filth and crime. Shut up in the apartments they receive free from the government, they plan the murder and destruction of their naïve hosts. And thus, in our misery, we have exchanged culture for fanatical hatred, creative skill for destructive

skill, intelligence for backwardness and superstition. We have exchanged the pursuit of peace of the Jews of Europe and their talent for hoping for a better future for their children, their determined clinging to life because life is holy, for those who pursue death, for people consumed by the desire for death for themselves and others, for our children and theirs. What a terrible mistake was made by miserable Europe.[1]

This is no simple or easy admission by the citizen of a country who had forced mass conversion of Jews and Muslims to Christianity through its horrifying Inquisition and finally expelled the remaining Jews (and Muslims) who were not ready to abandon their faiths. The admission is not made easier either by the shameful submission of the Spanish public to Muslim terrorism, after PM Jose Aznar, who supported President Bush in his war on terrorism, was voted out of office following the massive terrorist attack in Madrid in 2004 and replaced by the Socialist Zapatero who pledged to withdraw Spanish forces from Iraq. The Spaniards remain cautious in their dealings with Muslims, for they continue to walk the tight rope between their continued colonization of the Ceuta and Melilla enclaves on the North African coast, and their declared support for Muslim and other third-world countries' independence. But nothing threw them out of balance and exposed their vulnerability as the trial that began in April 2006 in Madrid, where the details of the Muslim plot against them, and its worldwide context were revealed. A Spanish judge indicted 29 people for their alleged roles in the deadly 2004 Madrid train bombings and concluded that the attack was carried out by a local radical Islamic cell that was inspired but not directed by al-Qa'ida. After a two-year investigation, Judge Juan del Olmo handed down an almost 1,500-page report and the first indictments, charging six people with 191 counts of terrorist murder and 1,755 attempted murders. The 23 other people were charged with collaborating in the plot. Explosives-filled backpacks were detonated by cell phones on the morning of 11 March 2004, ripping apart four rush-hour commuter trains. One hundred ninety-one people died and 1,800 were injured in what remains Europe's second-worst attack by terrorists after the 1988 downing of Pan Am Flight 103 over Lockerbie, Scotland, by other Muslim terrorists dispatched from and by Libya.[2]

The bombers' alleged ideological leader and six other men blew themselves up three weeks after the attack as police closed in on their Madrid apartment hideout. But several of the people indicted by the investigating judge are described as senior members of the conspiracy. They include Jamal Zougam, 32, a Moroccan, accused as a material author of the synchronized attack and charged with murder, attempted murder and membership in a terrorist group. According to the indictment, Zougam supplied the cell phones that detonated the 10 backpacks used in the attacks. In addition, four witnesses identified him as having placed dark blue bags under different seats on trains that blew up. Youssef Belhadj, Hassam El Haski and Rabei Osman Sayed Ahmed—known as "Mohamed the Egyptian" and currently on trial in Italy on separate terrorism charges—are also accused of membership in a terror group, murder and attempted murder. Jose Emilio

Suárez Trashorras, a former miner who allegedly provided the bombers with plastic explosives stolen from a mine in northern Spain, was charged with 192 murders. They included that of a policeman who was killed during the attempt to arrest suspected bombers at the Madrid apartment. The judge discussed the local nature of the conspiracy at length in his report. "If it is true that the operative capacity of al-Qa'ida has lessened in the past few years, it is not noticeable in a sustained decrease in its activity," del Olmo wrote. "From the point of view of the threat, regional networks and local groups have acquired greater importance." Del Olmo highlighted a trend of Moroccans and Algerians working together in radical Islamic groups in Spain. "It is a very noteworthy change, given that until relatively recently Algerian groups in Spain were homogenous in so far as nationality, and the relationship between Moroccan and Algerian *jihadists* was scarce," he wrote. The 29 indicted people include 15 Moroccans, one Algerian, one Egyptian, one Lebanese, one Syrian and one Syrian with Spanish national- ity. Also indicted were nine Spaniards, most on charges of having helped the bombers obtain their explosives.

According to Del Olmo, the bombers studied a report posted on the web site of the Global Islamic Media Front in which a committee of al-Qa'ida experts suggested an attack in Spain before the general elections of March 14, 2004. At the time, Spain had 1,300 troops in Iraq as part of the U.S.-led forces. The indictment details Spanish intelligence warnings to then-Prime Minister Jose María Aznar that Spain was one of a group of European countries at high risk of an Islamic terrorist attack. The bombings took place three days before the election. Aznar initially blamed the Basque separatist group ETA. But as evi- dence mounted of Islamic involvement, Spanish voters turned against Aznar and unseated his Popular Party. The Socialist Party, led by José Luis Rodríguez Zapatero, won the election and quickly fulfilled a campaign promise to pull Span- ish troops out of Iraq. Some people in Spain have speculated that ETA helped the bombers in some way. The indictment draws no such link. "The judge has only addressed what evidence there is," a court spokeswoman said. A trial will follow the indictment.

In the annual festival of satire in Valencia in early 2006, the furor over Dan- ish cartoons of the Prophet Mohammed seemed to be present among the giant sculptures of the high and mighty, that are placed in the streets for the public to mock before being destroyed in an orgy of gunpowder and flames. This show which follows a 400-year old tradition, has survived attacks by the Roman Catholic Church, various puritanical rulers and the Franco dictatorship. This year's figures included President George Bush, several of the Spanish prime ministers, notably José Zapatero, and the Prince of Wales dancing, in Highland dress, with the Duchess of Cornwall. But self-censorship has seen Muslim and Arab figures modified to avoid offence. The Fallas season was underway until March 19 but before it began Valencians watched global protests against newspaper cartoons of Mohammed with growing alarm. At last the mayor, Rita

Barber, urged artists to "temper freedom with a sense of responsibility" when referring to religious subjects. At least one well-known local Fallas artist admitted to removing elements from his display of comic sculptures. He had sculpted three life-size figures of illegal Arab immigrants storming the Spanish border, in a reference to the previous year's crisis in Ceuta and Melilla, Spain's enclaves in North Africa, involving thousands of migrants. The artist removed details that identified them as Arabs.[3] This will not only be seen by the Muslims as a victory over the local public opinion, but as a sign on their part that all leaders, religious and otherwise, can be mocked, but respect is due, and is observed, only with regard to Islam, the only True Faith, which will only encourage more Muslim threats and rampages in the future. The point is that if self-censorship is observed vis-à-vis leadership in general or the clerics of all creeds, then that is a laudable self-restraint and a monument to sensitivity and consideration on the part of the artists. But when in this case the artist asked not to be named, partly for fear of reprisals, partly because he did not feel proud of such "self-censorship," and he felt that this year was "different," because "radical Muslim leaders appeared to be looking for excuses to cause trouble," then Spain itself is in trouble. Muslims would not appreciate that gesture as a voluntary concession born out of sensitivity for Islam, but as yet another surrender, like the one of March 2004 following the Madrid massacre, then we are bracing for more pressures on the one hand and more surrenders on the other.

The reluctantly self-censored artist also said: "We saw what happened in Denmark. Those artists may have had the freedom to draw Mohammed, but now they're living as virtual prisoners. They have much less freedom than before. I felt responsible not just as an artist, but as a citizen of this city." In another bout of *dhimmitude*, Felix Crespo, the senior official in charge of the Central Fallas Council that runs the festival, urged the neighborhood committees that raise funds to build the sculptures to avoid mixing humor with religion, not any religion, which might have made sense, but specifically with the Islamic one "because that can be misunderstood." Misunderstood by whom? Only by Muslims who wish to intimidate others by trampling daily on their religious symbols and desecrating their holy sites, while remaining themselves immune to any encroachment on this supreme faith. Indeed, everyone assumed these warnings referred to Islam because sculptures of Roman Catholic priests, nuns, even of God, are a central part of the Fallas. The British journalist reported Mr. Crespo added that the "ordinary people do not know all the intricacies of Islam, they just saw that there was a very extreme reaction to the Danish cartoons, they heard that embassies were attacked, and so people felt cautious,." In the countryside near Valencia, many villages have their own festivals, involving mock battles between "Moors and Christians," in an ancient recreation of the Catholic re-conquest of Spain from Arab rule. But according to Spanish reports there have been subtle changes this year, which no locals would discuss. In Bocairent, for example, villagers refrained from burning life-size mannequins of the "Mahoma," a traditional figure presumed to be based on Mohammed.[4] If this is not a total terrorization of a culture and a tradition, and if the Spaniards continue to cave in out of "consideration" for Muslims, then the worse is to come. As the imposition of Muslim standards proceeds without much of a hindrance, those standards that had allowed the destruction of the giant Buddhas by the Taliban in Afghanistan without any Muslim authority seriously protesting or countering that move, then the Muslim *reconquista* of Spain will gain momentum and add impetus to the Islamization of Europe.

In March 2006, a conference of rabbis and imams was held in Seville, to discuss the "deepening crisis between the two faiths" and their inability to settle the Middle Eastern conflict. The conference was convened by the French organization *Hommes de Parole,* which promotes dialogue between conflicting groups, and it brought up the questions of terrorism, the Israeli settlements, and the centrality of Jerusalem in both creeds. There were displays of conviviality between the parties though no fundamental issue was resolved, and it was easy to make general and unbinding statements denouncing the use of religion to justify violence and urging "respect for religious symbols," which was an apparent reference to the cartoon affair. This meant that the organizers of the Conference and the chosen venue for its deliberations used the Arab-Israeli conflict as a parable for the mounting conflict in Europe between Christianity and Islam, an issue that one does not raise and prefers to deny. So, while the joint declaration condemned any "incitement against a faith or people, let alone call for its elimination," supposedly referring to Iran's President and the Hamas leaders' declarations in favor of eliminating Israel, any Muslim could also interpret that statement as condemning the Cartoons against the Prophet. Secondly, the Conference dramatically illustrated the asymmetry between the rival parties in the Middle East, for while Israel was represented by its established Chief Rabbi, Muslim imams from Gaza admitted that they would have been shot had they walked the streets of their city with Jewish rabbis.[5] Conferences like that were held in Alexandria, Egypt, in recent years, but beyond the smooth declarations, which were sometimes reversed by the Imams who participated in them, nothing practical came out of them. Both parties were acutely aware that the influence of clerics on toning down the conflict is insignificant, because it is politics that decide these issues. But for the Europeans who convened the conference, first in Brussels a year earlier, at the height of European fears from terrorism, and then again in Seville while all Europe was shaken by the Cartoon controversy, this goes to show that the Middle Eastern and Jewish-Muslim dispute was only a test-case for gauging the solubility of the much larger Arab-European and Islamic-Christian tensions. If in the Middle East the effort to dialogue proved so futile on the political level, even though virtual conviviality was feasible between individuals in the intimacy of an hotel in a foreign land, so much more so when it came to the bigger problem of Islam in Europe which was the top priority in the minds of the conveners of that gathering.

As the trial of the 11 March 2004 Madrid bombers proceeded, more details of the mammoth plot were disclosed to the public. One of the leading figures indicted in the bombings used a simple trick that allowed him to communicate with his confederates on ordinary e-mail accounts but still avoid government detection, according to the judge investigating the case. Instead of sending the messages, the man, Hassan el Haski, saved them as drafts on accounts he shared with other militants, said papers issued by the judge, Juan del Olmo. They all knew the password, so they could access the accounts to read his unsent notes and post reply the same way, the judge said. This way, the notes left less of a digital trail that the government could track. Intelligence officials have said in the past that some terrorist groups were using the method, which investigators call a "virtual dead drop." But few concrete examples had come to light until now, and its possible use in such a major attack, along with the wide circle of contacts that Mr. Haski maintained, officials say, raise the possibility that it is much more widespread among terrorists than previously thought. Few details of this use of e-mail accounts were given in a lengthy indictment that was re-leased to news organizations and that named 29 suspects, most of them North African, in connection with the Madrid attack. But because of testimony from one of the suspects in the Madrid bombings, the government now contends that such shared accounts were apparently used by the conspirators as early as late 2003. "This is probably a common method of communication among *jihadists* in Europe," said the director of the Center for Security Studies and Analysis at the University of Granada. "Haski is a person who traveled a lot and had lots of contacts, if he used this method, a logical interpretation is that many others did, too." The indictment includes testimony from a man named Attila Turk, a native of Turkey who was arrested on terrorism charges in France in 2004. Mr. Turk was trying to flee Europe after the Madrid bombings, fearing arrest. He asked Mr. Haski for help, he testified: "Hassan had given me an address on the Internet the day that I left." The indictment quotes Mr. Turk as testifying: "I was to check the Internet address in question every day and to go to the draft menu to check for messages. The only way to get in touch with him was through the e-mail address Babana12002 with password Wahd11," Mr. Turk said. "Hassan told me that the address worked in Yahoo or in Hotmail." Spanish investigators contend that by saving the messages as drafts, the men did not leave the digital traces that are normally created when e-mail messages are sent, and can often be traced by law enforcement agencies.

But the expert said he was skeptical that the authorities were as unable as they claimed to track unsent messages. "There is still communication between the computer and the server," he said. "I wouldn't be surprised if the intelligence services have a way of monitoring that. "Mr. Haski, 42, a Moroccan who has lived in Belgium, is portrayed in the indictment as one of the three main conspirators who helped the bombers carry out the Madrid attacks, which killed 191 people. He was arrested in the Canary Islands nine months after the bombings, and his trial was to begin shortly thereafter. Before his arrest, Spanish investigators said, Haski was a top leader of a terrorist network described as having broad contacts in Europe and Morocco and many ties to the Madrid suspects. The network, the Moroccan Islamic Combatant Group, is described in the indictment as the "supreme point of reference for the *Salafist Jihadist* Movement in our country." That refers to the followers of an extremist interpretation of Islam. The indictment also says the group has sent "a large part of its militants to join the ranks or the insurgency in Iraq" and "constitutes the principal concern regarding the end of the conflict and the return of the volunteers to Europe and Morocco."[6]

But Spain, like the rest of Europe, which had streamlined its human rights policies to fit the high standards of normal days, has fallen victim to its own indulgence once acute conditions of terror necessitate more stringent rules, which when adopted for self-defense, are abolished by the courts, just like in England. Spain's Supreme Court indeed quashed the conviction of a Syrian-born businessman for conspiracy in the September 2001 terror attacks on New York and Washington. Although Imad Eddin Barakat Yarkas, known as Abu Dahdah, still has to serve a 12-year sentence for membership of the al-Qa'ida network, the Spanish court's decision leaves Zacarias Moussaoui as the only man anywhere in the world jailed for the 9/11 attacks. It also calls into question the extradition from Britain to Spain of the Moroccan Farid Hilali, who Spanish prosecutors say was a co-conspirator in the U.S. attacks. Yarkas, thought to have been the head of the al-Qa'ida cell in Madrid, was one of 18 al-Qa'ida suspects sentenced in Spain on September 2005. During the trial, prosecutors accused him of helping to prepare a meeting in Tarragona, northeast Spain, in July 2001 at which they said the 9/11 attacks may have been planned. Prosecutors demanded that he be sentenced to a total of 74,337 years for the murder of the 2,973 people killed on 9/11. But the court decided that there was no proof that he had taken part in the World Trade Center attack, although there was evidence that he had helped think it up, working with a radical cell in Hamburg run by Muhammad Atta, the leader of the 9/11 hijackers. After Yarkas appealed, however, prosecutors went back through the evidence and decided that it did not stack up. In April, they asked the court to dismiss the conspiracy conviction for lack of evidence. Mr. Hilali, 38, is wanted by Spanish authorities for conspiracy to murder. His extradition was approved by magistrates in June, 2005 and he lost a High Court appeal later. He now plans to appeal to the House of Lords— and the decision to quash Yarkas's conviction will give his lawyers an extra argument. Mr. Hilali is said to have spoken on the telephone with Yarkas on four occasions, before and after 9/11. In one wire-tapped call, he said: "They are giving very good classes ... we have entered the area of aviation," and "We have slit the bird's throat." Moussaoui was sentenced to life by a court in Virginia after having testified that he was—despite previous assertions and evidence from elsewhere—part of the 9/11 plot. He said that he and Richard Reid, the British shoebomber, had been supposed to hijack a fifth aircraft and fly it into the White House.[7]

Italy

Some years back, when Europe was still complacent about Muslim immigration, a famous Italian film director gave an interview to a major Italian daily where he deplored the outrageous conduct of the immigrants. He particularly lamented the fact that every Friday, a Muslim crowd squatted in front of the one of the most celebrated cathedrals of Europe in Florence, to perform their Friday prayer. As a liberal, he certainly could not deny Muslims their right to freedom of worship, but at the risk of being labeled "racist," he courageously stated the obvious when he asked "why do the Muslims come to this particular spot," sometimes from their far-away suburbs, just in order to state their challenge to the Christian symbol. The Muslims have their places of worship, even in the very heart of Rome the capital and no one interferes with them, so why did they need to provoke their Christian hosts? Italy has one of the lowest Muslim immigration minorities, nevertheless in some areas it has taken the most dramatic measures. In Italy, which experts agree is the most wiretapped Western democracy, a report to parliament in January 2006 by Justice Minister Roberto Castelli said the number of authorized wiretaps more than tripled from 32,000 in 2001 to 106,000 last year.   Italy passed a terrorism law after the 7 July subway bombings in London that opened the way for intelligence agencies to eavesdrop if an attack is feared to be imminent. Only approval from a prosecutor—not a judge—is required, but the material gleaned cannot be used as evidence in court.[8] But during the raucous election campaign of April 2006, two inter-related issues came up for debate: the mass Muslim immigration, which also lay demands for Muslim education, and the place of government sponsorship of Catholic education in the school system, that had been mandated by the 1929 Concordat between the Vatican and Italy that was renewed in 1984. The issues are interrelated because some officials of the Catholic Church have to show their overall concern for religious education for all, including for Muslims whom they invite to "dialogue," if they wish the one hour a week Catholic education to be preserved.[9]

Italy's largest Muslim group, the Community of Islamic Organizations in Italy, which controls mosques and has connections with the radical Muslim Brotherhood, has asked the government to substitute Muslim instruction to Catholic teachings when a large enough Muslim constituency demands it. The President of the Organization, Muhammed Nour Dachan, has refused to sign a document in which the Muslims pledged to accept Italy's Constitution, denounce terrorism and accept Israel's right to statehood. Catering to his demands would be then acknowledging a separate status for Italian Muslims. In this context one has to understand the rage that spread in the Italian media when Cardinal Renato Martino, a former Ambassador of the Vatican in the UN, made a remark in favor of allowing Muslim education in Italian schools even without reciprocity for the oppressed Christian minorities in Muslim lands. A master-journalist, Sandro Magister, proclaimed in Milan's *L'espresso,* that not only Martino's wish for dialogue recognized Islam's separate place in the country, but it also run counter Pope Benedict XVI who told the Moroccan Ambassador to the Vatican that he advocated religious liberty only if it was granted in all societies on a reciprocal basis. Milan's *Corriere del la Sera* decried in an editorial the attitude of Martino, which was antithetical to the Pope's and amounted to an "anti-Ratzingerian manifesto." *Avvenire,* the paper of the Italian Bishops' Conference, stated that Martino's proposal contradicted Italy's constitution and the place of Catholicism in Italian culture. In the face of these attacks, Martino tried an exercise in damage control and declared to the French *Le Figaro* that his hands-off proposal was a "sign of respect for Islam that would encourage Muslim nations to show similar respect for their Christian minorities."[10] But, reflecting the mood in Italy in general, and Prime Minister Berlusconi's government in particular, Carlo Cardia, a non-Catholic Professor of Ecclesiastical Law and a consultant for left-wing parties, declared that:

> There does not exist in Italy an organized Islamic confession that is recognized by the state. There are various groups, which are not infrequently in conflict among themselves. All this prevents the implementation of teaching that would not be based on any community, institution or confessional hierarchy.... And then, one cannot ignore the potential conflict between some of the features of Islamism in its present state and fundamental questions for our society—the matter of human rights, beginning with religious freedom, the principles of equality, between men and women, the monogamous structure of matrimony—which constitute the most valuable heritage of the secular—Christian tradition of Italy and the West. At a moment when Islamic fundamentalism constitutes a concrete reality in many countries from which immigration comes to Europe, it would be a mistake not to take note of the risk that a hasty legitimation in the sensitive channels of the schools could let in subjects capable of transmitting other messages, creating ambiguous connections, and placing at risk values that are fundamental for civil life. These are some of the obstacles that make an organic presence of Islam in the Italian schools unfeasible and not worthy of entertaining.[11]

Curiously enough, Mediterranean Italy, which ought to be a natural habitat for Muslims, does not figure very high on the Muslim immigration agenda, exactly like the Jews, who for some mysterious reason have kept throughout history a low profile in the country. Unlike France, where these two most numerous minorities have also clashed more intensely than elsewhere, the Jews and Muslims of Italy have been out of each other's way in the main. In Milan, prosecutors have arrested two Italian intelligence chiefs and issued warrants for the arrest of four Americans over the alleged CIA kidnapping of a Muslim terrorism suspect. Three of the Americans are claimed to have been CIA agents, while the fourth worked at a U.S. military base in Aviano, northern Italy. Prosecutors believe this base was used to transfer the Muslim cleric out of the country. Marco Mancini, second-in-command at Italy's Sismi military intelligence agency, was one of the men held for his alleged role in the kidnap. Another Sismi official has been placed under house arrest. All the arrests and warrants relate to the abduction of Hassan Mustafa Osama Nasr, also known as Abu Omar, in 2003. Prosecutors say he was seized by a CIA-led team on a Milan street in broad daylight, forced into a van and driven to the air base. He was then flown to Egypt and, according to Mr. Nasr, tortured under questioning. This was the first time that Italian spies have been linked to the kidnapping. An Italian court has already issued arrest warrants for 22 suspected U.S. agents over the abduction. If an Italian role is confirmed, it would support allegations that European countries, including Britain, colluded with Washington in the secret "renditions" of terrorism suspects.[12]

Another major Italian figure, this time of the Catholic hierarchy, Cardinal Camilio Ruini, the papal vicar of the Archdiocese of Rome, echoed the views of the Italians *vis-à-vis* Muslim terrorism, when he emphasized that there should be no conflict with respect to the state constitution, for example with regard to civil rights, religious freedom, equality between the genders and marriage. He also suggested that since there has been no one representative body of Islam that would be capable to establish an accord with the state, following the example of the 1929 Concordat, it was necessary to ensure that any teaching of the Islamic religion in Italy "would not give rise to socially dangerous indoctrination."[13] Other public and clerical figures joined the fray, including Oriana Fallaci, who blamed, in her book, *The Force of Reason,* the Catholic Church's lax policy on immigration and ecumenism that might generate the disintegration of European identity. In fact, she charged, following Bat Ye'or, that due to that laxity Europe was degenerating into Eurabia. In April 2006 Italian police announced that they thwarted planned terrorist attacks on a Bologna church and in the Milan subway system. The plot was revealed by Interior Minister Giuseppe Pisanu during a political rally in Sardinia, who boasted that the plot which involved seven terrorists, had been scuttled by the monitoring and preventive action of police. In the heat of the election campaign he declared that out of the seven, three were expelled, two arrested, one was under surveillance and the seventh remained at large. Unlike the church plaza in Florence, where Muslim squat every Friday, just for the defiance they pose to the heart of Christianity, the Milan church was apparently chosen as a target because some Muslim groups have interpreted a fifteenth-century fresco there as "insulting to Islam," since it represents Muhammed in Hell being devoured by demons. This means that external appearances of challenging Christianity are no longer sufficient for European Muslims, they are now examining the contents of churches and museums and anything they deem offensive will be doomed to destruction, either "voluntarily" by Europeans who cave in after extending their proper apologies to the "insulted" Muslim, as in the Cartoon Affair, or by car bombs at the hands of the Muslims themselves. One wonders how the Muslims worldwide would react if a demand to ban anti-Semitic rhetoric in their museums and mosques should be imposed on them.[14]

In a policy that will be significant only if Western states follow the Church's lead, new utterances by senior Catholic officials may be signaling a new era, away from the accommodating conduct of John-Paul II towards Islam." Enough now with this turning the other cheek! It's our duty to protect ourselves," thus spoke Monsignor Velasio De Paolis, secretary of the Vatican's Supreme Court, referring to Muslims. Explaining his apparent rejection of Jesus' admonition to his followers to turn the other cheek, De Paolis noted that the West has had relations with the Arab countries for half a century and has not been able to get the slightest concession on human rights. De Paolis is hardly alone in his thinking; indeed, the Catholic Church is undergoing a dramatic shift from a decades-old policy to protect Catholics living under Muslim rule. The old methods of quiet diplomacy and muted appeasement have clearly failed. The estimated 40 million Christians in *Dar al-Islam*, notes the Barnabas Fund's Patrick Sookhdeo, increasingly find themselves an embattled minority facing economic decline, dwindling rights, and physical jeopardy. Most of them, he goes on, are despised and distrusted second-class citizens, facing discrimination in education, jobs, and the courts. These harsh circumstances are causing Christians to flee their ancestral lands for the West's more hospitable environment. Consequently, Christian populations of the Muslim world are in a freefall. Two small but evocative instances of this pattern: for the first time in nearly two millennia, Nazareth and Bethlehem no longer have Christian majorities. This reality of oppression and decline stands in dramatic contrast to the surging Muslim minority of the West. Although numbering only around 30 million and made up mostly of immigrants and their offspring, it is an increasingly established and vocal minority, granted extensive rights and protections even as it wins new legal, cultural, and political prerogatives. This widening disparity, notes Pipes, has caught the attention of the Roman Catholic Church, which for the first time is pointing to radical Islam, rather than the actions of Israel, as the central problem facing Christians living with Muslims. Rumblings of this could be heard already in John Paul II's time. For example, Cardinal Jean-Louis Tauran, the Vatican equivalent of foreign minister, noted in late 2003 that "There are too many majority Muslim countries where non-Muslims are second-class citizens." Tauran pushed for reciprocity: "Just as Muslims can build their houses of prayer anywhere in the world, the faithful of other religions should be able to do so as well."

Catholic demands for reciprocity have grown, especially since the accession of Pope Benedict XVI in April 2005, for whom Islam is a central concern. In February 2006, the pope emphasized the need to respect the convictions and religious practices of others so that, in a reciprocal manner, the exercise of freely chosen religion is truly assured to all. In May 2006 he again stressed the need for reciprocity: Christians must love immigrants and Muslims must treat well the Christians among them. Lower-ranking clerics, as usual, are more outspoken. "Islam's radicalization is the principal cause of the Christian exodus" from Muslim lands, asserts Monsignor Philippe Brizard, director general of *Oeuvre d'Orient*, a French organization focused on Middle Eastern Christians. Bishop Rino Fisichella, rector of the Lateran University in Rome, advises the Church to drop its diplomatic silence; and instead put pressure on international organizations to make the societies and states in majority Muslim countries face up to their responsibilities. The Danish cartoons crisis offered a typical example of Catholic disillusionment. Church leaders initially criticized the publication of the Muhammad cartoons. But when Muslims responded by murdering Catholic priests in Turkey and Nigeria, not to speak of scores of Christians killed during five days of riots in Nigeria, the Church responded with warnings to Muslims: "If we tell our people they have no right to offend, we have to tell the others they have no right to destroy us," said Cardinal Angelo Sodano, the Vatican's Secretary of State. "We must always stress our demand for reciprocity in political contacts with authorities in Islamic countries and, even more, in cultural contacts," added Archbishop Giovanni Lajolo, its foreign minister. Obtaining the same rights for Christians in Islamdom that Muslims enjoy in Christendom has become the key to the Vatican's diplomacy toward Muslims. This balanced, serious approach marks a profound improvement in understanding that could have implications well beyond the Church, given how many lay politicians heed its leadership in interfaith matters. Should Western states also promote the principle of reciprocity, the results should indeed be interesting, in Pipes' view.[15] The Pope's speech in his native Regensburg in the fall of 2006, which inflamed outrage in the Islamic world, did not help to calm the tempers even after his voyage of appeasement to Istanbul where he tried to explain the "misunderstanding" that his speech had provoked.

The place that Muslim immigrants occupy in the hearts and minds of people reflects the degree to which Italian politics have enmeshed themselves in this issue. The Berlusconi-Prodi confrontation which brought the clash between right and left to its apex in the March 2006 general elections, also produced much debate on this matter. Italy has newly offered, at the outset, 170,000 work permits, which produced a long line of half a million Muslim immigrant applicants in Italy out of the 2.5 million immigrants there (4% of the population). Thus the competition for work places is very tough in the weak economy and mounting unemployment. But immigrants keep coming to Italian shores from North Africa on risky illegal journeys that may cost them their lives. So, the immigration problem was pushed to the front of the agenda, when two ministers in the outgoing Berlusconi government professed that the illegal immigrants should be arrested, not welcome, on arrival. Those two ministers from the right-wing Northern League claimed that the fact that so-many immigrants were showing up to apply to jobs demonstrated that it was illegal in the first place. One of those ministers, Roberto Castelli said plainly that "we witness the paradox of watching clandestine people line up at the post office," therefore the law was ignored. Berlusconi has boasted during his campaign that during his five-year rule immigration has declined by more than 50%, but Romano Prodi fired back that "one cannot use the immigrants for work during daytime and then hunt them down during nighttime. The law of 2002 imposes restrictions and quotas of immigrant workers, which have been criticized by both the Unions and Confindustria, the main industrial alliance, as inadequate for attractive skilled labor to the country, while at the same time there are thousands of immigrants who work illegally and whose very presence in Italy is "clandestine." But the fact that applicants themselves stand in line, instead of their prospective employers who were required to produce evidence of their service, itself meant that there is a breakdown somewhere in the system. So, instead of the employers obtaining permits to import directly from their countries of origin the skilled labor they need, it turns out that many unemployed are already in Italy vying for the vacant jobs. Those among the applicants who have no visas, must return to their countries to obtain them, but they have no means (and will) to venture back to their lands with no assurance that they would be welcomed back. In the heat of the election campaign, the right wing equated immigrants, especially the clandestine among them, with danger, while the left wing which won the elections was warning not to lump all immigrants together.[16]

After the razor-thin victory by Romano Prodi, the new Prime Minister announced, like his Spanish counterpart, that he would withdraw Italian troops from Iraq, signaling to the terrorists there that their struggle paid and that if they continue to cause casualties to the soft West, isolated and defeated America would have to withdraw too, leaving Iraq to its turmoil and to the danger of reverting to the horrors of another dictatorial regime. Thus, European countries as a whole have either condemned the United States who launched the war almost singlehanded, or hampered the best they could the American effort after it started, and now are trying to distance themselves from that endeavor and throwing themselves open to more terrorist blackmail and to outright capitulation. True to their post-war habit of short-lived governments, the Italians once again resort to changing government, and there is no telling whether Berlusconi might replace Prodi, throwing Italian policy of immigration into chaos once again.

Central Europe

Switzerland

Though Switzerland and Austria are not large immigration countries, many Muslim elements have found asylum there, chief among them the Ramadan family, a direct descendent of the founder of the Muslim Brotherhood in Egypt-Hassan al-Banna. While Tariq, the grand-son of al-Banna, has made a name for himself as a great orator and a favorite of European media, and he sought to expand his preaching into the United States until he was banned from entry there, his younger brother- Hani, who is less known, uses his lower profile to pursue the same line almost unnoticed if it were not for the *Swissinfo* website which promotes him and tells his tale.[17] The canton of Geneva has fired teacher Hani Ramadan, a Muslim cleric, for his controversial remarks published in the French newspaper, *Le Monde*. Geneva has strict laws separating church and state which restrict cantonal employees' freedom of expression. Ramadan told S*wissinfo* he would be appealing against the ruling. Geneva officials said their decision to fire Ramadan was based on the "anti-democratic" nature of his remarks. In the article, which was published in September 2005, Ramadan defended death by stoning for adultery as set out in Islamic *Shari'a* law. He also said that believers were protected from being infected with Aids. Unlike non-believers and sinners, they could only be infected through a botched blood transfusion. Ramadan is an Imam and the director of the Islamic Center of Geneva. An investigation into the affair commissioned by the Geneva authorities found that his role as a religious representative was incompatible with his status as a teacher in a state school. Church and state in Geneva, which is a Protestant canton, forbids any overlap between religious and secular authorities. The investigation—which was conducted by the former public prosecutor, Bernard Bertossa—also found that, as a state employee, Ramadan had violated his obligation to refrain from airing controversial views. Bertossa wrote in his report that Ramadan expressed "opinions clearly incompatible with the values that the public school must defend." Cantonal regulations stipulate that "state employees must remain non-religious or secular." An exception, however, is made for teaching staff at Swiss universities who have greater freedom to express their personal beliefs.[18]

The article caused a public outcry. The Commission against Racism publicly reprimanded Ramadan, saying he had damaged the image of the Muslim community in Switzerland. One month later, cantonal authorities suspended him from his post as a French teacher in a state school. This is not the first time that Ramadan has got on the wrong side of Geneva cantonal law. He previously received two warnings for publicly voicing his beliefs. On one occasion, he participated in a demonstration outside the United Nations in Geneva in support of Palestinians. Ramadan told *Swissinfo* that he would challenge Geneva's ruling. He said he would lodge an appeal at Switzerland's federal court, which is located in Lausanne. In an interview published in *Le Nouvelliste* newspaper, he rejected the point made in Bertossa's report that he is a religious figure. In his 20 years as an employee of the canton, Ramadan said he had never encountered problems expressing his views. Ramadan continues to stand by the content of the *Le Monde* article. "Muslims living in Europe have the right … to bear witness to their faith and their convictions," he said in another newspaper article, "even if it offends those who judge them before understanding them. I will pursue all legal means to assert my rights," he told *Swissinfo*. Ramadan is a well-known thinker in the Muslim world and has published several articles on Islamic life. Ramadan said the international community "has an unfortunate habit of confusing certain acts of resistance with barbarism." But leaders in Switzerland's Islamic community are concerned by the content of the article written by Ramadan. Taner Hatipogliu, deputy head of the society of Islamic organizations in Zurich, said that the furor surrounding Ramadan had served to take Switzerland's Muslim community "ten steps back. This type of publicity harms all the activities undertaken in the area of integration [into Swiss society]," Hatipogliu told *Swissinfo*. A Geneva-born teacher, Ramadan says he will appeal against the canton's decision to fire him for writing that newspaper article in which he defended the death penalty as set out in Islamic *Shari'a* law. Ramadan is also head of the Islamic Center of Geneva. In his appeal in a Geneva court he won his case. However, the cantonal authorities responded by saying Hani Ramadan, would not be reinstated. It was the second time the courts have ruled in Ramadan's favor, saying that his dismissal was unfair and demanding that the cantonal government recognize Ramadan's status as a public servant and resume paying his salary. He had been dismissed by the cantonal authorities in 2003, a few months after making his remarks in the French newspaper *Le Monde*. In 2005 the appeals board had already said that Ramadan was still a public servant, but the government refused to budge and went one step further a few months later by cutting off his salary. Ramadan refuses to comment for the time being pending official notification of the government's position. But his lawyer, Eric Hess, says his client now wants his job as a high school French teacher back. "He wants nothing less than full reintegration," he told *Swissinfo*. The attorney believes there is no reason why Ramadan should not have his job back. "The quality of his work was never in question and he was considered an excellent teacher," he added. Hess reckons the local media have a lot to account for in the affair. "It wasn't his students who noticed my client's remarks in *Le Monde*," he said.[19]

Officials had said in 2003 that Ramadan, who had taught for 20 years without any problem, was fired because of the "anti-democratic" nature of his remarks. The canton forbids any overlap between religious and secular authorities. The investigation also highlighted the fact that Ramadan had violated his obligation to refrain from airing controversial views. The appeals board had, in its first ruling, admitted that the teacher had overstepped the boundaries outlined by state legislation. But it added that firing him was a disproportionate measure, and that there were other ways of disciplining him. The board's second decision has not gone down well with the government. Its president, Martine Brunschwig-Graf, said the authorities do not agree with the assessment that Ramadan is still a public servant and a teacher. For Brunschwig-Graf, he is neither, and the government still refuses to put him back on the payroll. But the authorities say they are prepared to pay him a monthly "indemnity" instead. They fear that paying Ramadan a salary would be tantamount to admitting that he was still a public servant. But Hess says that any funds given to his client would be considered a salary, and he expects all benefits to be paid out in full. "The government has had an absurd attitude throughout this whole affair," he said. "The decision to cut off my client's salary in December was arbitrary and had no legal basis, especially since his status as a public servant had been confirmed." According to the attorney, the authorities have nowhere to run. "They cannot appeal to a higher court," he told Swissinfo. Hess has already warned that if the government does not play ball, he will ask the state prosecutor to intervene. As to whether some kind of settlement could be negotiated with the authorities, the lawyer also has his doubts."The government's attitude has been to not negotiate until now," he said. "And so far we have had no indication there will be a change of heart."[20]

The firm stand of the Swiss government, in spite of the constitutional complication involved, may have had to do with the links that are perennially suspected between Muslim fundamentalists and international terror, of which the Swiss authorities want no part. A story which implicates Hani Ramadan (what a coincidence!) has been unfolding in the Helvetic Republic, enough to make the authorities concerned about Muslim fundamentalist activities within their otherwise placid borders. A plot to blow up an El Al plane at Geneva's international airport has been thwarted by Swiss intelligence agencies. The authorities uncovered a terrorist cell that was plotting to strike an Israeli plane while it was taking off through an RPG rocket attack in December 2005. The plot to shoot down the plane was uncovered by Claude Covassi, a Swiss secret service member who worked under the codename Babylon. Swiss newspaper *Blick* reported that Covassi (alias: Kuvasi) was planted as an undercover agent in an Islamic center in Geneva to find out if a terror cell was operating there. The episode was kept secret for six months, until the Swiss agent exposed it on his own. Kuvasi, who became closer to the head of the Islamic center in Geneva, Hani Ramadan, feared that his new friend would face complications due to the fact that some of his students planned a terror attack. The French website of *Le Point* featured a report on 19 May 2006 saying that "intelligence of the Swiss secret services carrying the date December 2005 shows that two people, a Libyan and an Algerian, held a mortar bomb, and planned to carry out an attack against an Israeli airlines El Al plane at Geneva's airport." According to the reports, the cell members used the Islamic center of Genevais, headed by Ramadan, as a shelter for their operational preparations for the attack. Hani's father, Said Ramadan, had been expelled from Egypt by then-dictator Gamal Abdul Nasser. Going to Saudi Arabia first, Said Ramadan was one of the founders of the World Islamic League, a Saudi "charity" organization, whose goal is to spread worldwide the Islamic faith. He moved to Geneva, Switzerland in 1961. There he created the Islamic Center of Geneva, which was inaugurated in 1978 by Saudi King Khaled Bin Abdulaziz. According to Richard Labeviere, a French journalist who has written about the Brotherhood's ties to terrorism, Said Ramadan used Geneva as the launching pad for the Muslim Brotherhood's international expansion, the group even created its own Swiss bank, *Al Taqwa*,[21] with offices in the Swiss town of Campione d'Italia as well as the Bahamas. *Al Taqwa* Bank is one of the financial institutions allegedly used by al-Qa'ida whose assets were frozen after 9/11.[22]

The Islamic Center of Geneva, headed by Ramadan's son Hani, was linked to *Al Taqwa*. The Secret Service of Switzerland had long suspected that the center acts as the meeting and training location of terrorists from Algeria and Afghanistan. The Saudi Kingdom has established more than 1,350 mosques around the world at a cost of SR 820 million, including the Islamic Center Mosque in Geneva, Switzerland which was built with the Saudi King personal contribution at a cost of SR 16 million and receives annual support from the Saudi "King Fahd Foundation" of SR 19 million. It contains a large Mosque, a cultural center, a school and a lecture hall. Abdallah Obeid, the Muslim World League general director stated in 1977 that the Geneva Islamic Center is operated and supervised by his organization. The Saudi regime has invested billions of dollars in the past three decades (directly, and via "charitable" institutions) in support of its policy of exporting *Wahhabbi* Islam outside its borders. This money has gone to projects in Islamic countries and Western countries to build a worldwide network of Saudi Islamic institutions. This network of mosques, Islamic centers, various educational and "charitable" institutions, whose activists are mostly Saudis or graduates of the *Wahhabbi* ideology, has become the backbone of recruitment into terror organizations and has supplied these organizations with the required manpower and the religious justification for *Jihad* against the West. Throughout King Fahd's reign, the Kingdom of Saudi Arabia has played an active role in all these organizations, using its influence to nurture and encourage unity in the Islamic world amongst which the Organization of the Islamic Conference (OIC) and the World Assembly of Muslim Youth. In addition, the Kingdom of Saudi Arabia has played a role in nurturing Islamic unity through the Muslim World League, based in the Holy City of Mecca. The Kingdom of Saudi Arabia has supported and contributed to the establishment of many mosques and Islamic centers amongst which the Cultural Center in Brussels, Belgium which has received a total support of SR 19 million; the Islamic Center in Geneva, Switzerland, which receives an annual support of SR 19 million, and contains a large mosque, a cultural center, a school and a lecture hall; the Islamic Center in Madrid, Spain, which has had a total support of SR 27 million, and is one of the largest in Europe. It comprises a very large mosque, a prayer hall for women, a library, a lecture hall and a medical clinic; the Islamic Center in London, England to which the Kingdom has contributed some SR 25 million; the Islamic Center in Edinburgh, Scotland, which is located in the city center, and contains a mosque, which can accommodate 1,000 worshippers, and includes a library, a lecture hall and classrooms. It cost around SR 15 million. The Islamic Center in Rome, Italy that comprises a mosque, a library and a lecture hall. King Fahd donated US$ 50 million (some 70% of the total) to cover the cost of construction. The Center also receives an annual donation of US$ 1.5 million. The list also includes the Mosque of the Custodian of the Two Holy Mosques [that is the title of the Saudi King] in Gibraltar, which cost in excess of SR 30 million and comprises a mosque for men, a prayer hall for women, a school, a library and a lecture hall.[23]

An interview of Tariq Ramadan by a Muslim journalist sheds some light not only on the man but also on his vision of European Islam, which he pretends will grow peacefully, in the face of the accumulating evidence to the contrary. When queried about the non-emergence of a reformed Islam after 40 years of its implantation in European soil, Ramadan was visibly embarrassed. Well, he said, there is nothing very visible yet. In a way that is not surprising, these things take time. But he believed that a silent revolution is taking place and things are evolving very fast. Muslims are now talking about national citizenship in a more confident way. Women are much more involved in the process. There are pockets of resistance to change, especially among the elder generation, but this is not the only reality: there are new leaders, new understandings, new trends. Faced with the challenge that he often says in his lectures that liberal democracies like Britain are more Islamic than many undemocratic Islamic countries, he admitted that protection of religion, life, intellect, family, goods, and dignity is much more a reality in the west than under the Arab Islamic countries, and that he would prefer social mixing of Muslims in their host countries and mutual interaction. He is not opposed to Muslim schools in the West, not against Islamic schools in principle, and says he has seen some good ones in Britain. He is also aware that even in the mainstream system one often gets a lot of plain old segregation, with 80 to 95% of pupils coming from one group, and this has to be fought against too. Muslims should, of course, have the same right to faith schools as Christians and Jews. But there is a danger that self-segregation could be the result. So, it is legally right, but Muslims should not necessarily take up the right. He sees a contradiction between the recourse of Muslims in Europe to their leaders and organizations, and their need to turn to MP's like all the rest, in order to ensure integration. European governments want to see the emergence of leaders who can speak in the name of Muslims. In France, they have even set up Muslim bodies. But at the same time, they do not want to encourage too much identity politics. So, he hopes that in the future, those organizations will just play a religious role, while the state should deal with citizens. Asked whether he recognizes the separation of religion and politics, he retorted: "I'm just saying that we must follow the rules in the countries in which we live. We should not confuse everything and Islamise social problems. Social problems are social problems and we have to deal with them as citizens claiming our rights, not as Muslims defending their religion. It is true that there are some special problems that Muslims face, certain kinds of discrimination or prejudice based on faith, that we call Islamophobia. But most problems that Muslims face are faced by other citizens too.[24]

For Ramadan, Islamophobia means distinguishing between criticizing the religion and Muslims, which is not Islamophobia, for a critical attitude towards religion must be accepted; and to criticize someone or discriminate against him only because he is Muslim, this is what we can call Islamophobia, this is a kind of racism. How come then that devout Muslims would not accept seeing the film *The Da Vinci Code* which has even been banned in many Muslim countries? He admitted that he may be in the minority on this point and dissociated himself from the confusion and some very emotional reactions "in these difficult times." We need some intellectual critical distance, he counseled. He concurred that Britain has remained calm in terms of Islamophobia even after the 7/7 events, especially compared to some other European countries. "The BNP has been doing well and they are overtly anti-Muslim," he said, but mainstream politics is relatively immune and the British Muslims have a sense that they are quite privileged compared to Muslims in Europe. As to the question why Muslims are more troubled about living in Western societies than other religious minorities, as if something in the history of Islam as a great world civilization, and a pros-elytizing religion, makes it harder for Muslims to adapt, or perhaps gives them greater expectations about the degree of adaptation of the host society; Ramadan subscribes to that. He believes that things are harder for Muslims in secular so-cieties. The whole intellectual and religious apparatus of Islam perceived itself as not of the west, and tended to see the west as a monolithic entity. Also, the experience of colonization is something Muslims cannot forget. In North Africa, India and Pakistan, it runs deep. Then on the Western side there is the feeling that Muslims are especially difficult to integrate because of the indivisibility of religion and politics; that Islam is monolithic. We have to try to deconstruct these perceptions on both sides, he says, for perceptions can be self-segregating. It's not easy. When challenged with regard to the French secular tradition, which does not permit any religion to exhibit its symbols in public, he retorted that the practice of laïcité in France dates back to a law of 1905. If a law already exists, why a new law in 2004? This is because crucifixes were accepted under the old law. The new law was passed because of France's Muslim presence. The real-ity is that France's secular tradition is being adapted to target a specific group. French society is going through something of an identity crisis. He said that he told French-Muslim girls that, if they have to make a choice between going to school and wearing the headscarf, they must choose school. Just go. This is the law. But at the same time, being a democrat means that you continue to discuss the merits of the law and call for change. He admitted that the headscarf ban is not Islamophobia, but a kind of discrimination.[25]

Ramadan expressed opposition to the belief that British Muslims live in an Islamo-phobic environment. He said it was dangerous to nurture this feeling. Very dangerous. It is nurturing a victim-mentality, the idea that everyone is against us. He also said that to force any women to wear a scarf is against human rights and "Islamic principles." But other Muslim *'ulama,* and not necessarily among the lesser of them, have decreed the reverse. What is then Islamic or un-Islamic? Can anyone bend Islamic rules to one's desires and wishes? Did Ramadan initiate, start or sustain any movement of reformed Islam that posits itself as a viable alternative to traditional Islam? When asked about his writings and talks where he preached that practice of Islam must become less literalist;

for example, whereas the majority of Muslims are taught that every word in the Qur'an has to be obeyed, he claims that the Qur'an should be read in its historical context. "What I say is firmly rooted in the Islamic tradition. Islam is constructed on a number of principles that cannot change. They are: belief in God, in the Prophet, the books of revelation, and so on. These are immutable. Then there is the practice of Islam: praying, fasting, and so on. Here also there is agreement, among both Shi'a and Sunni traditions [that they are immutable]." But there is a third level that deals with Islamic ethics. In this field, he says, there are immutable principles and there are implementations that have to take history and societies into account. The answers here come from intellectual creativity, from *ijtihad*. But he knows very well that the gates of *ijtihad* have been closed since the tenth century for all Sunnites, and that trying to be creative and innovative is considered *bid'a*, one of the most reprehensible sins. Let Ramadan ask Qaradawi or Tantawi, they are the determining authorities, not he. If he should dare to voice his views in al-Azhar, if one assumes they are sincere, he would not emerge alive.   Now he says that this idea of creativity and innovation is also firmly rooted in the Islamic tradition. But we do need a shift in the sources of authority. People who have power to make Islamic rulings are what he calls *'ulama* [scholars] of the text." What we now need is more of what he would call *'ulama* of the context." These are people who are aware of modern knowledge and who can help the scholars of the text to be more creative in their answers. This requires an acknowledgement that there is a role for modern knowledge in Islamic law and jurisprudence, but that this need not betray the ethic of Islamic teachings.[26] Brilliant! The trouble is that Islamic ethics are not necessarily ours, and that the text continues to outrank the context, because even the context has been constrained by precedent. This is precisely the significance of fundamentalists such as the *Wahhabis* and the Muslim Brothers, who go back to the fundaments of the faith (Qur'an and Hadith), to the detriment of the human reasoning that is usually encapsulated in the devices of analogy (*qiyas*), consensus (*ijma'*) and local custom (*'ada*), as the sources of the *shari'a*. So, at most, one could venture that Ramadan is a "moderate" Muslim individual, maybe full of goodwill and good intent if we indulge in our generosity, but who cannot produce another acceptable Islam.

Hard-pressed to produce possible solutions via creative interpretations, in order to respond to the arising needs of the modern world, Ramadan referred to medicine as an instance, an easy one at that because it concerns borrowing from Western science to save Muslims lives (about non-Muslims they couldn't care less). He says that the need for such a new applied ethic is quite clear when we deal with medical sciences: Muslim scholars must work together with medical doctors when they tackle the issues of cloning or euthanasia. It must be exactly the same when we deal with economics or any human sciences. At the same time he reconfirmed that for him, the Qur'an is the very word of God. It is a revelation and this belief is a fundamental pillar of Islam (*arkan al-Iman*). It was revealed over 23 years, but often as a kind of answer to a specific situation. Whether it is created or uncreated had in fact nothing to do with the question of how to read the Qur'an. It is the very word of God, revealed in a specific period of time: the great majority of the scholars agree that there are immutable principles and teachings and other lessons that we have to conceptualize. Even the eternal teachings require human intellect to be rightly enforced in a new environment. But these rather evasive and contradictory answers, where Ramadan at the same time says that the Qur'an is the Word of Allah, which makes it immutable and eternal, but at the same time new ways have to be found to interpret it, did not prompt the interviewer to take him off the hook. He pressed on with an example.

For many Muslims, the verses that call on the wives of the Prophet to cover up are seen as a commandment for Muslim women to wear the headscarf. But would it also be possible to read these verses as general guidance to dress modestly; or to respect women and not see them in a sexualized way? Ramadan answered: "There are two things here. First, all Islamic schools interpret these verses as being an Islamic prescription for women to cover their hair. But at the same time, what we are seeing in most Islamic-majority countries is that this interpretation is contributing to the seclusion and segregation of women. So, the headscarf is an Islamic prescription and I agree that modesty needs to be protected. That's fine. But some scholars of Islam go on to conclude that women do not have the right to work. For me this is wrong and is against women's rights. And we can actually go back to the scriptural sources in order to promote the struggle for women's rights. We have two main problems at the present time. The literalist reading, which is: there is no history, there is no conceptualization. The other is when we read the Qur'an through our own cultures. This is also a problem." But he still could not settle the contradiction.[27]

Ramadan was then asked about "parts of the Qur'an," that accept other "people of the book," namely the Jews and Christians, while other parts are intolerant of anybody who is, say a polytheist, and by implication anybody who is an atheist. Wrong, there is no "part of the Qur'an," it is one text, indivisible, and Muslim theologians have already worked out the formula of abrogation of the old revelations by the new ones (*al-nasikh wal-Mansukh*); The people of the book were not accepted unless they were subject *dhimmis* that recognized and accepted the superiority of Islam. It is that obverted view of the People of the Book that has to be straightened, and neither Ramadan nor any other *'ulama'* could, even if they wanted, redress that clear designation of others, let alone the polytheists and the atheists, who are not included in the *dhimmi* category? It is here that Ramadan faltered, because his attempt to show that the Prophet himself had collaborated with non-Muslims during his difficult times of persecution, does not prove what he did later or how he tailored the Qur'anic verses that regard the Jews and the Christians. To claim that Islam, following the model of the Prophet, gave freedom of religion to the Arabs and others, is to deny the forced conversions to Islam, the massacres of Jews and Christians under the Muslim regimes of the *Muwahhidun* (Almohads) in North Africa and the Mamluks in Egypt, and the wars of apostasy which sank in blood all the Arab tribes who relinquished their Islam after the death of Muhammed. To pretend moderation when you use your intellect and smooth talk is one thing, but to re-write history in order to claim events that have no leg to stand on, or deny others that are recorded in blood in history, is quite another. It is precisely on this matter of the right to apostasy that Ramadan tripped once again. He says that his view is the same as that of Sufyan Al-Thawri, an eighth-century scholar of Islam, who argued that the Qur'an does not prescribe death for someone because he or she is changing religion. Neither did the Prophet himself ever perform such an act. This is untrue, because he massacred in his lifetime Jewish tribes of Arabia who refused to convert to his faith, and it was done again in his name, by one of the "Righteous" (*Rashidun*) Caliphs, in the horrific, cruel, bordering on genocidal, *Ridda* (Apostasy) Wars. And now rationalizations and stories begin: "It is different for someone who becomes a Muslim during a war with the purpose of betraying Muslims," which means that if the Jews can be unjustifiably accused of "betraying" the Prophet, as if anyone owed him anything, then the context justified their killings. But before he can make totally sweeping and unfounded statements that "Islam does not prevent someone from changing religion because he feels that this is not right for him, or if he is not happy," let him study the detailed records of entire Jewish and Christian communities which were massacred for their faith. When he recognizes that there are records of the Prophet saying that someone changing religion should be killed, he hastens to qualify those sources as "weak." Muwahhidun and Mamluk sources are not weak and there to be consulted.[28]

Ramadan admits that the "moderate" views of Islam that he fabricates and emits are not accepted by the majorities in Muslim countries, and that this has been the case for centuries. But, he apologizes, "now in our situation we have scholars and people more and more speaking about that. I wrote 15 years ago saying: this is not the only position we have in Islam." But he does not explain why no effect has been recorded that he and the "others" (unidentified) have made. To base a claim to moderate Islam merely on voices of isolated Muslims who live in the West, is more than misleading, it is dishonest. In view of the isolated few moderates and the overwhelming trend of the traditionalists and fundamentalists, Ramadan was at a loss to say who would decide what verse of the Qur'an could or should be re-interpreted, if we came to that at all. He says that: "There is a problem today. In the Sunni tradition we have a crisis of authority. The Muslim scholars are no longer considered as an asset [He is wrong again, millions swear by the names of Qaradawi, Khomeini, Hassan al-Banna, his own grandfather, Sayyid Qut'b and Mawdudi, to name only a few]. And you cannot have people just organizing themselves, as it will lead to chaos. There is a crisis of authority. We do have some authority figures. But are we happy with them? I don't think so. Do we need a platform of scholars, at least at the national level? We need scholars at different levels. In Britain, we need people who know the country, come from the country, are raised in the country, who know the fabric and the culture, the language and the whole collective psychology. We need people who come from diverse readings of the Qur'an. We need a platform which will give direction, and this is missing today. This is for national issues and we may think of another platform for international issues." Where does he suggest finding such people? He has been supposedly looking for them in the past decade, but in vain. If anything, all the main leaderships that count among the Muslims in Europe are aligning themselves more and more along the more radical organizations, so how does he propose to launch the line of moderation that he has been preaching on the surface? He says that some attempts have already being made with bodies such as the Fiqh Council in the United States, the European Council for *Fatwa* and Research, and the International Council of Muslim Scholars in this direction, but these are first steps, and Muslim scholars and leaders in every single European country must take the lead and create pluralistic platforms beyond their respective and closed schools of laws and thought. Time is needed but one cannot expect the Muslims to remain blind in front of such imperative challenges, though for the time being, Muslims are too passive and continue to blame "the others" for their own mismanagement, he says.[29]

He reiterates that although his own position on many things may well be a minority position among Islamic scholars, on the great majority of the issues, his position is mainstream among the new generations of Muslims in the west. On being European, on being a citizen, on being part of society, and on dealing with discrimination, this is all mainstream. If one speaks with the new generations, their questions are being answered in a new way. He also believes that these views will become mainstream also in Arab countries such as Egypt and Saudi Arabia though it will be a long process. In Islamic-majority countries, religion is instrumentalized by both sides: the government and the opposition. There is no freedom, no democracy, so even problems of homosexuality that the West has been contending with will be difficult to address in Islam. He says that one cannot expect to see homosexuality being promoted within the Islamic tradition. Homosexuality is not perceived by Islam as the divine project for men and women. It is regarded as bad and wrong. Now, the way we have to deal with a homosexual is to say: "I don't agree with what you are doing, but I respect who you are. You can be a Muslim. You are a Muslim. Being a Muslim is between you and God." "I am not going to promote homosexuality but I will respect the person, even if I don't agree with what they are doing," he says. He confirms that the moment one declares the *shahada* (declaration of faith, the first pillar of Islam): "I believe there is no god but Allah and Muhammad is His Messenger," that makes one a Muslim. Whether or not one prays is one's responsibility, but if one believes in Allah one is a Muslim. The problem is not that states want to define who is a Muslim. What they want today is to be seen to be protecting the rules of Islam even though everything around is hypocritical. Hypocrisy is the heart of the matter, in his view, but he asserts that as long as you say that you are Muslim, this should be respected. He agrees with King Abdallah of Jordan that because *ijtihad* was disallowed in the Middle Ages, and literalist interpretations took over, Islam's scientific advance in comparison with the West turned into a cumulative backwardness. But the problem is that neither he nor Abdallah are authorized representatives of the Muslim scholarly establishment, nor can they differentiate between fact and myth in history, as we have outlined above, therefore they cannot have a selective view of the world- to adopt what suits them and ignore what does not. They cannot re-write history as it fits their political views and hope to see other things straight, for if they delude themselves that truth is selective, they are likely to miss it all along. This is what scientific development is all about.[30]

Ramadan was questioned about the liking the British government took to him, at a time when in France he was considered an "extremist" and a "double-talker," inasmuch as he only urged reforms in Islam when he addressed Western audiences, thus leaving a lasting impression of moderation. He claims that his problem in France is not one of double-talk, but one of double-hearing. When he talks with non-Muslims, he uses different levels of language, different words, references, and so on, but when he speaks to Muslims, his references are mainly coming from within the Islamic tradition. But he denies that the content of his discourse is different, for if this were the case, he ought to have few problems with Muslims, or with Muslim countries. But he says he is not allowed to enter countries such as Tunisia (strange, the most westernized of the Muslim world), Egypt and Saudi Arabia, because "those countries know exactly what I am saying". What he is saying, includes criticizing the fact that they are dictatorships and that the Saudi government is betraying Islamic teachings. Now, making himself the supreme arbiter of what constitutes an "Islamic teaching," is like a scholar of Christianity criticizing the Vatican and claiming that he understands better the teachings of Catholicism. The question is not only to criticize, but also to have a following large enough to be able to discredit the Muslim establishment, and still attract crowds in the Muslim world, which is clearly not the case. When he called for a moratorium on Islamic punishments (death penalty, corporal punishment and stoning), he said it on French television when millions were watching, as well as in Islamic majority countries. Then why he only asked for a moratorium instead of delegitimizing those cruel punishments as plain wrong? Because in Islamic-majority countries, this is a minority position. What we cannot deny is that these punishments are in the texts. He is explaining to Muslim scholars that today's conditions are different, so in this context you cannot implement these punishments, hence the need for the moratorium. He invited Muslim scholars to come together and clearly answer: "what is in the texts, what conditions should apply to these punishments and what about the context in which these would be implemented." No one of consequence is known to have heeded the call, so Ramadan remains the lonely moderate Muslim pitted against a traditionist Islam that refuses to change. He also referred to the share of women in inheritance and acknowledges that the Qur'anic texts are quite clear on this matter, but claims, a lonely voice in the desert, that to implement these rules literally today without taking into account social realities is plain injustice. To make such a statement is very audacious on his part and not likely to endear him to Muslim audiences, but he insists that some mothers find themselves alone with five or six kids to look after, the husbands have left, and nobody is helping them get the inheritance they should be entitled to. Therefore he is in search of a holistic approach and the state must think of financial support and compensation for the women. Without such procedures he thinks that Muslims are presently betraying the teachings of Islam through a literalist implementation. It is plain injustice and has nothing to do with the objectives of the *Shari'a*, to his mind [31]

Shari'a is not about justice, but about a claim to a law of divine inspiration, he said. Mind- and heart-captivating as it may be, Ramadan's is not the *shari'a* that is enforced in the Muslim world. So, while many of the young generation of Muslims in Europe are enamored with Ramadan's teachings, he is suspicious about his reception in the Muslim worlds. He says that in North Africa he is welcomed (before he said that in Tunisia he is shunned), as well as in Turkey, Asia and many Arab countries. He believes that Muslim audiences, from students to scholars, are closely following what is happening with regards to Muslims in the West, and that the Arabic translations of his books, such as *Western Muslims* and the *Future of Islam*, have been read by many people in Islamic-majority countries. They know about his work and he is also criticized, but he accepts that as well. As to his association with the British government, who appointed him member of the Task Force after 7/7, and a participant in the "road show" that was designed to talk to young Muslims in Britain and dissuade them from violence, he says that he is involved in something which is important, because a task force to act against terrorism is important. He will sit with everyone, any government, even the American government, to talk and discuss, but there are conditions. He must be free to speak his mind, and he thinks that the British have great responsibilities as to the domestic situation of Muslims, when dealing with violence and exclusion. He strongly criticized the new British security policics, and continucs to say that the Iraq war was a mistake, or that the British army shouldn't have been involved, or that it was wrong for Tony Blair to deny any link between Iraq and the bombings of 7 July. But he emphasized that if one constantly worries about misperceptions within the Muslim communities, we will never do anything. When his United States visa was revoked, he says, he became a hero to some Muslims, and then, when he called for a moratorium, he was criticized and accused of working for the United States administration. Muslims are too emotional, unfortunately, he outlines. He says that he does not work for the British or any other government. He is open to any kind of dialogue as long as the rules are clear: free to speak out, free to criticize, free to resist and free to support when it is right. Muslims should stop thinking that to talk is to compromise, but the black and white approach is often the reality of Muslims today. Asked about *Hizb ut-Tahrir* and whether it should be banned, he answered: "Let us be clear. I am not an adviser to the British government. As to *Hizb ut-Tahrir*, I disagree with them but I think that as long as they are not speaking illegally, they must be free to speak and the society and Muslims should be free to respond. *Hizb ut-Tahrir* is not calling Muslims to kill or to act illegally, so it must be heard and challenged. To ban is the wrong way." Queried about the future of Muslim societies in both the West and the Islamic world in the long run, he was quite optimistic about one or two generations from now. He believes that the change taking place at the periphery of the Islamic world, in countries such as Indonesia, Malaysia and the West, is going to make an impact elsewhere. The European and American experiences are also going to have tremendous impact on Islamic majority countries in the near future. "What is happening is not on the margins of Muslim communities in the west. It is much more mainstream," he concluded.[32]

The "neutrality" of Switzerland and Austria also makes them a fertile ground for international intrigues and plots, including spying and Muslim terrorist plots. Claude Covassi, whom we already mentioned above in the context of Hani Ramadan, was an informant for Swiss intelligence in early 2004, converted to Islam and infiltrated fundamentalist circles in his hometown of Geneva. He followed the trail of holy warriors all the way to mosques in Syria where aspiring foreign "martyrs" are groomed for Iraq. But in February 2006, the secret agent went explosively public. He revealed his mission to its prime target, Hani Ramadan who has been periodically accused of extremism, and gave newspaper interviews accusing his handlers of trying to frame the cleric. Since then, Covassi has unleashed everything from confidential documents to details of clandestine operations. The former spy insists that he abandoned his masquerade because he found faith. "It is not great speeches that convinced me but the force of prayer and understanding of the Qur'an," Covassi said in a recent interview by e-mail from his refuge in Egypt. "Islam transformed my existence." But Swiss anti-terrorism officials reject his allegations and accuse him of a personal vendetta. It's unclear who was manipulating whom. Covassi's story gives a rare street-level view of the fight against Islamic extremism. All across Europe's Muslim communities, security forces conduct aggressive surveillance of mosques, prayer halls, bookstores, butcher shops, Internet cafés and other outposts where legal fundamentalist activity converges with terrorism. The case of the turncoat informant also reveals the risks involved for spy agencies—and for a scruffy legion of secret soldiers on the front lines. Covassi alleges that he was a pawn in a turf war between domestic and foreign services in Switzerland that resembles the conflicts among anti-terrorism agencies in other countries." I think the situation would not have degenerated so seriously if our different intelligence services collaborated even a little," he said. "In reality, I have been able to observe that they are in continual rivalry, trying even to damage each other." His war of words has shaken the anti-terrorism forces of his country for their alleged cooperation with a surprisingly active militant underworld. There are open questions about Covassi's motivations. Is he retaliating over money or a grudge? Is he in league with extremists? Adding to the uncertainty about his credibility, a court recently sentenced him in absentia to eight months in prison for dealing anabolic steroids while he taught Thai boxing at a gym in 2002. Some officials believe he's trying to pressure the government to avoid the prison term. "Sometimes you use a source and it goes wrong," said a Swiss security official, who asked to remain anonymous. "How much of what he says is rubbish to help him get out of the criminal case, I don't know."[33]

The Los Angeles Times confirmed essential parts of Covassi's story in interviews with Swiss legislative and security officials, European anti-terrorism agents and others involved in or familiar with the events. And Covassi supports his account by providing names and phone numbers of his handlers and confidential e-mail exchanges with agents. The intelligence oversight committee of the Swiss congress is investigating the case. But doubts persist, especially regarding Covassi's allegation that spymasters plotted to smear the controversial Islamic scholar Hani Ramadan by linking him to Iraq-bound militants. Ramadan's brother, Tariq, is an internationally known Islamic intellectual. Without commenting on specifics, Federal Police Chief Jean-Luc Vez said he knew of no wrongdoing. "The [domestic intelligence service] respects the law," Vez said. "We do not know of a case in which they can be blamed for illegal activity." But Vez said the Ramadans' history and high profile made them legitimate subjects for scrutiny. "Their writings are sometimes ambiguous," he said. "It is quite normal that they would get particular attention." Hani Ramadan says he might sue the government, but will await the result of the legislative inquiry. He has declined to comment further. "As I have always said, the Islamic Center of Geneva has nothing to hide," Ramadan said in a prepared statement. "The two years of secret investigations by an agent ... indeed prove that, because they have not resulted in any official investigation or sanction." Ramadan and Covassi are ambiguous figures in this city of shadows. Geneva has long been a crossroads for intrigue because it is a base for international institutions, including the United Nations, as well as a haven for dissidents and a repository of colossal and dubious fortunes from around the globe. Soviet and Western agents sparred in this nominally neutral territory during the Cold War. "It is a place that is crawling with spies," said former legislator and author Jean Ziegler, a friend of the Ramadan family. Since 11 September 2001, the cloak-and-dagger game has had a new focus. Authorities have frozen millions of dollars of suspected terrorist financiers and investigated local groups allegedly linked to al-Qa'ida. Muslims make up about 4% of the Swiss population of 7.5 million, mostly Balkan immigrants considered moderates. But Geneva also draws extremist Muslim ideologues and holy warriors, who have become top priorities for law enforcement.[34]

When Covassi entered this game, he was no average Swiss security operator who suddenly left the normalcy and tranquility of his life to engage the world of plots and terrorism. The son of an Italian immigrant laborer, he grew up in Geneva and went to Paris to study philosophy. But he also racked up two misdemeanor convictions for fraud in Switzerland. Bouncing around Europe, he befriended far-left activists in Italy and hung out with cocaine dealers on the hard-party-ing Spanish island of Ibiza from 2001 to 2003, according to his account. Those contacts helped him develop a sideline as an informant for narcotics police in his hometown. A boyhood friend in police intelligence introduced him to agents of the domestic intelligence service, the Service for Analysis and Prevention, or SAP. The agents helped him get out of jail after an arrest on charges of credit card fraud in February 2004, he said, and enlisted him in a mission dubbed Op-eration Memphis. "The SAP had the air of being worried about a terrorist threat in Switzerland," Covassi said. "I didn't know anything about Islam. The project of Operation Memphis seemed useful. I did not get a salary. I was repaid for expenses, along with some 'gifts.' I got paid a total of about $12,200." Covassi started attending the Islamic Center of Geneva, a mosque run by Ramadan. Ramadan and his brother, Tariq, have been watched by the world's spy services for decades. Their maternal grandfather was Hassan Banna, an Egyptian who in 1928 founded the Muslim Brotherhood, a radical, sometimes violent group seeking to revive Islam and rejecting Westernization. The group's philosophies have inspired Islamist movements across the world, including those that spawned al-Qa'ida. After Banna's assassination in 1949, their father, Said Ramadan, helped spread the group's influence across the Muslim world, but soon fled Egypt amid a government crackdown. The Ramadan brothers were born and raised in Geneva, where their father was granted asylum in the 1950s. The two scholars say they have renounced the intolerant aspects of their legacy. But several top European anti-terrorism officials and academics see them as sinister ideologues. The United States revoked a visa for Tariq Ramadan in 2004 as he was about to begin a professorship at the University of Notre Dame. "We have been interested in the Ramadans for a very long time," the Swiss security official said. "But we have found nothing for a criminal indictment. They are fellow travelers.... They are preaching. They are spreading radicalism."[35]

The Ramadans have defenders, too. The British government has appointed Tariq Ramadan, now a professor at Oxford, to an advisory committee on Islam. Ziegler, the former legislator, calls the brothers unfairly maligned moderates. There is a campaign of permanent defamation against the Ramadan brothers," Ziegler said. "Hani is an organizer, a pedagogue, less brilliant than his brother. But there is a social dimension to his work at the Islamic Center, assisting fami-lies.... If you want Muslim immigrants to become European, you should support the Ramadans." In order to infiltrate Hani Ramadan's inner circle, Covassi used his real name and a classic cover story: He presented himself as a troubled ex-convict looking for spiritual solace. Within two months, Ramadan encouraged him to convert, Covassi said. "With other Muslims I founded a newsletter, *Al Qalam* (the Pen), and an association to defend the rights of Muslims," he said. "I was therefore in close contact with Ramadan and I spent many afternoons with him in his office." The SAP had to resort to an informant because domestic spying laws prohibit its agents from undercover work and wiretaps. The tough restrictions even put agents overseeing informants in danger of breaking the law. In addition to trying to learn everything he could about Ramadan, Covassi investigated Islamic networks that recruit for Iraq, the new magnet for holy warriors. Radicalization is difficult to combat even in countries with robust anti-terrorism laws. The speeches and activities of many hard-core ideologues are not illegal, even if they ultimately push young men into violence. "What's illegal?" the security official said. "Telling the 'brothers' that the Iraq invasion was illegal and must be resisted? Giving someone the address of a friend in Jordan?" Covassi said he did not turn up anything connecting Ramadan to terrorism. "I won't tell you that all the Muslims who frequent the center are all saints, but … the only men I met who were in contact with terrorist groups belonged to intelligence services of foreign countries," he said. As Covassi spent time at Ramadan's Islamic Center and Geneva's larger, Saudi-run mosque, he says he realized they were swarming with fellow operatives for European and Arab spy agencies. He briefed his handlers about an ardent extremist at the big mosque; they told him the man was a Syrian spy recruiting militants for combat in Iraq, he said. Pursuing the Syrian connection, Covassi says, he accompanied Iraq-bound militants as far as Damascus, the Syrian capital, in January 2005. There, he spent time at the *Fateh* mosque and the Abu Nour Qur'anic school, which have been identified in other European investigations as hubs for international pipelines feeding the Iraqi insurgency. Militants there charged $600 for passage into Iraq and $4,000 for weapons, he said. At both places, Covassi alleged, "the Syrian secret services recruit for Iraq." If true, his findings reinforce accusations that Syria aids the Iraq insurgency, a charge Damascus denies. European investigators said Syrian spies probably permit militant activity in Damascus, but proving direct involvement was another matter. Upon his return, Covassi clashed with his handlers. He accuses them of pushing him to plant names of suspected Iraq-bound militants on computers at the Islamic Center to implicate Ramadan in the recruitment network. Covassi said that by then he had come to admire the cleric "for his human qualities and the help he gave me in my knowledge of Islam."[36]

As a result, Covassi distanced himself from the SAP, but not from spying. He promptly went to work for the Swiss foreign intelligence service, known by the French initials SRS, infiltrating terrorist networks across Europe and the Middle East. The new job embroiled him in the harsh rivalry between SAP and his new agency, he said. Covassi provided *The Times* with excerpts of confidential e-mail exchanges with his handler at the foreign spy service. Using code names, they discuss surveillance photos, a clandestine rendezvous at a train station and a suspected plot to attack an Israeli passenger plane with a rocket-propelled grenade at the Geneva airport late in 2005. Covassi and the handler disparage agents at the SAP, whom they codename "the Bears." In an e-mail dated 3 December 2005, an agitated Covassi complains that his former bosses had renewed pressure on him to spy on Ramadan, whom he calls "the Guru." He refers to an apartment used for surveillance operations on the Islamic Center. And he threatens to go public. "[The agent] talks to me every day about the apartment in front of the [Islamic Center] and has confirmed to me that the Bears want to use it to go after the Guru again," Covassi writes. "I want to emphasize some points: (1) It's out of the question for me to participate in this plan, and therefore to put names on photos that [the agent] shows me. (2) As I told you during our meeting in the mountains, if the situation degenerates for the Guru, I wouldn't flinch from blowing the lid off my collaboration with the Bears and the information in my possession." Covassi soon went on a rampage. He had two angry meetings with his old handlers. He gave an interview to the *Tribune de Geneve* newspaper denouncing what he called the "persecution of Ramadan." In the following days, he alleges, he received threats, his studio apartment was burgled and he was mugged on a street by two Arabs who beat him bloody. He decided to run. Despite his public tirade, Covassi says, his handlers at the foreign spy service assisted him in his getaway on 19 February 2006. An agent drove him to the airport, paid for a ticket to Spain and gave him about $8,000 in cash, he said. The SRS had already paid about $33,000 for his services, he said. Asked about the apparent conflict among spy agencies, Swiss officials said they were working to improve cooperation. "There is always a certain competition among services," Vez, the police chief, said. "It's endemic. I think the role of a leader is to ensure that the competition is not counterproductive." Covassi said he made his way from the Canary Islands to Mauritania, narrowly avoiding arrest, and then to Egypt, where he had friends. He says he has been there since March 2006. From his refuge, he fires off e-mails to journalists and politicians. He threatens to disclose well-documented secrets if the congressional commission does not bring him back to Switzerland to testify. Despite Ramadan's family and ideological links to Egypt, Covassi insists that the Muslim Brotherhood has not given him shelter. The runaway spy sounds plaintive, lost in his labyrinth. "I don't have money," Covassi said. "I have made an effort to avoid being helped by any Islamist group so no one can claim that I am being manipulated or what have you. I am absolutely alone."[37]

Ramadan has also accumulated in his wake many critics. Just days after the 7 July suicide bombings in London in 2005, England was in an uproar when the London *Times* reported that Tariq Ramadan, who has been accused by several nations of having longtime terrorist ties and who in the past has proved skittish at denouncing Palestinian suicide bombings—was scheduled to speak in

London at a taxpayer-sponsored event. As Europe's most outspoken Muslim and a self-proclaimed "moderate," Ramadan and the British Muslim community lashed back, decrying the protests as "Islamophobia." But less than a year after those murderous attacks and the public outcry surrounding Ramadan's visit to London, there was hardly a whimper of protest when on May 1st, 2006 Tariq Ramadan took over the primetime airwaves of Britain's Channel 4 (a not-for-profit, publicly-owned station) in an hour-long program scripted and presented by Ramadan himself. The program, *Dispatches*, transmitted various Muslim messages: The "Muslim Reformation," which was little more than a headline, was clearly intended to be a public response to Ramadan's international critics, and actively promoted his call to European Muslims to follow his plan of integration, confrontation, and cultural empowerment. Thanks to some friends in the United Kingdom, this viewer was able to preview the program. One may recall the tempest in 2004 concerning Tariq Ramadan when he was denied a visa to the United States just days before he was to assume a three-year professorship of "religion, conflict and peacebuilding" at the University of Notre Dame. The Department of Homeland Security provided no reason for their decision, but many suspected that Ramadan's ties to terrorist organizations, including the Muslim Brotherhood (founded by Tariq Ramadan's grandfather, Hasan al-Banna), and his open association with terrorist sympathizers, including Muslim Brotherhood cleric Yussef Qaradawi, were to blame. Almost immediately after the DHS decision was announced, Ramadan's visa denial was condemned by the *New York Times, Washington Post, Chicago Tribune,* and the *L.A. Times*, in addition to the usual suspects in academia who expressed their outrage over the supposed suppression of free inquiry and free speech. In early 2006 the ACLU filed a lawsuit against the U.S. government naming Ramadan as a plaintiff and challenging provisions of the Patriot Act for denying Ramadan an entry visa. An op-ed by Paul Donnelly published at the time by the *Washington Post* described Ramadan as a "Muslim Martin Luther." This was far from the first time that the U.S. mainstream media had rallied to Tariq Ramadan's cause and lavished him with praise: in 2000, *Time Magazine* had named Ramadan one of their top 100 Innovators for the twenty-first century, not suspecting that in Islam innovation (*bid'a*) is one of the most inexcusable sins.[38]

Just why has Tariq Ramadan's message of "moderate" and "contextualized" Islam raised so many suspicions? And what exactly was the message he conveyed during his Channel 4 program in England? The answers are important for understanding the social tensions in Europe between Westerners and the 30-odd million Muslims that have immigrated to Europe in recent decades, as well as taking a look into the future at the identical cultural conflicts that loom on the horizon for America. The 1 May 2006 program on Channel 4 presented by Tariq Ramadan serves as an excellent snapshot of the social problems in Europe and the ideology espoused by Ramadan and his supporters. The "Muslim Reformation" was part of Channel 4's popular investigative program, *Dispatches,* whose most recent groundbreaking *exposé* was catching RyanAir employees sleeping on the job in earlier 2006. Ramadan is also a regular fixture on Channel 4's *Shari'a* TV. Even though The Muslim Reformation was part of Channel 4's *Dispatches* investigative series, this should not be interpreted to mean that the program was a critical look at Ramadan: the program was filmed by a production company he is associated with (Crescent Films), and he scripted, narrated and presented the program in its entirety. Tariq Ramadan had total control over what was said and what was shown. It should be no surprise then that none of Ramadan's critics were interviewed to pester him with questions about his terrorist ties or his public statements that have been criticized for anti-Semitism, excusing Palestinian suicide bombings or challenging the alleged "moderation" of his view of Islam. Most of the program was dedicated to recording visits that Ramadan makes with certain Muslim leaders in the United Kingdom, as well as trips he makes to Paris, Copenhagen, Cologne and Pakistan. The key theme he centers on in his discussions is the doctrine of *ijtihad,* an Islamic legal practice that allows for the reinterpretation of Islamic texts, which he advocates for and tries to contrast with "literalist" Islamic interpretations of the Qur'an. Except that in orthodox Islam, the idea of *ijtihad* is dead and buried since a millennium ago. He states early on in the program that *ijtihad* is "an alternative to radicalism and the literal approach to Islam," which he says "has been my personal *jihad* for many years." He claims further "Muslims in Europe want to reopen the debate and look at the Qur'an with new eyes." Except that those ideas have no mass following, certainly not in Muslim countries where the radical guidance for European Muslims is coming from.[39]

Early in the Channel 4 program Ramadan gives his version of *ijtihad* a spin in a discussion he has with Dr. Musharraf Hussain of the Karimia Institute in Nottingham regarding the Qur'anic injunction to cut off the hands of thieves (Sura 5:38). This discussion of the application of *Shari'a* law is important because of previous statements made by Ramadan's brother, Hani, in a September 2002 article in *Le Monde* where he advocated for the stoning of adulterous women. Tariq Ramadan was later confronted with his brother's statements in a televised debate with French Interior Minister Nicolas Sarzoky at which time he advocated for a "moratorium" on the imposition of Islamic punishments. In answer to this public relations problem, here is what Dr. Hussain had to say: "I think we have no right as the slaves and servants of God in any way to challenge or change the divine decree. What it is doing to us is setting for us a very high ideal of a fair punishment and a very powerful deterrent to protect human societies and to rid them of the evil of theft. This verse is laying down a law which is to be applied in an Islamic context and an Islamic state. We're not talking about the application of this law in a non-Muslim democracy. The law itself, the divine law, is indeed very wise; it is very just. It would save our chief constables an enormous amount of headache. It is all about zero tolerance that crimes of this nature of burglary, of stealing, of theft are of a very severe nature and they have to be curtailed and they have to be stopped and this is a very powerful deterrent and just divine decree, really." In an attempt to contrast his "moderate" position with Hussain's "literalist" interpretation of the Qur'anic injunction in question, Ramadan responded: "My view is that these verses were revealed for a particular context which assumes a high level of social justice and equality. These conditions do not exist today, so the punishment should not be enforced." But when did such conditions exist? Muhammed is credited with having brought social justice to a *jahili* society, therefore, if anything, the condition of justice was then much worse than it is today. What is striking when these two positions are compared is that they are in effect saying exactly the same thing. Both affirm that the divine laws expressed in the Qur'an are immutable (Ramadan stating such prior to his interview with Hussain) and acknowledge the abiding validity of Islamic laws. Both agree that *Shari'a* law is not appropriate in the present context of a non-Muslim Britain. But they both view these extreme forms of punishment as representing a high view of "social justice and equality" that by inference mean that current Western norms fall short of. It is clear that both Ramadan and Hussain believe that this "social justice and equality" is something that societies should strive for. At best, Ramadan's moratorium on the imposition of *Shari'a* law is clearly temporary, maybe until Europe is Islamized, and the contrast he tries to represent between his position and that of Dr. Hussain is really a distinction without a difference.[40]

Later in the program, Ramadan travels to Paris to meet with an old associate, Yamin Makry of the Young Muslims of France organization, which Ramadan prefaces by saying: "Elsewhere in Europe, opportunities for Muslims to live their faith and to participate in society sometimes seem to be getting worse ... the French state has not allowed its Muslim and Arab citizens real equal citizenship." Both Ramadan and Makry accuse French society for harboring latent racism that they contend was the primary cause of the car-burning *Intifadah* in late 2005 throughout the cities of France. Ramadan bluntly states that the French riots by young Muslims "had nothing to do with Islam; it was an outburst of pent-up frustration" over the perceived inequality by Muslims in French society. Just like the pent up frustration of Muhammed Atta and his fellow-Islamikaze on 11 September, one might add. This theme of White European social guilt and dismissing violence by Muslims is picked up again as Ramadan traveled to Copenhagen to discuss the protests surrounding the publication of cartoons by the Danish paper *Jyllands-Posten* caricaturizing the Islamic Prophet Muhammad. As Ramadan explains, the international wave of protests and violence by Muslims that followed, including more than 50 deaths and the burning of several Western embassies in the Middle East, was the responsibility of Westerners, not the Muslims who were actually engaged in the violent activities: The Danish newspaper was deliberately provoking a reaction.... Publishing the cartoons was a calculated provocation aimed at all Muslims. What it has done, according to Ramadan, was to make his and other "moderate" Muslims' work more difficult, since the cartoon affair was just more fuel on the fires of hatred which are fanned daily by Western policy on the Israeli-Palestinian conflict and the occupation of Iraq. These issues polarize Muslim opinion and have led to the rise of extremist Islamic political groups in Europe, thinks Ramadan, who thus exonerates the Muslims from the killings. It would be interesting to see what European country will have to take the brunt of the responsibility for the killings perpetrated by Muslims against other Muslims in Iraq, day in day out, under the watchful eyes of the media, or in Darfour where nobody watches. Ramadan believes that this creates an us-and-them version of the world that looks back to the idea of the non-Muslim world as a "House of War"—a vision like that of the four young bombers who brought terror to the streets of London. Ramadan says that he is completely against these acts of terror carried out in the name of his religion, but many Muslims sympathize with the Palestinian leaders who have used Islamikaze bombers as a weapon against Israel. They claim that when the oppressor has the tanks and the troops, it is legitimate for young Palestinians to become human bombs.[41]

As Ramadan makes clear, the publication of the cartoons wasn't just intended to provoke Muslims—it was part of the Western pro-Zionist conspiracy. It is indeed telling how Ramadan seamlessly links the Danish Cartoon Intifadah with the Israeli-Palestinian dispute as if it were a part of an ideological feed-back loop—the West is always to blame for its racism and religious bigotry and Muslims are never responsible for their acts of violence. Also telling is his pretended rejection of "suicide bombing." While claiming to be "against these acts of terror," he immediately qualifies the reasonableness of those who advocate for terrorism against Israel. This position is taken straight from the American leftist playbook: "I'm personally opposed to suicide bombings, but I would never prevent someone from exercising their right to conduct one against the Zionist oppressors." Ramadan identifies these Western policies as the cause of the rise of extremist Islamic political groups and the source of the "us-and-them" worldview of the "four young" (and it should be noted—Muslim) 7/7 London "suicide bombers." Admittedly, not everything that Ramadan says in the program borders on the extreme. Take, for instance, this statement made early on in the program: "European Muslims do not see the world as their ancestors did, divided into a medieval "House of Islam" and the rest as a hostile "House of War." Maybe Ramadan has been persuaded to shed that medieval notion, but who allowed him to represent European Islam in this regard? This would be a major advance in Muslim-Western relations if it was proved true, but does this statement jibe with the state of affairs he presents during the program? Especially in his discussion of the recent French car-burning *Intifadah* and the Danish Cartoon protests, didn't he claim that young Muslims in Europe felt alienated from the Western cultures they inhabit? Doesn't his justification of violence by Muslims in reaction to this alleged alienation and in response to the West's "pro-Zionist" policies assume the Manichean dichotomy that he claims that European

Muslims have now rejected? And does he not identify a vision of "us-and-them" resulting from Western pro-Zionist policies that has increased "extreme Islamic political groups" and provoked the 7/7 suicide bombers? His rosy assessment of the shift in belief amongst European Muslims about their role in Western society is belied by the very evidence he presents throughout the program. To his credit, in Ramadan's closing remarks he doesn't hesitate to direct some criticism at the Muslim community in Europe and in the Muslim world: "As I come to the end of my journey I am convinced that Muslims in Europe have to find a path between the secular West and the traditional East. Islam in the Muslim majority countries is trapped; it is trapped by undemocratic regimes and reactionary clerics...." So far, so good, but he immediately qualifies his position with this reversal: "Resistance to change is reinforced by resentment at what Muslims see as the double standards of Western policies towards the Muslim world." Yet again, Tariq Ramadan contends that the problems of Muslims living in the West and the cultural adaptations they need to make to integrate into Western societies are not really in their own hands, but the hands of non-Muslim Westerners. The West is responsible for the alleged policies and double standards that fuel their resentment. Ramadan provides justification to Muslims in the West for their refusal to socially integrate until Western culture reverses its internal and foreign policies to their liking and abandons the very values that have made the West a bastion of personal and political freedoms that many of the Muslim immigrants in Europe could not find in their own Muslim countries.[42]

It might be tempting to dismiss Tariq Ramadan and the approach he advocates in his Channel 4 program as the isolated views of one Muslim man in the West. It should be kept in mind that not only is Ramadan a prolific Islamic thinker, writer and speaker with a dozen books in publication and hundreds of recorded lectures that sell more than 50,000 units per year circulating in the European Muslim community and beyond. Ramadan is also looked to as the "moderate" response to Islamist extremists and terrorists by Western academic, media and political elites, as witnessed by *Time Magazine's* designation of Ramadan as one of the top 100 Innovators of the twenty-first century. It is hardly an exaggeration to say that Ramadan has assumed the leading role in setting the cultural agenda for Muslims throughout Europe today. Just how many other Muslims would get their own free primetime program on Channel 4 or the BBC? What makes Ramadan's rhetoric so troubling is that it is far and away the dominant voice of Muslims in Europe today. Equally disconcerting is that it is built upon a paradigm of duplicity that underlies the "moderate" position of Muslims in the West, as well as justifying a policy of cultural blackmail by Muslims purposefully delaying their integration into the cultures of their adopted countries until the West accedes to their demands. In effect, Ramadan is telling the West that their mountain must come to Muhammad. In the end, any accommodation of Muslims to Western culture must be predicated by a compromise by Westerners of Western values. Ramadan's program of *ijtihad* is not a call for modernizing

Islam, but rather, a battle plan for his Muslim audience in the West to follow to Islamize the West. All evidence indicates that Tariq Ramadan's battle plan is succeeding, concludes Patrick Poole.[43]

It is hard to believe that such a small and neutral country as Switzerland can become such an international ground for intrigue and terror, fueled and manned by local Muslims. A terrorist cell plotted to shoot down an Israeli airliner over Switzerland but was foiled by intelligence services. Seven people of North African origin are under arrest in connection with the alleged plot, said a statement from the federal prosecutor's office. Officials declined to give further details. Israeli media reported in May 2006 that those terrorists had planned a rocket attack on a plane operated by the Israeli airline El Al the preceding December, during takeoff from Geneva. A series of arrests began in May 2006 around Zurich and Basle, and the investigation continues in Switzerland and other countries. "Those who were arrested in Switzerland maintained contact with similar cells in France and Spain, which were likewise smashed," the statement said. One of the members of the Swiss cell was said to have been in contact with Mohamed Achraf, an alias for Abderrahmane Tahiri, who has been indicted in Spain for an alleged 2004 plot to carry out a lorry bombing against Madrid's national court. Tahiri was extradited from Switzerland in April 2005. The Israeli authorities said that a plot had been uncovered by the Swiss and French intelligence agencies. An undercover agent is said to have heard three migrants of Arab origin boast of attempts to smuggle weapons from Russia with the goal of shooting down an airliner. After the Israelis were informed El Al changed the flight paths of its Geneva-bound planes, landing instead at Zurich. El Al is believed to have fitted an anti-missile system called Flight Guard to some of its planes. It is reported to be capable of staving off missiles, but is said to be of limited value against rocket-propelled grenades and other weapons that are not radar-guided.[44] In another case involving Muslims, Switzerland's federal prosecutor made at least four separate appeals for U.S. help over the year of 2005, asking for access to documents and other evidence linked to the nuclear black market run by the Pakistani scientist Abdul Qadeer Khan. In that time, the Swiss have received no assistance, or even a reply, a spokesman for the prosecutor said. "Swiss authorities are asking for additional assistance from U.S. authorities, but we haven't gotten an answer so far," Mark Wiedmer, press secretary for the Swiss attorney general's office, said in response to a reporter's inquiry. "We are confident the American authorities will provide the information we need." The appeals were directed to the United States Justice Department, which has a bilateral agreement with Switzerland on sharing information in international criminal cases, and to the State Department's undersecretary for arms control and international security, according to officials knowledgeable about the requests. The problem was brought to light by a U.S. weapons expert who is advising Swiss prosecutors on the technical aspects of the Khan case. In testimony before a subcommittee of the House International Relations Committee, David Albright said the U.S.

government had "ignored multiple requests for cooperation" in prosecuting members of the Khan network. "The prosecutors have not received a reply, or even a confirmation that the U.S. government received the requests," Albright, a nuclear expert and president of the Institute for Science and International Security, told the panel. He said the lack of assistance "needlessly complicates" an investigation of great importance to both countries. Swiss officials are seeking to bring charges against three businessmen who allegedly played pivotal roles in Khan's smuggling scheme. Swiss authorities have arrested Friedrich Tinner, a Swiss mechanical engineer, and his two sons, Urs and Marco, who are suspected of supplying the network with technology and equipment used in enriching uranium. Urs Tinner is also suspected of helping Khan set up a secret Malaysian (that is Muslim) factory that made thousands of components for gas centrifuges, machines used in uranium enrichment. Some of the components were en route to Libya by ship in December 2003 when they were intercepted by German and Italian officials in a raid that brought the smuggling ring to light. The United States, which provided key intelligence that led to the intercept, heralded the breakup of the Khan network as a major blow against nuclear proliferation. In July 2004, President Bush viewed some of the components supplied by the Tinners during a visit to the Energy Department's Oak Ridge National Laboratory in eastern Tennessee. Bush called the Khan network "one of the most dangerous sources of proliferation in the world" and attributed the successful breakup to the efforts of "allies, working together." Albright, in his testimony to the subcommittee on international terrorism and nonproliferation, said, "I find this lack of cooperation frankly embarrassing to the United States and to those of us who believe that the United States should take the lead in bringing members of the Khan network to justice for arming our enemies with nuclear weapons."[45]

Venomous Islamic propaganda also pours out of Switzerland. Swiss police arrested two African men who allegedly used the University of Geneva's computer system to disseminate Islamic fundamentalist hate messages and justifications for terrorist attacks, AFP reports. The two—a 27-year-old Moroccan and a 41-year-old Algerian, both staying illegally in Switzerland—were fingered by German-language newspaper *Weltwoche* which reported the activity to the university's authorities. The powers that be alerted the cops, who swooped on the pair. That the duo was able to access the computer system was apparently due to a "code that a student had negligently left lying around."[46] In another case, Swiss Muslim leaders hit out at airport authorities for banning prominent scholar Sheikh Wagdy Ghoneim from entering the country to attend a key conference, while slamming the conspicuous absence of invited officials at the two-day event. "This is not the first time, and probably not the last, that a Muslim scholar is denied access to the country," Gamal Al-Khatib, the organizer of the fifteenth annual meeting of the League of Muslims in Switzerland (LMS), told *IslamOnline.net*. He said the reasons behind the decision will remain as usual vague and unknown." The decision is driven by a bunch of opportunists who are playing the terror card to scare authorities and to provoke the Muslim minority." Airport authorities said Egyptian Ghoneim, who holds a valid Swiss visa, is accused of raising funds for the Palestinian resistance movement Hamas, has been arrested by Egyptian police and is a *persona non grata* in the United States. Federal police did not issue a statement on the incident. Swiss law does not ban individuals from visiting the country if they were arrested in other countries. Ghoneim, 53, agreed to leave the United States voluntarily rather than fight a legal battle with immigration officials. The Muslim leader, whose case has drawn widespread support from Muslims in Southern California, agreed to leave for Qatar, where he holds a work visa. The LMS harshly criticized government officials for failing to show up in their annual meeting, themed the Mercy to Mankind, in Fribourg. "This is unacceptable and inexcusable," LMS head Mohammad Karmous told IOL. "Ignoring the forum by Swiss officials, particularly those who tirelessly talk about the integration of the Muslim minority, raises many question marks." He said government officials were expected to attend to listen to minority leaders and address problems facing Muslims. "Ironically, some officials are accusing Muslims of not doing their best to reach out to the government while they themselves paid no heed to our invitation," Karmous added. The Muslim activist, however, said Muslims are resolved to pursue dialogue with the government at all levels. Switzerland is home to some 380,000 Muslims, representing a sizable 4.7% of the country's some eight million people. However, due to the many illegals, the number and its rate in the population is close to the European average of 5-6%. Islam is the second religion in the country after Christianity. Swiss Muslims are planning to establish a federation of Islamic organizations as an umbrella group for all Islamic bodies in the central European country.[47]

Front Muslim organizations, which make representations to the government, demanding that their right to disseminate hatred be respected, have also hidden agendas that the security police monitors and cautions against. Robert Spencer posted an article on Swiss Islam that is very telling as far as using Swiss territory for Muslim terrorism is concerned. Swiss investigators have established a link between at least three Arabs detained in a nationwide anti-terror sweep and a purported key al-Qa'ida member, the Geneva daily *Le Temps*, reported. It claimed having obtained a copy of a document written by Deputy Federal Prosecutor Claude Nicati in which he detailed his case against 10 people arrested in raids since December 2003, and ordered the launch of preliminary judicial proceedings. Five suspects have been released but remain under investigation. Swiss justice authorities routinely decline to comment on media reports or give details of ongoing investigations, and the Prosecutor's office spokeswoman Andrea Sadecky told *The Associated Press* she could not comment. "All I can say is that we regret the report has been made public," she said. In June 2004 Swiss Federal Prosecutor Valentin Roschacher said investigators had concluded that Switzerland likely was used as a base for financial and logistical support for al-Qa'ida. According to *Le Temps*, Nicati's report said two suspects arrested in Switzerland—both originally from Yemen—were in "close contact with several hardcore members of bin Laden's movement." The report cited the name Abdallah al-Kini and described him as an "operational al-Qa'ida agent" involved in the October 2000 attack on the destroyer USS *Cole* off Yemen, which killed 17 American sailors. Al-Kini, who has not been mentioned previously by Yemeni anti-terror investigators, currently is detained there, the report said.[48] In another story, Swiss authorities said they have detained five Islamic extremists suspected of using the Internet to show the killing of hostages—which reportedly included the beheading of an American—and to give bomb-making instructions.[49] And following the same pattern elsewhere in Europe, at the same time that they are aware of the schemings and the machinations of their coreligionists, Muslim leaders "innocently" urge their compatriots to "dialogue" with them and "understand" them. Hassan El Araby—the head of an Islamic cultural center in Chiasso, and the border town's newly elected councilor—is calling for more dialogue between the Swiss and Muslims living in Switzerland. In an interview, *Swissinfo* talked to Switzerland's first Muslim politician about ethnic tensions and Western perceptions of Islam. El Araby is in the custom of offering the visitors to his Islamic Cultural Center a warm welcome. It is thanks to him that the center has expanded to include a library and a prayer room, and that it's become a focal point for the Islamic community even well beyond Chiasso.[50]

But the 50-year-old El Araby, who is of Egyptian origin, stresses that the center is not just for Muslims. "I want the local population to come into closer contact with Islam and see it in its true light, not in the way it is portrayed in the media." When queried about his feeling at being elected as a councilor by the general population, he said that he and others had actually wanted to put forward someone young. And they thought that only someone who was born and raised in Switzerland could be charged with bringing the local and the Islamic community closer—but in the end they picked him. He said he was in contact with various political parties, but in the end he stood as an independent candidate. He mentioned that while hitherto he had been working on the integration of Muslims, now his role has changed, and he has to look after everything that's related to Chiasso. It's a big responsibility and he hoped he would be up to it. He emphasized that his Muslim community has always been very much in favor of integration, both internal between all the Algerian, Turkish and Kosovar Muslims as well, and so it goes for Swiss converts to Islam, and external *vis-à-vis* the community at large. For that purpose they began using Italian for their internal communications in counseling and sermons. That way, aside from the liturgy which is in Arabic, Muslims always speak the language of the town and they made efforts to teach the language to newcomers and this in turn has brought the Muslims people closer to the local residents. He admitted that he Muslim presence in Switzerland is fairly recent, and cannot be compared to other big countries like France. "It's only in the past ten years that immigration has increased and that communities have developed. Mosques and meeting places are gradually being set up and the League of Muslims in Switzerland was created in 1992." He also revealed that on a European level, Islam is becoming more organized thanks to the creation in 1998 of a new Council of [Islamic] Experts, made up of over ten people living in Europe. That doesn't mean that there'll be a European [branch of] Islam but it's still an important move that will make a big difference to the faithful in Europe. Life as a Muslim in Switzerland isn't the same as in Egypt or Saudi Arabia, he remarked. For him who toes the general line of Muslims in Europe, even as they pretend to want to integrate, the events in France have nothing to do with religious symbols: it's about taking away fundamental rights. Banning headscarves goes against the principle of religious tolerance. He said he did not really understand all these debates. Even at the time of Jesus Christ—bless his name—women wore headscarves. Therefore, for him it's clear that there is a growing fear of Islam.[51]

Judging from his remarks on secularism, which he pretends to teach the Europeans its real meaning, when he says integration, he certainly meant to be generous in integrating the Swiss into Islam, and the numbers of converts in his environment probably lead him to believe in the feasibility of that project. In any case, far from learning from the Swiss the significance of the secular society they have espoused, he thinks he knows better: Secularism is becoming a new religion of banning crucifixes, banning headscarves…. The whole idea behind state secularism is that everyone should have the same rights (where did he get that idea?). But if secularism restricts someone's identity then it's going against this principle, he contended. He claims that the state shouldn't take away the rights of any minority group, for the Qur'an says: "You have your religion, I have mine." He just forgot that the Qur'an is not yet the legal reference for the country, and that this is precisely the Western approach to religion, that religion is the individual's right in the privacy of his home and does not have to be exhibited in the public square. Rejecting any Muslim responsibility for the eruption of Muslim violence in Madrid, he diagnoses violence as a "growing problem within all sectors of society" and he finds the media as partly to blame for making people scared as they focus on bloodshed. He assures that it's wrong to portray all Muslims as terrorists and all Muslim women as segregated [from society]. Prejudices are also being reinforced by all the news coming out of the Palestinian territories and Iraq. Muslims are being unfairly attacked there and yet no one speaks of the thousands of dead. The war is founded on a lie and is deeply unjust. So why be surprised when the people revolt? Expectedly, instead of addressing the cases of Muslim violence, like 11 September and Madrid, he elected to throw the burden on others' violence towards Muslims. But he envisions "dialogue," that amorphic forum for airing Muslim grievances, as the only way of promoting understanding. If the money that went towards fighting wars, he says, went into development aid, humanity would move forward. But that was exactly the blame he could direct to Muslim regimes who make war and no development, instead of implying that the developed West is the author of wars. And then the ultimate citation from the most celebrated warrior in Islamic history, who had massacred peoples and wiped out their civilizations: "The prophet Mohammed—bless his name—says: "Even on judgment day we are each given a seed that we can choose to sow. What's the point in life if there's no hope? What are we doing if we can't look to the future?"[52]

Austria

As if all Muslim immigrants in Europe had coordinated their conduct in its minutious detail, all follow the same patterns, and no amount of categorization according to countries of origin or the countries of absorption, can help determine any peculiar traits of character and conduct of any particular group among them. The leader of Austria's Islamic community lashed out at Interior Minister Liese Prokop for suggesting that Muslim immigrants are not integrating themselves into Austrian society. Anas Schakfeh called on Prokop to show more restraint after she told reporters that as many as 45% of Austria's Muslims are resisting integration, and that their insistence on living separate lives was "a ticking time bomb." "There are different groups in the population" who would be offended by Prokop's remarks, Schakfeh told the daily *Die Presse*. "A politician in such an important function should choose her words more carefully." Austria, a predominantly Roman Catholic country of 8 million, is home to an estimated 200,000 Turks—Europe's largest Turkish expatriate community after Germany and France, and another 300,000 from other Islamic origins.[53] Austrian Muslims have expressed concerns at a modified immigration law, fearing Muslims would take the brunt of the new restrictions as they make up the majority of immigrants in the south central European country. "Many Muslims still don't hold Austrian citizenship, which makes them vulnerable to the new bill," Omar Al-Rawi, the Islamic Religious Authority (IRA)'s official in charge of the integration file, told *IslamOnline.net*. He said that the amendments, for example, regard humanitarian work and assistance for refugees as illegal and punishable by law. "The amendments stipulate that illegal and unregistered residents could face deportation and subject those who provide them with shelter to prison terms," added Rawi, who is also a Member of Parliament for the opposition Socialist party. According to estimates, there are some 750,000 immigrants in Austria, representing 10% of the country's eight-million population. Muslims, estimated at nearly half a million, make up some 6% of the population.[54]

Austria's right-wing coalition government on 10 May 2006 tightened its immigration laws, which are already considered among the most restrictive in Europe. A new law approved by the cabinet of conservative chancellor Wolfgang Schuessel, extends from six to 10 months the limit on administrative detention before expulsion. It also authorizes forced feeding for asylum seekers who go on hunger strikes and toughens the penalties for those who resort to fake marriages. An initial assessment of cases within 72 hours after their submission and immediate rejection, if necessary, are also imposed by the new bill. The legislation also sets a 20-day maximum for the assessment of an application for political asylum and restricts the movements of the applicants during this period. It further obliges new immigrants to attend a minimum 300-hour German-language course. Rawi warned that the new bill would help increase crime rates in Austria." "Jobless asylum seekers could resort to robbery to make a living," he said, thus bringing the Muslim level of threats against prospective host countries who hesitate to give them asylum to new and disturbing heights, which can only give them negative incentives to welcome them. Turfa Bagaghati, Deputy Chairman of the European Network Against Racism (ENAR), agreed that the restrictive measure creates a fertile ground for thefts and drug trafficking, meaning that if severe criminal activity of this sort is embraced by the Muslim immigrants, it is the host society, as usual, that will be to blame, not the criminals. He said it will further open the door for tax evasions as many employers would skip government insurance programs. Bagaghati also maintained that forced feeding contravenes human rights. "Prisoners go on hunger strike to draw attention to their distress and the injustice done to them, and they shouldn't be forced to do something against their will," he stressed, knowing the power of emotional blackmail inherent in this kind of suicidal protest. At the same time that he is reluctant to force the immigrants to eat against their will, and let the blackmail run its course, he does not seem to mind forcing the Austrians against their will to accept immigrants they do not want.[55]

Under the new amendments, 1,072 prisoners, who staged hunger strikes, have been released to be deported later. The amendments have further raised the ire of Austrian rights activists, who accused the government of ignoring Constitution. They said that the government failed to honor its pledges as the interior minister had promised to issue work permits for all foreigners living in Austria. The clauses of the new bill come from previous legislation on asylum seekers which were declared invalid in October 2005 by the constitutional court after it was passed by the ruling coalition of conservative and extreme-right parties in December 2003. The court ruled that it was unconstitutional to prohibit asylum seekers who had initially had their application dismissed, to present new legal arguments on appeal. However, this clause does not appear in the new bill that was approved. According to interior ministry estimates, some 5,918 immigrants were granted political asylum over a period of four months out of a total of 24,634 applicants. Since 2002, some 24,000 people have been granted political asylum from 72,000 applications made in Austria, which is ranked fourth in Europe for its number of political refugees behind Britain, Germany, and France. There are currently 30,000 people awaiting a decision on their applications for political asylum.[56] But the whole issue seemed to disturb Austria especially in the much wider context of Europe rethinking its safe-haven status. On the Ringstrasse in Vienna, tourists wonder about the Muslim dress that begins to feature in the streets of the old and glamorous Capital of the Empire. "Did you see that one girl—so young! And wearing a veil," a woman exclaims, staring out the window of the tram. "They will form a separate culture," she added as a matter of course. The sentiment isn't isolated. Earlier, Austria's Interior Minister Liese Prokop announced that 45% of Muslim immigrants were "unintegratable," and suggested that those people should "choose another country." Indeed, recent rumblings from the top echelons of governments across Europe suggest that the continent is rethinking its once-vaunted status as a haven for refugees as it becomes more suspicious that many immigrants are coming to exploit its social benefits and democratic principles. "The trend today more and more in Europe is to try to control immigration flow," says Philippe De Bruycker, founder of the Odysseus Network, an academic consortium on immigration and asylum in Europe. "At the same time we still say we want to respect the right of asylum and the possibility of applying for asylum. But of course along the way we create obstacles for asylum seekers," he acknowledges.[57]

A day after Prokop made her controversial statement on May 15, 2006, Hirsi Ali—the Somalian immigrant elected to the Dutch parliament in 2003—was informed by her own political party that her Dutch citizenship was in question. Dutch Immigration Minister Rita Verdonk, a former prison warden dubbed "Iron Rita" who has long promised a tough stance on immigration, said "the preliminary assumption must be that—in line with case law of the Dutch Supreme Court—[Hirsi Ali] is considered not to have obtained Dutch nationality." Hirsi Ali's case, heatedly debated across Europe in the days since Ms. Verdonk's announcement, was seen as particularly ironic. But it also highlights the dramatic change in Europe since the turn of this century. In the years following World War II, a chagrined United States and Europe vowed to follow the Geneva Conventions and create safe havens for refugees. Yet such lofty ideals were hard to uphold after massive influxes of workers in the 1960s and early 1970s were halted during an economic downturn. Those immigrant populations—often Muslims from North Africa and the Middle East—swelled with family reunification, yet often remained economically and socially distinct from the societies that had adopted them. The image of the immigrant began to change, and distinctions between those who came for work and those who came for safety began to blur. Now, says Jean-Pierre Cassarino, a researcher at the European-Mediterranean Consortium for Applied Research on International Migration in Florence, Italy, "asylum seekers are viewed as potential cheaters." Today, in once-homogenous Europe, tensions between immigrants and native Europeans appear to be increasing. The perception that an ever increasing number of newcomers—who neither speak the language of their adopted country nor accept its cultural mores—are changing the culture, has increased support for ideas once only advanced by far-right political parties. "France, Austria, and the Netherlands all have had very significant electoral success of the far-right parties," says Michael Collyer, a research fellow in European migration policy at the University of Sussex. Collier points to the success in France of a strict new immigration law proposed by then Interior Minister, and now President, Nicolas Sarkozy. Mr. Sarkozy's proposal would institutionalize "selective" immigration, giving an advantage to privileged immigrants of better economic and education status who are more "integratable." It would also change the rights of family reunification for workers already in the country; speed up the expulsion of undocumented immigrants who are discovered or whose applications for asylum are rejected; lengthen the amount of time it takes to apply for permanent residency status for married couples; and toughen visa requirements. Most controversial, Sarkozy announced deportations for undocumented immigrant school children. "We speak of the need to fight immigration but we don't have a clear position on whether we need immigrants," says Mr. De Bruycker, noting the precipitous dip in internal population growth in European Union countries in the last half century. He adds that a series of recent incidents have affected the image of immigrants in the European mind. For example, the murder of a Jewish man—Ilan Halimi—on the outskirts of Paris in spring 2006, by a band of Muslim immigrant youths. Or the murder of a Malian woman and a Flemish child in Antwerp, later in the summer, by the son of a founder of Belgium's most far-right party. "In Europe, we are still unable to accept that we are a continent of immigration," says De Bruycker.[58]

Like in other European countries, the problems of Muslims in Austria begin with immigration, but do not end there. In what some fear could be a curtain raiser for a major policy shift in a country considered somehow tolerant, Austrian Interior Minister Liese Prokop has called for banning *hijab*-clad Muslim women from teaching at schools."I consider now the legality of banning *hijab* in schools," Prokop told the state-run *Falter Magazine*, on 8 March 2005. "But, anyhow, I will throw my weight about the ban." She argued that wearing the *hijab* in schools runs counter to the values of Austrian society. "Muslim women suffer from oppression and their rights are down-trodden," the minister claimed, urging for stopping what she called "forcible marriage" and "honor killing" spreading among Muslims. Muslim leaders reacted by claiming that Islam roundly abhors the primordial honor killing practices as it holds every soul in high esteem and does not allow any transgression upon it. Likewise, Islam granted women full rights to accept or reject whoever proposes to them. Women's consent is vital for a valid marriage contract under Islam. A female Muslim delegation met senior Austrian officials in 2004, stressing that Islam enshrined inalienable rights for women and cleared stereotypes circulated by right-wing media. Expectedly, the minister's statements raised the ire of the Muslim minority and Austrian politicians as well. "It is strange that such provocative and offensive statements coincide with the International Women's Day," Anas Schakfeh, chairman of Islamic Religious Authority, formally protested in a letter to the People's Party (OVP), which dominates the coalition government. "It is unusual for the People's Party and other parties in Austria to descend to this repugnant rhetoric," he added, calling for an immediate action from the government. Austrian Christians have demonstrated their solidarity with the Muslim minority and supported Muslim women's right to take on the *hijab*. "Will this minister call for banning the cross as well?" wondered Richard Schadauer, head of the Christian Socialist and Democratic Association (ACUS). He further distanced Christianity from Prokop's statements. "Catholic Prokop has nothing to do with Christianity," he said. Weighing in, Chancellor Wolfgang Schuessel, said the interior minister is in no position to address such an issue, which falls under the minister of education. An official source at the office of the minister of education tried to reassure the Muslim minority, saying that Austria has no problem with the Muslim dress code.[59] The spokeswoman for the Greens Party's women's affairs, Brigid Weinzinger, dismissed Prokop's statements as "insulting." "She leaves the impression that domestic violence is only confined to Muslims as if it doesn't exist in Austria," she said. Islam, which was officially acknowledged in Austria in 1908, is considered the second religion in the country after Catholic Christianity. A law issued in 1867, which guaranteed respect for all religions, gave Muslims the right to establish mosques and practice their religion in Austria. However, Muslim rights in the country were enhanced by the signing of the Saint-Germain agreement in 1919, in which the Austrian government pledged its protection for minorities and affirmed the right of each citizen to assume important national posts regardless of his/her religious or ethnic backgrounds. The International Helsinki Federation for Human Rights (IHF) said in a report released 7 March 2006 that the debate surrounding the adoption in 2004 of a French law prohibiting religious attire in public schools helped encourage intolerance and discrimination against *hijab*-clad Muslim women across Europe. Other Muslim leaders found their way to protest more subtly.

Sheikh Adnan Ibrahim sounds every bit the type of moderate Muslim who Western governments hope will develop a "European Islam" to help integrate immigrants and form a bulwark against radical ideologies. From the *minbar* (pulpit) in his Vienna mosque, or a podium on the conference circuit, the 40-year-old Palestinian-born preacher urges Muslims to be loyal citizens in their new European homes and to adapt their traditions to modern life. But he bristles at recurring suggestions from Westerners that Europe's Muslims need to develop a "Euro-Islam," a British, Dutch or Italian Islam or even go through their own kind of French Revolution or Protestant Reformation. "There will certainly be an Islam with a European imprint someday," he told *Reuters* in his spacious apartment full of Oriental carpets and ceiling-high shelves of books in Arabic. "It won't be a Euro-Islam, but an Islam in Europe," insisted Sheikh Adnan, a soft-spoken man who is one of the most popular Islamic preachers in the Austrian capital, whose population is 10% Muslim. "There is a big difference." Muslim leaders attending a conference of European imams in Vienna at in April 2006, struck a similar chord. "What is Euro-Islam—an Islam of the euro?" Amir Zaidan, head of Vienna's Islamic Academy, asked sarcastically. "Any adaptation, updating or development of Islamic norms in Europe must be clearly anchored in the sources of Islam ... without being extreme, watered down, Europeanized or Americanized," he said to assenting nods from his audience. France has repeatedly urged its six-million-strong Muslim minority, the largest in Europe, to develop a "French Islam" that fits into its highly secular society. Officials in other European countries have voiced similar ideas. But when Paris banned headscarves in state schools, the Muslims heard a subliminal message that they should be less Islamic and more like the secularized Catholic majority that skips church, ignores priests and forgets its traditions. Many West European leaders seem unable to hear the message Western Muslims like Sheikh Adnan are sending them, according to John Voll, associate director of the Saudi-supported Center for Muslim-Christian Understanding at Georgetown University in Washington. "There is an incredible deafness," he said, adding that the secular outlook of many politicians and journalists made a religious outlook "seriously incomprehensible" to them.[60]

But the problem is not there. Quite the contrary, had the West not been deaf to a religious outlook, it would have understandably preferred its Christian discourse to the Muslim one, thus only enhancing the clash of civilizations, not diminishing it. Sheikh Adnan, who grew up in a refugee camp in Gaza and studied medicine in Yugoslavia before moving to Vienna in 1991, could hardly be clearer when he says Islam cannot be updated simply by mixing in a few Western secular views. "It's not enough to just have ideas," he said as he reeled off names of Muslim intellectuals in Europe whose reform proposals he said were not solidly based on Islam. "If you cannot read the Qu'ran correctly, don't know which sayings of the Prophet Mohammad are authentic or don't know Islamic history, you can easily end up on thin ice and no Muslim will accept you," he explained. Tariq Ramadan and his enthused Western supporters ought to heed those words coming from a religious leader that has not been labeled as "Fanatic" or "Radical." "I know the traditional teachings and can justify my views on the basis of Islamic teaching and tradition." Sheikh Adnan's views often go against what traditional imams say is Islamic teaching. Citing a recent case in Afghanistan, he rejected the idea that anyone converting from Islam to another religion deserved the death sentence, or any punishment at all. "In the Prophet's day, there were people who left the faith and nothing happened to them," he said. "This death sentence was meant for people who fought with arms against Islam." So, what is the difference? You are doomed to die for either leaving the faith or for resisting it. In his sermons, Sheikh Adnan urges worshippers to reach out to their non-Muslim neighbors (once again, the imperative of *da'wa*). After the London bombings in 2005, he issued a *fatwa* saying Muslims who hear of plans for a terrorist attack must report them to the police immediately. One sermon condemning female circumcision, a custom still practiced among some Muslims in Africa, sparked off a lively debate, he said, but he ended up convincing the congregation that it was against classical Islamic jurisprudence. "One man came up to me afterwards and said,'thank God, you have saved my three younger daughters'," he recalled. "But for the oldest one, it was already too late."[61]

The conference of European imams ended in Vienna in April 2006 with participants urging Europe's Muslims and their religious leaders across the continent to take part in all aspects of society. Integration, education, politics and women's rights featured on the agenda of the three-day conference, which brought together more than 130 imams and Muslim ministers from about 40 European countries and a further 100 from Austria. "[We need to] foster integration by participation and participation especially by imams for they have a particular role ... [to] encourage people to be and feel part of society," said Amina Baghajati, spokesman for the Austrian Muslim association (IGGIOe). The group's final declaration addressed a number of issues Western politicians have been calling on European imams to tackle in the face of radical ideologies coming out of the Middle East. "We have shown how to protect ourselves from *fatwas* from other countries," said the IGGIOe's Mouddar Khouja of the religious edicts pronounced by Europe's imams. "We have *fatwas* from imams living in Europe and they speak for themselves". The imams emphasized the need for dialogue, cooperation and efforts to be made on all sides to achieve better understanding between cultures and religions. In particular, they said it was essential for European Muslims of all ages to learn the language and culture of the country where they live. The imams also stressed that integration is facilitated by participation in political, economical, cultural, social and academic areas. "It is the principle of Islam that the Muslim in Europe be active and participate in all aspects of life," said Ahmed Al-Rawi, president of the British-based Federation of Islamic Organizations in Europe, for Imams have a positive role to play . The imams called upon themselves to play stronger roles in helping their communities integrate into society.

"Imams, as teachers and preachers, have a duty to emphasize to their congregations that they can play a positive role in addressing the plagues of Europe [these are no longer Islamic plagues that are inflicted on Europe, but have become European]: hate, bigotry, racism, extremism and terrorism," said Imam Abduljalil Sajid, president of Britain's Muslim Council for Religious and Racial Harmony. While Muslims have a responsibility to adapt to their host country, Europe too must give them the opportunity to become part of that society by "talking with and not about Muslims," the declaration concluded. "Integration is no one-way street, but should be seen as a mutual process," the declaration said, meaning that Europeanization must also include Islamization, in spite of the paradox involved. In light (or obscurity) of the recent Mohammed cartoon controversy, the imams underlined the importance of freedom of speech, while denouncing the violent protests as well as the media's focus on violence in Islam (again a paradox: freedom of speech, but do not report the downsides of Islam). "Muslims are under pressure to justify themselves, as in the coverage of crises, and their images of aggression and violence, often outside Europe, stand in the foreground," the imams said. An attack on an Islamic cemetery under construction in Vienna reminded the imams of the hostility Muslims meet throughout Europe. "Will be blown up," was sprayed on the prayer room's outer walls. "The graffiti shows this was an anti-Islamic attack," said Omar al-Rawi, head of integration affairs at the Austrian Islamic Community. He would have sounded more credible if by the same breath he had condemned the hundreds of far more serious attacks and acts of arson by Muslims against Jewish sites in Europe. A similar attack on a mosque happened after another Islamic conference in November 2005.[62]

A note of cautious optimism was introduced in this rather grim controversial outlook when a poll on attitudes was published in Vienna in May 2006 and revealed that "only" 40% of Austrians are biased against Muslims. Indeed, it turned out that four out of 10 Austrians have a negative attitude towards Muslims living in the Alpine country, according to an official survey. A summary of the report, released by Austria's interior ministry, also shows that 37% of Austrians have a neutral attitude towards their Muslim neighbors and that 23% have a positive mind-set. The report was based on telephone interviews with 2,000 Austrians, 251 Turks, and 253 Bosnians. Austrian Interior Minister Liese Prokop made the survey public at a conference aimed at fostering dialogue between different religions and ethnic groups sponsored by the Austrian government, which then held the rotating European Union presidency. Prokop had angered Islamic leaders and other critics earlier when she said 45% of Austria's estimated 400,000 Muslims were not making an effort to integrate themselves into mainstream Austrian society and represented a "ticking time bomb." "We are dealing with a debate about anxiety ... on all sides," study author Mathias Rohe of the University of Erlangen in Germany said. Praising the Austrian government for commissioning the study, he noted it was important to look at the facts and prevent the creation of a "parallel society." "We must not just talk about Muslims, we should speak with Muslims, so we can reach solutions together," he said. Prokop said the purpose of the study was to identify the situation of Muslims in Austria, to determine how people feel and to prevent radicalisation." We need the participation of all involved—on our side, that of the Austrians, those who were born here, but also on the side of those coming to us, those who live here with us," she said. The interviews with Muslims showed that "traditional conservatives" and "religious conservatives"—45% of those interviewed, according to Rohe—showed greater "distance" towards Austrian society than their more liberal counterparts. While Muslims tend to see discipline, punctuality and neatness as positive traits of their Austrian neighbors, they identified a lack of solidarity, poor family life and a lack of sociability as negative traits. The report also showed that about 38% of Muslims interviewed would like to see Islam having a bigger influence on Austrian politics and society. While a mere 12% of Austrians interviewed said they had frequent contact with Muslims, about 80% said they had not had bad personal experiences. Nearly 90% of Austrians distinguish between Islam as a whole and its misuse by extremists, the study said. Underscoring how immigrants have flocked to Austria in recent years, the government statistics agency released a separate report showing that foreigners account for nearly 11% of the nation's total population of 8.2 million, half of whom are Muslim, and close to 19% of the capital, Vienna. Immigrants from Serbia-Montenegro account for half the foreigners in Austria, but the predominantly Roman Catholic country also is home to about 200,000 Turks—Europe's largest Turkish expatriate community after Germany and France.[63]

Notes

1. Sebastian Vilar Rodríguez, a circulated article on Internet, end of 2005 and beginning of 2006.
2. Pamela Rolfe, " 29 Indicted for Roles In Madrid Bombings: Judge Says Al-Qaeda Inspired Local Cell" *The Washington Post* - 12 April 2006.
3. David Rennie, "Artists try not to offend Muslims as satire festival treads softly," *Daily Telegraph*, 10 March 2006.
4. *Ibid.*
5. Renwick McLean, "Imams in Spain say Muslims and Jews must confront extremism," *The New York Times,* 26 March 2006.
6. Reuter, 24 April 2006.
7. Philippe Naughton, "Spanish court quashes 9/11 conviction," *Times Online*—1 June 2006.
8. Richard Ford, "Curb on sham weddings ruled illegal" *The Times* 11 April 2006
9. This and the coming passages are based on Joseph D'Hippolito, "How Will Rome Face Mecca?" *FrontPage Magazine.com,* 6 April, 2006
10. *Le Figaro,* 13 March, 2006.
11. Carlo Cardia, *Avvenire,* 16 March, 2006. Translated and Cited by Joseph D'Hippolito, *FrontPageMagazine.com* 6 April 2006.
12. "Top Italian spy arrested over CIA kidnap plot," *Daily Telegraph* 5 July, 2006.
13. Address by Cardinal Ruini to the Conference of Italian Cardinals, 20 March, 2006. Reported by D'Hippolito,
14. "Terror Attacks Thwarted," *Sky News,* 6 April 2006.
15. Daniel Pipes, "The Vatican Confronts Islam," *FrontPageMagazine.com*, 5 July 2006.
16. Peter Kiefer and Elisabetta Povoledo, "Illegal Immigrants Become Focus of the Election Campaign in Italy," *New York Times*, 28 March 2006.
17. "Muslim teacher fired for violating Geneva laws " *Swissinfo*—19 December 2002 http://www.swissinfo.org/eng/swissinfo.html?siteSect=105&sid=1527150
18. *Ibid.*
19. *Ibid.*
20. Scott Capper, "Controversial Muslim scholar wins in court," *Swissinfo*—20 May 2005.
21. For the international involvement of al-Taqwa in terrorism, see R. Israeli, *The Iraq War*, Sussex Academic Press, 2004, pp. 144-145
22. Yoni Fighel, "Swiss authorities thwart plot to down El Al passenger plane" *Institute of Counter-Terrorism* (ICT), 20 May 2006.
23. Yoni Fighel, *Institute of Counter-Terrorism*, May 20, 2006. op. cit.
24. Ehsan Masood, "Interview with Tariq Ramadan," *Prospect Magazine*—Issue 124, July 2006.

25.   *Ibid.*
26.   *Ibid.*
27.   *Ibid.*
28.   *Ibid.*
29.   *Ibid.*
30.   *Ibid.*
31.   *Ibid.*
32.   *Ibid.*
33.   Sebastian Rotella, "Swiss Spy in a War of Words: An ex-informant who became a Muslim says his handlers wanted him to frame an Islamic scholar. Officials say he's on a personal vendetta." *LA Times*—22 May 2006 >http://www.latimes.com/news/printedition/front/la-fg-mole22may22,1,1426054,full.story?coll=laheadlinesfrontpage&ctrack=1&cset=true
34.   *Ibid.*
35.   *Ibid.*
36.   *Ibid.*
37.   Sebastian Rotella, *LA Times*, op. cit—22 May 2006.
38.   Patrick Poole, "Britain's Tariq TV," *FrontPageMagazine.com* 25 May 2006.
39.   *Ibid.*
40.   Patrick Poole, "Britain's Tariq TV," *FrontPageMagazine.com* 25 May 2006.
41.   *Ibid.*
42.   *Ibid.*
43.   *Ibid.*
44.   "Terror cell 'plotted airliner attack',"—*Guardian,* 9 June 2006.
45.   Joby Warrick, "U.S. Silence Impeding Swiss in Nuclear Case: Expert Says Calls Have Been Ignored," *Washington Post* 26 May 2006.
46.   Lester Haines, "Swiss cuff Islamic hate message duo: Geneva uni computer jihad," *The Register* - 31 October 2005. http://www.theregister.co.uk/2005/10/31/hate_message_duo.
47.   Tamer Abul Einein, "Preacher Denied Entry, Swiss Muslims Furious," *Islam OnLine*, 19 September 2005   http://www.islamonline.net/English/News/2005-09/19/article04.shtml
48.   Robert Spencer, "Jihad in Switzerland,"citing AP, 23 August 2004.
49.   Robert Spencer, "Swiss Seize Five Suspected Extremists," citing AP, 5 March 2005.
50.   Daniele Papacella (translation: Vanessa Mock), "Muslim councillor calls for dialogue with Islam" *Swissinfo* – 25 April 2004. http://www.swissinfo.org/eng/search/detail/Muslim_councillor_calls_for_dialogue_with_Islam.html?siteSect=881&sid=4889542&cKey=1082887270000
51.   *Ibid.*
52.   *Ibid*
53.   "Islamic leader criticizes Austrian interior minister for suggesting Muslims don't integrate," *AP Online,* 15 May 2006. http://www.khaleejtimes.com/DisplayArticleNew.asp?col=&section=theworld&xfile=data/theworld/2006/May/theworld_
54.   Ahmad Al-Matboli, "Austrian Muslims Concerned at New Immigration Law," *Islam OnLine*, 15 May, 2005 http://www.islamonline.net/English/News/2005-05/15/article02.shtml
55.   *Ibid.*
56.   *Ibid.*

57. Sarah Wildman, "Europe rethinks its 'safe haven' status," *The Christian Science Monitor*, 24 May 2006
     http://www.csmonitor.com/2006/0524/p07s02-woeu.html
58. *Ibid.*
59. *IslamOnline.net,* 9 March 2005.
60. Tom Heneghan "Vienna imam says yes to Europe, no to "Euro-Islam," *Reuters,* 12 Apr 2006.
     http://www.alertnet.org/thenews/newsdesk/L11156867.htm
61. Ibid.
62. "European Imams Stress Social Integration," *Deutsche Welle*—4 April 2006.
     http://www.dw-world.de/dw/article/0,2144,1965132,00.html
63. "40% of Austrians are biased against Muslims," *Khaleej Times Online,* 20 May 2006. http://www.khaleejtimes.com/DisplayArticleNew.asp?xfile=data/ theworld/2006/May/theworld_May727.xml&section=theworld&col=

4

Scandinavia in Disarray

The Scandinavian countries, considered to be the quietest, most generous, and most open towards Muslim immigrants, especially those who sought "political asylum" on their territories, have been rocked by disbelief in the face of the violence and social unrest that they have been encountering on the part of the refugees of yesteryear who have come of age and are now making impossible demands on their countries of shelter. Denmark and Norway, in particular, have been stunned by the violence of Muslim riots across the world for the Cartoons that were published in their papers in the name of freedom of expression, which for them is no less blasphemous to suppress than it is important for Muslims to preserve and defend the "honor" of their Prophet. It is hard for a freewheeling Scandinavian to understand that the honor of a religious figure, which is intrinsic to him in the eyes of his followers, could be tarnished because of what non-Believers might think of him. We conceive of belief in relative terms without necessarily passing judgment on the belief of others, nor is there an expectation that the others should respect our own faith; but for Muslims belief, that is Islam, is to be regarded in absolute categories and therefore respected by all, regardless of how we relate to other faiths. This yawning gap in the different ways Islam and other faiths conceive of belief is the key to understand the Cartoon Affair as it blew into the open in early 2006, though it had been brewing for a few months prior to that. Islam does prohibit a representation of the Prophet, as it forbids pictorial representation of any human, for fear of human worship, one of the worst violations of Islamic Law (*shirk*). Both prohibitions have been repeatedly contravened, for example in the famous miniature illustrations that have become part and parcel of the acknowledged Islamic art.

At times the Muslim state was lenient and did not prosecute the trespassers even when they were Muslims, at other times puritanical Islamic rule has strictly enforced this restriction, like under the Taliban in Afghanistan when the two giant Buddhas of Bamyan that were considered part of the world heritage, were blown up (1997), despite the protests of world opinion. The Christian world is not Buddhist, but its indignation was made clear in the face of the fanatic insensitivity of Kabul towards other faiths. Islam had converted hundreds of churches to mosques, the most renowned of them was the Aya Sophia in

2001/

147

Constantinople, and it did not consider that an offense to other beliefs, and if it did it was "natural" for it to have done so as their religion has superseded all the others. Therefore, something strange happened in the case of the cartoons: while the Danish drawings may have been offensive, they were not done by Muslims who may then be subjected to Muslim law and be punished by it, as was Salman Rushdie who lived under threat of his life, nor were they done in Islamic lands over which they have jurisdiction. Therefore suspicion was raised by Europeans that their guest-Muslims were preparing to impose their law over their hosts, as some of them had stated explicitly. In September 2005 the Danish paper *Jyllands-Posten* published a series of 12 cartoons about Islam, the most abusive of them showing the Prophet Muhammed wearing a turban with explosives strapped to it.[1] Leaders of the Danish Muslim community approached the Editor, but he refused to comply, because he upheld freedom of expression and could not understand why would Muslims be hurt by the beliefs of others instead of concentrating on their own faith. Had they left it at that, no one would have even noticed and the whole matter would have vanished into oblivion, exactly like the dozens of churches which are burned routinely in lands of Islam, like Nigeria, Egypt and Indonesia, or synagogues that were destroyed by Muslims in Paris, Nablus and Jericho, or Serbian monasteries and churches in Kosovo without for Christians or Jews declaring *a casus belli* and setting fire to the world, burning flags, killing people, threatening humanity and assaulting foreign embassies.

Strangely convinced that the strength and prestige of their faith hinged upon a formal apology by an anonymous editor of a remote country paper, 11 Muslim Ambassadors in Copenhagen demanded to see Prime Minister Rasmussen, who not only refused to take measures against the Editor, as it would be customary in Islamic lands, but also upheld the freedom of the press and candidly expressed his helplessness to act in a country of law and freedom, notions that they could not comprehend. As a result, not content of having humiliated their own creed by making themselves dependent on Western recognition and whim, Danish Muslims dispatched a delegation to the Middle East and other Islamic countries in order to consult about how to react to the cartoons, thus turning it from a minor local gossipy issue into an international affair with worldwide resonance. All religious leaders that they encountered, and through them the political leaders who needed something to hang on to in their paranoid fears from the West, were only too happy to grab the occasion and to turn the crowds who sighed under their dictatorships into devout Muslims who were only happy to demonstrate their frustration and to turn their violence against the West, much to the relief of their governments who were delighted to see the wrath of their populace directed at the Danish flags. A new European scarecrow has been recruited to join the perennially burned Israeli and American colors and effigies, thus diversifying the outlets of hatred and rage that they cannot do without. As 22 former Danish Ambassadors to Muslim countries criticized their Prime

Minister's handling of the growing crisis, without suggesting an alternative avenue to calm down the tempers, the public debate came into the open and arguments began in Copenhagen's streets, shopping malls and the press over the proper conduct, with some fiercely upholding freedom of the press, others criticizing the cartoonists for their insensitivity and still others demanding apology from their government.

Only a few people versed in Arab affairs understood the stakes: if one apologized, one would not gain gratitude from the Muslims for the self-demeaning effort, for they would have certainly said that "they taught the West a lesson," that unlike any other creed which is subject to current humiliation in the "value-less free world," Islam reigns supreme as the only one which can demand apology and be heeded. Instead of respect, the apologizing government would have gained scorn and contempt, and could be sure to face the same hatred and more in the future. The Muslims would have also said that their boycott of Danish goods "worked" and they would have applied it more emphatically in the future. Once again, the Danes who are accustomed to deal decently and generously with others, would have expected similar conduct from Muslims, but the suspicious Islamic world would have taught them that foreign relations are a rapport of force—economic, demographic, cultural and otherwise, thus nothing short of a total victory and vindication of their position was acceptable to them, therefore compromise, appeasement, apology would not satisfy them.[2] Moreover, had the Danish government listened to its critics which surmised that freedom of speech meant by definition tolerance of others and respect for other cultures and faith, it would have fallen once again into the Muslim trap where Muslims voice the same words but mean different things. For a Westerner, tolerating the others signifies accepting them as they are without passing value judgment on them; for a Muslim, tolerance means temporary accepting the inferior until he can be persuaded, or forced, to recognize the superiority of Islam. One who operates on the Western principle of tolerance would expect the other to reciprocate in kind; the Muslim interprets his toleration by others as a clear sign of recognition of his superiority. Muslims can have mosques anywhere in the Christian world, for that is the beacon that will ultimately make Unbelievers see the light of Truth, but Christian churches in the Muslim world are indisputably dark dens of sedition and heresy. Admittedly, the Danish government of the Liberals in coalition with the far Right, has been tougher on Muslim immigration than previous governments, as a lesson learned from 11 September; Muslims in Denmark and Europe in general are perceived by the Right as a fifth column or a Trojan horse, epithets they earned honestly by their often hostile subversion against their host countries. Moreover, the Danes adopted the "24-year-rule" which prevents Danish citizens from obtaining living permits in Denmark for foreign spouses if either of the parties is under 24 years of age. On top of that mixed Danish-foreign couples must fulfill an "attachment criterion" showing that their common attachment to Denmark is stronger than their attachment to any other country. That rule is rightly considered discriminatory by Muslims, because it was tailored to block further immigration to Denmark through marriage (real or fictional), and since immigrants are usually Muslims, if the mixed couple remains preponderantly connected to the Muslim country of origin of one of the spouses, both would have to live there even as one of them is Danish. This is pretty harsh, and it came under criticism both domestically in Denmark and by the High Commissioner for Human Rights of the European Council.[3] It is indeed stunning that one of the most hospitable and liberal nations of Europe should have been compelled by the subversive Muslim "invasion" of it under various pretexts which exploited the loopholes in the legal system and abused the generosity of the host nation, to act so drastically against its own tradition of openness and compassion. This goes to show the intensity of the threat that the Danes perceive on their society and the constraint under which they operate for self-defense, in spite of the criticism hurled at them. When the Danish government proposed to introduce into the school curriculum "Christian studies" which represent the "national spirit" instead of the diversified "religious instruction" now in force, which allows parity to all faiths but puts in jeopardy what the Danes consider as the core of their culture, the same Human Rights Commissioner sanctioned the Danish government, only to be rejected as "interference in Denmark's internal affairs." The Danes are intent on defending the cultural homogeneity of their country, and unlike the spirit of multiculturalism which has taken hold in Britain, France and others, they would rather have immigrants assimilate into their national culture than tolerate the transplant of other cultures onto their soil.

When the Cartoon Affair blew up there were only a quarter-million Muslim immigrants in the country, barely 2.5% of the total and one of the lowest percentages in Europe. Nevertheless, looking around them and observing the growing inter-cultural clashes in France and other high-rate Muslim population, including next-door Sweden where its half a million Muslims already constitute 5% of the total, they became wary of the outcome. They know that in the southernmost city of Malmo, just across the bridge from Copenhagen, which is blessed with a more moderate climate than elsewhere, some 25% of the 300,000 urban population is Muslim, entire areas of the city have become Muslim, the Sunday market is almost all dominated by Muslims and foreign languages, dress and customs; criminality has gone up, Swedish citizens are scared in what used to be their peaceful and secure land, and even police do not dare enter certain neighborhoods in pursuit of public order. This has become a negative model for the culture-sensitive Danes to emulate in their tiny and vulnerable country of bliss and prosperity. Therefore, the backlash to the Cartoon Affair [4] has already produced a cataract of measures adopted by individuals, political parties and NGO's who refuse to follow their government hesitation and shyness, due to its commitment to restore sanity to its international relations and economic presence in the Muslim world. It has become obvious to many previously unaware

Danes, and indeed many others around them who are watching developments with trepidation, that European Muslims have proven, if proof was needed, that they have no intention or desire to acculturate into their host countries. Danes, who regard themselves as secular (despite their Christian culture), democratic, modern, open, generous, law-abiding and European, have suddenly awakened to the reality, just like in Holland after the van Gogh murder, that they were cultivating in their midst a religious, undemocratic, backward, bigoted, unruly and alien element, which if permitted to prevail might overturn in the long run all cherished values of the Danes (and other Europeans for that matter) and cause irremediable damage to their image and self-image.

Danes, who were faced by the burning of their Embassies in Muslim lands, find full justification for their fear, hence the growth of public rallies, web sites, conferences, debates and open letters in the press addressing both their government for rectifying its policies and their public for massive support. Even though their image as peace loving and popular around the world, who extend generous aid to developing nations, has been irreparably damaged in Muslim countries, the Danes stand their ground, refuse to be intimidated and find solace in the great popular, if not governmental, support they encounter in the civilized world. The Swedes internalize their fears and suspicions, manifesting a high degree of restraint (or denial), and have so far avoided head-on collisions with their Muslim minority internally, the Muslim world outwardly. But following 11 September many press reports began to raise the issue, at first hesitantly then more assertively. An Internet report by *Dhimmi Watch* of 9 September 2004, cited Swedish press reports that police "admitted that they no longer control the situation" in Malmo, the third largest city in the nation; that Muslims who lived in the area of Rosengard in Malmo for the past 20 years still could not read of write Swedish; that ambulance personnel are attacked by stones or weapons and refuse to help anybody in the area without police escort, and that the immigrants spit at anyone who comes to help. For example, a case was cited of an Arab who stabbed an Albanian and left him to bleed to death, while the ambulance waited for police escort to rescue him. It was said that police themselves hesitate to enter certain parts of the city unless they have several patrols, and need to have guards to watch their cars, which would otherwise be vandalized. One of the local Swedes was cited as warning that "something drastic has to be done, or much more blood will be spilled." This has produced a record number of people emigrating from the city, something which prompted the remark that "Swedes who used to open their doors to Muslim refugees and asylum seekers, are now turned into refugees in their own country and forced to flee their homes, mentioning crime and fear for the safety of their children as the main reason for leaving."[5]

Another local paper complained that all the 600 windows at one of the schools in Malmo had been broken during the summer vacation, something which cost the city millions to repair. City buses have also been compelled to avoid the Muslim ghetto, as they are met by Muslim youth throwing rocks or bottles at them when they enter. In earlier 2004 it was reported that an Afghan boy had made plans to blow up his own school, and that workers of a major local hospital receive threats from Muslims every day, patients with knives or guns having become commonplace. The workers feel so terrorized that they refrained from setting up metal detectors at the entrance to the emergency ward for fear that it might be considered as "provocation." A woman' Lisa Nilsson, who had lived in New York for 25 years and moved back to Malmo, began to miss the safety of New York and avowed her fear to walk in town after dark, taking a taxi wherever she goes.[6] The *Expressen* has more horrors to tell: according to its reports, "rapes in Sweden as a whole have increased by 17% just since 2003, and as a whole have had a dramatic increase during the past decade. Gang rapes, usually involving Muslim immigrant males and native Swedish girls, have become commonplace. In the summer of 2004 five Kurds brutally raped a 13-year old Swedish girl." Another 22-year-old woman was raped by a gang of three who just hurled at her one word: "whore!!"[7] Even though the Swedish papers, out of intimidation or consideration, usually refrain from mentioning the ethnic background of the rapists and other violators of the law, one can read it between the lines. Politicians dealt with this situation by making it easier for Muslims to enter Sweden like, for example, allowing arranged marriages to bring into the country spouses for the sake of "family reunification." A university Professor, Jan Eckberg, who computed the cost of immigration to the Swedish taxpayer concluded that it amounted to some $3.5 billion annually, more than two billion out of that for social welfare allocations to the immigrants, compared to about one-third of that sum in Denmark. But, contrary to public opinion, which continues to believe that the immigrants are only interested in exploiting the generous system of grants, that did not seem to deter the Swedish government from continuing to facilitate mass entry of immigrants. It seems to believe that the new Sweden is by definition multi-cultural and that immigrants are a blessing to the country, resentment of the populace notwithstanding. Political parties on the left which stand to gain from Muslim immigrant support have, on the contrary, proposed legislation to ban "Islamophobia," Swedish universities are discussing whether to allow the veils in their campuses, and Swedish flags are shunned as decorations because of the "nationalism" (racism) involved. Swedish national radio broadcasts an Islamic sermon (in Swedish) every day and some city councils have suggested that Muslim festivals become public holidays.[8]

As mainstream media caught up with the worsening situation, when stone throwing against buses and trains spread to Stockholm and Uppsala, politicians like Annika Billstrom, still wanted to meet with the troublemakers and naively ask them "why do they do that?," as if there were any reason in the world that justified disturbing public order. Research teams that followed the process of absorption of hundreds of thousands of immigrants in the Stockholm area found out that in the neighborhoods worst hit by segregation, which received billions of dollars to facilitate integration since the 1990s, the percentage of non-Swedes had increased from 57 to 73%, and that more jobless and unfortunate new immigrants move in constantly to replace the few more fortunate who found jobs and moved out. The families which moved out simply wanted their children to "see more Swedes," for otherwise they would not be "living in Sweden." But those who stay in the ghettoes, and are by far more numerous, come under the sway of Muslim leaders who wish to perpetuate that situation of segregation which serves their purpose of establishing semi-autonomous Muslim enclaves into which less and less Swedes are inclined to enter and enforce law and order. This self-imposed segregation does not prevent them, of course, from keeping their channels open to the government agencies when they collect the welfare benefits that are showered on them. This is not unlike the situation in France where a criminologist, Lucienne Bui Trong, has found that the numbers of Muslim "no-go-zones" has increased from 106 in 1991 to 818 in 1999. These dangerous areas, that she euphemistically calls "sensitive areas," are those enclaves where any government institution like post-offices, fire stations, policemen, and mail-delivery firms are constantly ambushed with Molotov cocktails, and where firearms imported from the Muslim parts of former Yugoslavia (Bosnia, Kosovo, and Macedonia) are routinely found. In Sweden, crime has reached record levels, where one in every five households in Stockholm experiences burglary every year. Private security companies are swamped with calls for help and a serious shortage of policemen to fight crimes has been irritating Swedes who are tired of being robbed, maimed, or raped. Nevertheless, Sigtuna became the first municipality which has instituted multicultural holidays for its school pupils, with others, like Rinkeby and Huddinge due to follow suit. Some teachers and principals have simply realized that since Muslim children miss classes during Ramadan, adjustments have to be made by the entire system.[9]

As in France and other parts of Europe the Muslim upsurge in Sweden's large cities is directly related to anti-Semitic attacks. Anders Carlberg, the president of the Jewish community in Goteborg (Gothenburg), the second-largest city in the country, told an interviewer that "the fear of being attacked is the primary concern of Jews in Sweden today," after his son and friends were assaulted by a gang of Muslim youth in Malmo and rescued by police. Jewish storeowners were threatened by Muslims during the large anti-Israel demonstrations in Malmo in 2000. The city of Malmo, 40% of whose population is foreign born, and whose children constitute already more than half the children of the city, boasts that its inhabitants come from 164 countries and speak more than 100 languages. That is admirable for the immigrants who wish to assimilate and become Swedish, but how about those who refuse to abide by the laws and wish to drag the city and its environment into chaos and terror? Middle East restaurants and super-markets, the weekend open market in the center of town, certainly add flavor and variety to the city's *ambiance*, and business in these specialized shops is brisk due to the large numbers of consumers, mainly Muslim but also growing numbers of Swedes. But many Muslims think (hope?), and many Swedes are afraid, that Malmo may be the prototype of how Sweden might look in the future. When interviewed about this state of affairs, Swedish officials and community leaders—doctors, police chiefs and teachers, are extremely tame and cautious when first interviewed about their growing Muslim populations, but when they open up they admit that their city cannot handle such a large immigration and that it failed to absorb and integrate the new comers. If nurses and doctors are afraid to go to work because they might be threatened, abused or attacked for not delivering a quick enough treatment to their Muslim patients, then the dissolution of the "Swedish way," which many Swedes are proud of and accustomed to, might simply speed the rate of Swedish emigration from their city. Swedes, like other Scandinavians, are extremely wary of mentioning the ethnic origin or the religion of the violators of their normative system of conduct, lest they be accused, or even suspected, of racism. In grave cases of gang rape or blatant robbery, oblique reference may be made to "dark hair," "North-African origin" or "speaking Swedish (or Danish) with an accent," "Immigrant population" and " ghetto inhabitants," with the words "Muslim," "Arabs," "Iranian" of "Afghani" rarely heard; but everyone understands the sub-texts and the latent meanings. Paradoxically though, this PC which is calculated to avoid prejudices, has a reverse effect, because when you do not hear the facts stated officially, then assumptions abound which increase prejudices not diminish them.[10]

The Cartoon Affair, which particularly targeted Scandinavia, especially Denmark and Norway, put those countries in disarray for they were the most forthcoming in terms of humanitarian aid, to poor Muslim countries. Unlike Denmark which apologized saying that it did not intend to insult anyone, but still insisted on the principle of free speech, the Norwegian government instructed its Embassies in the Middle East to apologize to Muslim countries, backed by Javier Solana's sycophant apology that he presented in his tour of the Middle East, expressing "solidarity" with Muslim countries, which implied his moral support for their outrageous rampages, for their boycott of member countries of the EU and for the vain killing of 200 people, Muslims and Christian, for that silly and unjustified outburst of violence. Those *dhimmi*-like apologies, far from calming the moods, on the contrary increased the contempt that the Muslim world showed to those who came to admit their "guilt" and recognized that, unlike others faiths which can be trampled upon with impunity, supreme Islam is untouchable; and that for the sake of saving the face of Islam in the eyes of those who should be so certain of their faith that they would brush aside any insult to it, it was permissible to massacre so many innocent people. The apologies were counterproductive for they caused more moral harm to the West than the initial "insults" to Muslims. One example is what the Saudi media boast as the price Denmark had to pay for its "injury" of Islam: "Products of the Danish dairy conglomerate Arla Foods will be back on the supermarket shelves in Saudi Arabi. The unofficial boycott has been lifted and this is only for

Arla products…. The move comes following a recommendation made by five Islamic organizations which participated in an Islamic conference in Bahrain last month to debate the issue surrounding the blasphemous cartoons…. Arla Foods had issued an apology to Muslims worldwide… pledged to disseminate awareness about Islam and make donations to charity groups. Arla has a major dairy plant in Riyad... A new production facility planned for Saudi Arabia has been indefinitely put on hold …. "We have deferred plans to set up the multimillion dollar production plant because of the boycott of Danish products and its adverse impact on our sales in the region," said Pedersen, [the Danish manager of the firm]. Arla had already invested $70 million to build the new plant in cooperation with Danya Foods of Saudi Arabia.[11]

In the meantime, a group of prominent Muslim scholars in the United Arab Emirates has called for ending the boycott on Danish food. In the name of the International Conference for the Support of the Final Prophet (Muhammed is known to His believers as the Seal of Prophets), those scholars determined that Arla should be withdrawn from the boycott, "in recognition for its efforts to reach out to the Muslim world, after Arla put full-page advertisements in Arab papers in March 2006, condemning the cartoons as an "insult to Islam." So, dairy products, which disappeared from the shelves in January, found their way back in early April. The Danish Consul General in Dubai, Thomas May, said the resolution came after weeks of dialogue between Danish representatives and Muslim leaders. But many retailers who were said to have kept the grudge against Denmark said they would keep Arla's products off their shelves, meaning that the popular resentment over the affair was, as it were, much more persistent and rooted in the psyche of the people who had been indoctrinated and incited for weeks on end, than in the clerical circles who had raised the issue in the first place. If this were so, it would have been a classic case of raising a controversy and then being unable to keep it under control. A product manager in Sharja, another UAE member, who refused to be identified by name, said candidly that, "the boycott is not in our hands or in the hands of the government…. It is in the hands of the people, and ultimately the consumer must decide." But there is something disingenuous and unbecoming about these statements: first, it was not the decision of the people to boycott, for the populace knew nothing about the crisis until it was incited against Denmark by the clerics and the Muslim media; and secondly, it was the merchants who removed those products from the shelves, not the people. A housewife from Iran said in Dubai that she was very happy to find in the stores the "Three Cows" cheese once again. She avowed that "last week, when I saw it on the shelf, I thought this is my luck day, so I bought ten packages." Someone who retains resentment against a produce or its makers does not stock up for the event that the boycott is renewed, when some cleric or politician decides for her what she could or could not buy or consume. Consumers can chose to buy or not to buy what is on the shelves, but the pretense of letting them choose when they have no choice is totally dishonest. It is interesting that none of the consumers raised the issue of the cartoons, all they were interested in was whether or not there was cheese to buy.[12]

Danish Muslims, on their part, were in disarray. Those 12 drawings of Muhammad printed in a Danish newspaper have turned millions of Muslims against Denmark. And one man's mission has transformed the caricatures into the stuff of international diplomacy. The Arab world, though, isn't being given the full story. It was just 12 simple drawings published in a Danish newspaper. But they have triggered an international relations crisis for Copenhagen—and potentially the rest of Europe. The result has been not only protests and boycotts in the Arab world, and soul searching in Denmark and Europe, but also explosion of the tensions between Danes and the Arab World in particular and Europe in general, suspicions between Danes and Muslims in Denmark, and also ugly comparisons to a conflict of civilizations and uncomfortable memories of the *fatwa* issued against author Salman Rushdie in the 1980s over his novel *The Satanic Verses* which Muslim groups claim disparaged their religion's central figure, Muhammad. But Denmark's crisis had been simmering for months. For when the Muslims responded through letters to the editor and complaints within the community—they felt ignored. One group of Danish Muslims, led by a young imam named Ahmed Akkari, grew so frustrated by the inability of Muslims to get their message across in Denmark that they compiled a dossier of racist and culturally insensitive images circulating in the country and took them on their road show in the Arab World to "raise awareness of the discrimination they faced," so they said, but instead they instigated a worldwide outrage that broke into violence. "There is currently a climate (in Denmark) that is contributing to an increase in racism," the group warned in the introduction to a 43-page dossier it prepared before traveling to Egypt in late 2005. It dedicated the rest of the dossier to "drawings and pictures" that disparaged Islam and "denigrated the Prophet." The offending images included Muhammad with a bomb wrapped in his turban. The Muslim community in the small Scandinavian country erupted in anger for not only did the images denigrate Islam's central figure, but many felt the drawings also equated all Muslims with terrorism.To Muslim leaders in Denmark like Akkari and fellow imam Abu Laban, the images provided evidence of an Islamophobia that they believe permeates Danish society. Worse yet, they felt their protests against racism had been ignored. Newspapers failed to publish their letters to the editor and politicians seemed unwilling to listen. "As a group in society, we've simply been ignored," Akkari told the Aarhus-based daily *Stiftstidende* in the wake of the cartoon events.[13]

It was Akkari and his group who traveled together to Cairo, where they visited Al-Azhar University. Akkari said he wanted to draw attention to the racist climate in order to prevent a repeat of the Theo van Gogh drama in the Netherlands, as if he were a deranged youth whose desires have to be fulfilled immediately, or else. Kaare Quist, a journalist at the Danish daily *Ekstra Bladet*, who had been reporting on the story for a number of weeks, says the group found a number of highly placed officials in the Arab World keen to listen to its message. Quist told *Spiegel Online* they included representatives of the Arab League, Egypt's grand *mufti* and other high-level officials. The trip the group made, Quist believes, helped to raise attention to the political cartoons in *Jyllands-Posten* and prejudices against Denmark's Muslims. Quist says the dossier they shared in Egypt may have been far more damaging than the *Jyllands-Posten* episode—and it may have further exacerbated misgivings between Denmark and the Arab world. In addition to the now notorious caricatures published by the newspaper which have now spread like wildfire in the blogosphere, it also included patently offensive anti-Muslim images that had been sent to the group by other Muslims living in Denmark. The origins or authenticity of the images haven't been confirmed, but their content was nevertheless damaging. Quist says the dossier included three obscene caricatures—one showed Muhammad as a pedophile, another as a pig and the last depicted a praying Muslim being raped by a dog. "The drawings in *Jyllands-Posten* were harmless compared to these," he says. For his part, Akkari said the more outrageous images were clearly separated from those published by the paper when the group met with Muslim leaders. "They were at the back of the folder," he told *Stiftstidende.* By including them, the group sought to show the kind of hate they feel subjected to in Denmark. Stoking the fire? But Quist claims the group may also have perpetuated misunderstandings during its trip. The reporter says that Arabs who visited with the group later claimed Akkari's delegation had given them the impression that Danish Prime Minister Anders Fogh Rasmussen somehow controlled or owned *Jyllands-Posten.*[14]

"I believe that this misunderstanding was unintentional," Quist said, reviewing his research. "But I also think that they are also trying to profit from the agitation. "Still, whether the trip by Akkari's group had any impact or not, Fogh Rasmussen and the editors of *Jyllands-Posten* were on the defensive, dodging bomb threats and a growing diplomatic crisis. The episode also sparked a strong debate in the European media about free speech and whether editors in other European countries should stand together in support of free speech and of a Danish paper that pushes the wrong buttons, or whether they should scorn a series of cartoons that perpetuated uncomfortable stereotypes about Muslims. Even after the newspaper's editor issued an apology and the Danish Prime Minister, who earlier said it would be inappropriate for him to apologize for a newspaper's right to free speech, did say he hoped the apology would "contribute to the comfort of those who have been hurt," the sentiment against Denmark remained strong. Arab countries including Saudi Arabia, Libya and Jordan, have staged loosely organized, "*impromptu*" boycotts that have led many companies, including France's *Carrefour* supermarket chain, to remove Danish products from their shelves. In addition, Arabs have taken their protests to the street, to the Internet and to the sphere of official international diplomacy. Arab hackers have attacked the server of *Jyllands-Posten's* web site and several

Arab countries—most recently Syria—have recalled their ambassadors from Copenhagen.[15]

Muslim clerics who had sought asylum in Denmark and obtained it, began voicing their misgivings about their new homes as a result of the Cartoon Affair, though it was not clear that they were ready to give up civilized and prosperous living in Copenhagen for the violent dumps of some place in the Islamic world. Such a "seeker of peace and dialogue" via fanatic demagoguery, is imam Abu Laban, the country's most controversial Muslim cleric who "threatened" that he would be returning to his homeland in the Gaza Strip as soon as possible, the *Jyllands-Posten* reported. "I'm not willing to be manipulated all the time and associated with terrorism, when I have worked day and night, tooth and nail in an honest way for this country's welfare," he told the newspaper that printed cartoons of the prophet Mohammed. Abu Laban assumed a central role in the crisis that erupted after the publication of the cartoons. He was suspected of traveling with other clerics to the Mid-East to stir-up public sentiment against his host country Denmark in the Muslim world. When the crisis raged at its highest point in February, 2006 Abu Laban was also accused of being two-faced by telling media in Denmark he opposed the trade embargo in the Mid-East, while at the same time telling a Saudi Arabian station he was "happy" about the Muslim embargo. A French journalist also used a hidden camera to capture Abu Laban on tape saying he knew of someone in Denmark willing to conduct a "suicide bombing." Abu Laban later disclaimed the statement, explaining that it was merely a figure of speech. He attributed his decision to leave Denmark to the poor treatment he received in the media. "I could have created a hell here in Denmark," he threatened, " I could have encouraged Muslims to strike. I've tried to be a good guest in this country in every way. But I've been treated extremely poorly by the other side." The cleric came to Denmark in 1984 as a refugee from the Gaza Strip. He says he has now decided to return together with his wife and youngest children. "The dream of Europe and human rights has shattered for me. Islam has been a test for Western democracy, and I think Western democracy has shown that it hasn't secured equal human rights for everyone."[16] His prospects are great to find in Gaza an exemplary haven of human rights. Confusion over his future presence in Denmark underscored the difficulty the cleric has communicating with his host nation, for shortly after his explosion of anger and his "threat" that impressed no one, he announced, in English which he still uses after so many years in Denmark, that he only meant that he was "tempted" to return home. "I never said to anyone that I wish to move away from Denmark. I have no such personal wish. I was invited here as an imam, and I will only leave if Muslims are dissatisfied with me and ask me to go." That meant that he only owed loyalty to the immigrant Muslim community, not to the country that has given all of them asylum.[17]

Abu Laban attributed his dissatisfaction with Denmark to the poor treatment he received in the media, and the poor human rights record of Denmark that he was going to improve in Gaza, if he only could make up his mind to move there. Some believe that Abu Laban has been demonized for working against the government's efforts to integrate Muslims and has been excluded from the PM's dialogues with the Muslim community. But he and the scores of followers who attend his Friday prayer services maintain that he is a "seeker of peace and a channel for dialogue." His unclear message about his future in Denmark is not the first time he has been involved in a case of contradicting his own statements. His accusations of the media for "mistreating" him have been countered with claims that he does the same. A BBC documentary revealed that the pictures Abu Laban's group claimed were the *Jyllands-Posten* cartoons were not printed by the newspaper at all. The pictures included in the dossier, among them one of a man wearing a plastic pig snout, were defended by Abu Laban as pictures that had been used to harass Muslims in Denmark. Laban came to Denmark in 1984 from Gaza at the request of Danish converts. Educated as a mechanical engineer, he has lived and worked in a number of Muslim countries. Egypt and the United Arab Emirates, however, have declared him *persona non grata* due to his radical teachings. One of those converts, Imam Abdul Wahid Pedersen, credited Abu Laban with keeping young Muslims on "the straight and narrow." Despite his radical teachings and questions over his motives, Danish Muslim experts said his decision to stay in Denmark could be a blessing in disguise. "Losing Abu Laban could have been a problem if he were to be replaced by a more radical imam," said Helle Lykke Nielsen, a lector at the Center for Middle East Studies. "The new generation is far more fundamentalist, pro-Hamas, pro-*Hizb ut-Tahrir* and more radical than Abu Laban is.[18] Another curious outgrowth of the Cartoon Affair is the pretext Turkey found to prosecute the Kurdish leaders it despises. The Ankara Prosecutor sued 56 mayors in the Kurdish southeast over a letter they sent to Denmark's prime minister, Anders Fogh Rasmussen. The state prosecutor has charged the mayors with helping Kurdish rebels when they urged Mr. Rasmussen not to close the Danish-based Kurdish satellite broadcaster ROJ TV. If convicted, they face up to 10 years in prison. Turkey accuses ROJ of being a mouthpiece of the outlawed Kurdistan Workers Party, which aspires to independence for Turkish Kurdistan.[19]

Remote, naive and well-meaning Norway, which by hosting the Oslo Accords thought it was bringing peace and salvation to the world, and persists in allocating the Nobel Peace Prize annually, was jolted by the Cartoon Affair, not so much by the violence against some of its representatives and symbols in the Muslim world, but by what a prominent fundamentalist Muslim who has been generously sheltered by her for years, had to say to its papers. Kurdish-Iraqi *Ansar Al-Islam* (The Supporters of Islam) Commander, Mullah Krekar, gave a press interview in the aftermath of the controversy over the cartoons of Islam's Prophet Muhammad, to the Internet edition of the Norwegian daily *Dagbladet*. In it, Krekar expounded his views on relations between Islam and the West. Krekar, whose real name is Najm Al-Din Faraj Ahmad, came to Norway as a refugee in 1991, where he established the Islamist *Ansar Al-Islam* organization. While slated for deportation from Norway he gave this interview to the press:

On one side stands the Western way of thinking. This is a way of thinking that has taken its materialism, egoism and savagery from the ancient Greeks and Romans. This is a way of thinking that has altered true Christianity. An example of this is that Western Christianity [today] accepts men having sex with men. That was never accepted by Jesus. On the other side stands Islam, and now the West is trying to take over and change Islam in the same way that Christianity was debased. There is only one civilization. But there are different ways of thinking about it, and our way of thinking in Islam stands in opposition to the Western way of thinking. Today it is our way of thinking that comes in and shows itself stronger than theirs. Islam has a stable foundation: one God, one Prophet, one Qur'an, and one tradition. This generates hatred among [those with a] Western way of thinking, and leads the losing party to use violence. And that is the violence and war against Islam. Democracy is Just an Excuse—It's Islam the West Can't Stand.... The same with the hunt for Osama bin Laden—it's just an excuse. It is Islam that the West can't stand.... The attack on Islam is like a hand. One finger is the war in Iraq and Afghanistan. Another finger is the imprisonment of Muslims at Guantanamo Bay. The third finger is the publishing of the pictures of the Prophet Muhammad. We must see things as they are, and those pictures [of Muhammad] are one part of the military fight that the West is conducting against Islam.... By 2050, 30% of the European Population Will Be Muslim....

We have no fear of the Western way of thinking. It can never win. In Iraq the two sides stand one against the other. On the side of Islam stand men who love death and who are willing to become martyrs for what they believe in. On the other side stand soldiers who fight for $1000 a day. The number of dead American soldiers is proof of failure. The same is true in Afghanistan. From 2001 to 2004, there were five suicide attacks. In 2005 there were 17. While the front of the U.S. and its allies is becoming smaller, Islam is widening its front. The reports from Guantanamo show the same. They are trying to rip belief from the hearts of the Muslims. It doesn't work. In Denmark they published cartoons, but the result was only to encourage people to rally behind Islam. I and all Muslims are proof [of this]. They have not managed to change us. It is we who will change them. Look at the development of the population in Europe, where the number of Muslims increases like mosquitoes. Each Western woman in the EU produces, on average, 1.4 children. Each Muslim woman in these same countries produces 3.5 children. By 2050, 30% of the European population will be Muslim....

Muslims who go to Afghanistan and Iraq to fight, that is an honor. It is an honor in itself if it violates the laws here in Europe. Those who say that Osama bin Laden is a terrorist are themselves killing our women, children, and civilians. This is what we see and know. We are not influenced by the U.S.'s words against bin Laden, since they are talking about someone we know. We are fighting for the same goal, just under different circumstances. The goal is Islamic rule in an Islamic state. Shi'ite Muslims have achieved this goal in Iran, and they are so strong that the West doesn't dare attack. This is the only way we can maintain a balance [of power] and achieve a lasting peace.

Our Caliph is dead and we are orphans. Therefore we are fighting, like the Jews fought under David Ben-Gurion, for our own state, a state ruled by a true Islamic ruler. Bin Laden is a good person to rule the Caliphate. Borders do not matter. Things are born, and then they grow bigger. The essential thing is Islamic rule. That was why the West destroyed the Taliban's rule in Afghanistan. They feared the Islamic state.

The ruler doesn't have to be a cleric. A good human being is enough and Osama bin Laden and Ayman Al-Zawahiri are among several good people. Weren't Jewish leaders also terrorists before they had their own state?

Muslims in the West and in Norway don't want to understand that this is not their country. The Muslim state will be their home, no matter where it is located. Muslims in the West are like the Jews were. We are homeless and weak, and will remain so until we create our own country. Life here has no value for Muslims. Muslims can participate in elections and elect Carl I. Hagen or Kristin Halvorsen, but in itself they have no value for society. When we get our own country, like the Shi'ites created in Iran, then Muslims will have full political and economic control. We have no role to play in Europe at this point. Our position is to maintain our numerical strength. But now you are putting us in the role of the accused. It is you and the West who should be telling us what [the West] can do for us. The West should protect Islam, and not the other way around. I am protected by the law in this country, but it is not a law that protects Muslims in particular. Neither could it protect Muslims against the attack that these cartoons were. It is not the West that is the victim in this case.[20]

From talk to deeds. Videos showing men training with explosives in Sweden, and threatening it with "suffering in the name of Allah"; this is what a group using the name of the Iraqi *jihad* group, *Ansar al-Sunnah* (Supporters of Tradition), has released showing what it claims are members training for terror attacks in the Swedish countryside. In one video, dated 8 August 2005, the group says that viewers are about to see a "demonstration of the high explosives device, that we will use in the name of Allah. This was recorded somewhere in Sweden," says a message on the video in yellow letters against military camouflage colors. A large explosion is then seen in a heavily wooded area. While it is not possible to verify the location of the explosion, the scenery does appear to be northern European. A second video by the group, which is dated 29 August, contains images of men with blurred out faces setting off mock suicide explosives and roadside car bomb attacks. The video begins with a message that reads: "Demonstration of real high explosive device, that is filled with gas instead of ammoniate nitrate." It goes on to show men standing in a clearing in a forest. They are seen pulling chords attached to devices, and setting off explosions of white smoke around themselves. In the same video, a red vehicle is seen driving along a forest path, before suddenly being engulfed in an explosion of white smoke. The videos are available for download on *infovlad.net*, which frequently posts videos of *jihad* shooting and bomb attacks from around the world, along with documents containing bomb-making manuals. One user on the site, who identified himself as "dehex," warned that "Sweden will suffer in the name of Allah. "Referring to a well known Swedish reverend, Runar Soogard, who is reported to be under police protection after offending Muslims with a speech about Islam's Prophet, Dehex wrote: "Runar Soogard had a very bad and nasty speech about our greatest Prophet Mohammed. It's because he doesn't want to apologize to the *Ummah* Nation, at least on television, we are giving out this videos as a warning! There will be one more warning, if he doesn't apologize on television….," wrote the user, in an ominous warning. "dehex" also posted an image showing a bloodied knife plunged into a map of Sweden, accompanied by the message: "We will slaughter all who dared to attack our Prophet Mohammed.[21]

The bottom line of all these tergiversations has been that the more Scandinavians apologize and show a smiling face, the more they are considered as power-less, spineless and ripe for capture and subjugation by Muslims. This manifests itself not only in more attacks against Scandinavian societies, their targets of upcoming Islamization, but also against Scandinavian Jews who are usually more assimilated, respective of their host-culture and society, law-abiding and successful in all walks of life. Take for example the attitudes of Muslims in Sweden to their Ramadan holiday. The holy fasting month of Ramadan in Sweden gives Muslims a good chance to stick closer to their Islamic identity, with mosques teeming with worshippers and shops selling famous Arab food. Encouraged by a country that respects freedom of religion, Muslim families are trying their best to instill the Islamic values and Ramadanian traditions into their young generations. State schools, in turn, respect the desire of Muslim students to observe the dawn-to-dusk fasting, excepting them from having the obligatory lunch meal. So far, all is fair and square, no different from what Jewish children would do on their Yom Kippur fast. Except that here religion to elevate the soul ends in political propaganda, under the guise of religion which poisons the undiscriminating souls of children and youth. In fact, after their *Iftaar* (the meal to break the fast), Muslim children glue themselves to the TV and keep flicking Arab satellite channels, searching for religious programs. Among a plethora of serials, the Syrian-produced *Al-Shatat* (Diaspora) has succeeded in grabbing the attention of hundreds of children, which helps keep the Palestinian cause alive in the memories of those young generations. The 26-episode mini-series traces back Zionism at all political, economic and religious levels, and unmasking ways used by the Jews to create their "fictitious" entity in Palestinian territories. A big problem facing the Muslim community in Sweden is moon sighting. Cloudy skies and cold weather make it tough for Muslims to sight the new moon. Therefore, Islamic societies in Sweden declare the beginning of Ramadan following the astronomical calculations of some Muslim countries, such as Saudi Arabia, Egypt and Iran. Islam has become the second official religion in Sweden, after Christianity. This is in spite of the fact that the Swedish Muslim community is a relatively new one, unlike that of other European countries such as France.[22]

New or not, the Muslim organizations in Scandinavia engage in blunt anti-Semitism sometimes even more overtly than the Scandinavians themselves, since it is no longer taboo to talk of it in common discourse, and there is not even an attempt to disguise it. As someone wrote in another context—it has become the "only hatred that dares to speak its name." Anti-Semitism in Sweden, has become directly subversive against a Jewish minority that has lived in Sweden and fully integrated with Swedish culture for 250 years, and in favor of a Muslim minority that generally segregates itself from mainstream Swedes and has lived in the country for about 30 or 40 years. Here is a case—one of many—in which Hitler's racist-supremacy descendants are expressing the very same sentiments albeit in a different language, and the result is, once again, a politically correct shrug of public-office indifference. Hitler called upon his supporters to kill all Jews for what he claimed was the general social good. His call was to kill all Jews everywhere. In the Stockholm Grand Mosque, true believers are incited to murder in the name of religion. And they are incited to murder all Jews, everywhere. The similarity in intent is terrifying. As is the similarity in silence from those whose job it is to know better. The international media might want to put a question or two on this subject to Swedish Chancellor of Justice Mr. Goran Lambertz. Swedish Radio News (SRN) reported that a Stockholm mosque is selling cassettes calling for a genocidal holy war against the Jews. According to SRN, the cover of one of the cassettes shows a picture of the Statue of Liberty draped in a burning American flag. Sales of cassettes promoting genocide are illegal in Sweden, but a spokesman for the mosque blamed volunteers for stocking the mosque bookstore with the cassettes.[23] Even more ominously, as part of what Swedish Jews see an "open season on Swedish Jews": the Swedish Chancellor of Justice is cited as saying that Muslim calls for "Death to Jews are just part of the debate on the Middle East." Earlier in 2006 the Swedish Chancellor of Justice Mr. Lambertz decided to discontinue his department's pre-trial investigation into the Grand Mosque of Stockholm, where those audiocassettes with highly inflammatory anti-Semitic content were being sold. After Swedish radio program Dagens Eko unveiled the contents of the cassettes in November 2005, a charge of racial incitement was filed with the police against the Stockholm mosque. The Swedish Chancellor of Justice responded by closing the pre-trial investigation on the grounds that "the lecture did admittedly feature statements that are highly degrading to Jews (among other things, they are consistently referred to as the "brothers of apes and pigs)" but pointing out that such statements "should be judged differently—and therefore be regarded as permissible—because they were used by one side in an ongoing and far-reaching conflict where calls to arms and insults are part of the everyday climate in the rhetoric that surrounds this conflict." [24]

A Jewish press release which wondered at this state of affairs, put the question whether this was political correctness, election tactics or fear of radical Islam? There were several comments to be made regarding the Chancellor's remarkable statement. One is that it was important to remember in the election year of 2006 that there was a sizeable Muslim minority in Sweden (Muslims number close to half a million souls in Sweden out of a total population of close to 10 million, whereas there were only about 16,000 Jews living in that country). Another is that at the mosque, a curse was pronounced on all Jews everywhere and the audience were encouraged to participate in *Jihad* (holy war) against Jews, highlighting suicide bombers as an effective weapon and praising them as martyrs. The Middle East was not singled out. This would therefore appear to be a clear case of general racial incitement. Yet the Chancellor of Justice opines that "owing to the Middle East conflict such expressions, despite their content, cannot be regarded as racial incitement according to Swedish law." One might indeed wonder how the phrase "kill the Jews" needs to be expressed in order to be regarded as sufficient incitement to kill Jews, according to the Chancellor, who finds nothing inflammatory in the statement.   Obviously, the Chancellor was considered to be on very shaky legal ground indeed. Sweden already has a legal precedent that Mr. Lambertz has chosen to ignore: a case was successfully brought on grounds of anti-Semitic incitement in 1989 in the District Court and again in the Court of Appeal (1990) against Radio Islam's legally responsible publisher Ahmed Rami. Legal proceedings had been instituted by the then-current Chancellor of Justice and Rami was convicted on 17 counts. Then too the defense and many Swedish apologists tried to mitigate Rami's culpability by claiming that his statements should simply be regarded as robustly expressed comments on the situation in the Middle East. They failed and he went to jail. One consistent theme in these recent audiocassettes is a *hadith* (tradition of the Prophet) which claims that there can be no peace anywhere in the world until the last Jew has been killed. As narrated by Abu Huraira: Allah's Apostle said, "The Hour will not be established until you fight with the Jews, and the stones and the trees behind which a Jew will be hiding will say. 'O Muslim! There is a Jew hiding behind me, so kill him.' This argument-cum-citation, was intended to show the honorable but ignorant Minister that the *hadith* ordaining the killings of the Jews was prescribed by Islamic sources some 13 centuries *prior* to the onset of "that Middle East Conflict."[25]

Had the Swedish Ministers done their homework, the Swedish Chancellor of Justice may come to different conclusions if he was not eying election year and the votes he needed from Muslims. It is, quite simply, an age-old appeal to religious zeal aimed at fomenting anti-Semitism. To explain it away as part of religious tradition or political commentary when neither the dates nor the words fit, is more than political correctness gone mad—it is directly subversive against a Jewish minority that has lived and integrated peacefully in Sweden and in favor of a vocal and violent Muslim minority that generally segregates itself from mainstream Swedes and has lived in the country for about 30 or 40 years. It is never acceptable to cry "Wolf!" However, if Europeans had cried out their warning 67 years ago as Hitler rose to power and his calls to arms against the Jews had been taken at face value, the world would have been a very different place today. Not only for Europe's Jews, but for the many millions of Russians, Americans, Australians, Canadians, Japanese and Europeans—not least Germans—who would have been spared the horrors of a war fired by racist zeal and stoked by racist ideology. In any case, it is fair to bring the Chancellor of Justice's standard response that he sent to all protesters:

Dear everyone who wrote to me about hate speech. I understand your reactions. But you were cheated. The press release you must have read was seriously misleading. My decision was a purely legal one, interpreting Swedish Law on hate speech. And it is quite safe to say that the Law does not make it a crime to sing battle songs or utter war cries related to the conflict in the Middle East. This is true even if suicide bombers are called heroes and abusive speech is used about Jews. Insults can sometimes be regarded as hate speech, but not in a context like the one that was under my judgment. It is also quite safe to say that the Law in this country does not make it a crime to quote and to analyze a so called *hadith,* which is a centuries old part of Islamic Law, even if the *hadith* is utterly offensive—as this one was—to the Jews. If, however, the author or the speaker makes statements which must be regarded as supportive to a *hadith* like the one in question, then this is definitely a crime. But this was not the case. The basis for my judgment was Swedish Law on freedom of speech. This is protected by the Constitution, and the freedom goes very deep. The Law on hate speech is one of the few exceptions to this very important human right. It is expressly stated that expressions must be clearly in conflict with freedom of speech to be a crime. I found some of the expressions under my judgment utterly provoking and quite unacceptable. But they did not constitute a crime under Swedish Law. My judgment is supported not only by national Law of this country. Freedom of speech is also protected by the European Convention for the Protection of Human Rights and Fundamental Freedoms. I am convinced that it would have been in conflict with the Convention to declare the statements in question a crime. My decision is final and cannot be tried by any Court or another organ here in Sweden. There is furthermore no reason for me to review my decision as long as such re-examination would concern the same material. But if new material is put before me I am of course ready to make an assessment of that. I will just mention one item from the totally off the point press release. The author of it implies that it would be politically correct in Sweden to refuse prosecuting hate speech against Jews, and that my decision had something to do with the upcoming elections in Sweden. Nothing could be more false. The author also accuses me of not daring to prosecute. This is highly insulting. I certainly dare. I am not going to pass any kind of judgment on any of you. But I have never before in my life been awarded so many ugly names or received so many indirect threats. And let me thank all of you who were good enough to make reservations concerning the correctness of the press release, or who were otherwise respectful enough to be friendly.

Kind regards,
Göran Lambertz Chancellor of Justice of Sweden.
Postadress Gatuadress Telefon (växel) Telefax E-

If this were a mere academic argument, it would have been left there. But there are two glaring faults in the Minister's argument. The quotations of the *Hadith* were not made by the Muslims for debate sake or to promote knowledge of Islam, but as an instruction to Muslims to act likewise, just as the Rami case of 20 years ago dealt with citations from the Bible that the Court in Stockholm then found offensive enough to prosecute. If the Minister cannot judge the local context in Sweden unless against the general background of the conflict between Muslims and Jews in Palestine, then the coming to power of the Hamas, which upholds the same principles against the Jews and uses the same citations, has been the basis on which Americans, Europeans and Israelis have founded their refusal to deal with that organization, precisely because they realized the operational import of those words of abuse. If that statement by the Minister distances him from the suspicions of an election year, it is interesting what he would do with the news about huge government expenditures for Muslim religious facilities during that year, which in fact reward Muslims, at the same time that he refuses to prosecute them for incitement. Indeed, the Islamic Centre in Malmo is to receive three million kronor in government funding for rebuilding and repairing damage "caused in the latest attack on the mosque." The government said that the donation was based on the fact that the Islamic Centre is important and contributes to "creating the image of Islam in Sweden" (which one, the negative or the positive?)."The Islamic Centre is a significant player in integration and its work- religious, social and cultural, reaches many people in southern Sweden," said Lena Hallengren, minister with responsibility for religious issues, but added nothing about the incitement, anti-Jewish and otherwise, that emanates from that center. Sweden's government is also to send three young Swedish Muslims to Egypt and Jordan, with the aim of counteracting the image of Sweden as anti-Islamic, but only where they are also sure to learn more anti-Jewish hatred that runs routinely in those countries even one or two decades after the peace treaties signed between them and Israel.[26]

The Swedish government said that negative images of Sweden have been fostered in the Arab world following the publication in Denmark of caricatures of the Prophet Muhammad. The delegation that it planned to send to the Arab world was to "talk about how Muslims live in Sweden," foreign minister Laila Freivalds told newspaper *Sydsvenskan,* "They will travel round for nine days, talking to students, politicians and opinion formers about their own lives." The trip was to have taken place in March 2006. "There is a need to exchange experiences," said Freivalds during a visit to Malmo. All the young "ambassadors" came from Skone. They were Othman al-Tawalbeh, 33, an imam who works in the information department of Helsinborg council, Hanin Shakrah, 24, who works on a youth project in Malmo, and Nadja Jebril, 23, a journalist from Malmo. The sociological and psychological phenomenon here is fascinating, because as a result of the Cartoon affair, it is Scandinavian countries which find themselves soul-searching, despite the fact that their embassies and institutions were the victim of Muslim violence, not the other way round. In Sweden, it has brought questions about freedom of speech, political correctness and minority groups rights back to the heart of public debate. Sweden was itself forced to deal with publications of cartoons of Muhammed on the web site of the far-right Sweden Democrats (*Sverigedemokraterna,* SD), which were reported to be causing an uproar in Syria. The site was taken down by its hosting company after information was brought forward to it by the foreign ministry and the security service. Foreign Minister, Laila Freivalds, while denying government pressure on the hosting company, has said that "there are those who still clearly want to offend and provoke in this way, and I think that they too ought to show some responsibility." SD's secretary, Bjorn Soder, protested against the censorship but said the party has received threats and eventually removed the cartoons from the site with the safety of Swedish citizens abroad in mind. He said that the episode was another illustration of the dilemma facing Sweden and other countries. While the government security, diplomacy and racial harmony demanded a harsh response to papers publishing offensive cartoons, principles of freedom of speech appear to require the state to take a hands-off approach. When asked what he would have done if Muslim countries had complained that a Swedish newspaper had published the cartoons, Swedish Prime Minister Goran Persson said he would have called in the (Arab and Muslim) ambassadors: "I would have explained what freedom of the press is about, what democracy and the formation of public opinion mean for us and made it very clear that this has nothing to do with ridiculing or scoffing at another religion."[27]

But this did not stop the media debate: can total freedom of expression avoid ridiculing and scoffing? The Swedish example shows that this is no simple issue. Sweden's constitution gives all individuals a fundamental right to express their opinions and disseminate them without censorship. Press freedom in Sweden dates back to the eighteenth century, and Swedes have always been very proud that things there can be discussed in the open. Today, however, these principles are set against a constant struggle to reconcile free speech with a modern tradition of strident political correctness and a desire not to offend minorities (or most often for different minority groups not to offend each other). But is this an attempt to square a circle? "Unlike many other Western societies, this is a country where women are thought to have a natural place in working life, where homosexuality is not a crime, and where same-sex marriages and women priests no longer raise any eyebrows" says Alexa Robertson, a lecturer at the Department of Political Science at Stockholm University. "The problem, of course, arises if you think freedom of speech should apply to extreme right wing groups and Pentecostal ministers who say homosexuality is a disease, for example. There is an inevitable conflict of principles here and it is very difficult to resolve. It seems to me this is the same conflict we have been experiencing when it comes to the Danish cartoons." Sweden enacted a new hate crimes law in 2003, which makes any expressions of "disrespect" or "incitement" towards individuals and groups of people illegal. The law was motivated by attacks on racial and religious minorities, and also criminalized speech against people because of their sexual orientation. The last couple of years have seen many examples of this conflict. In 2004 the Israeli ambassador to Sweden, Zvi Mazel, attacked a piece of art depicting a Palestinian suicide bomber. Following this, subway posters advertising the exhibition with the bomber's face on them were removed by local transport bosses. In spring 2005, Sweden's biggest ice cream maker, GB Glace, was accused of racism after launching an advertising campaign for its new ice cream, Nogger Black, and more recently, a subway campaign for bras was stopped because its slogan, "We Love Boobs," was found offensive. "The boobs are still there of course, but not the slogan," says Alexa Robertson, "so whatever the issue, there is obviously sensitivity towards ruffled feathers and the public sphere in Sweden"[28]

This sensitivity isn't always enough though. In a famous case Sweden's Supreme Court acquitted Pastor Green of charges of hate speech arising from a sermon he preached in July 2003 denouncing homosexuality. The pastor said, amongst other things, that "sexual abnormalities" were a social tumor. In another very recent case authorities closed an investigation into an extreme right-wing Christian web site which lists famous homosexual Swedes and makes death threats against them, quoting passages from the Bible. The chairman of gay rights group RFSL said, following Green's trial, that the judgment showed the need for protection laws to be strengthened. "Agitation and threats, such as those uttered by Green, limit lesbian, gay, bisexual, and trans-sexual people's rights and opportunities to participate in debate." One of the ironies about the long-running debate on freedom of speech in Sweden is that in many cases ultra religious and conservative groups were the ones fighting for the freedom to speak out, while secularists and left-wingers were the ones arguing for curbs on it. For Sweden's 500,000 Muslims, the cartoon scandal is just another issue in their attempt to build a functioning Muslim community in this modern, secular society, where freedom of speech is almost a religion. But some argue that the 'right not to be offended' is just as important." The Danish cartoons are a provocation against Muslims all over the world and can't be seen as a statement of freedom of speech even with good will" says *Sveriges Muslimska Rd* (The Muslim Council of Sweden). The organization claims that the cartoons are similar to those depicting Jews in the 1930s; anti Semitism, they say, has become Islamophobia. What elegant way of avoiding the issue of Anti-Semitism by Scandinavian Muslims, who complain about Islamophobia! They also accuse the Danish government for failing to "maintain tolerance and an open dialogue and turning its back on Danish Muslims." However, the organization has also strongly condemned acts of violence in the Middle East and stresses the importance of a non- violent debate.[29]

"We are glad the climate of debate in Sweden is considerably better than in Denmark," says the organization, which has also called for a conference of politicians and Islamic organizations from all over Scandinavia to discuss minority politics, integration issues, religious rights and freedom of speech. Some commentators have claimed the Danish cartoons have nothing to do with freedom of speech; they are a provocation, which is part of the Danish attempt to tighten immigration laws and part of a struggle to fight the "Islamization of Europe." Others claim the Muslim demonstrations in the Middle East were only a tool for authoritarian regimes to deal with domestic pressure from Islamic opposition forces. In any case, the fact that Muslims in Europe have not been as violent as in the Middle East, though their part in riots and criminal attacks has been noted, does not necessarily emanate from their more peaceful attitudes, but from the realization that embarking on the road of violence might end disastrously for their very existence on the European Continent. Yet the essential problem for Sweden remains the same as that in many other countries: there can never be a guarantee that freedom of speech will be exercised responsibly. There is a temptation to believe that the calm and measured way that Sweden has faced up to these clashes is largely a sign that respect for minority groups is firmly anchored in the mainstream media. But one thing is for sure—the examples of the Sweden Democratic case show that anything the government does to try to control the debate is likely to blow up in its face. Swedish publishing company *Liber* stopped the sale of a religious education book which contained two images of the Prophet Muhammed. The book's section on Islam included those two pictures taken from medieval religious artwork. The book was aimed at the intermediate level of high school and was published in 1993. One of the illustrations came from a fourteenth century Persian manuscript from the 1300s while the other was taken from a thirteenth-century Iraqi manuscript. Both featured images of the Prophet. The decision to take the book off the market came after Haga School in Varberg removed the book from its religion education syllabus. "We will return the books to the publisher. They are a bit old—we have other books which we use today," said school head Roland Fallstrom. Abd al Haqq Kielan, a spokesman for Sweden's Muslims, said he found it "painful" that pictures of the Prophet were still used in education. He added that he was dissatisfied that the people responsible for Swedish teaching books had not shown consideration. However, he said that it was a consolation that the pictures in the book were not prejudiced or defamatory. Liber announced its agreement to withdraw the old books, and posted a short message on its web site. The company declined to comment further on the decision.[30]

The generally conciliatory, ambivalent and at times even self-flagellating attitudes of the Swedes towards terror and terrorists, generate also an atmosphere where no Muslim can be wrong, and even if a Muslim is caught red-handed, he has plenty of others to blame before he recognizes his own fault. A Swede being held in the Czech Republic on suspicion of planning terrorism has accused the domestic U.S. intelligence agency of "manufacturing" a case against him, adding that it was "politically directed against Islam." "The whole thing against me has been manufactured by organs of the FBI" said the 39-year-old in a statement released by his Czech lawyer, Jan Cervenka. "This is a political thing, when the United States wants to embarrass the Swedish and Czech governments. It is politically directed against Islam," he added. The man, the subject of an international arrest warrant for allegedly abetting terrorists, and wanted by Interpol, was arrested as he stepped off a plane at Prague airport in early December 2005 on his way from Stockholm to Beirut. The U.S. indictment against him charges him with conspiring to set up a "*jihad*" (holy war) camp in Oregon in the northwest United States that would offer military weapons training for Muslims interested in fighting in Afghanistan. But the Muslim Swede rejected the charge." I was never in Oregon, I never even considered that I would set up some sort of training camp in the United States. I went there with my wife and children as a tourist on the basis of a valid visa. If I had allowed myself to be involved in some sort of illegal actions, I do not understand why I was not immediately detained. I do not understand why these alleged crimes are being discussed after six years," he said. Cervenka said his client is being held on his own in Prague's Pankrac prison. He had been flying to Lebanon to see his mother in Beirut and also to get medical treatment, he added. The Czech lawyer said he was trying to contact the 39-year-old's lawyer in Sweden to find out if evidence in court cases there could be used to help defend him against extradition to the United States. Sweden has never agreed to extradite the man, who originates from Lebanon and has Swedish citizenship.[31] Even had the 19 perpetrators of 11 September been captured before they could carry out their horror, they would have said that they were merely tourists in the United States, they learned piloting for their spare time entertainment, they conspired for fun, and it was only a fabrication of the FBI that they were caught and indicted. So we hear from all prospective terrorists. The fault or responsibility is never theirs, they only do it for Allah, any lies and fabrications are allowed, all the seized prisoners, in Afghanistan or Iraq, in Guantánamo or in Sweden, are "victims" of American machinations. And since anti-Americanism is rife, there is no better way to gain sympathy among the host populations of Europe than to accuse the Americans of all evils. The Scandinavians, much like others in Europe, find that easier to believe than to take firm steps that might further infuriate their restive Muslim populations against them.

Based on these assumptions of "American falsehood," the principal actors in the string of terrorist-related events in Sweden which went concurrently with the Cartoon Affair and its aftermath, took advantage of the permissive mood in general, and the Swedish sense of guilt and apology that accompanied the Affair in particular, to articulate some denials and make-believe "convictions" that would detach them from any suspicion. Some claimed that four out of ten Muslim organizations in Sweden have been threatened, thus rendering suspect Muslims the real victims of the wave of terrorism while it was left to the host societies to soul-search and repent for their mistreatment of their innocent guests. According to an investigation by Swedish Radio's Ekot program, three out of ten Muslim associations have been attacked, vandalized and damaged. Ekot interviewed 100 organizations that together represent 80,000 Muslims in Sweden. The alleged abuse against them ranged from graffiti to attacks with firebombs. Bejzat Becirov, who runs the Islamic Centre in Malmo, said that the mosque there receives threatening mail "almost every day." One example was a newspaper cutting showing victims of the recent earthquake in Pakistan. On it, someone had written "dead Muslims cannot come to Sweden." According to the responses from the 100 organizations, Muslim women who wear veils are particularly likely to be harassed and discriminated against.[32] Granted that persecution of, and vandalism against, unsuspected Muslims must be prosecuted by the authorities, how much more credible it would have been if those same Muslims showed similar concern for the incitement against Jews in their same community, or for the mounting crime rate in Malmo, which had made certain neighborhoods virtually out of bounds for law enforcement agents? A Swedish teenager being held in Sarajevo on suspicion of terrorist offenses, visited the leader of al-Qa'ida in Iraq, Abu Musab al-Zarqawi, according to the British newspaper *The Times*. In an investigation into al-Zarqawi, one of the world's most wanted terrorists, the paper stated that "there are signs that al-Zarqawi wants to mobilise cells in Europe." An example given by the paper is the arrest of that 18-year-old Bosnian-born Swede with a Turkish man in the Bosnian capital of Sarajevo on 19 October 2005. Police found 30 kilos of explosive materials, weapons, and a so-called "suicide vest" in the man's apartment. On a video the men are seen "praying to Allah for forgiveness," according to a local journalist, and stored on their computer were pictures of the White House. Or was that also a fabrication of the FBI? Or perhaps, Zarqawi has never existed and all those stories are the figment of American imagination and persecution of Islam?[33]

The Swedish man, reported *The Times*, is alleged to have spent time in Iraq with al-Zarqawi and run one of his web sites. *The Times* cited police and intelligence sources, and said that British detectives are also investigating the Swede." His defense lawyer has told reporters that British, American and Danish police have interrogated him," said a journalist on the weekly paper *Slobodna Bosna* (Free Bosnia) to   journalists. According to earlier Bosnian reports, the Swede was identified as an Islamist who, under the code-name Maximus and from a computer in Sweden, is said to have recruited fighters to Iraq. Sweden has also begun an investigation into the man. Representatives of the Swedish embassy in Sarajevo have visited the man in prison on two occasions, most recently on October 28, 2005. He was in jail for almost a month before the next court hearing was to be held.[34] In another piece of news, that Swedish terror suspect was investigated by a Bosnian court, together with his Turkish co-conspirator. The state court of Bosnia said the two men were being investigated for "terrorism and the illegal possession of weapons or explosives." The pair were arrested on October 20, 2005 in an operation that involved a raid on two Sarajevo houses, yielding weapons and explosives. A Bosnian national who was detained the same day was later released. Later, police in Denmark have arrested seven men in connection with the two men in Bosnia, saying they were suspected of planning a terror attack in Europe. Later in October, a NATO commander in Bosnia said the alliance was closely monitoring about 10 terror suspects in the former Yugoslav republic. U.S. Brigadier General Luis Weber said that "camps" existed in Bosnia, which was at risk from suspected terrorists who were able to pass through the Balkan country thanks to a lack of security. Hundreds of foreign Islamic militants had entered Bosnia to fight alongside local Muslim soldiers during the country's 1992-1995 war. Some of them remained after gaining Bosnian citizenship. This means that the tremendous war effort expended by NATO, mainly the United States, to "free the Muslims of Bosnia from Serbian yoke" has finally backfired on America, who should henceforth be more distinguishing between long-term interests and short-term "friends" of fortune.[35]

And, explaining the rush of the Swedish government to allocate money for the refurbishing of the Malmo Islamic Center, it sufficed for it to declare that it was "facing ruin," namely that Malmo mosque "faces ruin" for government funds to be provided. One wonders if a similar call by a Jewish or a Lutheran organization should have received such generous allocations if it were in such distress. The Islamic centre in the Malmo said it was threatened with financial ruin after arson attacks earlier in 2003 and then in 2005 left it damaged. Now the centre's insurance company has said it can no longer provide cover because of the risk of further attacks. Bejzat Becirov, the Chief Executive of the centre, has asked Prime Minister Persson to help the mosque. The lack of insurance means the centre is likely to face difficulties getting credit for business funding and investment in the future, according to Becirov. "Next time we're under threat of sabotage and terrorism it will become impossible to rebuild the centre, we won't be able to get a loan to do so either," Becirov wrote in a letter to the Prime Minister. Persson visited the mosque during election-campaign party rallies (and they say no relation to elections) and gave "half a promise" of financial support. He said the repeated attacks on the mosque show that Sweden "sadly has become a country with European norms." He should have added that Swedish Islam had also stooped to the level of the rest of Europe. It was difficult to find an insurance company that would offer cover to the centre after the first attack in April 2003. The policy had a higher risk assessment than normal and the insurance company that approved the Islamic Centre at the time, has since withdrawn its cover. Approximately 57,000 Muslims are members of the centre.[36]

An Italy-based Moroccan terrorist group with links to al-Qa'ida has members in Sweden and Norway, according to Italian intelligence sources. The group is said to have been involved in the terrorist attacks in Madrid in 2004 and in Casablanca in 2003. According to the newspaper *Corriere della Sera*, the Italian military's intelligence service SISMI has since 2005 made several warnings concerning groups of volunteers who fought against the U.S.-led forces in Iraq and who are now returning to Europe to carry out attacks. Among these volunteers, said SISMI, are people who were brought up and recruited from Sweden and Norway, reported the Norwegian news agency NTB. One of these groups, the Moroccan Islamic Combatant Group (GICM) is said to have cells in northern Italy. These cells in turn have contacts across Europe, including in Sweden and Norway, wrote the paper. "Generally you can say that all terror groups have participants and sympathizers in Sweden, although I don't recognize this one," said Anders Tornberg, who is head of information at the security police and formerly worked with terrorism issues. Tornberg said that Sweden is also used in certain cases as a fundraising base for terrorist organizations, but he pointed out that it is not illegal just to sympathize with a terrorist group. GICM, according to the Norwegian defense expert Brynjar Lia, is a primary target for those fighting terrorism in Europe, not least for its suspected branches in Europe, including Scandinavia.[37] It serves no purpose, then, to pretend that there is no terrorism to fight, or that Sweden or other Scandinavian countries are relieved from it due to their "humanitarian" attitudes and "understandings" with their domestic Islam. Scandinavia is learning the hard way that more appeasement will always certainly increase the will and the daring of the terrorists to try some more. They have no sentiments, no obligation or gratitude towards their lands of asylum, they are committed only to their kin and to their ideals of Muslim dominion in Europe. The 39-year-old Swede, suspected of involvement in the London bombings has said that Sweden would be "punished" if he was handed over to a foreign power. The man, who is originally from Lebanon, has lived in Sweden since he was 18. In an interview with *Dagens Nyheter* he denied that he had met Osama Bin Laden but said that he "loved him." "I am proud of Osama bin Laden. "I am proud of everyone who wages war for justice." The man also told *Dagens Nyheter* that he thought the 11 September attacks against the United States were "very good." The man refuted accusations that he had been at a terrorist training camp in Oregon in 1999. He admitted, however, that he had lived with Abu Hamza, the controversial Muslim preacher at the Finsbury Park mosque in London, who is currently awaiting trial in Britain on terrorism and race-hate charges. This man, was obviously confident that Scandinavia was a no-man's land, where no one would prosecute him and he threatened that those who did "would be punished," which was enough to deter the authorities and thus pave the road for the next act of terror.[38]

The Swedish man says that he lived with one-eyed, hook-handed Hamza "for medical reasons, as a nurse. He is described by the FBI as "very dangerous," denies that he was involved in the London attacks of 7 July. In an interview published by *Expressen*, he says that he has not left Sweden in the past three years. Responding to reports that he had flown to the United States in 1999 in the company of Haroon Rashid, suspected mastermind of the London bombings, the man said he does not know who Rashid is, and has never met him. While denying involvement in the London bombings, the man said that the suicide bombers who attacked three underground trains and a bus were "martyrs," adding that he hoped also to become a martyr one day. "They are not terrorists, as they are doing what Islam requires," he said. Sweden, he said, is not threatened by al-Qa'ida, although he told *Expressen* that this could change if the Swedish government handed him over to the British or American authorities. "If Sweden hands me over to another country then it will only have itself to blame. Sweden will then be punished with the greatest punishment."[39] Another, or the same, Swedish citizen is being hunted by the FBI in connection with the bombings in London on 7 July. He is thought to be linked to the suspected British al-Qa'ida leader, Haroon Rashid Aswat, who is currently being interrogated after a swoop by Pakistani police 90 miles from Islamabad. According to *The Times*, British police suspect that Aswat played a crucial role in the London attacks, which killed 52 people as well as the bombers themselves. Mobile phone records have been found which detail his calls with the four suicide bombers and Aswat is believed to have come from the same town as one of them. He is thought to have visited all the bombers' hometowns in the fortnight before the attacks and flew out of London hours before the atrocity. But the interest of the Swedish press has focused on the Lebanese-born Swedish citizen who traveled to the United States with Aswat in 1999.

American security services believe the man, who, according to *The Times,* described himself as "a hitman for Osama bin Laden," could be involved in the London attacks. The two men apparently investigated the possibility of using a remote ranch in the Seattle area as a training camp. They allegedly received firearms training and some months later the Swede was still in Seattle, preaching to young Muslims. In 2003 the 39-year-old, by then based in Stockholm, was sentenced to ten months in prison for possessing illegal weapons in his flat in the south of the city. *Aftonbladet* said that the Swede was also suspected of plotting a terrorist attack, but charges were never brought against him." The allegations against him were obviously very weak since he was never charged," said his then lawyer, Bengt Soderstrom, to the tabloid. "I defended him then but I haven't had contact with him since," he added. The Swedish security police refused to confirm the man's identity or that he was part of the London investigation. "When it comes to operational questions we never confirm or deny reports. And here we're talking about one of the largest police investigations ever," police spokesman Anders Thornberg told AFP, referring to the massive international efforts to track down those responsible for the 7 July blasts. "We are doing our best to help our British colleagues," was all Thornberg would say.[40]

In the middle of these turbulences, lawsuits ran their course, including some dealing with the all-European plight of "honor-killings" among Muslim immigrants. A landmark verdict found nine people guilty for conspiring to kill a young Pakistani woman and her husband in the largest honor killing case ever tried in Europe. The High Court of Eastern Denmark delivered a "guilty" verdict to all nine defendants in the most far-reaching honor killing ever tried in Europe. The verdict is considered a landmark finding, since not only the brother who fired the gun that killed Ghazala Khan was found guilty. The court also found Ghazala's father and seven others guilty of conspiring to murder the young Pakistani woman and her husband for disobeying orders not to marry in September 2005. Jurors determined that a group of uncles, aunts and acquaintances apparently plotted to lure the couple to the train station of Slagelse in western Zealand, where the brother waited with a loaded gun. Ghazala suffered fatal wounds while her newly wed husband narrowly escaped death. Although lawyers of seven of the defendants sought a reduced sentence for their clients, jurors rejected their plea that mitigating circumstances should release a milder sentence. The verdict came as no surprise to Vagn Greve, a law professor at Copenhagen University. Jurors merely made use of Danish law's broad guidelines in defining who acts as an accomplice in a crime, he said. "From what I have heard and read, I cannot see that we have done anything new. The jurors found that existing rules should be put to use." Legal experts in Germany, Sweden and other countries have followed the case closely, since it marks the first time accomplices have been found guilty in an honor killing.[41]

All these tribulations within the Scandinavian public and authorities, and the statements of their politicians cannot hide the fact that massive terrorist activities are being plotted and launched from their territory. No matter how skilled they become in semantic platitudes, in order to avoid saying "Muslim terrorism," or to take to task their Muslim population for the terrorists it has been hatching and protecting, or ignoring the threats from the terrorists that the country would be punished if it dared to interfere, one can discern the slippery road on which Sweden has embarked and would finally bring her, in the immortal words of Churchill about Munich and the initiators of appeasement, who ignored their honor to avoid war, to ultimately both lose its honor and wage war. The Swedish Radio program *Kaliber* reported that "almost all" Islamic schools and congregations in Sweden have contacted potential sponsors in Saudi Arabia. Many of these Saudi foundations ask for influence in return. However, an expert thinks the chances are slight that violent organizations will gain a foothold in Sweden's Muslim communities. Islamic organizations have received help from the Saudi embassy in Stockholm to find potential donors. Many community groups can only afford simple basement premises. But with Saudi money, they can build mosques. "Kaliber" featured the *Al Salam* school in Örebro, which takes children from nursery age to Year 5 and receives between 150 and 200,000 crowns a month from an Islamic foundation. In return for their money, sponsors often demand a seat on the board or the right to appoint *imams* or school leaders. Saudi Arabia practices the strict *Wahhabi* and *Salafi* traditions. Women are required to be completely covered and are not allowed to socialize with men outside the family. Men must have long beards and dress in the style of the Prophet Muhammed. Music and art are banned. It's not clear how many schools or other organizations have accepted sponsorship or acceded to demands of influence. But four of Sweden's 11 Islamic schools have said that they wouldn't accept donations if demands were attached. Two headmasters have said they wouldn't accept gifts from Saudi sources because the country was associated with terrorism. Now the government have taken an interest in the issue. Schools Minister, Ibrahim Baylan, was concerned that teaching could be affected: "Our legislation is very clear. In order to qualify for state support, a school's syllabus should be objective and comprehensive. Schools shouldn't alter their teaching in return for money. It's *Skolverket*'s (Ministry of Education) job to make sure that doesn't happen and I'll check to see if they've received any reports on this issue." Children and Young People's Minister, Lena Hallengren, also expressed concern. She said that it was primarily the responsibility of the Muslim communities to consider the implications of accepting sponsorship. "It's a serious matter if these Saudi sponsors are making demands which don't match the community's beliefs," she said. The Minister also said that the government provides a total of 50m crowns in funding to faith organizations and it will never be able to compete with Saudi billions. But Jan Hjaerpe, professor in Islamic studies, thinks any fears that fundamentalist or terrorist organizations will infiltrate Sweden's Muslim communities are exaggerated. And he doesn't think Muslim parents would allow such a development in their children's schools. "Saudi Arabia is very anxious that extreme, violent groups are not allowed to spread. Obviously they don't stand for the most liberal form of Islam either, but parents are more interested in the children getting a career." Except, that he prefers to ignore the fact that Hamas schools, for example, where violence and terrorism are cultivated among young Palestinians, are financed with Saudi money. Mehmed Kaplan of Sweden's Young Muslims feels the Swedish government could help solve the financial difficulties of many community groups by being more creative with their funding: "I think it's up to the government to come up with a constructive solution, for example by providing some form of state credit."[42]

According to a report of AFP several hundred Muslims protested on a Sunday at a Pentecostal church in Stockholm against a preacher who denigrated Islam's Prophet Mohammed. According to police, about 400 Muslim protesters, including women and children, gathered in front of the Philadelphia Church, the main site of the Pentecostal movement in Sweden. In March 2005, at the same church, a 37-year-old Norwegian preacher living in Sweden, had made comments about several religions including Islam. "Mohammed, he is not God, he was a confused pedophile…. Read the story of what Mohammed did. He married girls at age nine, 11," he said in a sermon which was sold on a CD by his followers. A statement signed by "Muslims of Sweden" called that pastor's remarks "immature and ridiculous," noting that at the time when the prophet lived girls were married at very young ages. After the sermon was reported in the Swedish press, the preacher has tried to justify his remarks. "I made humorous descriptions of different religions, including Christianity," he said in a television interview. Pastor Runar Sögarrd, who is not a member of the Philadelphia Church but has his own religious group, has been under police protection having received threats, according to his followers.[43] In some ways, that was a preview of the Cartoon Affair, with the difference that this time no violence was used, meaning that not every "insult" to the Prophet necessitates violent reactions, and that when law and order are enforced, and Muslims are made to understand that respect for them and their Prophet also entails their own respect of the Christian and Jewish faiths which they denigrate, order can be ensured. In this regard, the Cartoon Affair is a break with civilized practices, as self-enamored Muslims felt strong, self-confident and unassailable enough to dare to cross the red lines.[44]

And finally, even in the neutral business of IKEA, Muslims have interfered. Norwegian Prime Minister Kjell Magne Bondevik has attacked Swedish furniture chain IKEA over the depiction of women—or rather, lack of—in its assembly instructions. Bondevik is outraged that none of IKEA's product-assembly guidelines actually show women putting the furniture together. The reason for the men-only policy, according to IKEA's Norwegian information chief Camilla Lindemann, is the fact that "in Muslim countries there's a problem with using women in instructions." Norwegian media said that the Prime Minister, who once went on sick leave because he was "burnt out," was unimpressed by IKEA's explanation. "That's not good enough," Bondevik told Norwegian tabloid VG. "Promoting attitudes of equality is at least as important in Muslim countries. They should just change this." Apparently, VG sent out intrepid reporters to talk to Muslims in Oslo and found that none of them could understand IKEA's explanation."Islam is not the way it was in Afghanistan," said Fahrid Ismail of Jordan. "Women can study, they can do anything. IKEA has now promised to rectify the lack of female assemblers in its instructions. "Now we'll make sure that there's an equal distribution," said Fredrik Wahrolen, in the Swedish information office.[45] And if proof were needed that Europe is gradually becoming the backyard of the Muslim *umma,* here you have the inexplicably docile conduct of the Swedes towards their new Arab masters whom they fear and obey. Sweden has indeed decided to withdraw from an international air force exercise to be held in Italy after learning that units from the Israeli air force will participate, announced a Swedish government spokesman. Sweden had originally agreed to send eight jet fighters to the Volcanex 2006 exercise in Italy between 8-26 May 2006. Foreign Ministry spokesman Christian Karlsson said the aim of the drill was to prepare for future cooperation in international peacekeeping operations, but added that "the participation of the Israeli Air Force has changed the prerequisites of the exercise." Defense Minister Leni Bjorklund said in a statement that Sweden pulled out because a state "that does not participate in international peacekeeping missions" would be part of the exercise, but did not mention Israel by name. Sweden has a long-standing policy of neutrality, but is actively involved in UN-peacekeeping missions. Its armed forces also participate in NATO exercises under the Partnership for Peace program. The Volcanex 2006 exercise was to be held in cooperation with the European Air Group as part of the Italian Air Force exercise Spring Flag in Decimomannu, Italy. The EAG was established to further develop the collaboration between British and French air forces in the first Gulf War. It now has seven member nations.[46]

The depth of the ridicule the Swedish government brought upon itself while trying to placate Muslim votes in the period leading up to general elections of 2006, is made clear by these excerpts from a press editorial:

Sweden claims that its decision to pull out of a NATO air force exercise has nothing to do with the participation of the Israeli Air Force in the event. But as a [an Israeli] Foreign Ministry spokesman put it, both Sweden's decision and its strange denial of the obvious are "insulting and unacceptable." The Swedes, indeed, did not mention Israel by name in announcing their withdrawal from the exercise. Swedish Defense Minister Leni Bjorklund, however, said that her country was withdrawing because "the Swedish Armed Forces were notified at a late stage that a state not belonging to the Partnership for Peace, and with which Sweden did not previously have bilateral military cooperation and which does not take part in international peacekeeping missions, was to take part in the air exercise." That country has a name. It's Israel. In case any confusion remained regarding which country Sweden intended to snub, Swedish Prime Minister Goran Persson told reporters in Stockholm Thursday that Sweden withdrew from the "Volcanex 2006" exercise in Italy because "We are careful about joining exercises with countries that we won't cooperate with in international missions under UN or EU mandates. That's our principle, that's our history. The Israelis have another, more warlike, history, which I find regrettable for that matter."

Israeli spokesmen might have responded that, come to think of it, it does have a "more warlike" history, and it is regrettable. Israel regrets that in 1948, 1956, 1967, and 1973 it was compelled to fight wars against the Arab armies poised to wipe it off the map. It regrets that Iranian leaders and the Hamas and Hizbullah movements and Iran continue to fund terrorism and remain openly dedicated to this same cause, the destruction of Israel. Israel also regrets that immediately after Israel formally offered, in 2000, to create a Palestinian state in more than 95% of the West Bank and Gaza, the Palestinian's launched a wave of suicide bombing that took over 1,000 Israeli lives and has not fully concluded to this day. Moreover, in the wake of Hamas's election victory, terrorist attacks are on the rise again, and formally justified as "natural and understandable" by Hamas officials. This sequence of events, where Israel can wholeheartedly agree with her Swedish "friends," is both warlike and regrettable. But by what logic should it lead to boycotting Israel and welcoming Hamas officials, as Sweden has done? Sweden's foreign minister, Jan Eliasson said, "There is no reason to dramatize this. It has nothing to do with our relationship to Israel that we want to protect and promote. It is a purely practical judgment based on the "exercise needs we have." It is unclear why the judgment and the "exercise needs" of France, UK, Germany, Belgium, Netherlands, and Spain—all members the European Air Group that organized Volcanex 2006—seem so different than those of Sweden. Even more mysterious is the nature of the relationship with Israel that Sweden seeks to "protect and promote." Israel is a peace-seeking democracy that is under attack. We don't appreciate it when countries boycott us and welcome our attackers, as Sweden has done by granting visas—contrary to European policy—to Hamas officials. "If a country believes that Israel is not good enough to participate in peacekeeping maneuvers, Israel will be entitled to think that that country is not qualified to play a role in the Middle East peace process," Foreign Ministry spokesman Mark Regev said. This is certainly the case. It is unfortunate that Sweden has shown such a gross inability to understand Israel's position that—in the name of promoting peace, of all things—it has removed itself from any constructive role in such a quest. Far from advancing peace, Sweden's extreme positions, however inadvertently, encourage terrorism against Israel, resulting in the deaths of more Israelis and Palestinians.[47]

These confused and pathetic rationalizations of a policy that while seeking justifications in European politics and policies was exactly violating them in a most blatant way, did not add to the clarity of Swedish policies, where disarray only continued to rule, pending the election period that Persson and his associates wished to wade without trouble, but in vain. Something is rotten in the State of

Sweden, one might conclude. In view of this uncertain attitude, Muslim organizations in Sweden can do one thing and its reverse, attempting to test the limits of Swedish tolerance towards their demands, precisely when in the pre-election period the government has been "flexible" and forthcoming in its responses to them. Thus, while one Muslim organization makes exorbitant demands to try Swedish readiness to acquiesce to them, another Muslim organization puts on the mantle of "moderation" by rejecting those demands when the unified negative Swedish reaction was deemed impossible to overcome. The list of Muslim demands keeps growing, the more the Swedish government yields to threats and blackmail. The more crumbs it throws to the Muslims to appease them, the more voracious their appetite for more. Consider, for example, Sweden's largest Muslim organization's demand that the country introduce separate laws for Muslims, according to Swedish television. Sweden's Integration and Equality Minister Jens Orback called the proposals "completely unacceptable." At the same time, the Swedish Muslim Association, which represents around 70,000 Muslims in Sweden, has sent a letter to all Sweden's main political parties suggesting a number of reforms, according to another TV program. The proposals include allowing imams into state (public) schools to give Muslim children separate lessons in Islam and their parents' native languages. The letter also said that boys and girls should have separate swimming lessons and that divorces between Muslims should be approved by an imam. The letter provoked an instant, and damning, response from integration and equality minister Jens Orback. "We will not have separate laws in Sweden. In Sweden, we are all equal before the law. In Sweden, we have fought for a long time to achieve gender-neutral laws, and to propose that certain groups should not be treated like others is completely unacceptable." Orback said he had spoken to representatives of the Swedish Muslim Council, and they did not support the association's position. "We have freedom of speech, we have the right to opinions and we have the right to make proposals—but if a law is going to be changed, it must be the same for everyone. "Asked whether the proposal plays into the hands of racists, Orback said that it did. "I think it is very problematic and unfortunate that people who have been in Sweden for so long make proposals such as this that are so opposed to our intentions, when we are fighting for women's rights and the right to divorce," Orback replied. Liberal Party leader Lars Leijonborg also slammed the idea of separate laws. "Sweden has equality between men and women. To introduce exceptions for Muslims so that women can be oppressed with the support of the law is completely unacceptable to me," Lars Leijonborg wrote in a statement.[48]

In another report on the same issue, more nuanced views came to the fore, throwing more confusion into the Muslims ' real position towards these issues. The Muslim Council of Sweden has added its voice to the criticism of the suggestion that the country should have separate laws for Muslims. The idea was expressed in an open letter to the Swedish political parties by Mahmoud

Aldebe, the chairman of the Swedish Muslim Association. It was Aldebe who suggested allowing imams into state (public) schools to give Muslim children separate lessons in Islam and their parents' native languages. The letter also said that boys and girls should have separate swimming lessons and that divorces between Muslims should be approved by an imam. We have seen that initially this provoked a swift and fierce response across the political spectrum and was described as "completely unacceptable" by Minister for Integration and Equality Jens Orback. Now other Muslim organizations, including the umbrella organization, the Muslim Council of Sweden, have distanced themselves from the letter. "This has absolutely no support in any of our organisations," said Mehmet Kaplan, the council's spokesman, to *Svenska Dagbladet*. "It's a non-issue for us. I have also spoken to the vice-chairman of the Swedish Muslim Association and he didn't know anything about it either." At a crisis meeting following this open debate, other Muslim organisations confirmed that they did not support the controversial proposals. "This is sad. There are other important issues which are now being obscured," said Kaplan. Speaking to Swedish Radio, Mahmoud Aldebe said that the furor following his letter was the result of a misunderstanding. "I'm not demanding parallel laws, I'm not demanding special legislation for Muslims. I just want to adapt our laws so that the Muslim minority feels safe in society," Aldebe told Swedish Radio.[49]

An anonymous Swede, who was reluctant to identify himself due to "certain Swedish laws and attitudes," says he translated the Muslim demands to all political parties from their original Swedish language. The document, assuming its authenticity due to its nature as an "open letter" whose words and intentions cannot be hidden, would be an eye-opener for all Europe, not only for the Swedes, because if it, or parts of it, should be accepted, that would be the beginning of the "slippery road downward" for all Europe, who, once the plug is removed from the dam, would no longer be able to stem the flood. The document also genuinely reflects the very same problems faced by other Muslims throughout Europe, hence the imperative of becoming aware of its details and their significance. In the open letter to all Swedish political parties that were participating in the 2006 election, purportedly signed by Mr. Adebe, the Secretary of the Muslim Council of Sweden, a long litany of demands, grievances, threats and expectations were formulated, which can send shudders down the spine of every European (the translation is not always adequate, but it was altered here only in extreme cases of awkwardness or of obfuscation). One suspects that it may have served as a trial balloon to test the forthcoming attitude of the parties the eve of elections, but was criticized and withdrawn only due to the harsh wall-to-wall rejection that it encountered. Had the Swedish politicians caved in as is their wont, this would have been the outline of the Muslim blueprint contained in that letter:

> Hello!
> If we are to succeed in engaging Swedish Muslims so that they will participate in
> the election in September 2006, we should take note of the following demands and

wishes from the Muslim minority in Sweden. I have not seen clear signals from all parties as to whether they'll accept such wishes. We want to see the most important demands as a part of the political programs. Otherwise there is the risk that the majority of the Muslims will remain on their couches on election day. Muslims are fed up with broken election promises, and therefore they wish concrete suggestions to show that we care. It won't hurt if our elected representatives or new candidates would set aside an hour to read our open letter that is sent to all established parties.

Kind regards,
Mahmoud Aldebe

THE FORGOTTEN MINORITY

Islam in Sweden, a short history.

Sweden didn't really get its first contact with Muslims before immigration began during the 1940s, when the first Muslims came from the east, that is from Finland and Estonia, they were Tatars and it was they who established the first house of prayer assembly in Stockholm 60 years ago. The Muslims who immigrated during the 1960-1970 period were part of the big labor immigration. Between 1970 and 1990 the immigration changed character, a flood of refugees began to make up a much larger share of the number of Muslims in Sweden. The Islamic community calculates the number of Muslims in Sweden to be roughly 470,000 people. Everyone that through birth belongs within a tradition [culture] traditionally dominated by Islam, who accepts the Islamic declaration of faith, belongs to a Muslim people, is descendant of Muslims, have a first name that belongs in an Islamic tradition, and who themselves identify with or considers themselves part of this religion or tradition, are Muslims. There are some immigrant Muslims that don't want contact with the Islamic community and that considers themselves secularized, and on occasion we have heard that they are objecting to being considered Muslims. It is hard to calculate the exact numbers but from our analysis and mapping, we can assume that there are approximately 15% of the Swedish Muslims that want nothing to do with Islam and that want to be considered as Swedes with an ethnic background.

Swedish Muslim rights and duties, special laws for religious freedom

Regarding the problems that concern the legal status of Muslims—concerning everything from laws regarding residency- and work-permits, denominational issues and the legal status of their religious functions to possibilities, with the support of religious freedom, to practice and live according to the message of Islam—the situation varies enormously. We have struggled, often with little progress, to make Islam accepted on the same terms, and with the same (legal) rights, as any other religion in the country. Despite that you talk about the same general rights for all religions, there are still in practice big differences between the ability of different religions to work in the community. We require special laws protecting religious freedom since all the conventions regarding human rights that Sweden has committed itself to, and we are thinking especially of the UN Declaration of Human Rights and the European Convention for the Protection of Human Rights (ECPHR) all imply the right to create special laws protecting religious freedom. Creating such specific laws is really about religious freedom since here in Sweden there has been full religious freedom since 1951. Swedish Muslims have become more and more politically aware of their rights in the community and now they wish for these rights to be respected. To be able to affect Swedish politics and to maintain an effective dialogue and conversation between

Swedish Muslims and the different organs of the community (state in this context) we present these practical and necessary solutions that must be carried out if you wish a successful integration policy and a diversified Sweden religious freedom should apply to everyone, and the UN different declarations in this regard are applicable even in Sweden. So in reality all laws should be altered or adjusted after the needs of all minority groups in Sweden. We Muslims are a large minority group in Sweden, but lack status and the laws created to protect religious freedom must be applied in their widest meaning so that they don't just apply to certain minorities and the majority, but rather they should be applied even to the Muslim minority in the country. The problem that exists in regards to the Swedish religious freedom is that it is a pietistic understanding of individualized religion, that lies behind the Swedish laws regarding religious freedom, whereas for the Muslim minority it is the collective expressions of the religion that are central. One considers the religion more like a way of life than a belief system. It is also a part of ordinary life, with its social rules and judgments, through which religious allegiance is displayed, and the religion practiced, not primarily through prayer and sermons and the common religious language that is Arabic. This is why certain Islamic religious practices come outside what is covered by religious freedom. The Muslim minority criticizes this narrow definition of religion that is the basis of the Swedish laws regarding religious freedom. Specific laws are required when it comes to the legal protection of the Muslim minority. With such protection we can request corrections of the Swedish family law to adapt it to Islam. It is this law that is the most important to Swedish Muslims: marriage, divorce, child protection, and raising underage children. It is also a matter of having the right to take a vacation on some of the two major religious holidays, and to be allowed a few hours time off in the middle of the day on Friday to participate in the Friday prayers. In such matters special legislation is seen as essential to protect the Muslim identity of the Swedish Muslims. The ability to live entirely according to Islamic family law if you wish to do so is very limited in Sweden (it is very difficult to do so), unless we get status as a separate minority.

Islamic religious community in Sweden

In Sweden there are more than 185 local Islamic assemblies, but only a very few mosques. Several mosque projects are underway. The community views this as a threat and many individuals and groups are loudly protesting. Counties and provinces ought to elevate all the so-called basement- and apartment mosques around the country to equal status with Churches, if the local politicians want to bring about a practical integration in the country. The resistance to mosque building comes from certain persons and from organized groups. The arguments that are most often used against mosque building are those linked to the environment (surroundings) in that a mosque would lead to increased traffic, and among other things increased air pollution, and noise. The mosque has been seen as an encroachment on parkland. The negative views on mosque building also contain comments and questions about Islam and Muslims. People talk about the immigration numbers and if they'll increase, about friction between Swedes and Muslims as well as internally between Muslim groups that frequent the area. Many people are openly saying that the limit has been reached, and that the Muslims should accept the customs of the place they've come to. The threat (damage) to Swedish values and culture is often held up as an argument. That one thinks ill of, or is afraid of Islam as a religion or movement is also often given as a reason among those that argue against mosque building. This strong ill will can hardly be changed by counter argument and is nourished by ignorance or mythology (bigotry, fantasy) about what it (Islam) stands for. Construction of mosques and financing this construction is a big problem for Muslims in Sweden, the basement facilities that exist are no longer sufficient as they are getting much too cramped

"Basement People"

Muslims are called the basement people by young Muslims that are loathe to participate in activities in such underground facilities, often hinting at the problems caused by the local environment such as poor air quality in basements that often lack proper ventilation. Many get sick from underground facilities or bicycle sheds. Swedish Muslims wished and hope to have a mosque in every city or county and that would have significant value to the Muslims of the country. It would be seen as a recognition of the existence of Muslims and Islam's right to exist in Sweden. The right to be a Muslim in Sweden is strengthened if there is legislated religious freedom that gives Muslim groups the right to build their own mosques without any obstacles and it would be a sign from the Swedish majority community that religious freedom can work in practice as well. A mosque has several roles other than simply being a place of worship. The mosque is the house of a great people that functions as a social and cultural institution, a place to meet, where the contact with the Swedish community and its fellow citizens happens daily. The demand to be allowed to build Mosques is a step in a process of Muslim integration that is occurring in Sweden. It is a matter of fundamental needs to keep and practice one's religion, but also to be able to improve the status of Muslims and gain respect and understanding. In such a situation it would greatly increase the sense of loyalty towards Sweden as one's new homeland, despite being a Muslim.

The creation of interest free loans

The construction of mosques ought to be financed by interest free loans as an alternative to voluntary contributions from abroad. The counties should take the responsibility to either provide security for these interest free loans or to lend money without interest for the construction of mosques for its Muslim inhabitants. The Swedish state should introduce the term "interest-free loans" and borrowers should have the right to deduct payments on interest free loans from the tax returns on the same grounds as loan interest

Islam and the school

To integrate Islam into Swedish schools reduces the demand for separate private Islamic schools. This includes elevating native language and religion [Islam] to the level of normal subject in the curriculum, where Muslim children have the possibility of being educated in homogenous groups using their own native language and their own religion in the County schools. Imams and native language teachers should have status as ordinary teachers in second native language and religion. In this way the demand for separate private schools would lessen and many of the problems Muslim students meet daily in school would easily be eliminated. Education in school would not be held in a different language from the Swedish, aside from the traditional Native Language education and the increase religious education in their own religion.

Islamic schools

To support the establishment of Islamic elementary schools in densely populated areas with many Muslims where Muslim students would have the opportunity to study in homogenous groups could reinforce the students cultural and religious identity and this way many of the problems that Muslim students meet every day would very simply be eliminated, among other things—Native Language, religious education, the issue of Muslim food, the gymnastics [physical education] question, and there could be a concrete way of helping girls and boys from Muslim countries to participate in segregated swimming classes and thereby graduate with a school diploma. Many Muslim students finish their High School education without being able to swim at all.

Health and Physical Education

Every county ought to have one night a week that should be a woman's evening, and respectively a man's evening, in the gym and the swimming hall. The entire hall [facility] should be open only for women or men, whereas other evenings would be for both genders. This is among other things about giving young girls from Muslim countries the opportunity to participate in swimming education and thereby getting a passing grade [equivalent to anything above an F] in gymnastics [physical education]. The prerequisite for this is that there are no young boys or adults in the swimming hall. The very presence of the opposite sex prevents certain girls with an immigrant background from taking advantage of the swimming education. Among other things ethnic and religious causes means that Muslim girls may not bathe together with young boys and men. It is both dangerous and unfair to that the girls are often not able to swim at all. Thousands of immigrant women can never use the swimming hall and training facilities. This is a pity. Exercise and activity is required by all and the problem with swimming education and training in the official locales is very great for immigrants, men and women.

Demands

We demand that county politicians should deliberate this matter immediately. The counties are responsible to make sure that school children get their degrees. All youth regardless of background shall have the opportunity to get a passing grade in gymnastics [physical education]. With good will this could easily be done.

Muslim holidays

That the riksdag [Parliament] create a law that gives Swedish Muslims the right to take vacation time during the Islamic holidays of Eid al fitr and Eid al Adha is a demand from all Muslims. Currently it is impossible to take time off to celebrate the vacation along with one's family. We demand special legislation in this matter that is the right to two days paid vacation in connection to the celebration of these holidays and that these two days cover the need to celebrate the holidays for Sunni and Shia Muslims and it proves that our religion and culture are accepted by the community.

Wishes and hopes

To solve the integration problem requires a true adjustment of legislation to accommodate the Muslim demand for vacation during the celebration of their holidays. To be able to keep one's religious way of life at the same time as the Muslims are integrated into the Swedish community, creates a real diversity in the community. Muslims demand that the government shall investigate the possibility of whether a special law is possible and how in this case it shall be motivated given existing legislation in the religious freedom law [Just as incomprehensible in the original, R.I.] Muslims, in other words, demand special treatment in terms of legislation as they are a minority and this would increase their status and protect them from the majority community.

UN and EU conventions

In Sweden one is often pointed to the constitutionally protected freedom of religion and, since January 1995, the equally constitutionally protected European convention about human rights and the fundamental liberties. The support for special legislation can be found even there, but Sweden today chooses to interpret the laws and conventions in such a narrow way that religious freedom is in practice reduced to a level that is unacceptable. Muslims as a religious minority has, like any other religious minority, according to, among other things, the UN international convention on civic and political rights, the right to have their own culture, the right to profess and practice their own religion or use their own language.

Friday prayer and time off

Two hours of time off for Friday prayer, between 12-14 o' clock wintertime, and between 13-15 o' clock summer time. The Friday prayer is an obligatory prayer that must be conducted collectively in the mosque. Employers are loathe to even talk about the matter with their Muslim employees. The state, as the biggest employer, ought to be an example for other employers in the private sector. Religious minorities' interests and struggle to preserve their identity coincides with both the legislation regarding religious freedom and the established legal minority rights. It would be good to investigate if there is support for special legislation in the relevant parts of the declarations, conventions, and legislation for our just demands.

Halal butchery (permitted foods for Muslims)

To contribute to giving the Muslims and Jews dispensation or special legislation to perform the Islamic and Jewish butchery. In a series of international speeches and conventions it is established that religious freedom is a human right. That certain food items are prohibited to Muslims, especially any products of pigs, is now commonly accepted in the Swedish communities. Institutional food halls have therefore been adapted to providing special food for Muslims and Jews. Since pig products are often used in food items and other every day objects, it has become more difficult for Muslims to determine what can be considered permissible foods. The Department of Food Items has therefore created a listing of any food items that contain pig products as a guide to Sweden's Muslims and Jews, but access to permitted Swedish meat (halal) can still be a problem. In Sweden animals may not be ritually slaughtered before anesthesia, but you are permitted to import food to be used for our permitted meals. It is imported meat that is used in institutional dining halls in, among other places, all schools. Halal butchery has become a special problem for Muslims. This is especially true in connection to the sacrificial feast (Kurban or Eid al Adha) where Muslim families slaughter a lamb due to religious traditions. Since 1937 it has been prohibited in Sweden to ritually slaughter large animals without preceding anesthesia. The demand for anesthesia was part of a larger reform initiated to protect animals. However the law did not only have animal welfare in mind, but an important argument was also a distaste for foreign customs. This prohibition against slaughtering according to Jewish and Muslim traditions remains all the same. It has several times been brought up in the *riksdag* [Parliament], but the decision makers have been unwilling to change their attitude. As late as 1992 a study made by the ministry of agriculture determined that ritual slaughter cannot be accepted in Sweden. Now, however, there is a new study being made by the department of agriculture and we hope that the decision makers will come to a positive conclusion.

Burial Grounds

Despite the fact that Islam has existed for 32 years as an organized religion in Sweden, the construction of burial grounds has been constantly hampered. Other than in the forest churchyard in Stockholm, there are Muslim burial grounds in 20 something counties, but that is not enough. Today there are Muslims in nearly 100 counties that lack burial grounds. The biggest general problem that Muslims encounter is that their dead are to be buried as quickly as possible, according to Islamic custom, and by a Muslim burial in their home county. Muslims demand that the Union of Congregations [head organ] in the Swedish Church co-operates with the country's counties to reserve burial plots in all counties that have Muslim inhabitants. Muslims also demand that the ombudsman in each province will, in matters of funerals, take full responsibility to accommodate the Muslim demands for burial grounds.

Imam education in Sweden

Starting Imam education in Swedish universities and colleges is a demand from the Muslim nations and from Swedish authorities. The education can be based partly on theology education, partly on Native Language (Arabic) education. Students can get permission to function as language and theology [religion] teachers. This education can create a natural integration of Islam in Swedish schools, and reduce the demand for private schools.

Opinion making

That the Swedish legal system is democratic and non-discriminating is fine, but this isn't always enough as the Muslims see it. People that belong to minority groups can require special rights to be able to exist on an equal footing with the majority. The biggest problem that Muslims face is the opinions of the majority. The community is responsible [or guilty] for trying to assimilate the immigrants of the nation. Both in daily speech and learned discussion the community uses such concepts and expressions in regards to Muslims that are untrue, distorted, and laden with negative undertones. Borders are made between "us" and "them." As members of the dominant majority culture you're equipped with your own cultural blinkers that give you great trouble when it comes to seeing the whole picture. The stark one sided focusing on certain problems strengthens the already widespread idea that "the immigrants have forced their way into Sweden and they are a burden on the country's natural resources," and that "they're the only ones to blame for the high unemployment and economic crisis, as well as the cause of their own problems." Today you openly speak about the Muslims as if they are not proper, full members of the Swedish community. The negative image of Muslims is maintained and strengthened by the media and not least by the Swedish educational system. Muslims immediately pick up on the negative connotations [subtext, undertone] that are used to describe their existence. It cannot be denied that this will affect their self-image and the end result is that they are kept outside of the community. Many Muslims experience discrimination, especially at work or when they are looking for housing. The biggest problem in the integration politics is that second generation children and youths cannot find their place in every day life. This should be seen as an expression of negative Swedish cultural influence that has rubbed off on the youth.

Wishes and Hopes

Sweden's Muslims express displeasure towards those local politicians who are not doing anything to support the struggle against Islamophobia in Sweden. The Muslims express displeasure towards employers, both in the private and the public sectors, since they [the Muslims] cannot get work because of their origin, skin color, foreign name and religion. Muslims demand that the community should treat them in the same way as you treat native Swedes and the Muslims want to live under the same conditions as their Swedish neighbors. Muslims want help to create a creative future on the basis of their cultural background and religious allegiance; if this is done, they will feel at home in their new homeland. If the Security Police will continue to consider Islam a violent religion and Muslims as a security risk, the community will force young religious Muslims to segregate and that is not good either for the community or for the Muslims. Islamic culture should be a part of the multi-cultural community. It is up to the community as the maintainer of the dominant culture to recognize Muslims as full fellow citizens, and give Muslims the same social, cultural, economic, political, religious, and personal rights as the "native Swedes" enjoy themselves.[50]

Mahmoud Aldebe
Swedish Muslim Association

The link has been established between the pressing demands of Swedish Muslims on the eve of elections and the shamefully sycophantic policies of the Swedish government towards Muslims and against Israel, even as they run bluntly counter to the European consensus of which it purports to be part. After coping out of the air-maneuvers where Israel participated, the Swedes indeed invited and gave a visa to a member of the Hamas government in Gaza, which is shunned even by the French. The invited Minister of Refugees, Atef Adwan, gave a speech in Malmo, the third largest city in Sweden, during the "fourth international conference concerning the right of Palestinian refugees to return to a free Palestine," which means a Palestine free from Jews and Israel, or in other words an end to Israel. According to the Swedish daily paper *Sydsvenskan*, Adwan made the following remark: "By allowing me to travel here the Swedish government is sending a clear message to our people that somebody is at our side." Perhaps he is right. That a representative of the Hamas terrorist organization chose to begin his European tour by visiting Sweden, and that he was given a visa to do so, is telling of the soft mentality among European socialist governments towards terrorism. Swedish politics is full of similar examples. Two members of the Swedish Parliament have recently attempted to invite the group leader of Hamas, Salah Mohammed al-Bardawil, to the Swedish Parliament. The fact that Hamas is a terrorist organization with the blood of innocent civilians on its hands does not seem to bother the Swedish politicians too much. Indeed, as the September 2006 elections drew closer, it seemed as if the Swedish left was openly embracing radical Islamic groups. Recently, Swedish public television revealed that the leading Social Democratic party has started fishing for votes with the help of radical Muslims clergies. For several years the Christian wing of the Social Democratic party, called The Brotherhood, has been working with the influential Muslim leader Mahmoud Aldebe, president of Sweden's Muslim Association. But the new ally of the Social Democrats is anything but democratic. Already in 1999, Aldebe went on radio proposing that *Sharia*—the Islamic law—be introduced in Sweden. In addition, Aldebe has in a letter to the Swedish minister of Justice in 2003 involved himself in a heated debate regarding an incident of honor-related murder where a Kurdish girl was murdered by her two uncles; shot several times in the head. Aldebe did not condemn the murderers—rather he forcefully defended the perpetrators. Aldebe sees the entire debate regarding honor-related murders as an attack against the Islamic religion and claims in his letter that a public debate regarding these acts of murder risk to "encourage immigrant girls to revolt against the tradition of the families and their religious values."

One might ask how a democratic party can justify co-operating with Sweden's Muslim Association. During the above-mentioned documentary the Social Democrat Ola Johansson referred to the book *Social Justice in Islam* by the Islamic ideologue Sayyid Qutb as proof that the social democratic ideology could find common ground with Islamic ideas. As the Swedish paper *Expressen* has exposed, Sayyid Qutb was not only a social thinker; he was also inspired by the German Nazi movement. He was an important figure in the Egyptian Islamic movement in the 1950s and remains an inspiration for Muslim extremists. Sayyid Qutb calls for an all out war against the Western civilization; he hates liberal democracy, views capitalism as a sick idea and is an extreme anti-Semite. Perhaps it is not a coincidence that Qutb's writings were translated to Dutch by Mohammed Bouyeri, the murderer of Theo van Gogh. There is little sign that the unholy alliance between the Swedish Social Democrats and radical Muslims is ending. After the election in 2002, Sweden's Muslim Association sent a letter to the re-elected Social Democratic Prime Minister Goran Persson, congratulating him on his victory and hoping that Persson would work for implementing some of the demands of the Association in the future. It will be interesting to see if this emerging alliance will become part of daily political life in Sweden.[51]

Even more embarrassing was Persson's attempt to justify the invitation of the Hamas Minister, which in fact amounted to acceptance of his bid to wipe Israel out. He backed the granting of that visa to a Hamas Minister after saying earlier that leaders of the group could not receive visas to enter European Union countries. Israel expectedly expressed "its regret" over Sweden's decision to be the first European country to grant a visa to a Hamas minister, but Persson persisted that the consulate official in Jerusalem who granted the visa to the Palestinian minister Adwan was only following the rules. "I appreciate the position by Sweden which dealt with the issue not on political grounds but on purely academic grounds," said Adwan, echoed by Persson's declaration to Swedish Television, that "this (decision) follows a body of regulations which our civil servants handle." He added that "If decisions to grant visas become party politics and are made by the prime minister, we are on a slippery slope. It is important for me to say that we must not mix up the facts here. Hamas has been labeled a terrorist organization and there are people who are more or less loosely tied to it, but that does not mean their rights to get visas disappear." What "right to get a visa"? If everybody had a right to get a visa, then nobody would have needed it. It is exactly to screen out terrorists and indecent applicants that right is given to the granting countries to approve or deny visas. The Swedish PM said he had not been informed of the decision to let Adwan visit Sweden, made by the consul-general in Jerusalem. By the same breath Persson dismissed the possibility that Hamas legislator Salah al-Bardaweel would be granted a visa to enter Sweden."We have no national interest in inviting them and will therefore follow the guidelines that Hamas leaders cannot have visas to visit Schengen countries," Persson told TT news agency during a visit to Finland.[52] But, who could then take his statement seriously after a visa was granted and justified?

While Israel was furious and its Foreign Ministry spokesman Mark Regev slammed the decision "because the way to promote positive change in the Palestinian Authority is to resolutely support the Quartet's benchmarks, and giving recognition to an unreformed terrorist cannot help that process," Hamas spokesman, Sami Abu Zuhri, understandably regarded that as a victory, since it was the first time an official in the new Hamas-led government was given a visa to a European country. "We encourage other European countries to follow the brave move by the Swedish authorities," Zuhri said. The European Union, of which Sweden is a member, has severed political contacts with the Hamas-led Palestinian Authority, which took power on 29 March 2006. The bloc has temporarily suspended payments to and through the Palestinian government because it has not met the international community's three conditions of recognizing Israel, renouncing violence and accepting past peace agreements. But Persson was not impressed, and on the back of Israel and in contravention of European consensus, he elected party politics over his country's international and moral commitments. News of the invitation spread just one day after Sweden's prime minister ruled out a visit by another Hamas politician, Salah al-Bardaweel, saying Sweden would not give him a visa because the European Union brands the Islamic group terrorists. Palestinians living in the southern Swedish city of Malmo, home to the biggest Muslim community in Scandinavia, had invited the Hamas delegation, including the Hamas politician, to visit in mid-May, 2006. They were also due to meet members of parliament. France has already denied Salah al-Bardaweel a visa, but the Hamas lawmaker said Monday he would apply to other countries to join a delegation of four Palestinians from other parties on a tour of Europe, including Sweden's neighbor Norway. Upon arriving to Malmo, Adwan said he hoped that the Palestinian Authority under Hamas will now establish further contacts in Europe. "I saw no protests as I was coming here," he said after arriving at Folkets Park ahead of the conference. "I believe that this corresponds to the wishes of the Swedish people. They respect human rights," he said at a press conference. Adwan said that he was representing the Palestinian administration, not Hamas. "With great resolution we will build up the confidence of the Europeans," he said, although he did not believe that the visit to Sweden was a breakthrough. "But it serves peace," he added. "We have many friends in Europe."The conference he was visiting was the fourth of its kind for Palestinians exiled in Europe. Its focus is on demands for the rights of Palestinians to return." We must not forget that we once had a country. It is important that we get the right to return," Adwan said. Before his speech, 700 conference participants chanted "With our souls, we protect you, Palestine." In his speech Adwan attacked the blockade started against the Palestinian territories after Hamas's election victory." It was a free and fair election, but we were punished afterwards. It is aggression without parallel. The only crime we committed was to undergo a democratic process," he said. According to Adwan the blockade has led to children suffering from lack of food and healthcare. In a speech shown to the conference hall, Sweden was also thanked by Ismail Hania, the Palestinian Hamas Prime Minister, for making Adwan's visit possible. He also called the blockade unjust and an attempt to force the Palestinians to their knees. Adwan described Israel as an enemy that wants everything without giving anything.[53]

Scandinavia is renowned for its welfare system, which immigrants, legal and illegal, have been attracted to and learned to exploit to their ends. The policies of the welfare state can in the short term reduce the economic poverty of low-income takers. But in the long run, the same policies tend to create a dependence on the state and reduce the capability of individuals, families and the civil society to take care of themselves. Also, left of center governments usually put the interest of labor unions before that of ordinary citizens, creating unemployment as a consequence of labor market regulations. Nowhere is this more evident than among immigrants in the Swedish welfare state. During the 1950s and the 1960s, Sweden experienced strong economic growth. The combination of a relatively free economy and the fact that Sweden did not participate in the Second World War (due to a submissive policy towards the Nazis) allowed Swedish industry to rapidly expand. During this period, some 600,000 people came to Sweden as work force immigrants. Their absorption into the labor market was successful and the immigrants could contribute to the economic well-being of Sweden. From the immigrants point of view, they were able to function and prosper in the society. However, the labor unions became threatened by the competition from foreign labor and influenced the Social Democratic government to change the immigration laws, forcing employers to supply foreign workers with 240 hours of lectures in Swedish. Since employers not only had to provide this education, but also pay full salaries during this period, it became uneconomical to hire workers from abroad. Under the false pretense that they were caring for the well-being of foreign workers, the unions managed to bring labor immigration to a halt. During the following decades, Sweden experienced sizable refugee immigration. These immigrants usually came from non-European countries and had a relatively high degree of education. Still, they found it very difficult to find jobs in Sweden, as the political system was shifting evermore towards high taxes, generous welfare benefits and labor market regulations. As the massive Swedish welfare state was taking form, Sweden experienced a drastic change in the labor market participation of immigrants. The percentage of the adult population active in the labor market for those with a foreign citizenship was 20% higher in 1950 compared to those with a Swedish citizenship. As more and more immigrants became dependent on welfare benefits, this figure gradually fell to 30% below that of those with a Swedish citizenship in 2000.[54]

Since labor market participation in Swedish statistics can include involvement in government labor market programs, this figure actually underestimates the problematic development in Sweden. The average yearly income from labor for those with a foreign citizenship was 22% higher than those with a Swedish citizenship in 1968. In 1999 it was 67% lower. This drop more accurately shows the change from workforce to welfare. The waves of immigrants that arrived to Sweden particularly during the 1980s and the 1990 systematically became dependent on various forms of government subsidies, rather than work, as a means of income. The role of families and civil society diminished and crime rates rose to high levels. As the entry into the labor market was difficult, many immigrants never got the chance of establishing themselves in the Swedish labor market. Groups that flourished in the United Kingdom or in the United States due to a combination of good education and entrepreneurship, such as immigrants from Iran or Lebanon, remained dependent in the state in Sweden. In 2001 persons born outside of Sweden on average received seven times more social security than those born in Sweden. Today, both first and second-generation immigrants in Sweden, most of whom are Muslim, are strongly dependent on various government handouts. Those growing up in immigrant dense neighborhoods come from environments where individual responsibility, respect for families and the rule of law are much less strongly rooted compared to the rest of society. Many young immigrants are disillusioned regarding the opportunities to make a living for themselves through hard work and education, while crime levels remain high. The welfare state does help immigrants in the short run by supplying generous handouts beyond measure. But in the long run, the effect of the policies is clear: the arguably strong social capital among many immigrant groups has diminished due to welfare dependence. These policies have been damaging both for the Swedish society and the immigrants arriving to it. It is a clear reminder that socialism might very well be the cause, rather than the cure, for poverty. But in terms of Muslim immigrants, the temptation to improve their living by joining the welfare system, by far overwhelms the economic consideration about their future, much less the future of Sweden. Socialist parties which more and more depend on their votes, are trapped in their policy of maintaining the system, leaving to the future generations the job of cleaning up the ramifications of the welfare policies.[55]

Another sideline of the policy of the Swedish government to please its Muslim population, has been the adoption by Sweden's state-owned alcohol retail monopoly, *Systembolaget*, of labeling Israeli *Golan* and *Yarden* wines as "made in Israel-occupied Syrian territories." According to the company's spokesman, Bjorn Rydberg, the decision was made after clients complained about the previous label, which stated the wine was made in Israel. The change was made after the company consulted with the Swedish Foreign Ministry. "It's the ministry's recommendation that we are following," Rydberg said. However, "because of the criticism, we will consider changing the label again," he said. Although Swedish Foreign Minister Jan Eliasson and his Israeli counterpart, Tzipi Livni met recently to discuss the visa granted to Hamas, some tension still remains over the labeling issue. In April 2006, Sweden pulled out of a European military exercise because of Israeli participation. And in May, Sweden hosted Hamas minister Atef Adwan. Adwan, who was invited by local politicians, was granted a visa to visit Sweden, which he also used to visit other European countries, which had declared Hamas to be a terrorist organization. Systembolaget's decision is "upsetting and unfair," said Annelia Enochson, from Sweden's Christian Democratic Party. "It means Israel receives special treatment, and it also politicizes the state-owned alcohol company." Rydberg maintained that the company was not trying to make a political statement. "We have no foreign policy ambitions," he said. Systembolaget was created in the nineteenth century to minimize alcohol-related problems by selling alcohol in a responsible way.[56] It would have been interesting for the Swedes and their other Scandinavian partners, who constantly criticize Israel over the "collective punishment" she inflicts upon the Palestinians, to ponder over the collective punishment inflicted upon them by the Palestinians, and their necessity to resort to the forces of the "Occupier" to rescue them from that punishment. On February 8, 2006, in the context of the Cartoon Affair, 60 international observers from TIPH (Temporary International Presence in Hebron)—including 20 Danes and Norwegians—were forced to flee their headquarters, after being attacked by a group of Palestinians. Since the PA police were unable to defend them from the demonstrators, the IDF had to be summoned for the job. The irony of the situation lay in the fact that it was the Palestinians who had insisted upon having these international observers—after the 1994 Baruch Goldstein massacre of a group of Muslims praying at the Cave of the Patriarchs in Hebron—as protection from Israel. Now the TIPH leadership was asking Israeli soldiers for protection from a Palestinian onslaught, and the *protégés* were Norwegians and Swedes who were lumped together with the Danes, the stars of the Affair, in what amounted to collective punishment.

The Muslim threat in Sweden often radiates outwardly, for even if that country is not immediately and directly menaced for now, it serves as a very fertile and adequate grounds to mount plots against other European countries. British police busted into a Swede's apartment in Gothenburg and confiscated books, mobile phones and computers, *Aftonbladet* has reported. The tenant, Abu Usama el Swede (the "Swede"), told *Aftonbladet* he didn't know why British police with the help of the Swedish Security Service (Sapo) raided his home. Four apartments were hit during the raid in the Hammarkullen area. Two men were detained and one woman was questioned. Sapo spokesman Anders Thornberg confirmed that the British police had submitted a rogatory letter, which can be used by authorities in one country to request help from counterparts abroad, to deputy chief prosecutor Agneta Hilding Qvarnstrom. "A rogatory letter was received from British police. This was then examined, Agneta Hilding Qvarnstrom," told *The Local*. "Use of such rogatory letters is quite normal procedure," she added. The 28-year-old Swede was born in Sweden and converted to Islam at the end of the 1990s. He became known after putting messages on the Internet after controversial Christian preacher Runar Sogaard called Muhammad a "confused pedophile," the paper reported. Abu Usama has congratulated suicide bombers and also written, "May Allah help us destroy Islam's enemies and terrorize this scum," *Aftonbladet* reported. "They haven't given me any evidence," he said about the raid, which according to *Aftonbladet* took place in May 2006. His detainment could be regarding an e-mail sent from a man who is in custody for terrorist crimes in England, said the paper. *Aftonbladet* also said he was also on a telephone list that belongs to a Swede suspected to have prepared an attempted attack in Sarajevo.[57]

Notes

1.   Most of the narrative for this affair relies on Ulla Holm's "The Danish Ugly Duckling and the Mohammed Cartoons," *DIIS Brief*, Dansk Institut for Internationale Studier, Copenhagen, February 2006.
2.   See for example, the apology in the *Berlingske Titende*, 8 February 2006.
3.   *Ibid.*
4.   For a more elaborate expansion of this theme, which is a watershed in the relation of Europe to its Muslims minorities, see Chapter Seven.
5.   Citing the *Aftonbladet*, Dhimmi Watch, 9 September 2004.
6.   *Sydsvenskan, Ibid.*
7.   *Expressen, Ibid.*
8.   *Ibid.*
9.   *Dhimmi Watch*, 28 October 2004.
10.   *Ibid.*
11.   Ghazanfar Ali Khan, "Products of Danish Dairy Company Return to Supermarket Shelves" *Arab News* (Saudi Arabia) 4 April 2006.
12.   Hassan Fattah and Nada al-Sawi, "Possible Crack in the Boycott of Danish Goods," *New York Times*, 5 April 2006.
13.   Yassin Musharbash and Anna Reimann." Crisis in Denmark," *Spiegel Online*—1 February 2006 http://www.spiegel.de/international/0,1518,398624,00.html
14.   *Ibid.*
15.   Yassin Musharbash and Anna Reimann." Crisis in Denmark," *Spiegel Online*—1 February 2006. http://www.spiegel.de/international/0,1518,398624,00.html

16. "Imam gives up European dream: Western democracy has failed to give equal rights to Muslims, says the controversial imam, Abu Laban, as he announces plans to leave Denmark," *Copenhagen Post*, 11 May 2006.

17. "Controversial imam threatens to return to Gaza," *Copenhagen Post*—18 May 2006.

18. *Ibid.*

19. "Turkey: 56 Mayors Face Trial," *New York Times*—20 June 2006.

20. *Dagbladet* (Norway), 13 March 2006.

21. Yaakov Lappin, http://www.ynetnews.com/articles/0,7340,L-3135697,00.html, 1 September 2005 This site is accompanied by videos showing men training with explosives threatening Sweden with "suffering in the name of Allah."

22. Yahia Abu Zakariya, IslamOnline.net—8 November 2003, http://www.islamonline. net/English/News/2003-11/08/article08.shtml.

23. Gothenburg, Sweden, http://www.upprop.net/pressrelease.php?

24. *Ibid.*

25. Hadith collected in Sahih Bukhari, Volume 4, Book 52, Number 177, cited by the Hamas Platform, see R. Israeli, "The Charter Of Allah: the Platform of the Islamic Resistance Movement," in R. Israeli, *Fundamentalist Islam and Israel*, University Press of America, Lanham and NY, 1993

26. This and the following passages are based on a selection of stories, all from *The Local* in English, and on the government's announcement about the funding of the repair of the Malmo Mosque. http://www.thelocal.se/article.php?ID=3392&date=20060327 27 March 2006.

27. *Ibid.*

28. *Ibid.*

29. *Ibid.*

30. David Stavrou's school book depicting Muhammad was withdrawn, as a result of the controversy regarding the cartoons. See http://www.thelocal.se/article. php?ID=2998&date=20060206, *The Local*, 6 February 2006.

31. *The Local*, 15 December 2005, http://www.thelocal.se/article.php?ID=2696&date=20051215

32. *Ibid*, 24 November 2005.

33. *The Local*, 18 November 2005. http://www.thelocal.se/article.php?ID=2525&date=20051118

34. *Ibid.*

35. *Ibid.*

36. *Ibid.* 16 November 2005.

37. Al-Qaeda "recruited from Sweden," *The Local* 1 October 2005 http://www.thelocal.se/article.php?ID=2197&date=2005

38. *Ibid.*

39. "Man linked to London bombings threatens Sweden," *The Local*, 22 July 2005 http://www.thelocal.se/article.php?ID=1775&date=2005

40. "Swede suspected of links to London bombings," *The Local*, 21 July 2005, based on AFP. http://www.thelocal.se/article.php?ID=1766&date=20050721

41. "Court finds family guilty of honour killing," *Jyllands-Posten* 27 June 2006.

42. "Muslim schools seek funding from Saudi "fundamentalists," *The Local*, 7 June 2005. http://www.thelocal.se/article.php?ID=1559&date=20050607. based on reports by Andy Butterworth, for *Dagens Nyheter*, and *Sveriges Radio*.

43. "Muslims protest against celebrity preacher," *The Local*, 25 April, 2005. http://www.thelocal.se/article.php?ID=1327&date=20050425

44. Muslims protest against celebrity preacher," *The Local,* 25 April 2005 http://www.thelocal.se/article.php?ID=1327&date=2005042

45. Norwegian prime minister slams IKEA, http://www.thelocal.se/article.php?ID= 1085&date=20050310

46. "IAF participation a deal breaker," *Jerusalem Post,* 26 April, 2006; see also Jerusalem Post Lead Article of 30 April 2006.

47. "Sweden's anti-peace policy," Lead Article, *Jerusalem Post,* 30 April 2006.

48. "separate laws for Muslims' idea slammed," *The Local*—(Sweden's News in English)—28 April 2006 http://www.thelocal.se/article.php?ID=3674&date=20060428

49. "Muslim Council: no support for special laws," *The Local*—29 April 2006 http://www.thelocal.se/article.php?ID=3688&date=20060429

50. "Post subject: The List of Musulman Demands to Swedish Political Parties," *Divine Salamis BBS: The discussion board for the Divine Salamis community 29 April 2006.* http://www.divine-salamis.com/phpBB/viewtopic.php?t=1447

51. Nima Sanandaji, "Sweden's Unholy Alliance," *FrontPageMagazine.com*, 19 May 2006.

52. "Swedish PM defends decision to grant visa to Hamas minister," www.haaretz. com, 5 May 2006.

53. *Ibid.* See also "Hamas minister thanks Sweden for visa" *The Local*—Sweden's News in English, 6 May 2006 http://www.thelocal.se/article.php?ID=3738&date=20060506&PHPSESSID=0 4d908160f98e39972b6afe9e01248b5

54. Nima Sanandaji, "Sweden's Immigration Nightmare," *FrontPageMagazine.com*, 2 June 2006.

55. *Ibid.*

56. David Stavrou, "Swedish company labels Golan wines," *Jerusalem Post,* 6 June 2006.

57. Adam Ewing. *"British police in Gothenburg 'terror' raid," The Local: Sweden's news in English,* 30 May 2006.

5

The Re-Islamization of the Balkans

The Problem

On 12 February 1997, on the occasion of the 'Id al-Fitr Festival, the Uighur rebels in Chinese Central Asia published in their Internet site an appeal to all Muslims to heed the unfolding events in Bosnia. "What kind of festival is this," asked they, "when 250,000 Muslims are being murdered, tortured and raped in Bosnia?" They sent their heartfelt thanks to the "Iranian people who are sending help in spite of the West's embargo," and accused the West of "stopping the Muslims when they were about to win, while aiding at the same time the Serbian Fascists." Evidently, the Uighurs in China's Northwest had their own axe to grind when they used the universal festival which linked all Muslims together to draw attention to their own plight in Xinjiang, where their own land was being "robbed" by the "fascists" of China. However, as they thanked the Iranians for their assistance to the Bosnians, they might have also been referring to the backing that Islamic countries in the Middle East were providing the Uighurs and other Islamic groups in China,[1] something that was recognized by and caused alarm in the midst of, the China leadership.[2]

In April 1998 the State Department published its annual report on global terrorism. Among other things it referred to the unidentified terrorists who acted against the international presence in Bosnia, and especially to the Mujahidin who had served in the Bosnian army during the civil war, but were now engaged in warrant killings. According to that report, the Bosnian government began arresting some of those loose terrorists, and by November 1997, it had incarcerated twenty of them, who were identified as Arabs or Bosnian Muslims.[3] In the same year of 1998 there were reports that Iranian intelligence agents were mounting extensive operations and even infiltrated the American program to train the Bosnian army. According to those reports, more than 200 Iranian agents were identified as "having insinuated themselves into Bosnian Muslim political and social circles … to gather information ant to thwart western interests in Bosnia." Those agents, it was believed, could be helpful in planning terrorist attacks against NATO forces or targets.[4] Taken together, these reports do identify the "unidentified terrorists" mentioned above. Moreover, these reports link together into an Islamic International centered around Iran, most of the major terrorist activities that are carried out by Islamists, from the Israeli Embassy in Buenos Aires (1992); the international gathering of Islamic terrorist organizations in Teheran (1997); the Hizbullah stepped-up activities against Israel in the late 1990s; the arrest in Israel of Stefan Smirak, a would-be "suicide-bomber" for Hizbullah (November, 1997); the attacks against American interests in the Gulf, East Africa and on American soil (throughout the 1990s)[5] to say nothing of the Muslim separatists in China, and the Islamic resurgence in Bosnia and Kosovo.

People today speak of the clashes between Serbs and Muslims in Bosnia, Serbs and Albanians in Kosovo, in terms of ethno-national conflicts, with the more numerous Serbs figuring as the oppressors and their rivals as the underdogs and the oppressed. *Prima facie,* the very usage of the terms Serbs (and Croats for that matter) against Muslims, equates the latter (essentially members of a faith and civilization) to the former who clearly belong to religio-ethnic groups. This points out to the fact that not only did Yugoslavian statism and universalistic communism fail to obliterate ethnic and kinship identities (real or imagined), but that communal interest overrides the state umbrella, economic interest or even sheer common sense. But this also raises the question of whether Islam, a universal religion predominant in more than 50 countries around the world, is or can be perceived as a nationalism that is particularistic by definition.

The Historical Underpinnings

After the Arab conquests had exhausted the immense primeval energies released by Islam since its inception in the seventh century and up until the ninth century, the Turks of Central Asia who arrived on the scene in the eleventh century gave a new impetus to Islamic expansion, this time into the heart of Europe. As Bat Ye'or put it:

> The Islamization of the Turks within the Muslim Empire integrated new and unlimited forces. Uncouth and hardy, they had, since the ninth century, supplied contingents of slaves exclusively reserved for the Abbasid Caliph's guard and for military service. Thus, quite naturally, the ideology and tactics of jihad inflamed the warlike tendencies of their tribes, already roaming the Asiatic borders of the Greek and Armenian lands. They joined its ranks with the enthusiasm of neophytes, and their ravages facilitated the Islamization and Turkification of Armenia, the Greek territories of Anatolia and the Balkans. Yet, it is also true that their depredations could not be controlled by the Muslim state and often harmed its economic interests.[6]

The Ottoman state, which reached Vienna at the pinnacle of its existence, was multi-ethnic and multi-religious, and under its Muslim-majority dominance Christians, Jews and others lived side-by-side for many centuries. However, this coexistence was not born out of a modern concept of tolerance of the other on the basis of acceptance of differences and equality to all, but on a sense of supe-

riority, which tolerated the others in spite of their inferiority. Thus, even though
Turks, or Muslims, may have constituted the minority population in some areas
of the Empire, they reigned supreme by virtue of their Muslim master status,
while the various Christian groups (and Jews for that matter), were relegated to
the status of "protected people" (the *dhimmi*).[7] Christians and others who had
integrated into the Ottoman system by embracing Islam, speaking Turkish and
going into the Imperial service, soon became part and parcel of the Ottoman
culture even when they kept their attachment to their ethnic origin and to their
mother tongue. The case in point were the Bosnians many of whom felt privileged to go into the *devsirme* system of enrolling their boys to the prestigious
Janissary corps, and in the course of time were Islamized though they preserved
their Slavic roots and language.[8]

The Balkans were conquered by the Ottomans from the middle of the fifteenth
century on. Serbia fell in 1459, and four years later Bosnia with Herzegovina
succumbing to the conquerors in 1483. Caught between the economic interest of
milking the tax-paying *dhimmis*, which necessitated maintaining the conquered
population in place instead of expelling or converting it by force, and the military
and security needs which required that the Muslim population be numerous
enough to ensure the loyalty to the Empire, the Ottomans tended to implement
the latter choice in the Balkans. They adopted a policy of deporting the native
populations and settling their own people, or other conquered people, in their
stead, thus ensuring that no local minority should envisage any insurgency among
a Muslim population. In Bosnia, the process of Islamization was reinforced by
the turncoats who flocked to Islam and became the worse oppressors of their
former coreligionists. So much so, that the Bosnians were notorious for their
role in the Ottoman administration, military and especially the Janissaries.[9]

As late as 1875, way after the introduction of the tanzimat reforms which
were supposed to redress the situation of the non-Muslims throughout the Empire, the British Ambassador in Istanbul reported that the Ottoman authorities
in Bosnia recognized the impossibility to administer justice in equality between
the Muslims and the Christians, inasmuch as the ruling Muslim courts accepted
no written or oral evidence from Christians. One 1876 report from Bosna-Serai
(Sarajevo) by the British Consul in town, tells the whole story:

> About a month ago, an Austrian subject named Jean Udilak, was attacked and robbed
> between Sarajevo and Visoka by nine Bashi-Bazouks. The act was witnessed by a
> respectable Mussulman of this time named Nouri Aga Varinika, and he was called
> as a witness when the affair was brought before the Sarajevo Tribunal. His testimony
> was in favor of the Austrian, and the next day he was sent for by the Vice-President
> and one of the members of the Court and threatened with imprisonment for daring
> to testify against his coreligionists.[10]

As Majer tells us, Muslims, Christians (and Jews for that matter), could keep
to themselves in their own communities, with their lifestyles, rituals and festivals
running without hindrance, except in case of inter-marriage. For here, the only

allowed combination was Muslim men taking in Christian (or Jewish) wives, which consecrated their joint offspring as full-right Muslims. The result was that while non-Muslim culture merged into the predominant Islam, there was also an outside input into the Muslim culture with material culture (food, dress, habits, language) growing to become common to all. All this was acceptable to the Ottoman authorities who were reluctant to interfere, but as soon as the *dhimmis* became wealthy and were conspicuous in their dress and demeanor, that was considered a provocation to the Muslim population and dealt with accordingly. Christians who wanted to improve their lot in Bosnia and Albania could always do so through conversion to Islam or seek the protection of their Muslim family members.[11]

Towards the end of the Ottoman rule, as economic problems arose and the state was no longer able to enforce law and order in the face of the nationalist awakening in the various provinces of the Empire, local rule grew more despotic in an attempt to hold on to the territories that were slipping out of the Porte's grip. The notions of equality coming from liberal Europe, which made the maintenance of legal and religious inequities untenable; conjugated into national terms, and spelled out independence from the Ottoman yoke since the idea of a ruling Empire held together by Islam was no longer operative. It was ironically the Ottoman attempts at modernity, opening up the system, addressing individuals instead of traditional communities, which brought to its downfall and opened the new vistas of nationalism and independence in the Balkans as elsewhere, a situation not unlike Eastern Europe after the Gorbachev Perestroika in the late 1980s and early 1990s. But in view of the Greek and Bulgarian plans for a Balkan Federation under their aegis, to take over from the Ottomans,[12] and the tax repression imposed by the Bosnian Muslims, the Serbs rose up in arms (1875), and many of them ran into hiding, leaving behind children, the old and women, something reminiscent of the horrors of the Bosnian War and then the Kosovo War more than one century later. Preydor and Banja Luka were the most harmed by the insurgents when Serb churches and homes were burned.[13]

According to reports from the time of the rebellion, the Bosnian Muslims, descendants of converted Slavs who had become the landowners and acceded to the status of aristocracy by virtue of their conversion, now practiced their faith fanatically and ruthlessly towards their Orthodox compatriots who would rather die in battle than submit to the tax exactions. What made things worse, again like in the recent events in Bosnia, was that the Catholics allied to the Muslims against the Orthodox Serbs. An eyewitness of the time reports:

> United under oppression, it was natural that the Serbs should respond by rebellion. But in the entire northern part of Bosnia and Turkish Croatia … the antagonism between the two [Catholic and Orthodox] denominations is vast enough for us to have eye-witnessed Catholics marching on the heels of the Turks against Greek insurgents…. By an inexplicable aberration, the priests of the two denominations entertain hatred [towards each other] and we could say without exaggerating that, if

given the choice the Catholics would rather be dominated by the Turks than by the Orthodox Serbs.[14]

The reporter concluded that the Muslims of Bosnia maintained their loyalty to the Ottomans, and therefore there was no chance of a fusion between the populations, in view of the fact that those Serbs whose ancestors had embraced Islam as a political expediency, were now too imbued with it and too captured by the teachings of their Holy Book to relent from their intense hatred which had germinated in their bodies and taken them over completely.[15] But this was to be only a foretaste for things to come, as henceforth the politics of Bosnia would be dominated by the alliance of two of its major religious groups, and later ethno-national communities, against the third. After the Berlin Congress and the occupation of Bosnia by the Austro-Hungarian Empire, the Serbs allied with the Muslims against the occupiers, who were supported by the Catholics in the province. The Hungarian governor of the province tried valiantly to create a new Bosnian identity merging together its three principal communities but he failed.[16] But the annexation of Bosnia by the occupiers in 1908, created a new alliance: the Serbs, who wished their merger with Serbia, were pitted against the Croat-Muslim coalition who would rather reconcile to their occupation than allow the Serbs to implement their dream. As a result, repression of the Serbs in Bosnia, coupled with the expulsion of Serbs from Kosovo, brought to a record level the bitterness of the occupied Serbs against their oppressors. Sukrija Kurtovic, a Bosnian Muslim, sought the differentiation between ethno-nationality and religion, and pleaded for the unity of the Bosnians with the Serbs in one single national group by reason of their common Serbian roots, arguing that Islam was a common religion of the Bosnians and the Turks, but that in itself did not make them share any national common ground.[17] The idea of Yugoslavism, a larger entity where all the ethnic and religious groups could find their common identity, came to the fore after the Balkan wars and precipitated World War I following the Sarajevo murder of the heir to the Austro-Hungarian throne in 1914. That war reinforced the Croat-Muslim alliance in Bosnia, which swore to expel the Serbs from Bosnia altogether and acted upon its vow by perpetrating large-scale massacres of the Serbs, and demonstrated the vanity of an all-Yugoslavian identity.[18]

A Yugoslavian state was created in 1918 nevertheless, which once again attempted to fuse its components in the ethnic and linguistic domains and leave, as befits a modern European state, the question of religion to the realm of each individual. However, while the Serbs and the Croats of Bosnia could look up to Belgrade and Zagreb, respectively, the Muslims were left to vacillate between their Muslim, Ottoman, local, and Slavic roots. At first they allied with the stronger Serbs and turned their eyes on Belgrade where they ensured for themselves some privileges, but wary of the competition between the Croats who championed their nationalism and the Serbs who regarded themselves as the guardians of Yugoslavian unity, they focused more and more on their local and religious identity in the form of a Muslim Party (JMO), while the Serbs and the Croats continued to claim that the Muslims of Bosnia were of their respective origins.[19]

During World War II the renewed Croat-Muslim alliance had tragic consequences inasmuch as under the shelter of its collaboration with the fascists and the Nazis, it brought about the murder, forced conversion or expulsion of a million Serbs. After 1945, Yugoslavia was reconstituted this time on its Soviet model, with its various components recognized on ethnic or linguistic grounds, and since 1971 on religious grounds for the Muslims of Bosnia. Since then, what was ethnic and religious sentiment for the Bosnians turned into a national identity, in spite of the paradox under which communism offered them nationalism based on faith,[20] something which immediately reinforced their coalition with the Croats in order to scuttle Serbian hegemony in the federated communist Yugoslavian state, especially in view of the demographic presence of Serbs in all the federal republics, especially in Bosnia and Croatia. So, once again, instead of using the idea of Yugoslavia to merge the populations of Bosnia-Herzegovina, the idea of faith (Islam and then Orthodox and Catholic Christianity) became a vehicle for reinforcing the hatreds and suspicions, which only waited for the end of the Tito rule and the Communist regime to burst out in violence and war. After the disintegration of Yugoslavia in the early 1990s, the Croats and Serbs of Bosnia expressed their wish to join their respective national republics, while the Muslims naturally regarded such a dismantling of what they viewed as their national state as detrimental to their national existence. None of the rival national groups possessed a demographic majority to claim legitimacy to rule all the rest, and the road was wide opened to war.

The Ideological Underpinnings

In 1970, well before the collapse of the Yugoslavian order imposed by Tito and the outburst of communal nationalism which instigated the process of its disintegration, a political manifesto was written by an unknown Muslim in Bosnia—Alija Izetbegovic (born in 1925)—but not immediately released to the public. It was, however, duplicated and made available to individual Muslims who circulated it among their coreligionists apparently to serve as a guide of a Muslim order to replace the Godless communist system in Bosnia. That pamphlet, known as the *Islamska Deklaracija* (The Islamic Declaration). In 1983, after Tito's death but while the communist state was held together, a trial took place in Sarajevo where the author and some like-minded individuals were prosecuted for subverting the constitutional order and for acting from the standpoint of Islamic fundamentalism and Muslim nationalism. Significantly, after the fall of communist power, the accused were publicly rehabilitated, and the Declaration was then officially published in Sarajevo (1990). Izetbegovic, at the head of his Democratic Action Party (SDA) won the majority of the Muslim votes in the first free elections in Bosnia-Herzegovina (November 1990), but his pamphlet was obscured and not heard of again. However, judging from the wide appeal of his later book, *Islam Between East and West*, which was published in English in the United States (1984), then in Turkish in Istanbul (1987), and in Serbian in Belgrade (1988), and from the developments in the Bosnian war in the mid-1990s, one might be well advised to take a look at it.

The declaration, which in many respects sounds and looks like the platforms of Muslim fundamentalists elsewhere (e.g., the Hamas Charter),[21] assumes that its appeal will be heeded by Muslims around the world, not only by its immediate constituency, accuses the West of wishing to "keep Muslim nations spiritually weak and materially and politically dependent" and calls upon the Believers to cast aside inertia and passivity in order to embark on the road of action.[22] And like Muslim radicals such as Sayyid Qutb of Egypt, who urged his followers to reject the world of ignorance around them and transform it on the model of the Prophet of Islam, the Declaration of Izetbegovic also calls upon the millions to join the efforts of Muslim individuals who fought against the *Jahiliyya* (the state of ignorance and godlessness which had preceded the advent of the Prophet),[23] and dedicates the text to the memory of "our brothers who have laid their lives for Islam,"[24] namely the *shuhada'* (martyrs) of all times and places who had fallen in the cause of Islam.

The manifesto, again like other Muslim radicals, not only addresses itself to the restoration of Islam in private life, in the family and society, but also expressly shuns local nationalism of any sort and substitutes for it the creation of a universal Islamic polity (the traditional *umma*), "from Morocco to Indonesia."[25] The author awakens his people to the reality where "a few thousand of true Islamic fighters forced England to withdraw from the Suez Canal in the early 1950s, while the nationalist armies of the Arabs were loosing their battles against Israel," and where "Turkey, an Islamic country, ruled the world," while when it tried to emulate Europe it dropped to the level of a third-world country. In other words, it is not nationalism that makes the force of Muslim nations, but their abidance by Islam in its universal version. Therefore, it does not befit Muslims to fight or die for any other cause but Islam, and it behooves Muslims to die with the name and glory of Allah in their hearts, or totally desert the battlefield.[26] Translated into the Bosnian scene, Muslims ought not take part in, or stand for, any form of government, which is not Islamic, and any cause, which is not connected, to Islam. To the Bosnians, whom Izetbegovic addressed, there were only two options left: either to subscribe to Muslim revival and its political requirements, or be doomed to stagnation and oblivion.[27]

The Manifesto then goes into a long dissertation explaining the reasons and history of "backwardness the Muslim nations" (pp. 5-11). Basically, it refutes modernists who regard the notion of the Islamic *din* as only religion in the European sense, and insists on viewing it and living by it as an entire religious, cultural and political way of life, which unifies "religion and science, ethics and politics, ideal and interest."[28] In the typically fundamentalist fashion, it attacks established conservative Islam and its "hodjas and sheikhs, who organized themselves as a caste unto itself and arrogated to itself a monopoly over the interpretation of Islam, and placed itself in the position of mediator between the Qur'an and the people."[29] It also mocks the modernists for emulating the West and worshipping its material life, ultimately producing corruption and decadence instead of spiritual uplifting. In this context, the author belittles the role of Mustafa Kemal in modern Turkey because he wrongly thought that by ordering the *fez* out, the heads, which wore it, would also be transformed.[30] That was the reason, in the author's mind why Turkey and Japan, which began from the same starting point at the turn of the century grew in totally different directions: Japan, who knew how to integrate its own culture with modernity, but kept her traditional writing system, became a great power, while Turkey, who abolished her Arabic script which "ranks among the most perfect and the most widely used alphabets" to introduce the Latin script, remained a third-world country.[31]

This total rejection of Kemalist Turkey's model of course stands in contradiction to Western hopes to "sell" that very precedent of modernity, Europeanization and moderation to the emerging Muslim entities in Central Asia and the Balkans. As against the perceived failure of Turkey and other Muslim countries due to "the weakening of the influence of Islam in the practical life of the people," the author posits that "all successes, both political and moral, are the reflection of our acceptance of Islam and its application in life."[32] Therefore, while all defeats, from Uhud at the time of the Prophet to the Sinai War between Israel and Egypt, were due to "apostasy from Islam," any "rise of the Islamic peoples, every period of dignity, started with the affirmation of the Qur'an" But in the real world the Qur'an, complains the author, is being recited instead of practiced, mosques are "monumental but empty," the form took over from substance, as the Holy Book turned "into a mere sound without intelligible sense and content."[33] This reality was caused, laments the author in line with other Muslim fundamentalists, by the western-inspired school system in all Muslim countries[34]

Secularism and nationalism, the products of that foreign educational trend, took over the minds and hearts of the new generation of Muslims. The masses, who do not submit to these fleeting concepts which are foreign to Islam, chose indifference; but if they are rightly guided they can rise to action provided they are spurred by "an idea that corresponds to their profound feelings, and that can only be the Islamic idea," instilled by a new intelligentsia that "thinks and feels Islam" and would ultimately "fly the flag of the Islamic order and together with the Muslim masses initiate action for its realization."[35] This new Islamic order should unite "religion and law, upbringing and force, ideals and interests, the spiritual community and the state, free will, and coercion," for "Islamic society without Islamic rule is incomplete and impotent; Islamic rule without Islamic society is either utopia or violence."[36] This in effect means, in the vein of other Muslim fundamentalist platforms, that the Muslim state ought to enforce ("coerce") the Islamic order, short of which violence would erupt by necessity. For, according to this scheme, and contrary to the European concept of a liberal society where the individual is prized, a Muslim "does not exist as an individual entity," and he must create his Islamic milieu in order to survive, by way of changing the world around him if he does not want to be changed by others.[37]

The manifesto holds that there is no point to legislate laws, as is Western wont, because they end up corrupting society. Better to educate people and teach them to obey the decree of Allah, and that would put an end to corruption and lawlessness.[38] This is the reason for the "incompatibility of Islam with non-Islamic systems"; therefore "there can be no peace nor co-existence between the Islamic faith and non-Islamic social and political institutions."[39] This means in effect that Muslims should not submit to a non-Islamic rule and that they should strive to create one where none exists due to the assumption that "Islam clearly rules out any right or possibility of action of any foreign ideology [supposedly including democracy, pluralism, tolerance. freedom, equality, etc.] on its turf." As a result, "there is no room for the lay principle, and the state should be an expression of the moral concepts of [the Islamic] religion and supportive of them."[40] In light of these principles, which shun mysticism and stagnation and assume the right of innovation to make things adaptable to every time and place, the pamphlet defines and traces a long series of rules and regulations which ought to guide the individual Muslim (pp. 25-40) in practically all spheres of his societal life. The core of this orientation is that "Islamic society may not be based upon social or economic interest only, or on any other external, technical factor of association as a community of believers, it is based on a religious and emotional aspect of affiliation. This element is most clearly visible and enshrined in the *jemaat* as the basic unit in Islamic society."[41] This would mean in the Bosnian context that only a religiously-based society, on the model of religious associations (*jemaat*), is viable, and no provision is made for non-Muslims or for a multi-religious or multi-cultural society in its midst (See the question of minorities below).

The question of life in such a Muslim community is left unclear. On the one hand, the manifesto assures the "equality of all men"[42] and discards divisions and groupings according to race or class. But, if man's value is determined according to one's "integrity, and spiritual and ethical value,"[43] and these noble qualities are grounded in Islamic creed and value-system, then only if one is a good Muslim can he be considered worthy. This is all the more so when the concept of the *ummet*, the universal congregation of all Muslims is taken as the "supranationality of the Muslim community," and Islam and Pan-Islamism define its boundaries: "Islam determines its internal and Pan-Islamism its external relations," because "Islam is its ideology and Pan-Islamism its politics."[44] By Islam, the author means certain limitations on private property in order to ensure a fair distribution of wealth based on Qur'anic precepts. The restoration of *Zekat* (paying of alms, one of the Five Pillars of the Faith) to the status of a public obligation as of old, and the enforcement of the Qur'anic prohibition of collecting interest, are seen as the instrument to achieve social justice.[45]

Izetbegovic, in intending to establish the "Republican Principle," namely that power should not be inherited, defeats his purpose by positing at the same time the Qur'anic "recognition of the absolute authority of Allah, which means the absolute non-recognition of any other omnipotent authority," for "any sub-mission to a creature which implies unsubmission to the Creator is not permis-sible."[46] This, or course, would have a direct ramification on the entire question of sovereignty, democracy, authority and power. In this scheme, the idea of the inviolability of the individual is totally rejected, as it is made clear that, state-ments of equality of all men notwithstanding, and "irrespective of man's merits," he must submit to the Islamic order where there is a "synthesis of absolute authority (in terms of the program) and of absolute democracy (relative to the individual)."[47] It takes a lot of intellectual acrobatics to extricate the meaning of this "absolute democracy" that is strapped to the "absolute authority" of the Divine Qur'anic message under which the Believer is expected to operate. For, while the author subscribes to the idea that all men, including the Prophet, are fallible and worshipping them is a "kind of idolatry," he assigns "all glory and praise to Allah alone, because Allah alone can judge the merits of men."[48] This, of course, would render any process of election between men impossible, and anyone who reaches a position of authority can only gain legitimacy if he submits to the "absolute authority" of the Koranic teachings.

Part of this brand of democracy is insinuated to us when the author suggests that in his envisaged Islamic order the mass media "should be controlled by people of unquestionable Islamic moral intellectual authority. Perverts and degenerates should not be allowed to lay their hands on these media ... and use them to transmit the senselessness and emptiness of their own lives to others. What can we expect if people receive one message from the mosque and a totally opposite one from the TV relay?"[49] The author does not spell out the criteria to judge the "emptiness and senselessness" of journalists under his regime, nor does he explain how he, or anyone else, can judge any person when all judgment is left to Allah. But he dares under the heading of "Freedom of Conscience"[50] to suggest all those limitations on the media, which would certainly make them anything but free, the protestations of the author notwithstanding.[51]

While the statement that "there can be no Islamic order without indepen-dence and freedom" may still sound plausible, in view of the Islamic regimes of Iran, Afghanistan and Saudi Arabia, its vice-versa, namely that "there can be no independence and freedom without Islam"[52] seems a bit presumptuous by any stretch of the imagination. For that would mean, that the freest and most democratic nations of the world are in fact deprived of freedom and independence as long as they do not see the light of Islam. Unless, of course, he means that the idea applies only to Muslim peoples. In that case, the author argues, only if the Muslims assert Islamic thought in every day life, can he achieve spiritual and political liberation. Moreover, he claims that the legitimacy of the ruler in any Islamic nation will always depend on the extent of the ruler's commitment to Islam, short of which he turns for support to foreigners who maintain him in power.[53] Conversely, if he acts according to Islamic requirements, he thereby achieves the true democracy by consensus which is inherent in Islam and which alone makes violence redundant.[54] But the road to this utopian state of affairs is not obtained in "peace and tranquility, but in unrest and challenge."[55] That means, that like other Muslim fundamentalist movements who promise their constituencies sweat and blood, and they earn credibility and appeal in so doing, the Islamic Declaration under discussion treads the same road to contrast with the empty promises of rulers in the Islamic world who make sweeping pledges of peace and prosperity but are unable to deliver.

Now comes the problematic issue of the relations between the Muslim host culture and minority guest cultures under the Islamic order. The manifesto provides religious freedom and "protection" to the minorities, "provided they are loyal," something that smacks of the traditional Muslim attitude to the *dhimmi* (protected people) under its aegis. The interesting aspect of all this is that when the situation is reversed, namely Muslim minorities dwell in non-Muslim lands, their loyalty is made conditional on their religious freedom, not the other way around. Moreover, even under such conditions, the Muslims are committed to carry out all their obligations to the host community "with the exception of those that are detrimental to the Muslims."[56] The question remains unanswered as to who is to determine what is detrimental to Islam, when and where. Assuming that the status of Muslim minorities would depend on "the strength and reputation of the Islamic world community," means two things:

1.   That there was a possibility for Izetbegovic that the Muslims of Bosnia would remain a minority; indeed, their rate is about 40% of the total population (and growing, due to higher birth-rate) and if the Catholic Croats and Orthodox Serbs of Bosnia should gang up against them (something quite unlikely), this manifesto still provides them with a chance for survival;

2.   In either case, the Bosnian Muslims are counting on the intervention of the world Muslim community, something that was to be corroborated during the Bosnia and then the Kosovo wars.

Again, like the Hamas and other branches of the Muslim Brotherhood, this manifesto proclaims the primacy of education and preaching, in order to conquer the hearts of the people before power, a prerequisite of the Islamic order, is conquered. "We must be preachers first and then soldiers" [57] is the motto of the manifesto. Force to take over power will be applied "as soon as Islam is morally and numerically strong enough, not only to overthrow the non-Islamic rule, but to develop the new Islamic rule," because "to act prematurely is equally dangerous as to be late in taking the required action":[58] The author is confident that this can be done, because "history is not only a story of constant changes, but also of the continual realization of the impossible and the unexpected."[59] The model for the new Islamic order, which the manifesto puts on the pedestal, is Pakistan, the Muslim state that, in spite of its many deficiencies, remains the "great hope" of Izetbegovic.[60] But his great goal is the unity of the Muslim people, and in the meantime every Muslim country should be concerned about all the rest: Egypt ought to care for the Muslims of Ethiopia and Kashmir,[61] and by inference, the Muslims of Bosnia and the Balkans should be the business of all the rest of the Islamic world. The fact that feelings of affinity for oppressed Muslim brothers everywhere are not translated into action, is the fault of the Western-educated Muslims who substitute nationalism for Pan-Islam.[62]

Under the heading "Christianity and Judaism," the manifesto determines the future relationships of the envisaged new Islamic order with those two faiths, which the author considers "the two foremost religions" and the "major systems and doctrines outside the sphere of Islam."[63] Nonetheless, the author distinguishes between Jesus and the Church. The former says he, in line with Qur'anic teachings, is part of divine revelation while the latter, as embodied in the Inquisition, is abhorrent to his heart. At the same time, however, as is the normative Islamic wont, he accuses Christianity of "distorting certain aspects" of the divine message while accusing the Church of intolerance.[64] Similarly, he differentiates between Jews and their national movement- Zionism, idealizing the times when they lived under Islam, but he totally rejects their plea for independence and nationhood.[65] So, as long as the Jews are submissive and stateless in their *dhimmi* status within the Islamic state he envisages, all is well, but to dare to declare independence and stand up to the Islamic world, that is unforgivable. He claims that Jerusalem is not only a Palestinian city but first of all a Muslim one, and therefore he warns the Jews, who "have created themselves" the conflict with the Arab regimes (not the Arab or the Muslim people), that a prolonged war will be waged against them by Muslims until they release "every inch of captured land." He threatens that "any trade-offs or compromises which might call into question these elementary rights of our brothers in Palestine will be treason which can destroy even the very system of moral values underpinning our world."[66]

In sum, this passionate message of Izetbegovic, based on the Qur'an and the revival of Islam, addresses the universal congregation of all Muslims, and strives to establish an Islamic world order based on Qur'anic precepts. The idea of nationalism, any nationalism, is totally rejected in favor of the Islamic Republic, which alone can respond to the challenges of their modern world and restore to Islam its glory and preponderance. Like the platform of the Hamas and other fundamentalists, the text of Qur'an, rather than the commentaries of the Muslim establishment, provides the rationale for the cultural, social and political revolution that the author proposes to undertake. Indeed, the profuse citations from the Holy Book that we find interspersed throughout the text of the Declaration, bear witness to Qur'anic hegemony in the thought and plans of the author. Moreover, by positing the listed principles as deriving from the Holy Scripture, namely the eternal and immutable Word of Allah, the document creates the impression of a divinely guided program, which is not given to debate or consideration. The vow insinuated in this declaration, that Islam would reconquer its people peacefully if possible, by force if necessary, might throw some light (or rather obscurity) on some of the events that took place in Bosnia in the 1990s, including Iranian and other *Mujahideen* which participated in the battles, and seem to be accelerating in Kosovo at the turn of the millennium.

When in Serbia in 1998 and 1999, when I met academics, politicians from the opposition and journalists who did not hold much sympathy for their government, but were at the same time concerned about the revival of Islam in the Balkans, I was given more details about Izetbegovic and his Islamic activities. It is said that immediately after World War II, in spring 1946, as a member of the "Young Muslims," he together with Omer Behmen (later Vice President to SDA Party), and Dr. Shachirbay (father of Muhamed Shachirbay, the Bosnian Ambassador to the UN), started an illegal magazine, *The Mujahid*, in which the following poem was published:

> The earth throb, the mountains quake
> Our war cry resounds through the land
> Heads held high, men old and young,
> In a holy *jihad* our salvation lies
> Chorus: The time has come, onward brethren
>   Onward brethren, onward heroes
>   To the Jihad, to the Jihad let us go.
> Proudly the green banner flies,
> Close ranks beneath it in steel-like file,
> Let the brotherhood of Islam bind us,
> Let us scorn death and go to the battle
> Chorus: The time has come...
> With our war-cry "Allah Akbar"
> Rot the old and corrupt world
> For the joy and salvation of mankind
> Boldly, heroes, let us go into battle!
> Chorus: The time has come...

These themes are strikingly similar to those propagated in cassettes by the Hamas organization[67] to glorify the death for the cause of Islam in the course of Jihad. They also strikingly from the same thinking which produced the Islamic Declaration analyzed above. It is not surprising therefore that as early as 1992, at the genesis of the Bosnian War; the Islamic community newspaper in Sarajevo "Prepared" published the following poem:

> Go into battle with a clear mind and with full confidence
> In Allah. If you survive, you will be a *ghazi* [a Muslim fighter]
> If you die, you will be a *shahid* [martyr]. Otherwise,
> You will not be one or the other, and most surely you will be
> humiliated.
> Go into battle, if possible with *abdest* [ritual ablution] and, obligatorily,
> With Allah's name in your heart and on your lips.

On no account must you go unbathed, because any such individual can be the cause of disaster both to himself and to others.

> During the attack on the enemy, or in combat with him, shout the *tekbir*
> [Allahu Akbar- Allah is the Greatest].
> If possible, carry the Qur'an with you.
> After all this the Muslim must know that he is fighting
> on the side of justice and is following the path of Allah.
> Allah promises assistance to such men. The man on whose
> side Allah is, no one can defeat. This and next world are his.[68]
> In yet another song popular among the Muslim fighters, one could hear:
> Wake up soldiers, it is dawn, it is time for prayers
> We are the army of the Jihad, there is no god but Allah
> This is the remedy for every pain; there is no God but Allah
> In the Bosnia river valley, an army corps is being formed
> We are brothers like steel, every Chetnik fears us
> And every Ustasha, there is no God but Allah.
> We are the army of the Jihad; there is no God but Allah.[69]

The Concept of Greater Albania

During the turmoil, which swept the Balkans on the eve of the Berlin Congress (1878), the Albanians, as an ethnic group, came up with the concept of including within their fledgling national entity all the Albanians of the Balkans, beyond the geographic boundaries of Albania itself. Being Muslims, the Albanians, like the Islamized Bosnians, enjoyed a privileged status in the Ottoman Empire. In 1878 the Albanian League was established in Prizren, which presented the Greater Albania plan. While the Albanians constituted the majority in the core areas of Albania proper, their proportion in the Kosovo did not exceed 44%.[70] Like in the case of Bosnia where ethnicity was religion-bound, namely that there could not exist an Orthodox Croat, nor a Catholic Serb, nor a Bosnian who was not Muslim,[71] so in Albania Islamized Serbs, Greeks and Bulgarians became *ipso-facto* Albanians. In 1912 an attempt was made under Austro-Hungarian auspices to implement the idea, followed by another such attempt under the Italian fascists in 1941. The third attempt, initiated at the end of the 1990s as a result of the collapse of the Soviet Union and Yugoslavia, translated into tearing Kosovo, by now predominantly Albanian-Muslim, from Serbian sovereignty, following up on the Bosnian experience which had subtracted that province from Serbian-Yugoslavian hegemony.

The precedent of Bosnia, which had allowed in 1971, ironically under the communist rule, the recognition of Bosnia's nationalism as Muslim, would now propel the ethnic Albanians to revive their Islamic heritage and claim their Muslim identity which *ipso-facto* would justify their separation from the Serbs. At first, the awakening of the Albanians was undertaken along the ethno-national track. Prior to 1971, the break between Maoist Albania and Yugoslavia had occasioned the Albanian revolt in Kosovo (1968), but after the normalization of their relationships in 1971, the Albanians turned to cultural propaganda by peaceful, if subversive, means. Interestingly enough, like the Palestinians who are competing with Israel over their ancestral land by conveniently claiming that they are the descendants of the ancient Canaanites who had preceded the Israelites on the land, the Albanians now advanced the claim that they inherited the ancient heritage of the Illyrians who were the original inhabitants of Kosovo.[72] This resulted in the Albanian rebellion of 1981, in which they demanded the status of a republic (no longer an autonomous region within Serbia, like Voivodina in the north), still within the 6-republic Yugoslavian Federation. After the fall of Communism in Albania, the new regime recognized, in 1991, the self-declared Republic of Kosovo, and its head, Ibrahim Rugova, opened an office in Tirana.[73]

The disintegration of Yugoslavia by necessity revived the old dreams of the Greater Albania, which now eyed not only Kosovo, but also parts of Macedonia, Greece, Serbia and Montenegro where an Albanian population had settled over the years. The rising of Muslim consciousness in the Balkans, after the Bosnian precedent, and the spreading of the Izetbegovic doctrine, now acts as a catalyst to draw together, under the combined banners of Greater Albania and Islam, all the Albanian populations of that region. In 1992 Albania joined the Conference of Islamic Countries, and it has been working to attract support by other Islamic countries to the Greater Albania plan, actually presenting itself as "the shield of Islam" in the Balkans.[74] It has been noted that while the Albanian demographic explosion in Kosovo, which has allowed them to predominate and demand secession, has not taken place in Albania itself,[75] perhaps an indication, as in Palestine and Bosnia, that the "battle of the womb" heralded by nationalists and Muslim fundamentalists, is not merely a natural growth but may be also politically motivated.

Conclusions

While in Serbian national terms the loss of Kosovo to the Albanians is equivalent in their eyes to Israel losing Jerusalem,[76] in international terms, the importance of this issue lay in the emerging pattern of the re-Islamization of the Balkans. True, the immediate concern of the Serbs is to what extent can a minority which achieves a local majority within their sovereign territory, demand the right of secession, especially when that demand is backed up by irredentist claims of a neighboring country. If that should be the case, then entire areas of the United States populated by Mexican-Americans, or parts of Israel where the local Arab population has achieved the majority, or the Kurdish populations of Turkey, Iraq, Iran, Syria, or Arab enclaves in France, could raise the question of their autonomy and ask for their right to secede. For that matter, the Croats and Serbs of Bosnia could also revert to their initial demand at the outset of the Bosnian crisis to merge with their respective national entities. The larger concern, however, is to what extent the settling patterns of the Albanians can disrupt the physical continuity between the major Christian powers of the Balkans: Greece, Macedonia, Serbia, Bulgaria, Romania; or, more importantly, whether a new continuity of Islamic settlement, from Bosnia through Kosovo and now southern Serbia, can link up with the Muslims of Bulgaria to achieve a geographical continuum with Muslim Turkey. In view of the Islamic Declaration analyzed above which does not accept the present state of affairs in the Balkans and Turkey, and makes provision for an Islamic revolution to redress the situation to its liking, the Bosnia and Kosovo events seem only as an ominous precursor of things to come.

These concerns have been raised due to the pervert link that has been established in real politics between Muslim fundamentalist powers like Saudi Arabia and Iran who seek to further the penetration of Islam into the Balkans, against Western interests, and the inexplicable rush of that same West to facilitate that penetration which is already turning against it. From the Muslim point of view, things are easy and goals are clear: to ensure the continuity of Muslim presence from Turkey into Europe, namely to revitalize a modern version of the Ottoman Empire. True, the present successive governments of Ankara are committed to secularism of the Kemalist brand under the guardianship of the military. But as the Erbakan experience has shown (1996-1998), when democracy is allowed to operate, then the Algerian scenario may have the upper hand and an Islamist government may be elected to power that may also opt for the strengthening of the Islamic factor in Europe. Muslim fundamentalists across the world, from the Uighurs of Chinese Turkestan to the Arabs of the Middle East; from the Mujahidin of Afghanistan to the disciples of Izetbegovic in the Balkans, do not hide their designs to act for the realization of this new world order.

A summon by the Saudi scholar Ahmed ibn-Nafi' of Mecca, which was circulated to all centers of the Pan-Islamic Salvation Committee, at the outset of the conflict in Bosnia, states in no uncertain terms:

> Let it be known, brothers, that life in this ephemeral world differs immensely from the life lived in keeping with the principles of Jihad.... Fortunate is he whom Allah enlightens in this life ... by waging a Jihad for Him. Following Allah's instructions, the Pan-Islamic Salvation Committee has devised a holy plan to clean the world of unbelievers. We entrust you to see to the imminent establishment of the Caliphate in the Balkans, because the Balkans are the path to the conquest of Europe.

Every individual Imam in our states, and especially Turkey, is ready to help. Know, therefore, brothers, that time is working for us. Let us help our brothers who are fighting for the holy cause in Bosnia. Let us help them for the sake of Allah, by sending them as much money and weapons as we can, by sending them new Mujahidin. Furthermore, in keeping with this holy plan all women and children and some men must immediately be given refuge in Europe. And you, brother Muslims, must care for them as for your own, so they will spread everywhere and preach our religion, for our sake and for the sake of Allah. Brothers, give women and children refuge in each center, collect money and weapons and send them to Bosnia. Gather *Mujahidin* and send them to Bosnia! This is your obligation. Help them so that Islam will spread as soon as possible....With all your heart and soul and everywhere, fight the unbelievers! This is your duty! The Caliphate is at hand! ... May Allah reward you![77]

This appeal was by no means an isolated case. In the same month of August, 1992, a poster was plastered on walls in Sarajevo, signed by the spiritual head of the Iranian Revolution, Imam Khamenei, which accused the Western nations for not preventing the genocide against the Muslims of Bosnia, due to their innate hostility to Islam, and urged them to clear the way for Iranian *Mujahidin* and other young Muslims to wage the war and "drive the Serbs from this Islamic country."[78] In Zagreb, at the time the ally of the Muslims against the Serbs, a local journal echoed that call:

The Muslim nation in Iran began its revolution with "Allahu Akbar!" and succeeded. On the territory of Yugoslavia, the Serbs could not tolerate a Muslim [Izetbegovic] as the President of Bosnia-Herzegovina. Their only rival is Islam and they fear it. The time is approaching when Islam will be victorious.[79]

While the traces of Iranian and other Muslim volunteers' Jihad in Bosnia were rife, Western reactions seemed more and more obtuse. Except for the theory that the United States had to please Saudi Arabia as it had done during the Gulf War when it desisted from occupying Baghdad, other explanations range from sheer misunderstanding of the dangers that Islamic fundamentalism poses to the West to cold- blooded. Commercial gains in the short run which obscure the long-term strategic considerations. If that quandary raised many eyebrows in the West during the Bosnia War, where the United States and European powers supported Bosnia at the detriment of the Serbs, so much more so for the intransigent, costly and destructive military intervention of NATO in Kosovo. As it is known, war does not determine who is right, it only determines who is left. It is time to draw the balance of who is left and what is left from that war.

The "Good Guys" of NATO had set out, under the cover of a barrage of propaganda, to address the humanitarian problem of "ethnic cleansing," forgetting the "ethnic cleansing" that the Serbs had suffered over centuries in Bosnia and Kosovo. While accusing the Serbs of inflicting collective punishment on the entire Kosovar-Albanian population for the sins of the Kosovo Liberation Army, they have themselves destroyed the lives and livelihoods of millions of innocent Serbs, depriving them of bridges, potable water, supplies, municipal services, broadcasting stations and what not. And all that while relentlessly repeating in their harrowing press briefings that they held no grudge against the Serbian people, only against their leader. The real questions for the horrors of that war were never raised by NATO, and certainly never answered: What has caused the mass uprooting of people from Kosovo, including Serbs? Was it only Serbian abuses against the Albanian population, or perhaps also the fear of people who were caught in the crossfire? Why were only the old, women and children who ran away to safety in refugee camps? Was it only because the Serbs callously imprisoned or exterminated able-bodied men, or perhaps because they were recruited into rebellious KLA troops who aided NATO's designs? Was Serbia encouraging or preventing ethnic cleansing? One day we were told that the refugees were pushed across the borders of Kosovo, another time we were told that they ran away by themselves, and yet another time we were assured that the Kosovars were prevented by the bad Serbs from crossing in order to serve as human shields. Who could take these inconsistencies seriously?

The havoc that was wrecked on Kosovo, far from settling the issue on the contrary aggravated it: the Serb population was almost totally forced out of the province, and those who stay can only do so under the protection of the NATO or UN forces. Two months after they had "established order" there, a *New York Times* editorial had this too say about it:

> Kosovo remains lawless and violent. There are no local police, or judges.... NATO is doing an uneven and unsatisfactory job of preserving order.... Local thugs, rogue fighters of the Kosovo Liberation Army and Albanian gangs slipping [from Albania] across the unpatrolled borders, have taken advantage of the law enforcement vacuum to terrorize the Serbian and Gypsy minorities and drive them from their homes.... The same violent elements also prey on Kosovar Albanians subjecting people to extortion, and potential political rivals and suspected collaborators with the previous Serbian authorities, to intimidation and murder....

NATO must rethink its overly indulgent attitude towards the KLA, which has been permitted to postpone the deadline for surrendering heavy weapons and expects to see its former fighters included in the new local police forces.[80]

One year later, in July 2000, and things had not changed much, chaos still prevailed and the parties determined: the Kosovars wanted independence from Serbia, and the Serbs to prevent it lest the Greater Albania plan comes to be implemented, with the related instability in Macedonia and other areas inhabited by Albanians.[92] The UN troops were supposed to impose a "substantial autonomy" for the Kosovars under Serbian sovereignty, but that was not to be. By the time the Albanians who live in Serbia Proper wanted to draw UN troops across the border to expand its protection over them, reports from the spot identified a "Kosovo-wide problem of attacks on [Serb and other] minorities, harassment, intimidation and persecution" and the "vicious Albania-based mafia that is spreading crime."[93] The irony in all this is that while the problem of Bosnia remains unsettled, with the Serb and Croat entities there entertaining their hopes to join their mother lands, and the Kosovo issue was still festering as an open wound, NATO found itself backing, or at least seeming indifferent to, the Islamic takeover in the heart of Europe. In 2007, talk in Europe and the UN was of imposing Kosovo independence on the reluctant Serbs, whose new democratic leadership opposes as vehemently as Milosevic any separation of Kosovo from Belgrade. If it were not for Russian opposition, the West might have foolishly celebrated the severance of Kosovo from its Serbian nexus faster than it did in early 2008, when the Kosovars declared independence against the adamant opposition of Serbian authorities, coalition and opposition alike.

Robert Cohen-Tanugi, in his series of articles which has drawn world attention,[94] proposes the thesis that the USA is basically interested to promote Islamic radical states to create the "Green Belt," loyal to it, around Russia and China, and its subsidiary, the "Green Diagonal" designed to link Central Europe with Turkey, in order to restore the power and hegemony of this pivot of American strategy to its Ottoman times. That is the reason, he claims, for American determination to advance the cause of Islamic revival in Bosnia and Kosovo and, conversely, to eliminate nationalist Serbia which stands as the major obstacle on that road. However, rising fundamentalist Islam, which is inimical to the United States in particular and Western culture in general, will not necessarily play the American game and may turn against its benefactors sooner and with more vengeance that either the U.S. or its European allies suspect, just as it did in Afghanistan. The daily flights from Teheran to Sarajevo do not carry nuns or chocolate for children, but Muslims from the Middle East and Asia who now converge on Bosnia en route for other European countries. While many of them seek their economic fortunes through the porous borders of Bosnia into the West, there is no telling how many of them might, in the future, become agents of trouble and Islamic revolution when their numbers and local circumstances in Europe permit.[95]

The elections in Turkey of 2002 brought to power the Muslim party headed by Erdogan, who had been incarcerated several years earlier, when as the Mayor of Istanbul he made fiery declarations much in the Izetbekovic style. The previous incarnation of the same party, headed by Erbakan, won the plurality in 1996 and became Prime Minister, but he was ousted by the military in 1998 and his party outlawed. Under those circumstances, the thought about linking moderate Turkey to the Balkans may have had some justification. But in view of the new situation where the Islamist party gets the majority in Parliament (no longer the plurality as in Erbakan's times), so much so that they could defy their alliance with the Americans and deny them the right to open a northern front in the war against Iraq in 2003, the dreams of a moderate continuity of Islam evaporates. Certainly, Turkey is interested to show the pretty face in her struggle for access to the EU, but at the same time Erdogan is nominating his own men to the upper echelons of the army, so that when the day comes of shifting demonstratively to Islam, no military, who now hold themselves as the "curators of Ataturk's heritage," could topple his government as they did to Erbakan. In that perspective, retaining a Serbian Kosovo and a Christian Macedonia would at least arrest Islam's advance into the heart of Europe and scuttle the recreation of the Muslim Ottoman Empire in the Balkans.

Notes

1. See Lillian Craig-Harris, *China Considers the Middle East*, Tauris, London, 1993, p. 275.
2. Xinhua News Agency, 20 February 1990.
3. Patterns of Global Terrorism, The U.S. Department of State, April 1998.
4. Policy Watch No. 296, p. 3., 1998, The Washington Institute, citing reports by *The New York Times* and the *Washington Times*.
5. *Ibid.*
6. Bat Ye'or, *The Decline of Eastern Christianity under Islam: From Jihad to Dhimmitude,* Fairleigh Dickinson University Press, Madison, 1996, p. 52.
7. For the details of the dhimmi status within the Empire, see Hans Majer, "The Functioning of a Multi-ethnic and Multi-religious State: the Ottoman Empire," in Slavenko Terzic (ed), *Islam, the Balkans and the Great Powers (XIV-XX Centuries),* The Serbian Academy of Science, Volume 14, Belgrade, 1997, pp. 61 ff.
8. *Ibid.*, p. 63.
9. Bat Ye'or, p. 132.
10. Cited by Bat Ye'or, pp.176-7. For documents about the inequities in Bosnia against the Christian population, see also pp. 421-427.
11. Majer, pp. 67-68.
12. Vrban Todorov, "The Federalist Idea as a Means for Preserving the Integrity of the Ottoman Empire," in S. Terzic, op. cit. pp. 293-296.
13. Revue ded Deux Mondes, Paris, 1876, Vol II, No 1, pp. 237-254. Cited by Jean-Paul Bled,"La Question de Bosnie-Hercegovine dans La Revue Des Deux Mondes"; Ibid., p. 330.
14. *Ibid.*, pp. 331-332.
15. *Ibid.*, p. 332.
16. Dusan Batakovuc, "La Bosnie-Herzegovine: le System des Alliances," in Terzic, op. cit. pp 335- 343.
17. *Ibid.*, pp. 343-344.
18. *Ibid.*, p. 346.
19. *Ibid.*
20. A. Popovic, "La Politique Titists envers les Religions et ses Consequences," in M. Bodzemir, *Islam, et Laicite: Approches Globales et Regionales*, Paris 1996, pp. 98-102.
21. See Raphael Israeli, "The Charter of Allah: the Platform of the Hamas," in Y. Alexander (ed), *The Annual of Terrorism, 1988-9*, Nijhoff, the Netherlands, 1990, pp. 99-134.
22. Introduction to the Pamphlet, pp.1-2.
23. *Ibid.*, p. 2.
24. *Ibid.*
25. *Ibid.*, p. 3.
26. *Ibid.*, p. 4.
27. *Ibid.*
28. *Ibid.*, p. 5.
29. *Ibid.*, p. 6.

30.   *Ibid.*, pp. 7-8.
31.   *Ibid.*, p. 9.
32.   *Ibid.*, p. 12.
33.   *Ibid.*, pp 14-15.
34.   *Ibid.*, pp. 16-17.
35.   *Ibid.*, p. 19.
36.   *Ibid.*, p. 20.
37.   *Ibid.*
38.   *Ibid.*, pp. 21-22.
39.   *Ibid.*, p. 23.
40.   *Ibid.*
41.   *Ibid.*, pp.25-26.
42.   *Ibid.*, p. 26.
43.   *Ibid.*, p. 27.
44.   *Ibid.*, pp. 27-28
45.   *Ibid.*, pp. 29-30
46.   *Ibid.*, p. 30.
47.   *Ibid.*, p. 31.
48.   *Ibid.*
49.   *Ibid.*, p. 33.
50.   *Ibid.*
51.   *Ibid.*, p. 34.
52.   *Ibid.*, p. 35
53.   *Ibid.*
54.   *Ibid.*, pp.35-36.
55.   *Ibid.*, p. 37.
56.   *Ibid.*, p. 40.
57.   *Ibid.*, p. 45.
58.   *Ibid.*, pp. 45-46.
59.   *Ibid.* p. 46.
60.   *Ibid.*, p. 48.
61.   *Ibid.*, pp. 49-50.
62.   *Ibid.*, p. 51.
63.   *Ibid.*, pp. 55-57.
64.   *Ibid.*, 55-56.
65.   *Ibid.*, pp. 56-57
66.   *Ibid.*, p. 57.
67.   See e.g., R. Israeli, "Islamikaze and their significance," in *Terrorism and Political Violence*, Vol. 9, No. 3 (Autumn 1997) p. 112-113.
68.   "The Future Saints," in Vesna Hadzivukovic and others (eds), *Chronicle of Announced Death*, 1993. p. 46.
69.   *Ibid.*
70.   Jovan Čanak (ed.), *Greater Albania: Concepts and Possible Consequences*, the Institute of Geo-Political Studies, Belgrade, 1998, pp. 8-11.
71.   Jens Reuter, "From Religious Community to Nation: the Ethnogenesis of the Bosnian Muslims," in Tezic (ed.) op. cit. pp. 617-623.
72.   Canak, op. cit. pp. 42-43.
73.   *Ibid.*
74.   *Ibid.*, pp. 47-48.
75.   *Ibid.*, p. 49.
76.   Duro Fuletic, " Consequences of a Possible Creation of "Greater Albania," *Review*

of International Affairs, Vol. L, No. 1085-6, October-November, 1999, p. 23.

77.   The hand written Arabic text of the epistle of 17 August, 1992, appears in Hadzi-vukovic, op. cit. p. 52.

78.   The text of the summons, with Khamenei's picture, appears in Serbo-Croat *ibid*., p. 54.

79.   Vecernui List, Zagreb, 9 August, 1992.

80.   The New York Times Editorial, 6 August 1999.

Summary

What is There to Do?

When it is the stated purpose of Muslim fundamentalists to Islamize not only their own societies, which is strictly their own business, but also their Western host societies, must Western societies wait for demography and proselytization to run their course, or can or should they do anything to arrest the trend? Certainly, the Muslim minorities would brand as "racist" any attempt in that direction, posing the very "innocent" question of "What is wrong if the United States or Europe should become Muslim via a democratic process?" Nothing is wrong in principle except that while democracy and tolerance allow Islam to prosper, proselytize, expand, immigrate and become part of Western societies, it has been a unilateral flow as long as Muslim countries do not allow, and are not attractive enough for reciprocity. Moreover, Muslims preserve their "bastions" of Islam in their purity, and in Saudi Arabia, Iran and Sudan, Western countries are told to dissolve, to alter their Christian values that are not acceptable to Islam and to give up, ultimately, their traditions of democracy in favor of totalitarian Islam, although it is those very traditions which afford Islam a foothold on Western soil. Does a political and cultural, never mind religious, tradition possess the right to preserve itself against an evident Muslim onslaught, in the face of the mounting and pressing waves of both militant Islam, which does not hide its goals, and Muslim immigration, especially illegal, to Western countries?

There are admittedly many Muslims who live in the West (upward of 25-30 million), who are content, as a minority, to accept the culture, values and way of life of the majority. Many North African intellectuals and others, who have found their way to Europe, have integrated into their new societies and seek nothing other than assimilating into the system as fully fledged Europeans. There is, however a growing trend, especially among Muslim immigrants and converts, which rejects Western civilization and strives to replace it by a Muslim order. It is difficult to fathom what percentage of the Muslim population this represents, since we usually only see the tip of the iceberg while the bulk of the problem is hidden until an eruption of terrorism or violence brings it to our attention and reveal its depth and full scope. We have seen above the cases of Abu Hamza's and al -Bakri's virulence against the very British system that sheltered them and from whose hand they ate. Cat Stevens, the popular British pop-singer who became Yusuf Islam and contributed much of his fortune to the Islamic Movement in Israel, grew particularly relevant to the Islamic cause since the 1980s.[1] After the events of 11 September, another British citizen, Richard Reid, re-baptized Abdel Rahim, the "shoe-bomber," who had converted to Islam, tried to blow up an airline but was foiled, and came to world attention.[2] Roger Garaudy in France, the notorious Sho'ah denier, also converted to Islam and is making tours of the Muslim world where he is widely acclaimed. Tariq Ramadan, the grand-son of the founder of the Muslim Brothers in Egypt, Hassan al-Banna, was raised in Geneva as a European and has been very successful in crisscrossing the Continent and spreading his Islamism in gentle ways. But when he tried to conquer the United States as well, under the guise of an innocent academic appointment, he was banned by the authorities there who recognized his potential for trouble-making after 11 September. There are thousands like them in Europe who are there but did not gain notoriety. Thus the Muslim radicals in Europe, who are for the most part immigrants and sometimes local converts to Islam, want to transform Western societies within which they dwell into Islamic ones, run according to Muslim precepts, because they consider the latter superior to the former. A former Muslim chaplain at Yale University in the United States, someone who supposedly absorbed something of American values in one of the intellectual bastions of the country, was cited by Daniel Pipes as saying that: "Muslims cannot accept the legitimacy of the existing American system since it is against the orders and the ordainments of Allah.... The orientation of the Qur'an pushes us in the exact opposite direction."[3]

A word of commentary is needed here, to awaken the public to the danger posed to Western systems by this sort of thinking by someone who has made it to the elite of American society and benefited from its bounty. In Western thinking sovereignty pertains to the people who, through their elected representatives, control the legislative process. This is precisely the concept that the Islamists reject lock stock and barrel, because to claim sovereignty, which is Allah's exclusive province, amounts to blasphemy. And since the Almighty has already dispensed to humanity the most perfect of legal systems, encompassed in the Qur'an, it constitutes another blasphemy to pretend to better it. Pipes rightly and incisively pointed out that the debate within the Islamic camp in the United States (and the rest of the West for that matter) is not about the desirability of Islamizing Western society—that is a foregone conclusion-, but about the pace of that transformation: gradually, through conversion and *da'wa*, or in one stroke through a traumatic act of violence, like the events of 11 September. He cites as examples integrationist Siddiqi, of Pakistani origin, as advocating mass conversion over time, and the blind, convicted Sheikh abdul-Rahman, who proposed conquest of the land from the American Infidels.[4] It is not the elusive, apparently the majority of the gradual integrationists who will determine the outcome of this debate, but the purposefulness, the single-mindedness and the burning conviction and devoted activism of the radicals, backed by the sympathy of their masses.

People's imagination is much more likely to be carried by acts of daring and promises of sweat and blood than by cajoling assurances of a good, but remote and uncertain future. Passion is impatient, and the Islamists in the West, being the most active and militant, also provide the leadership and the initiative for the Muslim communities in the West in mosques, Islamic centers, publications, web sites, schools and "charity" organizations that they control and raise money for in Saudi Arabia, the Gulf States, Iran, Libya and wealthy individuals who believe they would thus fulfill their share of good deeds to gain Paradise, without directly dirtying their hands in work of subversion and violence.

One of the greatest mistakes the Bush Administration has done in its quest to eradicate terrorism has been to commit itself to democratization of the Islamic world, while at the same time combating Muslim fundamentalism which is usually associated with terrorism. The problem is that that sort of policy, far from being efficacious, on the contrary presents America and the West as hypocritical insofar as they are unwilling to accept the consequences of democratization when they bring to power precisely the fundamentalist Muslims whom they wanted to dethrone or denigrate, in the first place. That happened in Algeria, partly in Egypt and Iraq, and more recently in the Palestinian Authority which heralded the rise of the Hamas. Therefore, it should be the concern of the West what type of regime prevails where. Democracy, in spite of all its drawbacks was found to be best fitted for Western culture, but no one can determine what is adequate for others. Any civilization ultimately gets the regime it deserves, for tyranny has been more of a norm in Muslim countries than otherwise. If this is their domestic choice, or as long as they do not rise against it, it should not concern outsiders.

Where the West should be concerned is the outward conduct of the regimes in Muslim countries. When they adopt policies that threaten their neighbors, intimidate them or harm their interests, and those interests coincide with the West's, then the latter has the right, indeed the obligation, to retaliate in order to check Muslim expansionism, remove its threats and secure its own and its allies' interests. The Iranian quest for nuclear power, or the aggressive conduct of al-Qa'ida under the Taliban in Afghanistan, or the invasion of Kuwait by Iraq, or the menace to cut off oil-supplies, are cases in point. The Muslim world should not be permitted to hold to its belief that only its religious tenets are holy and all the rest are violable. Christians are not happy to see the crosses on the national flags of the Scandinavian countries, Britain and its former colonies, Greece, Austria, and Switzerland being trampled upon and burned at will throughout the Muslim world. Israelis and Americans are very dissatisfied when they see their national flags being torn apart and set afire by Muslim crowds, and Jews in general are very injured when they see the unbridled anti-Semitic cartoons and denials of the *Sho'ah* advertised day in day out in all Muslim media, with Muslim leaders either encouraging them or looking the other way. Unlike the West, where governments cannot interfere with freedom of speech and expression, the rulers in the Muslim world interfere in their state-owned press when they are personally attacked, or when it serves other perceived interests of their regimes, but ignore anti-Semitic broadsides and anti-Western intimidations under the pretext of a "freedom of the press" that they neither understand, nor cherish or protect.

Muslims across the world must be taught that if they wish their holy places or religious rights to be upheld and respected, they cannot at the same time deny the same to others. For example, during the anti-Semitic outbursts in Europe in the fall of 2000, hundreds of Jewish synagogues and cemeteries were burned or otherwise desecrated by Muslims, the Joseph Tomb in Nablus was destroyed and burned to the ground by the Muslim crowds and the ancient Jewish synagogue in Jericho was set aflame, despite Palestinian obligation to protect them under the terms of Israel's withdrawal. At the same time, Muslims demanded that hostilities in Afghanistan should be ceased because they violated the holy month of Ramadan, and that their prisoners be released from Israeli jails due to the holiday that ought to be taken into consideration by non-Muslims, while they felt no compunction about attacking Israel in 1973 on the holy day of Yom Kippur or in 2000 during the Jewish High Holidays when the Intifadah broke out. Muslims had built their Aqsa Mosque on what they knew was the emplacement of the ancient Jewish Temple, as they did when they turned the Tombs of the Patriarchs in Hebron into the Abrahamic Mosque. Israel could have done the reverse in 1967 when it took over those places, but it did not. It recognized the rights of Muslims, but while in Hebron it imposed the sharing of the facilities between Jews and Muslims, in Jerusalem it neglected its duty in deference to the Muslims, and since then Muslims have come to interpret that generous and considerate move as a total renouncing of Jewish rights there. An absurd reality was allowed to crystallize whereby the Muslims who deny the rights of the Jews who preceded them, are the masters of the place, while the Jews who wish to share with Muslims, and have the power to enforce that view, remain totally dispossessed of their right.

In 1995 a young Israeli woman waved in the face of horrified Muslims in Hebron a poster which insulted Islam and the Prophet Muhammed. She was arrested and duly sued by the State Attorney for causing religious incitement, and convicted to jail. The day she was released coincided with the first week of the Intifadah in October 2000, when newspapers carried the picture of an anti- Jewish procession in Ramallah, where a donkey wrapped with a Jewish prayer shawl and sporting a swastika on its forehead, was led in the street, with Palestinian crowds, including their police force, clapping their hands in rejoice at that sight. The difference in attitude between the respective forces of law in the two events could not be more striking, one expressing the rule of law in a civilized country that can legislate and enforce the law to protect others' faith, the other echoing the wild and emotional outburst of the mobs in a lawless society that has no concern for others. So, if the Muslims worldwide today are not self-confident enough to ignore others who may denigrate their faith, as in the cartoon affair, they must make sure that they have clean hands when they come to complain against others, who are self-confident enough to absorb Muslim insults to the Christian and Jewish faiths without resorting to violence to show their discontent. Many movies, books and posters ridiculed Christianity and Jews, but none of the latter burned any embassies or issued death verdicts against the perpetrators. This is the essence of freedom and lawful behavior in a civilized society, in contrast with uncontrollable mobs who in their inferiority complex cannot bear to be "humiliated" and must resort to violence to compensate for their frustration.

Only few Westerners understand that by yielding to Muslim demands and unnecessarily apologizing for anything their private citizens, politicians and journalists may have innocently said or done without using violence, they only ignite the fires of fanaticism among Muslims who regard these concessions as recognition of the immunity of their beliefs against any criticism. No Muslim country has apologized for the Rushdie verdict or for taking Western hostages or chopping their heads live on television. Thus, one-sided considerate apologies by the West can only justify what the Muslims do with impunity and encourage them to do more, which amounts to intellectual terrorism every bit as dangerous as the other manifestations of terror. In one noted example of resilience in the face of the Western baffling conduct, President George Bush, in his address to the National Endowment for Democracy, said:

> We are facing a radical ideology with immeasurable objectives to enslave whole nations and intimidate the world.... Our commitment is clear—we will not relent until the organized international terror networks are exposed and broken and their leaders held to account for their acts or murder.... With every random bombing and with every funeral of a child it becomes evident that the extremists are not patriots or resistance fighters, they are murderers.... There is always a temptation in the middle of a long struggle to seek the quiet life, to escape the duties and problems of the world and to hope the enemy grows weary of fanaticism and tired of murder....[5]

As a sociopolitical systems where law prevails, Western countries might certainly take steps to protect other faiths and minorities by legislating against abuse and provocation which might incite public unrest, and draw the lines between freedom of speech and wanton incitement. Then, like in cases of libel, it would be left to the court system to decide in each instance which is what and administer law enforcement accordingly, without in any case condoning violence or the threat of violence to settle differences between individuals, groups, or organizations. But civilized and lawful conduct and legal standards within Western countries will not apply on Muslim countries which make their own laws. Therefore, new rules have to be adopted on the international arena which will govern the relations between countries who abide by the civilized standards of law and all the rest who do not. International treaties and conventions are of no use, because we have seen many countries that sign them up only in order to contravene them. Thus, unilateral measures should be agreed upon and abided by in the Western world, to be joined by others who would commit themselves to comply, under the sanction of being ejected from the organization of civilized countries if they do not. Among other things, the present UN, which has proven totally inadequate to deal with terrorism, and only knows how to condemn member-states for "executing without trial" terrorists at large that cannot be caught or brought to justice, must be left to wither away under the burden of its own inadequacy and replaced by a new ADS (Association of Democratic States), or LOD (League of Democracies) to which admission will be conditional on proper conduct according to set standards.

On its part, the West has been naively convinced that if only it could cultivate its relations with the Arabs and Muslims, trade with them, enrich them with its dominant culture, teach them its ideas, innovations, technology and modernity, help develop them, admit their students to its best institutions of learning and open itself up to them and their religion and culture, sign alliances with them, collaborate with them and show goodwill towards them, they would respond in kind. In fact, many of the Muslim fundamentalist luminaries, such as Sayyid Qutb of Egypt and Hassan Turabi of the Sudan, knew the West well, took degrees in its institutions, and then wrote the most vituperative attacks against it from their position of "knowledge." Was it because they hated that West which they could not imitate and to which they could not resemble? Or perhaps they were afraid of the viable and more attractive alternatives it offered to Muslims? We are talking, in other words, about two worlds apart, separated by an unbridgeable cultural gap: one modern, open, tolerant, advanced, meaning well, law-abiding, democratic, orderly, eager to live and to let live, oriented to progress and the future, accepting and self-confident to the point of running the risk of self- destruction by generously allowing into itself Muslim elements bent on altering, terrorizing and destroying it; the other narrow-minded, bigoted, jealous, backward, lawless, bent on restoring past glory, intolerant of others and other ideas, tyrannical in rule, unable to accept and include, suspicious and fearing plots, taking shadows of things as the things themselves, vengeful and vindictive, prone to humiliation and shunning exposure to shame, and ready to waive its own life and to take down with it its Western enemy.

The component elements of this yawning gap which no policy, "understanding" or declaration can bring together were discussed in detail in my own *Islamikaze*[6] and here we will only recapitulate their essentials. All the cajoling, the courting, the "compromises," the concessions and the "agreements" of the past were taken by the Muslim world in general, and the fundamentalists in particular, to mean that the West was weak, decadent, soft and decaying, and that if only the Muslims kept pushing, it would collapse under the weight of its own imperfections. All the West could hope for, therefore, is not to adopt a policy line that would be acceptable to the Muslim fundamentalists, for nothing short of surrender to their absurdities would do, but to delineate red lines beyond which Muslim aggression would find a determined, united and resolute West, ready to fight for its values and the very survival of its culture. It is not a foreign policy towards the Muslim world that the West needs, only foreign relations with it, and readiness to react, strongly and massively, when it feels threatened. After all, the battle against *Islamikaze* terrorism, the only brand of terrorism that has been systematically sustained, protected, sponsored, justified, idealized, defended and idolized by a wide array of peoples, countries and cultures that come under the heading of Islam, is not only a military or economic or territorial confrontation, but a clash between two world views, creeds and approaches to life (and death).

The Contours of the Confrontation

This is a confrontation because, unlike Western culture which, at least in theory, accepts to co-exist with others, even when they are weaker, the Islamic world shows respect towards, and at the same time feels humiliated by, the stronger—technologically, militarily, economically and culturally. The frustration at their inability to match up to the strong, especially that they were themselves the strong of yesteryear, makes the Muslims eager to destroy the bearers of strength rather than try to lift themselves to their level. Frustration generates shame, and aggression is used to displace the shame. Several areas of comparison may be suggested which point out to the differences between the two cultures, and which were substantiated by the massive instances and quotes in the above chapters:

The Attitude towards Human Life and Death—while Islam does not permit suicide of the faint-hearted individual who runs away from the difficulties of life, and enjoins him to face up to his fate and count on Allah, the Muslim fundamentalist champions have found a way to sanctify death as "martyrdom," and to idolize it to such an extent as to turn it into a desirable pursuit, sanctioned by Allah, Islam, the precedents of the Prophet and his *tabi'un* (followers). Gradually, on the footsteps of the medieval *fida'iyun,* the revived idea of sacrifice and of the Shi'ite ideal of suffering under the Khomeini Revolution, its application in the Iran-Iraq War (1980-88) and then by Hizbullah in Lebanon, against the United States and Israel; and then through the adoption of the idea by extremist Sunni Muslim radicals, such as Hamas and Islamic Jihad, it developed as a popular, effective and universal strategy of warfare among other Muslim fighters, especially the Palestinian nationalists of the *Tanzim* and the Aqsa Brigades in their Intifadah against Israel. Finally, Muslim women and children were brought into the widening circle of Islamikaze which, though still limited to hundreds, and potentially appealing to thousands, finds wide support among tens of thousands of clerics, columnists, political leaders and professionals, including some "enlightened" by their own standards; and hundreds of thousands, if not millions, cannot contain their sympathy and adulation for them and express it openly in public. For this reason, one can no longer speak exclusively of the war

declared by militant Islam against the West, but of a growing circle of support
in the Muslim public in general for the radicals, especially when they can show
"positive" results to their credit. The most harrowing and callous in this attitude
to human life has been the dragging of teen-agers and women, by Palestinians
and Hizbullah, into their relentless battles of terrorism against Israel.

This attitude to human life has other dark aspects to it, both internal, within
the Muslim community and *vis-à-vis* the enemy. During the Intifadah of the
Palestinians, or the insurgency of the Islamic Groups in Algeria, for example,
we have seen massive slashing of throats of other Arabs/Muslims just for belonging to the "other camp," or for suspicion of "collaboration with the enemy,"
be it domestic or external, without any concern for human life itself, for the
families of the murdered or for the destructive impact on the minds of innocent
civilians and children who grow up to accept, as a matter of course, that sort of
massive use of murder and hanging in public squares before their eyes, which
blunts their human sentiments. This is accompanied by a masochist display of
wounds, blood, lynching, abuse of the bodies of the dead, dragging bodies in
the streets, and the chants of the onlooking crowds, who are mesmerized and
maddened by this orgy of cruelty, violence and inhumanity. Funerals for their
own favorite dead, for example in combat, or as a result of targeted elimination
by their enemies, or of the remains of Islamikaze bodies, are also accompanied
by shoutings, shootings in the air, huge processions where the body of the dead
is arraigned by the masses out of control, and tossed from hand to hand, by
vows of vengeance for the life of the departed martyr and for his replacement
by many others who would volunteer in his footsteps, and the like. Compare that
to the funerals of the victims of terrorism, in the United States or Israel, which
are silent and dignified, intimate and inward-turning, and you have one of the
keys to comprehend the difference between the two cultures.

If this is the situation with regard to Muslims-to-Muslims, how much more
so when foreigners-enemies are concerned. We have seen the chilling scenes
of indiscriminate blowing of unsuspecting civilians in restaurants and cafes,
the cold-blooded murder of passengers in buses, airplanes and check-in coun-
ters; the shooting of passers-by in streets and of hostages, on a scale and with
a frequency unknown in other times and other cultures, save the Mongols and
the Nazis. What is more harrowing is the jubilation of the masses of Muslims
in support of such massacres, and the "learned" rationalizations that many
clerics, intellectuals and public opinion makers produce to justify them. But
that is not all: enemies can be abducted, killed, murdered, tortured, and jailed
indefinitely, and no information about them is given to the families, no access
to them is allowed to the Red Cross or anyone else, and expensive prices are
extorted for just releasing any piece of news about their whereabouts or their
putative fate. No other culture in modern memory has behaved so cruelly, so
inhumanely and so obtusely with captured enemies and their loved ones. They
know the sensitivity and concern in the West for human life, therefore they

exploit them to the maximum, either by keeping silent, thus raising the price of the extortion, or by hiding behind non-governmental organizations such as the Hizbullah in Lebanon or the Hamas in Palestine, or the Islamic Jihad in Syria, in order to escape responsibility. We have also witnessed live on television, the use of bare hands to tear Israeli soldiers to pieces and then the exhibition of the blood-soiled hands to boast before an approving public seized by inhuman frenzy and demanding more cruelty. We have seen Israeli teen-agers ambushed by Arabs and their skulls appallingly crushed by rocks and left laying in the open. The worse part of all this is that when the Arab authorities are confronted with these inhumane situations, they "condemn" acts of "murder of innocent civilians on all sides," as if there were two sides to this story, and as if these were natural calamities without murderers that could be identified, called to task and prosecuted to justice.

This callousness in the attitudes of Muslims towards their victims is supplemented by the horrendous re-enacting of scenes of murder, as if they were sublime human experiences worth replaying and memorizing, and models to educate their public and their young generation to emulate. This, of course, goes a long way to demonstrate how cold-bloodedly these murders are planned, and are not the spur-of-the-moment act of "frustration" by some ill-fated or "desperate" Palestinian or al-Qa'ida member. For, when the scene of an Israeli café or a paper-model of an Israeli bus is carefully and meticulously reconstructed in a public place at the heart of an Arab or Muslim city, flying limbs of Israeli children, dripping with blood are hung around as part of the scene, explosions are re-played and sounds of dying victims are amplified for the impact of their despair, and all this to the frenzied cries of joy of the assembled masses, including children, then something is decidedly sick in the psyche of this society. If no amount of explanation or justification can excuse the horrible acts of murder themselves, where the murderers become hallowed martyrs, how much more so the sheer madness of reproducing those acts, once and again, as if a recorded reel is replayed in a slow motion to satisfy the sadism of its producers. There are reports of Nazi murderers who delighted in projecting on screens to their private audiences their "feats" of mass murders, but even they did not stoop so low as to screen them, let alone replay them in detail, to the wide public. Only now do we understand that those re-enactments are the outcome and derived extension of the terrible ta'zia ceremonies celebrated by the Shi'ites at large during the 'Ashura day, where the Believers relive the suffering of Hussein in Karbala by inflicting pain and injuries on their bodies. But while the Shi'ites exhibit a masochistic sense of identification with their own kin, out of their own volition and without inflicting pain or damage upon others, the Hamas scenes express their hatred towards, and sadistic joy at the suffering of their enemies.

A new addition that threatens to descend on the civilized world is the fundamentalists' menace to use non-conventional weapons for mass extermination, as if the mass-killings of satanic proportions, by mechanical means, were not sufficient to quench their thirst for blood. Palestinians and Hizbullah are known to have experimented with gas and poisons contained in the shells and bombs they use against Israeli civilians. The best sign of what is coming is when they begin, in a process of projection, to impute to their enemy what they plan to do. The massacres that they perpetrate or plan against others, which for them are licit and to be expected, become in their minds the "crimes, atrocities and massacres" that the enemy did or will do, and as they were experimenting with gas and poison, they spread the rumors about Israeli use of depleted uranium in the territories, "like NATO in Kosovo," or of "poisoned sweets" and "HIV-positive virus" among Palestinian children. This means that before they use those materials for mass killings, they wish to inject in the minds of the world that they were not first and that they only responded to the "massacres" carried out by Israel with American connivance. The eyes of the Arab world were for long longingly and hopefully directed to Saddam Hussein, to see what kind of arsenal he will deliver against America and Israel, United States dares to attack. No public voice was heard in the Muslim world, attempting to dissuade him from that folly, for any moral reason, with a view of restricting the loss of human lives, and even not for the practical reason of avoiding a holocaust to his people. For if the Twin Towers were a "big success" for them, so much more so the lesson that Saddam is about to teach the West. Hamas and al-Qa'ida, as well as Egyptian fundamentalists, have actually been adding their voices to those in Iran[7] who threaten Israel and the West with poisoning their waters or infecting them with viruses.[8] It is only hard to see who will be left to be brought under Muslim dominion, in accordance with the fundamentalists' dream, if and after the nuclear, chemical and biological annihilation of the enemy is completed.

Intolerance Built into the Culture—Bernard Lewis has made the point that, unlike other civilizations which are essentially regional, Islam and Christianity are, by their very pattern of expansion, become universal, and exclusive in the sense that not only do they consider themselves the "fortunate recipients of God's final revelation to mankind, and therefore their duty to bring it to the rest of humanity," but the clash between them becomes inevitable.[9] However, while Western culture has forsaken the use of violence to spread its message, and pursues it by ways that the Muslims regard as devious (mission, the pop culture of jeans, fast food, music and Coca-Cola, television, cinema, alcohol, etc.), militant Islam and its supporters do not shun violence, as the *Islamikaze* phenomenon has been dramatically evincing. In other words, the humanistic idea of tolerance of the other in European culture, which has come to mean that the other is accepted as is, without value-judging him, has become predominant, and has paved the way to the free market of ideas that prevails in the West today. That thinking has not only permitted the renouncing of force, at least in principle, to spread Christianity, democracy, free trade and other Western ideas, but has also allowed for Islam and other creeds to compete within its own turf, without ever suspecting that the competition would ultimately grow over the turf itself.

Moreover, since the West accepted the idea of separating the Church from the modern secular state, the faith has become the domain of the individual while the public square was made impervious to it. In the Islamic world, practically all the "secular" governments, which for the most part lack legitimacy, must pay lip service to the Islamists, at times by even including them in their governments. Even so, the Islamists appear as the most popular claimants of power, and if allowed to operate as political parties, can often show their mettle and gain access to government. Therefore, no Muslim turf can be made neutral towards other faiths, and the frequent use of violence against them goes a long way to prove that, day in day out.

Furthermore, Muslim radicals regard the defeat of their own illegitimate government as a prelude to their restoration of the universal Caliphate of all Muslims, and therefore treat the Western governments who protect, aid, and sponsor the dictators in place as the direct enemy of the Muslims. From their point of view, then, not only is Western culture despicable in its own "right" and faulty due to its own deficiencies, but it invaded their turf in order to subvert it and undermine it from within, until it falls off like a ripe fig. It is the West which came to them, not they to him. This creates a paradox nevertheless, for while Muslim fundamentalists decry the Western cultural invasion, which is "worse," in their eyes than the physical invasions of the medieval Crusades, they and their less militant coreligionists at the same time crowd the queues in front of American, Canadian, Australian and European Embassies and Consulates across the world, to gain visas of entry into those bastions of "decadent" Western values that they love to hate. Some explain their quest as a simple will to study in the West, especially value-free technical professions which are not "soiled" by Western thinking, ignoring the fact that Western learning and protracted sojourns in the West by necessity will have an impact on them, to the point that they might at the end elect to stay and become Western; others wish from the start to improve their economic lot by immigrating to the West, but once they get there they congregate around their kin and constitute fertile grounds for Muslim fundamentalist *da'wa* (Call, Mission); still others, the likes of Sheikhs Bakri and al-Masri in Britain, have migrated to the West as "refugees," because there was no other place left as a safe haven for them in their countries of origin, and the West was generous enough to accommodate them.

Paradoxically, it is the latter who place themselves at the forefront of Muslim fundamentalism in the West and who, beneficiating from the hospitality and social welfare arrangements in their host-countries, recruit local converts or already naturalized Muslims for training abroad, for indoctrination at home and for activities in the Path of Allah. It is they, who were tolerated by societies against whom they are operating ideologically, who are the least tolerant towards their hosts. Their objective is loud and clear: to Islamize their host societies and let Islam take them over. If until now, under the decisive impact of the integrationists who wished to assimilate into society, fit into its political, economic and social institutions and become part of it culturally if not religiously, the penetration of Muslim fundamentalism into the West has begun to change these trends around. More and more Muslims "rebel" against their host cultures and demand, as full-fledged citizens, that their culture be recognized as a component of the national make up, that state symbols (for example the cross in Scandinavian national flags) be altered to become inclusive of them, that mosques, foreign Muslim languages and Muslim education should be subsidized by the state. In France, following the scandal aroused by Francois Bayrou, the Education Minister in the 1970s when he refused to allow veiled Muslim women into the secular education system of the state (*l'affaire du foulard*), it is young French Muslims, the sons of immigrants from North Africa, ("beurs" in local parlance) who frequently boo the *Marseillaise* when it is played on football fields prior to the matches.

All this emanates not only from the absolute conviction of the Muslims that Allah's message to them, being the most recent is also the most "updated" as it were, but also that their way to Allah is the only valid one. In contrast to Christianity, the other universal monotheistic religion which claims the same, however, the Muslims did not preclude force to enforce their beliefs and to "save the Infidels from themselves," by their own volition if possible, by violence if necessary. Therefore, when they speak of "tolerance" they mean some sort of temporary measure of accommodation towards the Infidel, who clearly embraces an inferior creed, until Islam is strong enough to prevail. The miscalculation of al-Qa'ida on 11 September, and before and after that of the Hamas and the Islamic Jihad, was that Western societies, including Israel, were so ripe for their demise that a shocking trauma, or a series of smaller but frequent and consistently growing blows, would in the end overwhelm the enemy. Thus, every time the enemy responds more forcefully, or in more unconventional ways than expected under their imaginary scheme, like the Americans in Afghanistan or the Israelis in the West Bank, they cry "foul game!" This is not how the enemies of Islam are supposed to behave, their very resistance to their subjugation by Islam is regarded as "blasphemous" for its failure to recognize the will of Allah, and their retaliatory strikes against Islam are seen as "signs of distress and despair" which augur their approaching end. Hence the stepped-up activities to speed that process up, and bring it to its conclusion, and so on and so forth. That point of view does not recognize the right of the attacked "for the sake of Allah" to self-defense. The Muslims can, indeed are bent upon, expanding, conquering, killing, enslaving, dominating and ruling, for the entire universe is theirs to be included in *Dar-al-Islam*, but woo to who resists that "noble" process entrenched in the Will of Allah, and if he does, he is decried as "aggressor," "killer of civilians and children," "arrogant," perpetrator of "massacres."

Thus, any hideous attack upon Western enemies, even when it involves innocent lives, as in the Twin Tower case, is "inevitable" and "blessed" and "well deserved," and a "great success," and causes masses to jubilate and writers to sing its praise throughout the Muslim world, while every retaliation is lamented, condemned and blasted as "unjustified," "out of proportion," "cruel," "wanton massacre" and "proof," if proof was needed, of the enemy's inherent evil. The idea of fair play, of attack and counter-attack, and in consequence of casualties inflicted on both parties to a conflict is misunderstood in Muslim circles. Even the issue of aggressive and defensive warfare is foreign to them, because the Muslim definitions of warfare do not follow the accepted objective norms prevailing in the West, but strictly abide by the subjective rules drawn by Muslim jurists who have formulated Muslim political theory and international relations.[10] According to these rules, any attack by non-Muslims on Muslims is inherently illegal and immoral, and therefore it is incumbent upon all Muslims to assist their co-religionists, regardless of what they did to provoke the attack. Conversely, any Muslim attack on the West, for example, since it can be justified as a defensive war against the heretical West, or as an act of self-defense against the spiritual invasion of the West, or as a battle to repulse the enemy from *Dar-al-Islam* (for example Palestine, Andalusia and Southern France), is *eo ipso* a just war that all Muslims are called upon to sustain. In other words, once a war against the enemy had been entitled "*Jihad*," and any of the latter examples justifies a *Jihad*, the arena is wide open for war. Guerilla warfare, or *Islamikaze*, terrorism and the like, are means of warfare that are hallowed by Islam, with all the attending ideological and doctrinal elaborations attached thereto.

The West has no standing in these definitions and what it says or thinks does not matter, because the Islamic position is Allah-inspired and *Shari'a*-dictated, which means that it is beyond discussion, compromise, debate or concession. Therefore, while external wars in the West are considered quantitative issues (over territories, interests, assets), and when they are terminated, then compromise, concessions and negotiations are led until an agreement emerges, and when it does it is binding on the parties who signed the treaty, cease-fire or convention; in Islam the wars are qualitative (over ideas, doctrines, "justice," "redress of wrongs"), are never terminated until the victory of Islam and the imposition of its rule, and when an "agreement" is signed under duress (like after a military defeat) it always derives from the precedent of Hudaybiyya that was established by the Prophet, namely that the agreement is temporary (*hudna* = armistice), and it is to be violated at the first opportunity, when Muslims feel they have regained superiority, or have found new ways of warfare that the enemy is unable to counter (like the *Islamikaze*). *Sulh* (peace-cum-reconciliation) can be concluded only under the terms of a *Pax Islamica*, when the non-Muslim has accepted the hegemony of Islam and submitted to its rule.[11] This is the reason why Muslim authorities in Egypt and Saudi Arabia justified the Camp David Accords of 1977, as well as the Oslo Accords of 1993, in terms of a temporary Hudaybiyya-like truce which is open-ended and reversible, if and when the circumstances so allow. Like the Prophet's precedent, these "agreements" were only necessary to extort concessions from the enemy, but once they are made and cashed, they no longer necessarily bind.

This worldview, where rules of war and peace do not apply equally on the belligerents, and clearly beneficiate the Muslims while they are expected to obligate only the non-Muslims, are the very reason why the Muslims see themselves free to violate their "agreements," while they constantly accuse their adversaries of "violating all agreements and commitments," at a time when they themselves faced no reproach because they had never expected to live up to their "commitments" in the first place, and their adversaries who were truly obliged by them were expected to keep them to the letter. Thus, when the Palestinians, for example, committed themselves in Oslo (another Hudaybiyya, in the words of Arafat), without reserve or qualification, to end terrorism and violence in general, not to introduce to their territory any category of unallowed weapons, to maintain their armed force at agreed levels and under one command, to put an end to incitement against Israel and the Jews, to arrest terrorists and pursue them to justice or extradite them, as a *prerequisite* to receiving more territory from Israel and advancing into the peace-process, they only remembered the Israeli part of the agreement, and when not fulfilled they heaped *all* the blame on Israel, while their consistent violations of their main commitments did not matter. They became accustomed by the Rabin Government that they could break their commitments, but that Israel, for fear of arresting the "peace process," would swallow all violations and proceed with its one-sided concessions, and so it was. But when a new Israeli government came in, which made further Israeli concessions in accordance with the peace accords contingent upon Palestinian parallel implementation, they cried "foul game!" once again, and that brought the process to an end.

Intolerance based on a concept of superiority, whereby the superior does not have to conform like the inferior, is apparent also in the daily conduct in the Muslim world towards other religions. Rampant are the instances where Christian churches are burned down in Egypt and Indonesia, and synagogues are attacked and destroyed by Palestinians (notably the Joseph Tomb in Nablus and the Jewish Synagogue in Jericho during the Intifadah), and by Muslims throughout the Western world since the outbreak of the Palestinian insurgency in late 2000, but rare are the occasions where Muslim mosques are attacked by anyone anywhere. The Muslims do not take this, and the fact that they can build their mosques anywhere in the West, as an indication of Western tolerance and acceptance of the other, but as a sure sign that no one dares to resist Islamic expansion while they, in their countries of origin can curtail or totally prevent the construction of any Christian, let alone Jewish, houses of prayer. Muslims can be the inhabitants of any country in the world, including the Christian world and Israel on whose doors they knock for immigration or "right or return," and still dub those countries "racist" for not completely surrendering to their will, but Jews and Christians are severely restricted in various areas of the Muslim world. That suggests to them, once again, that while the whole universe is their domain as of right, other faiths are not, by their very nature, entitled to the same rights in the lands of Islam.

No country in the West witnesses its citizens follow the shameful scenes, current in the Muslim world, where American and Israeli flags, and the effigies of their leaders, are burned ritually as a matter of routine, save when Muslim communities in the West practice the same ritual. But no sustained burning of Arab or Muslim flags or effigies is known as a phenomenon in the West or in Israel. Once again, the inability of the Muslim world to accept as their equals the national symbols of others is striking, at a time when the West respects theirs as a matter of course. This, far from awakening the consciousness of the Muslims to their own intolerance, in contrast with the publicly advertised and exhibited Western tolerance towards them, on the contrary has confirmed them in their belief in the hegemony of their faith and symbols that no one dares to challenge, at a time when they openly challenge with impunity other creeds and symbols. This has encouraged the Muslim communities in the West and in Israel, to demand the right to construct their mosques, or to perform their Friday rituals, in places known as holy sites to other faiths. On Temple Mount in Jerusalem they built their mosques on a site that they knew was the holiest for the Jewish creed, they transformed many churches and synagogues into mosques during their conquests and expansion, and turned every occupied land into a *waqf* (Holy Endowment) that cannot revert to non-Muslims.[12] But woo to anyone who dares to turn a mosque into another house of prayer, or to occupy land that is or was Muslim, for that is intolerable. More recently, new challenges rose when Muslims began constructing illegally their mosque on the grounds and in defiance of the Basilica of the Annunciation in Nazareth, to squat for the Friday prayers near the main cathedral of Florence, to seek to construct the largest mosque in Europe on the grounds of the London Olympics in 2012, and to deny any historical rights to the Jews over Temple Mount, thereby declaring to Christianity and to Judaism, in Lewis' memorable words: "Your time has passed. Now we are here. Move over."[13]

This is not exactly tolerance. Incidentally, and significantly, the verse from the Qur'an that Bernard Lewis mentioned in connection with the inscription in the Dome of the Rock, to wit: "He is God, He is One. He does not beget, He is not begotten," which was meant to reject the basic dogma of Christianity about God and His Son, when the Muslims took over Jerusalem in the seventh century, was also inscribed on the temporary tent-mosque in front of the Annunciation that awaited the building of the permanent mosque until it was dismantled by Israel, obviously with the same intention and meaning. Coupled with the denial of Jewish rights on Temple Mount, this signifies, in the eyes of the Muslims, that they intend to indeed supersede both Judaism and Christianity, as Islam had taught them of old. Hence the hatred of the Muslims to the construct "Judeo-Christian tradition," which they regard as a passing episode in history, once the Seal of the Prophets had dispensed to humanity the latest divine message. "Your time has passed. Now we are here" is not only the statement of a factual chronological sequence, but also a declaration of mastery, dominance, hegemony and exclusivity, backed by the will and the power to make it happen in the real world. For, a creed that was designed by Allah to replace all others and to bring all humanity under its aegis cannot be expected to tolerate other faiths, let alone competitors for the same world constituency.

The Eternal Victims—In stark contradiction to the dreams of world domin-ion that they entertain, Muslims tend at the same time to regard themselves as eternal victims of the West that they hate and want to displace, but whose help they need and implore, and they rationalize this contradiction by the plots and conspiracies constantly woven around and against them, as if the West had no other concerns than them, or could not do very well without their lachrymose complaints. First and foremost for them is the need to explain to themselves and to the world why and how they, who had pioneered civilization and sci-ences in medieval times, and had caused Europe to tremble and fear from their successive mighty empires, found themselves, without preparation, warning or transition at the bottom of the civilisatory heap and of the hierarchy of world powers as the modern era dawned. For a shame society like theirs, it is difficult, nay impossible, to take responsibility for their deeds and to devise a policy of adaptation that could help them pull out of the quagmire, for that would amount to admitting the deficiencies of their culture, the stifling restrictions of their faith, the pipe-dreams of their leaders and the insufficiencies of their social systems. Thus, rather than admit their inabilities and seek succor elsewhere, it is easier to project their own ill-will on others, masquerade their jealousies and bigotry as "revivalism" and accuse the all-powerful West, the colonizer and imperialist of yesteryear, of all their ills, including their demise, suffering, backwardness, population explosion, dictatorial rule, corruption, and what not. They do not want to recall that when they were the powerful, the conquerors, the coloniz-ers and the imperialists, they did not stop one moment to ask themselves what they were doing to their conquered peoples and civilizations that they gradually decimated.

Arabs and Muslims have resources, human and mineral, a great tradition of learning and a vast ambition to restore themselves to where they were before they began slipping in the modern era. But their self-inflicted deficiencies in government, economics and antiquated social structure do not permit them to take off. Perhaps most stifling of all is the array of dictatorships of all sorts, monarchical and republican, one-party and military juntas, rulers who were never elected, and self-declared Presidents-for-life. Illegitimate rule spawns corrup-tion, helplessness and hopelessness, which often generate also haplessness; and the near non-existence of civil society and non-governmental organizations and voluntary associations with the necessary clout to fill in when the government is deficient, make change difficult and nearly impossible. Uncontrollable poverty and population explosion are hardly the requisite processes to arrest these trends. When allowed to operate, Islamists often step in to fill the gap, but they are closely monitored or harnessed to the regime's goals, and therefore their operations are often circumscribed and cause them to become part of the problem instead of the solution. In this state of affairs, where the Western world, and Israel at their doorstep, advance and increase the gap between themselves and the poor Muslim world, an eye-poking gap that is observed on television screens and in neighboring Israel daily, people find refuge in self-victimization: it is not their fault, it is the fault of others. This state of mind is aided in those societies by the dependence of the commoner on his corrupt government for food subsidies, for employment, for education and social services, for development and for the individual's well-being. But the governments are incompetent, illegitimate, bent on staying in power and lack a blueprint for resolving the ever-aggravating problems of their countries and societies. The stronger the regimes, by virtue of the modern weaponry which affords them a superior power of enforcement, the more disaffected the populations who sense that their government's interests are not theirs; all the more so, since the maintenance of the rulers in their place is often made possible by their Western "allies" who provide the money, the economic aid, the weapons and the food that keep this explosive situation from getting worse and blowing up in the West's and the regimes' faces. Another paradox develops: because they are dispossessed, unemployed and hopelessly classified as have-nots, the masses in those countries not only are victims of their rulers and Western "allies," and therefore are "entitled" to demand that both provide for their needs, but the more they receive to sustain themselves and ascertain their survival, the more humiliated they become from that dependence, the more enraged they are by it, and the more violent-prone as the only way to air their frustration that only keeps increasing. In other words, the West and the local governments, who are held jointly responsible for the poverty and frustration of which the masses are the victims, not only are expected to alleviate the burden of the impoverished and the disadvantaged, but when they do so they are all the more resented and likely to become the targets of the frustration. A no-win situation. A case in point: Bin Laden is no less enraged against America and Israel than against his own Saudi government which is sustained by its alliance with the United States. If it is so with a Saudi system which is not needy, and a Bin Laden who is not impoverished, how much more so with other Arabs and Muslims where both government and people are in dire poverty!

The eternal victim also believes that not only everyone owes him everything, and they themselves are exempted from any self-strengthening effort, but also that they can use violence to be redressed. So, for example, Palestinians who have been living on UNRWA's handouts and sacks of flour for the past 50 years, and their population in the squalid refugee camps has quadrupled since then, believe it is the duty of the world to continue to feed them indefinitely. They make children and the West has to take care of them. They have resisted all attempts at resettlement in their host countries, which are also Arab and Muslim, but prefer to leave the refugee problem seething, and to continue to depend on the world's goodwill for survival, rather than force the refugees to take up a constructive life and end their refugee status. Because a refugee standing is the ultimate victimhood, and they are not about to relinquish it. What is more, the United States, and other Western countries that take the brunt of the UNRWA budget, are also the most hated and threatened by the Muslim fundamentalists who feed from their hands. If they had learned, if they had been willing to learn, from Western nations and Israel how to absorb refugees on their own and put them on a productive track, rather than to implant in them the mentality of the eternal victims, much of the bitterness and frustration which engender violence and terrorism could have been spared. And this is not only a matter of money or of development (Bin Laden and Saudi Arabia being the ultimate example), but a matter of culture. If one is educated to not accept any handouts, to rise on his feet and help himself, to shed the feeling of victim and be proud of a self-made and self-sustaining livelihood, then dignity is restored, the humiliation effaced or diminished, and the paralyzing jealousy and stifling apathy replaced by aspiration, ambition, and action.

No wonder then that among Palestinians some 80% were found to support terrorism, which is for them, to be sure, the "right" of the eternal victim to both avenge his situation and to have it redressed. How exactly, they do not say, unless they think, as part of their delusions that we shall address below, that they can bring the West to submission. There is also no wonder that al-Qa'ida, the Hamas, Hizbullah and the rest rationalize their wild terrorism as "retaliation" for their humiliation and victimhood by the strong, the arrogant and the powerful who had rendered them victims. Therefore, while their terrorism is to be "understood" in their eyes, and justified as the cry of the desperate victim, as Mrs. Blair or Secretary Straw have themselves intimated, any Western counter-attack or defensive act, must be construed as "aggression" against and "massacre" of the eternal victim. For every one of their orgies of death one must seek the "roots" and comprehend the "reasons," and address the "causes," exactly as for every burning of a church or a synagogue, but if a mosque is hit, or children are hit incidentally, that is "desecration" and "blasphemy." For that reason, they do not recognize the difference between intentional damage and collateral casualties. It is the result that counts, no matter what the intention of the enemy planners may have been. America and Israel are always "children killers," "heretics," aggressors, arrogant and performers of massacres. Americans "kill" Iraqi children by "preventing food and medicaments from reaching them," even if it is Saddam who prefers to purchase weapons or compensate the families of the Palestinian *Islamikaze,* rather than import food and drugs for the sick. The dead corpses of the Iraqi children were there for display, they are clearly the victims, then the Americans are their killers.

Thus, a reversal of roles is effected, whereby the West and Israel become the "terrorists" and the Muslims the victims thereof; it is the West who terrorizes the Muslim world and is arrogant and condescending towards it, and the Muslims merely act in self-defense. Hence the failure of Muslim countries, including in their Kuala Lumpur Conference of June 2002, let alone in international *fori*, to accede to the Western definition of terrorism, which is, in essence "the use of violence against innocent civilians for political goals." They refuse to relinquish the mantle of victimhood to others, therefore terrorism is what is done to them, not what they do to others. They struggle at all international *fori* to show that the Palestinians and Hizbullah cannot be considered terrorists, whatever they do, because they fight for "liberation" from "occupation"; many of them also rationalize the Twin Tower horror as "liberation" from the choking American tutelage, or a "message" to the "real terrorist," which is America (or Israel for that matter), or a "lesson" to the arrogant, or a new "mode of warfare" against the threatening and aggressive West; or the "desire for death" of the audacious *Islamikaze* martyrs, matching up to the "desire of life and comfort" of the cowardly and decadent West. That is also the reason why they remind America of its own "terrorist attacks" against Hiroshima and Nagasaki, proof that what matters is not what is done and to whom, but who does it. Victims of the world, Unite! If, of course, America or Israel are the authors of your misery.

Other victims, such as the Americans murdered on 11 September, or Indians obliterated in Kashmir, or the Israelis who are blown apart in pizza parlors, or in the bus on their way there, are no victims in the eyes of the Muslim fundamentalist, and more and more of plain Muslims, but the perpetrators of that terror in all those cases. They do not deserve compassion, because they "had brought that upon themselves," or better, "have concocted it themselves" in conjunction with the CIA or the Jews, or the Mossad. The wide acceptance of those theories of conspiracy, including among intellectuals and opinion makers as we have noticed above, add to the universal sense of victimhood that is rampant in the Islamic world. Another important corollary of this attitude is that, while in the Judeo-Christian tradition martyrs are usually the victims of external aggression inflicted on them in the pursuit of their faith; in Islam it is the perpetrator of the aggression, who also immolates himself in the process, who becomes the *Islamikaze* martyr. In other words, it is not he who suffers death or torture or misery on his way to martyrdom, since he had chosen that course avidly and advisedly, but he must kill in order to gain his place in the hierarchy of martyrdom. This dramatic shift, from those who were killed in battle or by accident and became thereby martyrs in classical Islam, to the *Islamikaze* intentional mass-killing of others in order to go to Paradise and enjoy the 72 virgins promised by the Qur'an, is the mind-boggling thought that baffles the West today.

Self-Delusion, Fantasy and the Real World—The proverbial Arab enamoring with words, to the point of ecstasy, has been studied by scholars, such as Gibb and Patai, and found related to the strength of the Arabic idium, as exemplified in the Qur'an, in the ancient Arabic poetry of the time of the *Jahiliyya,* and in the subsequent Arab and Muslim literature. The ability of the word to move people and to incite them to action, a key element in the training of the *Islamikaze,* is supplemented by a rich world of fantasy, which defies rational analysis, and where wishful thinking replaces facts, mantra-like slogans supersede policy ("Jerusalem will be liberated by one million *shahids*"; "if the Israelis do not like it, they can drink the waters of the Gaza Sea/the Dead Sea"), and the unpleasant is denied as if it did not exist (No Muslims have committed the Twin Tower murder; The Israelis/ Jews did). For that reason, commitments are ignored, as if they had never been undertaken (Oslo, smuggling in weapons by Palestinians, arresting terrorists), promises are forgotten the moment they are made (to stop incitement and terrorism), slogans are coined and repeated (Israelis inject HIV positive to Palestinians; Oslo is like Hudaybiyya), propaganda and incitement thrive (the Karine A and Suntorini weapons smuggling never took place; Israelis and Americans are children killers), boasting one's exploits (Egyptian democracy is more authentic than Israel's) and denigrating the enemy are rife (the Jews are cowardly, the descendants of monkeys and pigs), lies are made up to cover up deficiencies (Palestinians economic suffering is due to Israel's policies, not to terrorist activities by the Palestinians), and denial is exercised when one is faced with facts (No Karine A, no blowing up of the Twin Towers). History is invented (Palestinians are the descendants of Canaanites), false analogies are made (Palestinian leaders and the founding fathers of America), facts are denied (the Holocaust, or involvement in terrorism), and self-embellishment and self-aggrandizement are sought (the future belongs to Islam, the West's demise is imminent) for consolation. Palestinian and other Arab and Muslim textbooks for children tell the entire story with such eloquence that not much needs to be added.[14] But enough examples will be cited, especially in connection with Islamic terrorism, its incitement, and its praise after the acts of murder, to illustrate the main assumptions of this chapter.

Each of the fantasies undergoes several stages: first the fabrication of a web of lies that has no relations to facts, and which Muslims think that if it is repeated often enough, it becomes a reality, in which they begin to believe themselves, even when they cannot prove it. Because no rules of evidence apply to them, and what matters is the manufacturing of "facts" and their diffusion in their midst and across the world, the latter swallows the stories, unsuspecting that hoaxes of that dimension can be invented, and out of believe that even if the Israelis or the Americans did not "do it," it is likely that they would, because it is in their nature. A classic case in point is the blood libel against the Jews, which we see repeated by the Minister of Defense in Syria, and reiterated by nearly all Muslim media, without criticism. In the same vein, the Palestinian delegate at the Commission of Human Rights in Geneva, of all places, can stand up and accuse the Israelis of injecting AIDS virus to Palestinian children, or Arafat lambasting the Israelis for spreading poisoned sweets to kill Palestinians, or the Saudis and Egyptians claiming that Israel had distributed an aphrodisiac which increased the sexual appetite of women in order to corrupt their morals, or that the Israeli armed forced used depleted uranium bullets to harm the Palestinians. During the battles of Jenin in April-May, 2002, for example, a Palestinian father was produced on television cameras, crying and weeping for his nine children who had "perished" before his eyes and whom he "had seen with his own eyes" under the rubble. A very horrible and heart-tearing experience indeed, except that all nine children were fortunately found sound and safe. Perhaps the most chilling hoax that was fabricated by the Palestinians, actively supported by all Arabs and Muslims, and passively accepted by much of the European press, was the "Poison Affair" of 1983, when the Israelis were blasted for "poisoning Palestinian schoolgirls in Jenin," and then in other areas of the West Bank, with a view to "sterilizing them before their age of reproductive activity" and thus "battle against Palestinian demography." These condemnations were made throughout the press of the world, and even when it was proved that the "poisoning" was a case of mass hysteria, what professional medicine recognizes as "hyper-ventilation," the accusations did not recede.[15] Any accusation goes, and when the accuser is not held responsible for providing evidence, accusations and libel become cheap and no one has to account for.

Self-delusion operates on other levels as well. Convinced of the righteousness and exclusivity of their Islamic universal message, the Islamists cannot understand why the West and Israel pursue them, do not let them act with impunity in the Path of Allah, or wage war against them. For the message of Allah is clear and unambiguous, it declares the Jews monkeys, it forbids Muslims to befriend Jews and Christians,[16] enjoins the Muslims to "kill Unbelievers wherever we find them,"[17] to "murder them and treat them harshly,"[18] "fight and slay the Pagans, seize them, beleaguer them, and lie in wait for them in every stratagem,"[19] then what do the Infidels want? That word of Allah was intended against them, and they cannot deny or resist it, because Allah himself said it, and that is written, word for word, in His Divine Message—the Holy Book which applies to all humanity. They also believe that Allah and His Messenger had announced that it was acceptable for Muslims to go back on their promises and obligations with Pagans and make war on them whenever Muslims find themselves strong enough to do so[20] or that Allah had taken away the freedom of belief from all humanity and relegates those who disbelief in Islam to Hell,[21] calls them "untouchable and impure,"[22] and orders its followers to fight the Unbelievers until no other religion except Islam is left,[23] and more and more. Then, why should they spare non-Muslims, make any agreement with them, or honor any of their commitments to them?

The hardcore Islamists are therefore shocked that the West battles them and resists them, instead of submitting to them and recognizing that Islam is their only salvation. We have seen appeals to President Bush to convert to Islam and astonishment at his procrastination to do so. They cannot comprehend how and why the westerners are failing to see the light and do not hurry into the fold of Islam. In their world of delusion, they already see "thousands of Americans" repenting for their previous obtuse misunderstanding of Islam, and their "coming to tears when they listen to the Words of the Qur'an recited to them." Their worldview, which cannot accept a plurality of creeds, cannot also understand why they, the disseminators of the good of Allah and his message, should be held in low esteem, feared and persecuted by the West. All they did on 11 September was the fulfillment of the Word of Allah: "For them [the Unbelievers], garments of fire shall be cut and there shall be poured over their heads boiling water, whereby whatever is in their bowels and skin shall be dissolved and they will be punished with hooked iron rods,"[24] and that they will not only have to live in "disgrace in this life, but in the Day of Judgment He shall make them taste the penalty of burning."[25] To have precipitated the Day of Judgment upon the victims of that massacre was therefore nothing anomalous, just the early fulfillment of the Word of Allah.

Then, the stage of denial sets in, when the Muslims realize the outrage and havoc that their delusions have impelled them to commit. Be they acts of terror against Israel, the Karine A weapon smuggling, or the 11 September horror, they first of all deny they ever did, intended, knew or participated in those acts, paradoxically while at the same time evincing unrestrained jubilation about them. In their stage of denial, they wish both to dissociate themselves from the atrocities they had committed and to "enjoy" their results at the same time. The first major terrorist act against Israel, committed at the height of the Oslo euphoria in mid-1994, for example, where 21 young Israelis perished, was immediately denied by Arafat, who "had no knowledge" of it, and as "proof" of his innocence, he denounced the "act." In an interview to Israeli media, he speculated that it must have been the "deed of the Israeli services" who "were interested to wreck the Oslo agreements." Why wreck them, when the Rabin government who signed them was in power, full of goodwill and leniency towards Palestinian violations, and eager to show to his suspecting constituency in Israel that they "worked," Arafat did not explain. His conspiracy theory and mighty sense of denial was stronger than any rational consideration he might have invoked. When the *Achille Lauro* was hijacked by Palestinians in the Mediterranean in 1986, and an American citizen was murdered on board and callously tossed into the sea, the highjackers retired to Port Said where they were arraigned, but President Mubarak denied that he had any knowledge of the mastermind of that terrorist act, at the same time that he gave him shelter in his country. The affair of the ship Karine A, which in early 2002, was seized by the Israeli Navy in the Red Sea, illicitly carrying weapons to the Palestinians, under the command of one of Arafat's associate, was totally denied by Arafat and the Palestinian Authority as an "Israeli plot." Then when presented by the facts and the shipment of weapons was exposed to world media, Arafat said that he "had no knowledge of it personally," and only when he was confronted with the documents he had personally signed, he had no choice but apologize to President Bush.

In the aftermath of 11 September, similar patterns of behavior were detected in the Muslim world. In spite of their joy that they could not contain, Muslims from Pakistan to America, from Egypt to Afghanistan, denied that any Muslim could "commit such horror," because it was patently against "the compassion and tolerance of Islam," and verses were cited in support of that contention, such as that Islam "was opposed to compulsion in faith," or to the execution of "innocent civilians," unless they challenged Islam or "humiliated it." They also contended that an act of terror of such proportions could not have been possibly planned, let alone executed, by any Muslim state or organization, thus exonerating themselves in advance, even if that implied their admitting their incompetence in carrying out operations of such a scale. Even as the evidence was being gathered and divulged of the al-Qa'ida involvement, and demands were mounting for its indictment, they continued to insist that "unless America provided decisive and undisputed evidence for Muslim involvement," it was wrong on the part of the West to "smear the entire Muslim world," which was "opposed to terrorism," on account of the "yet unproven" deeds of the few. And so, the roles were again reversed: the Muslims, who needed no evidence for their delusions, and never stop to reflect on the irrationality of their accusations against the West and Israel, suddenly find themselves scrupulous about "evidence," when the accusations are laid at their door. And so they found themselves pledging that should any evidence emerge of Muslim involvement, the culprits ought to be pursued to "Muslim justice," and dealt with according to Muslim legal procedures, which meant in effect exonerating Muslims altogether.

But the facts kept pressing at the door, and the Muslim claims of "innocence" having become ludicrous in the eyes of world opinion, the stage of projection and laying the blame on others began. Like in the cases where Israelis were accused by Palestinians of "provocations," in mounting terrorism against their own citizens in order to blame the "innocent and peace-loving Palestinians," or of concocting the Karine A arm smuggling in order to smear the Palestinian "impeccable reputation" of "law-abiding" and "respect for its commitment," the Muslim world orchestrated such a campaign of projecting on others the evils of 11 September. First, it was claimed by Muslims in Egypt and Pakistan, America and Saudi Arabia, that the Jews, the CIA or the Israeli Mossad "did it," with countless "indications" indicting, successively or simultaneously, either or all of them. Again, becoming suddenly meticulous about "data gathering" and the provision of "conclusive evidence," they began to fabricate piecemeal fantastic stories about Israelis or Jews who "had been pre-warned and evacuated the premises of the Twin Towers prior to the blast," or the takeover of control towers by "suspect elements," also presumably Jewish, who "collaborated with the hijackers," or other hoaxes that never cease to raise our admiration for the boundless imagination of their inventers. Indeed, even though the reality of Muslim daydreaming is not itself limited by imagination, it proves to us more fantastic than their fantasies. From the concept of imagination we often use the constructive derivative of the "imaginative," but they are bent on the cultivating the "imaginary" full throttle, for that seems to fill their world and satisfy their emotions.

In this Kafkaesque world of the unreal, only non-Muslims are supposed to sin, and therefore anything projected on them is either true, or could be true even if it is not proven. This is the foundation of the vicious and sustained campaigns of denigration and diminishment of the West and the Jews in Muslim circles, countries and societies that we commonly call incitement and that is the pre-requisite for terrorism against them. Incitement often means delegitimation of the enemy, making it look corrupt, decadent, an inherent enemy of Islam and Allah, and therefore deserving of annihilation through terror. To that end, any means is justified, even inventing lies, making up false quotations from unexist-ing sources, like the "citation" by Palestinians in their textbooks of Talmudic passages that never were, which "prove" the Jews' conspiracy, their "evil" and their ill-intentions against Islam and the rest of humanity; or the ritual repetition of the blood libel as a fact of history, or liberal quotations from the forged Proto-cols of the Sages of Zion as if they were true documents, etc. It seems amazing to us that they care little not only for the truth as long as this serves their goals of libeling Israel and the West, but even less about educating their children on falsehoods and training them to consider imaginary texts as "citations."[26] In May 2002, when the Israeli armed forces launched their Defensive Shield Operation against terrorist bases in Jenin, which was led extremely carefully and sparingly with regard to civilians, the Palestinians immediately shouted:" Foul Game!." They had conducted a series of murderous attacks against Israeli civilians, and blown up one hundred of them within one week, including during the Passover Seder where entire families were wiped out (29 killed in all), and that passed in the Palestinian public as a matter of routine; but when Israel decided to root out the bases of terror in the West Bank, immediate accusations of "massacres" began, echoed by the Arab and Muslim press, (and also by the European press, and the numbers of "massacred" people kept increasing, reaching the peak of 3,000 according to Saeb Arekat, the Chief Palestinian negotiator. Then it turned out that "only" 50 Palestinians were killed in that center of terror, and for the most part amid very heavy fighting. There was no massacre, in short. Moreover, the total number of Israelis killed in the Pessach massacre (29) and in the Jenin operation (22), was still above the numbers of the killed Palestinians, but for them theirs was a massacre, Israel's was not.

Similarly, when the Americans opened their counter-attack against the Taliban in Afghanistan, and thoughtfully attempted not to harm civilians, to the extent possible, in the process, and even dropped significant quantities of food to sustain them during the fighting, it was the stories of "massacres" of "innocent civilians," "poisoning of the dropped food parcels," the "intentional bombing of schools and food depots," the "cruel arrest of Taliban POW's" and their transport to Guantánamo where they were treated "inhumanly" like "the Nazis would," that dominated the Arab and Muslim reporting of the operation, not the intentional atrocities, committed by the Taliban themselves and their supporters. For the Arab and Muslim audiences in both cases, the story was not about reporting a balanced truth, where the evils and motivations of both parties were recounted, and where the cause and effect sequence had to be explained, of horrendous terrorist attacks against civilians which had to be retributed and rooted out, but only the "callous and senseless American and Israeli aggressive attacks against civilians", without reason or cause, just to satisfy the evil instincts of Bush and Sharon. For them, vilifying, debasing, calumniating and libeling their enemies was the only way to delegitimize them as inhuman predators, so as to pave the way for future additional terrorist attacks against them. Projecting on the enemy, by heaping lies and pipe-dreams against him by way of pure and primitively simple incitement, however, does not only permit his delegitimation and encourages more attacks against him, but also, more significantly, belies and exposes the hidden dreams of what the Muslims would do to the Americans and the Israelis, if they could. Projection-cum-incitement, therefore, reveal to the West what fate is awaiting him, should the Muslim world win this confrontation. Wasn't it the Secretary General of the Arab League, 'Azzam Pasha, who declared on the day the Arab armies invaded nascent Israel in 1948 in order to eliminate it, that a "massacre would ensue that the world had never seen since the Mongols?" He meant a massacre of the Jews, exactly as the Muslim terrorists mean and implement today, but instead of piecemeal—in one big stroke.

Thus, while Americans and Israelis, in their reprisals in self-defense, have espoused the strategy of saving civilian lives to the extent possible, and would rather fight surgically, at the risk of their own casualties, to minimize the enemy's civilian losses, rather than blanket-bomb entire cities or population centers, Muslim terrorists act differently. Their stated aim is to maximize civilian casualties in the enemy's ranks, as evidenced in the Twin Towers and in the massive explosions in crowded civilian places in Israel, where nails and bolts are added to the bombs for maximal effect, and sometimes poisonous substances were tucked on to the bombs. In other words, while the West operates with a considerable restrain of its forces, for fear of their devastating impact, terrorists act with maximum unleashing of their power, something that leads to the fear in the West that they would not hesitate to use unconventional weapons if they laid their hands on them. That is exactly the soft-belly of the West, which ties in with its concern for human life, for due process of law and for restraint in use of power, which the Muslim terrorists who are not shackled by those limitations seek to exploit and strike at. To make that happen, roles are once again reversed: "We are not the terrorists!, You are!," they shout at the West. For, what Muslim martyrs do in terms of wanton killing, not only is it justified, because it is in the Path of Allah, but by delegitimizing the West as terrorist itself, the fight against it is called for, to be fought by all means available to the Muslims, precisely those that the West has restrained itself from using.

Pathological anti-Semitism—Perhaps since Nazi Germany no amount of vitriol was poured on the Jews as such, not only Israelis and Zionists, and has been the case in the past few years. We have seen nauseating citations of anti-

Semitic attacks in the high echelons of Arab politics, not only in intractable Syria, but even in the Egyptian mainstream press, which shamelessly recounts its lies and fabrications as "history," and avidly "quotes" from the Protocols of the Elders of Zion that never were, and recounts with a sadistic delight that can only match its joy at the carnage in the Towers, the Blood Libels of which Jews have been accused. Not one voice is there to stand up to the calumniators and intercede for ceasing that orgy of hatred. All one has to do is to rummage through the hundreds of hate sites that are fed by Muslims and Arabs across the world, to realize the width and depth of anti-Semitic sentiment in the Muslim world. There has also never been any society since the Nazis which so boasted of its hate towards the Jews as Muslim society today. Its preachers denigrate and humiliate them, incite against them, justify massacres against them, and associate them with America and the evil West. The reason for this new outburst of hatred, which has been manifest also throughout the democratic West where Jewish and Muslims communities live side by side, is perhaps because Jews represent the successful middle-class that has made the West prosperous. For the Muslims it is painful to admit that Jews succeeded where they have failed, and the jealousy in their regard cannot be contained or suppressed. They compensate themselves by their prophecies about the "cowardly" Jews who in the end of days will run away and hide from the Muslims who will seek their destruction.

There is no need, as some counsel, for Israel (and the West for that matter) to go into any soul-searching and to dig up the "reasons" (there must be reasons, right?) for this hatred, anymore than there was one when the Jews were made the scapegoats of the Nazis, and were murdered for what they were, with the burden of the "guilt" accruing to them. If anything needs to be investigated, it is the sick minds of the anti-Semites, today and of old, but this does not seem to be the moment, beyond the enumeration of some traits of character of the Muslims which make them so prone to accuse others in general. For if the Muslims and Arabs are so fond of Hitler and of citing him, and they miss no opportunity to analyze "scientifically" the "reasons" for his victimization of the Jews, and they naturally find the Jews themselves guilty, then words (like "reason" and "cause") have been depleted of their meanings, and one is dragged to the realm of the incomprehensible. But then, side by side with that, the Holocaust that the Jews were supposed to have brought upon themselves, is vehemently, and again "scientifically," denied, and the Jews are relegated to the role of the Nazis themselves in their dealings with the Palestinians. Such a web of lies, presumptions, pretenses, denials and contradictions, only the modern Arab and Muslim mind could create. In any case, the delegitimation of the Jews, Israel their state, and Zionism-their movement of national liberation, are so thorough, total and irreversible, as to turn them into the target of the coming *Islamikaze* massacres, which they deserve *a priori*.

The details of Muslim and Arab anti-Semitism have been studied elsewhere[27]. By turning their hatred to Jews into so pathologically inseparable from their physiology, they immunize themselves against any human compassion. Otherwise, it is hard to understand how crowds would jump of joy in Palestinian and Egyptian streets, at the sight of Jewish children blown to pieces, or entire families wiped out in one stroke of madness. They have turned so obtuse and cruel when Jewish victims are concerned, that it is necessary to remind them, from time to time, that they are evil to pursue civilians and murder them in streets, restaurants and buses; even more evil are those who rejoice with them, and they must be excluded from the human race. If they call their massacres *Jihad*, and their murderers martyrs, that does not mitigate their crime; on the contrary, it discredits the faith that motivates them and the God in whose name they act. But the Muslim fundamentalists' judgment is blunted by hatred, to the point that they can no longer differentiate between good an evil, human or inhuman. They profess the evil of indiscriminate killing that is dictated by their blind hatred, even if they should be consummated by its fire. They have no use for facts (for example the Holocaust), nor respect to values (the mass-murders they commit without a hitch), nor concern for the victims. Because only they, the fighters of *Jihad*, who are awaited in Paradise, count and anyone in their way should be eliminated. They turn their own plight onto the Jews and accuse them of their backwardness, oppression and poverty; and impute to Zionism the "oppression of freedom" of which they themselves suffer. Only a twisted mind beyond repair can accuse the Jews of the Twin Tower massacre, begin to believe it itself, and then come to the conclusion that because of the "Jewish failure" to achieve their goals, the "future of Muslims in America looks bright."[28]

The Challenge to the West

Contrary to what some Muslim apologetics in the West, who stretch their leniency towards, and their "understanding" of the radicals to the exasperating limit; and regardless of whether they are motivated by their naïveté, ignorance, goodwill or sheer wishful thinking, or whatever hidden agenda may hang in their skeleton-closet, it is time to call a spade a spade, to stop playing into the hands of the terrorists and to ply to their manipulations, to stand up tall and determined, and fight back, pure and simple, as President Bush has taught all of us. For a plan of war to succeed, it has first of all to understand the motives and convictions of the enemies, something that we have tried to accomplish in the harrowing chapters of this book; and then to assess the enemy's war-plan and try to foil it, as a prerequisite to counter-attack and victory. This too was addressed in the previous pages of this chapter. We shall now attempt to develop ideas for counter-measures, taking into account that certain things, like verses from the Qur'an, or commonly accepted interpretations thereof, cannot be altered, and if they were that would only create more outrage and havoc. Secondly, in spite of the fundamentalists' perception that their war against the West is total and perpetual, until it succumbs, the latter, or any civilized society for that matter, cannot gear itself, nor educate their young on such a grim prospect of permanent war *ad infinitum*. And thirdly, it is not the business of the West to educate others, to look for "enlightenment" where it does not exist, or to determine unilaterally scales of values that must apply universally.

Departing from these premises, one can then devise some sort of accommodation by co-existence, not by changing others to please us, or adopt ourselves to please them, for their choices, like ours, must be respected, if we wish others to respect ours, as long as they do not interfere with ours or do not try forcibly to change them or to force theirs on us. In other words, it is the *modus vivendi* with others that the West has to choose over the *modus operandi* against them, as long as the live-and-let-live formula is accepted on both sides and none of them tries actively to undermine the other. But, unfortunately, the test of whether the rule is respected has to remain subjectively within the domain of each party, the present international organizations having shown us that politicking often takes precedence over decency and fairness; and we must be aware that conflicts of opinion, which might erupt into armed conflicts, will remain the constant characteristic of international relations in the foreseeable future too. This means, that though politics of consensus remain a choice course of action, the West has to be prepared to go its way all alone, when it considers that its vital civilizational, economic, perhaps existential, interests are at stake. Because the present rifts, suspicions, jealousies and bitterness between rich and poor countries and societies: Western and non-Western, northern and southern, developed and under-developed, and their struggles over resources, environment, immigration, social justice, population growth and standard of living, will not only deepen, but will create coalitions of the disadvantaged against which the West will find itself outnumbered and outvoted at any international forums. That is very much the case today already.

The West has tried over the past century, and especially after decolonization in the past half century, with the help of the emerging modernized elites in the liberated colonies, one must say, to introduce its own modern values of democracy, liberalism, human rights, peace for its own sake, free choices, education, development, technology, accountability in government, and an improving standard of living. The results were far from spectacular, save a few exceptions, and in any case in the 57 countries that label themselves "Muslim" today, with their over a billion (and growing) population, spanning two continents, the total failure is resounding. Yes, the perennial model of Turkey is cited, but since westernization was enforced brutally there, rather than grew organically from within by consensus, its coarse seam-lines are still visible almost a century later, and when allowed, the reaction of the fundamentalists erupts to the surface. This means to say, that should the West pursue its dictated "reforms" in Islamic countries, as it has been trying in the Palestinian Authority, Iraq and Afghanistan at the beginning of the new millennium, it will not get very far, because reforms by foreign pressure are doomed to fail under the internal counter-pressures of the Islamists. In consequence, it is not new reforms that the West should demand or expect in Muslim (or other non-Western for that matter) countries as prerequisites to dealing with them, but the fulfillment of two conditions in the aggregate: renouncing the use of force externally, and grant a minimal base of human rights domestically.

The West, on its part, cannot attain credibility if it only insists on the enforcement of those conditions differentially. For example, it cannot, on the one hand, detach itself from the domestic politics in Muslim countries, but on the other hand interfere in internal struggles for power between Islamists and others. It is its business to declare that it refuses to deal with a certain regime, for example, because of its blatant violations of human rights, but it is not its business to decide what regime would hold power, how it should behave domestically or externally, so long as it does not resort to violence, or whether it is illegitimate or not. We have seen that current American support to illegitimate rulers in the Muslim world, has only augmented popular resentment against both. If America does not ally itself with violators of human rights, though it does not interfere in their policies, then it cannot make the provision, at the same time, that those who own petrol are exempted from this requirement. This would otherwise be laughable and no one in the Islamic world would take it seriously. Let the peoples of the Islamic world struggle for their own form of government, and they will emerge, at the end, with the order (or the chaos) they deserve, or that is best suited for them, or that they are prepared to suffer. If and when they reach the end of the road with it, like the Shah's regime in Iran, then let them rise, struggle and come up with a new arrangement, all their own. And their "choice" must be respected by the West, whether it is Islamic, monarchical, military or otherwise. In view of the results of that internal struggle, the West might decide to deal or not to deal with the new emerging order, and only when it shows clear indications of using violence, conventional or non-conventional, or of resorting to terrorism against Western targets or interests, or against others who are allies of the West and whom it is interested to preserve, will the trouble-making ruler encounter the unified resolve of the West, deployed to defend civilization from havoc.

In these terms, stability is a fetish that has no longer room in the new world. Would we have preferred the continued "stability" of the "Empire of Evil," over the instability that followed its demise, until things took finally shape there (for now)? Or the "stability" of the Thousand Year Reich over the instabilities and horrors of the War, which ended that evil reign of the Nazis? Or do we prize the "stability" of stagnant economies over the social mayhem and instability that rapidly growing societies may incur? Similarly, buying "stability" in the Muslim world, at the price of perpetuating corrupt rulers and illegitimate regimes that the West supports, is not necessarily a superior choice over some domestic political struggle which may shake up those societies until something acceptable to them emerges. In the same vein, massive military and economic aid by the West to those countries it judges "vital" to its interests, does not necessarily serve that purpose in the long run: we have seen in our generation the Western-supported

Shah of Iran, and the Kings in Egypt, Iraq and Libya crumble, and with them Western influence, and the transfer of weaponry and funds from the West to the hands of its enemies. That very process can happen tomorrow in Egypt, Saudi Arabia, Jordan, Pakistan and elsewhere in the Muslim world, where Islamists are waiting in the aisles for their local illegitimate rulers to falter, or for American aid to be suspended. In the meantime, all America and the West are getting out of those heavy investments, is strengthening the illegitimate rulers they protect, by handing them more lethal power to hold their rule in place, thereby causing the pressures of anti-American resentment to build up and ultimately explode in their face.

This hands-off policy from the Muslim world will not necessarily harm Western interests. The West needs oil, all right, but the Muslims are no less interested to sell it than the Westerners to buy it, they cannot drink it or deflect it to any other use without bringing disaster upon themselves. Quite the contrary, if the West decides that the track record of the Muslims on human rights is unsatisfactory, it can also punish them differentially by reducing its purchases of oil from them, and increasing them from others. And if the present corrupt sheikhs, who immorally and illicitly appropriate to themselves the legendary wealth of their kingdoms, decide to launch hostile acts of boycott against the West in order to strangulate it economically, then perhaps it can help the people of those countries to take over their wealth, rid them of their absolute rulers and exploiters, and put the income to a better and fairer use than finance the obscene debauchery of the princes, who have no more legal and moral rights over the resources of their country than all the rest of their fellow-citizens. There is nothing more just, democratic, fair and indisputable that the West can help create, and the fear of that happening alone, will insure the unhampered flow of oil. And if it should happen, no one, save for the princes, would shed a tear.

But the predicament of the West will not end with its hands-off policy towards the Muslim world. Enough fundamentalist rogues will remain in the midst of Islamdom to concoct plots, violence and acts of terror, the bitter foretaste of which we have all shared on 11 September. A unified West must devise a long series of long-term, both defensive and offensive, measures to learn to coexist with the Muslim world in good neighborliness, with mutual respect if possible, in rough stand-off if necessary, where boundaries are drawn, red lines are clear, the rules of the game honored, and their violation swiftly retributed. But if terrorism, or other kinds of violence are unleashed against the West, its citizens, its allies or its interests, then measures will have been rehearsed to contain the situation and prepare for combating it. Those measures must cover: prevention and deterrence, punishment and reward, coping and eradication.

Rules of Coexistence—Coexistence between the West and the Muslim world, if not peaceful then at least non-belligerent, cannot exist or last unless a system of unilateral measures of self-defense is adopted by the West, but advertised and made clear to all, on the one hand; and another system of reward and non-lethal punishment is put in place, as a menu for every Muslim country or organization to choose from, if it elected to enjoy the goodies of the West, on the other. Both do not require any agreement on the part of the Muslim countries, but do assume a united and uniform policy of Western countries, who are willing to participate in the effort and also to benefit from its fruits, those who belong there today, or prove in the future that they respond to the cumulative criteria, set by the West itself, for joining in, such as a certain per-capita income, a certain GNP judged necessary to maintain Western norms, a regime of liberal democracy- elected, with pacific transfer of power, accountable, a-personal, non-hereditary; a free press, transparency of government, human rights and freedoms; free enterprise, freedom of property, transaction of real estate and funds; freedom to create in the arts, the humanities, literature, and protection of one's creation; and a strong and independent judiciary to oversee all this. Such countries that would be accepted to LOD (League of Democracies), or ADS (Association of Democratic States) at the center of which will be the United States, Canada, Australia and Western Europe, will add other applicants as they prove their adaptablity to its rules and their willingness and capacity to live by and up to them. This system may sidetrack the chaotic situation in the UN today, where politics and shifting majorities, composed of dictatorships for the most part, determine the moral and other standards of behavior in the world body. Durban 2001, should remain forever a warning to the level of hatred and bigotry that the UN today is capable of stooping to.

ADS will announce that it is organized to fight in unison terror, but is open not only to cooperation with Muslim countries who so desire, as long as they meet the two criteria of renouncing violence externally and enhance human rights domestically, but would even consider co-opting them into the organization if they should wean themselves from terror and develop political systems acceptable to it. Thus, without threats, recriminations, forced reforms and all the rest, a powerful incentive is introduced in the international arena for change, the Western way, if a country so elects, or stay in the putrid marsh of UN politics. The West will then determine whom to get into ADS, and once there what sort of obligations every country has to meet, proportionately to its strength, population and wealth, in contrast to the universality of the UN, which permits that any group of evil terrorist countries, such as Algeria, Syria, and Sudan can determine the agenda and resolutions of, for example, the Commission on Human Rights in Geneva. Handing public order and morality to the heads of the mafia, is not exactly the most efficient way to achieve peace and equity. It is important to emphasize, that in order to come across the most horrendous incitement, libel and hatred in the Muslim world, one does not need to look for the most radicals of fundamentalists. It is there across the board, in mainstream and opposition newspapers, among the populace and amidst students and intellectuals, in official chanceries and in Arab and diplomatic missions abroad.[29]

Before anything else, however, an iron-clad definition of terror has to be adopted unilaterally and announced by ADS, as there is no chance that Muslim countries would agree to any Western definition or abide by it. For them, things are clear: the United States and Israel are terrorists, while the Arabs and Muslims are either "freedom fighters" or they "fight back" out of "frustration" and "despair."[30] Even should the West agree unanimously on the formula of the State Department, there will remain the problem of who are the states which support terror and that President Bush pledged to regard also as terrorists. For example, Lebanon's government does not support terror openly, but it lets the Hizbullah operate in its territory, in conjunction with Iran and Syria who do support it. Or Saudi Arabia and Egypt, who are supposed to be aligned with the Americans, not only for fear of their wrath, but mainly because they are themselves threatened by domestic terrorism which jeopardizes their regimes; so, while they do not strictly encourage terror of give it shelter, Saudi Arabia does finance the Hamas and Islamic centers around the world which spawn terror, and both she and Egypt have permitted such a high level of home-grown incitement and hatred against the West and Israel, including in their state-controlled media, that it is doubtful whether they can be released from responsibility. American reactions to that incitement in the press of those "allies," are unaware of the venomous anti-Western and anti-Jewish sermons in the Saudi mosques, and of the violent student demonstrations in Egyptian universities where not only support is voiced for the Palestinian *Islamikaze*, but horrendous scenes of massacres of Israeli civilians were re-enacted on campus while the police was looking.

Thus, only after having arrived at an internally agreed formula, fine enough not to let anyone slip through, and being aware that even though the West did not declare war on Islam, Muslim fundamentalists did vow to wage war on America and Israel, ADS can then announce its rules of engagement with the Muslims, and the rest of the world for that matter:

1.   Immigration from those countries to ADS, will be strictly curtailed, in view of the Muslim undergrounds that have been festering in the past years in Europe and America, due to the extremely liberal policies of the West, which have been abused, right and left, by Muslim terrorist organizations. Control must not rely on the countries where immigration originates, not only because they are unwilling to stem the tide of their *reconquista* of Europe and of setting a Muslim foot in all continents, but even had they been willing to arrest the immigrants, their chaotic and corrupt systems would be incapable of implementing the decision. Therefore, only stringent defensives around ADS countries, interception of illegal immigrants and their repatriation without ceremony, and the expulsion from their territory of operatives who assist them, will slow down the invasion.

2.   Immigration, tourism and study by Muslim aliens in the West will be allowed only to nationals of Muslims countries which themselves allow

such an unhampered flow of Western immigrants, students and tourists, without discrimination towards other races, faiths or nationalities.

3. Economic aid, food grants, technical assistance, health and education, and development projects outside ADS will be offered only centrally by the organization if certain conditions are met by the applicants/recipients, such as: accountability, progress in democratization and human rights, a tangible effort in population control, renouncement of force in dealing with others, monitoring and taking steps against their centers of incitement in the media and the mosques, and the like. The central choice of programs by the organization will not only eliminate the current competition between member-states, which generates a waste of funds and a disruption of priorities, but will act as a positive incentive on candidates to aid to improve domestically in order to qualify.

4. No military assistance or sales of weapons will be permitted by ADS to non-member states, experience having shown that armed dictators are more lethally equipped to perpetuate their brutality and to divert their national wealth to undesirable ends; ADS will also announce that any weapon-manufacturing third party which sells or transfers weapons to those regimes, will itself be disqualified from dealings with ADS members.

5. Muslim assistance, especially by Saudi Arabia to building mosques and other Muslim institutions in the West, and their continued funding thereafter, will be made contingent upon parallel permission to build religious institutions for other faiths in Muslim countries, including the Arabian Peninsula, and on the contributor and the recipient's commitment that no incitement and no hatred would be propagated therein.

6. Import will be allowed to the West of Muslim cultural assets, in the form of books, movies, art shows and exhibits, performing art groups, missionaries and clerics, newspapers or tapes, only from countries that allow a free flow of the same Western assets to their territory, forbid by law the dissemination of hate and act upon that law..

Rules of Confrontation—ADS ought to be the main world body to fight terrorism, when the rules of peaceful engagement have been violated, or in preparation to such an eventuality. The struggle against terror is a continuous, never-relenting process, involving governments and populations, overt and covert means, punitive and preventive measures, legal and political, diplomatic and military initiatives, national and international efforts, education of the population to help avert catastrophe, and to deal with it when it strikes, morale, combat tactics and an overall strategy, intelligence gathering and analysis, and sometimes plain luck or sharp intuition can make the difference between disaster and relief. If ADS does not establish, lead and operate an integrated system of this sort, the world efforts against terror will remain diffuse, uncoordinated and inefficient; every country, organization and intelligence machine will remain suspicious of the others and jealous to preserve its own gathering networks and analysis staff, and every operational unit will continue to elect its reputation and glory over the general good of the Western world. The very joining of ADS should be a sign by its members that they are willing to surrender some national pride and resources for the sake of eradicating terrorism and neutralize its causes. It is understood that the West has little patience for the tremendous waste in human power and resources which terrorism forces on it collectively by compelling it to spend so much energy and attention to prevention and watching. But it is exactly the challenge to the West to show to the terrorists that their goal of sagging Western strength into submission will not happen. As we have said before, a succession of three dichotomic concepts will have to be addressed: prevention and deterrence, punishment and reward, coping and eradication.

Prevention and Deterrence—When ADS is established, its goals stated and the necessary resources, chains of command, operational tools and organizational frameworks wielded together, that in itself will signal to the Muslim terrorists that the West has taken up decisive steps to eradicate terror, and will no doubt act as a deterrent and preventive measure. But the list of deeds only begins: preventive arrests of suspects worldwide, not only in the United States; concerted intelligence efforts to penetrate terrorist rings, by all the means that human, electronic and communications intelligence can afford; stringent monitoring of ADS countries borders, less generous visas, eviction of students originating from countries who support terrorism, and more difficult access for those in doubt; a blanket prohibition of the use of weapons and explosives by non-governmental agencies; outlawing operations and fund-raising for terrorist, or otherwise "charitable," Muslim organizations, and freezing/confiscating their funds; a total ban on importing foreign money to build mosques for ADS countries Muslims, or to finance their activities or other Muslim activities, unless the same is allowed to other faiths in Muslim countries. Also, the special forces trained to battle terrorism or to curtail its activities, should be given high visibility, and the ADS budgets for that purpose should be advertised, both to explain to its own population the burdens it is asked to bear, and also for the sake of deterrence of the prospective terrorists, who should know that they face an impregnable wall if they want to penetrate ADS countries, and if they do succeed, their bodies would be returned in bags to their homelands, with great fanfare to deter others. Select pre-emptive operations could also be held against bases of terrorists prior to their setting out for action against the West or its allies.

Punishment and Reward—Deterrence works only when a credible and devastating force of punishment (not revenge, as the Muslims would have it) is ready to be unleashed every time an identifiable act of terrorism is perpetrated or being prepared. Naturally, since the *Islamikaze* themselves are likely to perish in their own blasts, the rapid detection of their sponsors, dispatchers, financers, supporters and trainers is crucial for swift and deadly retribution. No terrorist organization should escape unscathed by hiding under the apron of its sponsor state: just like the Taliban in Afghanistan, so the Hizbullah in Lebanon, the

Hamas in Jordan or in the Palestinian Authority, the *Tanzim* and Aqsa Brigades under Palestinian rule, or the Islamic Jihad in Damascus, all should be aware that any terrorist activity emanating from their territory would bring destruction and devastation to their sponsoring country. This is the only way to make those countries responsible for eradicating terrorism in their midst or to signal to them that they cannot escape economic and political pressure to conform, in addition to military strikes, unless they relent. Conversely, if those authorities battle terrorism themselves, which for them may amount to a domestic insurgency that they are unable to control, like in the Philippines, ADS would step in to help, to allocate generously equipment, funds and expertise, and to assist the self-purging society to make its steps towards even joining ADS itself, if it meets the requirements.

Coping and Eradication—While total eradication of terrorism is apparently impossible, bringing it to manageable levels, like in the 1960s, is quite feasible, if the pressure on terrorist organizations keeps escalating to the point that their own societies would have to eject them from their midst. The irony may be that, while Muslim countries may be willing and able to adopt the requisite steps to eradicate terror, if only to allow their regimes to survive, it may be that European countries themselves, who had allowed for years al-Qa'ida bases to thrive on their turf, would have difficulties to invoke the necessary legal and political steps to wipe out would-be terrorists in their lands. In any case, no program of long-term eradication is possible if the citizenry of ADS is not taught to cope with the new situation in the long haul. It is not only a matter of patience in long security lines, alertness to suspicious people or parcels, precautionary steps entering a building or exiting from it, night-watching in urban areas against terrorist mischief under the cover of darkness; but also training to be calm in the face of adversity and not to panic, how to assist the injured after a blast, how to block off an affected area, to identify non-conventional blasts, to self-inject anti-dotes and to self-administer treatment, how to evacuate to hospital oneself and others, and how to accept placidly additional outlays that are not usually anticipated. A well-prepared, well-rehearsed and determined citizenry has proven, as in the case of Israel, that it can not only reduce the panic and face up to the disaster, but also act as a deterrent in the final analysis, when the terrorist enemy knows that his initial scheme of sowing terror and fear had been *a priori* aborted.

These measures seem harsh, even inhuman and undemocratic to the squeamish and faint-hearted among us. But they are needed by democracies to defend themselves in this hour of emergency. Other optimistic minds believe that by explaining and apologizing, the West's righteousness shall prevail and the bad spirits that have been threatening all of us shall be soothed and mitigated. Still others are expecting "other interpretations" of Islam to emerge, which will be more enlightened, accommodating and modern. Such interpretations do exist, but in the underground, they are based more on apologetics than on moral grounds, and their authors have been attacked, killed, maimed or disgraced. The masses of the Arabs are not exposed to free speech and to liberal media with contradicting opinions, they are subjected to the uniform and repetitive message of hate and illusion that is hammered into their heads, day in day out, in the form of incitement, therefore they do not know any better. No enlightenment can be expected to emerge from a conservative Islam, which does not even possess the humanity of compassion to victims of terrorist massacres, and no liberal Muslim individuals will have the courage, let alone the power and stamina to enforce their dissenting marginal views on the terrifyingly deluded and incited masses. Therefore, the West has no much choice but to go all the way all alone in thinking, planning and implementing its measures of self-defense and survival.

Notes

1. See R. Israeli, *Muslim Fundamentalism in Israel,* Brassey's, London, 1993, p. 147.
2. *Jerusalem Post,* 4 January 2002.
3. Daniel Pipes, "Fighting Militant Islam without Bias," *City Journal,* Autumn 2001.
4. *Ibid.*
5. *The Jerusalem Post*, 7 October, 2005, p. 9.
6. R. Israeli, *Islamikaze: Manifestations of Islamic Martyrology,* Frank Cass, London, 2003, the Concluding Chapter.
7. Former President Rafsanjani spoke of using a nuclear bomb against Israel. See Iran News (English), *Kayhan* (Farsi) and *Al-Wifaq (*Arabic), 15 December, 2001. Memri 325, 3 January, 2002. See also *Al-Sha'b* (Egypt), 23 September, 2001.
8. Al-Qa'ida spokesman, Suleiman Abu Gheith, in an article titled "In the Shadow of the Lances," and also Ayman al-Zawahiri's article in *al-Mujahidin.* For both, see Memri, 12 June 2002.
9. Bernard Lewis, "How did the Infidels Win?," *National Post,* 1 June, 2002.
10. For the most comprehensive and authoritative study to date, see Majid Khadduri, *War and Peace in Islam.*
11. See Moshe Sharon, *"Hudna* and *Sulh* in Islam" (Hebrew), *Nativ,* Summer 2002.
12. See repeated references to this in the Charter of the Hamas, referred to above.
13. Bernard Lewis, see ftn.1 above.
14. R. Israeli, "Identity and State-building: Educating Palestinian Children after Oslo," *Journal of Terrorism and Political Violence,* Spring 2002.
15. See R. Israeli, *Poison: Modern Manifestations of a Blood Libel,* Lexington Books, Lanham and NY, 2002.
16. Qur'an, Sura 5:51.
17. Qur'an, Sura 2:191.
18. Qur'an, Sura 9:123.
19. Qur'an, Sura 9:5.
20. Qur'an, Sura 9:3.
21. Qur'an, Sura 5:10.
22. Qur'an, Sura 9:28.
23. Qur'an, Sura 2:193.
24. Qur'an, Sura 22:19-22.
25. Qur'an, Sura 22:9.
26. For examples see R. Israeli, fn. 6 above.

27.   See, eg. The above cited:*Islamikaze* book, especially Chapter 8, pp. 281-344.

28.   See for examples, Itamar Marcus, "Islam's Mandatory War against Jews and Israel in Palestinian Authority Religious Teaching," *Studies on Palestinian Culture and Society,* Study No 4, 2 July 2001. By Palestinian Media Watch, Jerusalem; and James Cox, *USA Today,* 28 September 2001.

29.   Note, e.g., the virulent anti-Semitic terms with which Assad of Syria spoke about Israel during the visit of the Pope in Damascus, the Blood Libel that is promoted by his Defense Minister, or the statement by the Saudi Ambassador to London in support of the Islamikaze martyrs.

30.   Regarding the heated debates in the Arab world on the definition of terrorism, see *Al-Hayat* (London) 25, 28, 29 September, and 1 October, 2001; *Al-Ba'th* (Syria), 1 October, 2001; *Tishrin* (Syria), 3 October, 2001; *Syria Times* (Syria), 2 October, 2001; *Al-Safir* (Lebanon), 25 and 27 September, 2001. All in Memri's *Terror in America* Dispatch 18 (Hebrew), no date.

Bibliography

Newspapers, News Agencies, Websites, and Journals

Agence France Press (AFP)
Aftonbladet,
Al-Ahram Weekly, "Beyond the Vacuum," 13-16 April 2006.
(The) American Thinker
Arab News (Saudi Arabia)
Associated Press (AP)/AP Online
Atlantic Monthly
Avvenire
(Al)-Ba'th (Syria),
Berlingske Titende
brusselsjournal.com / Brussels Journal
Christian Science Monitor
City Journal
Commentary
Copenhagen Post/ Online
Dagbladet (Norway)
Dagens Nyheter
Daily Telegraph
Deutsche Welle
Dhimmi Watch
DIIS Brief, (Dansk Institut for InternationaleStudier, Copenhagen)
Divine Salamis BBS: The discussion board for the Divine Salamis Community
Economist
(The) European Magazine
Expatica (center of Extremist Studies, Amsterdam)
Expressen
FrontPageMagazine
Gazet van Antwerpen
Guardian
Haaretz
Al-Hayat (London)
instapundit.com/archives/028869.
Institute of Counter Terrorism (ICT)
Iran News
IslamOnLine,

Jerusalem Post
Journal of Terrorism and Political Violence
Jyllands-Posten
Kayhan
Khaleej Times Online
Lawrence Auster@att.net,
Le Figaro
(The) Local (Sweden)
Los Angeles Times
MEMRI (Middle East Media Research Institute)
MSANews *(The) New York Times*
(al)-Mujahidin
National Post
Nativ (Israel)
NIS News Bulletin—Netherlands, National News Agency ANP
Palestinian Media Watch
Patterns of Global Terrorism, (The U.S. Department of State)
Policy Watch, (The Washington Institute)
Post-Holocaust and Anti-Semitism Series, (The Jerusalem Center for Public
    Affairs).
Prospect Magazine
(The) Register
Reuters
Review of International Affair (Belgrade)
Revue des Deux Mondes
(Al)-Safi r (Lebanon)
(al) Sha'b (Egypt)
Sky News
SliwaNews@aol.com, Daily report
Spiegel Online
Studies on Palestinian Culture and Society
(The) Sunday Times
Sydsvenskan
Syria Times (Syria),
Sveriges Radio
Swissinfo
(The) Times /Times Online
Tishrin (Syria),
USA Today
Wall Street Journal, Europe
Washington Post
Washington Times
(al) Wifaq (Iran)
Xinhua News Agency
ynetnews

Books

Bat Ye'or, *The Decline of Eastern Christianity under Islam: From Jihad to Dhimmitude,* Fairleigh Dickinson University Press, Madison, 1996.
Bodzemir, M., *Islam, et Laicite: Approches Globales et Regionales*, Paris, 1996.
Burns, Robert, *The Crusader Kingdom of Valencia,* Harvard University Press, Cambridge, MA, 1967.
Canak, Jovan (ed.), *Greater Albania: Concepts and Possible Consequences*, the Institute of Geo-Political Studies, Belgrade, 1998.
Craig-Harris, Lillian, *China Considers the Middle East*, Tauris, London, 1993, p. 275.
Etzioni, Amitai, *From Empire to Community,* McMillan, NY, 2004.
Hadzivukovic, Vesna and others (eds), *Chronicle of Announced Death*, 1993, Belgrade.
Israeli, Raphael, *Fundamentalist Islam and Israel*, University Press of America, Lanham and NY, 1993.
Israeli, Raphael, *Muslim Fundamentalism in Israel,* Brassey's, London, 1993.
Israeli, Raphael, *Poison: Modern Manifestations of a Blood Libel,* Lexington Books, Lanham and NY, 2002.
Israeli, Raphael, *Islamikaze: Manifestations of Islamic Martyrology,* Frank Cass, London, 2003.
Israeli, Raphael, *The Iraq War: Hidden Agendas and Babylonian Intrigue,* Sussex Academic Press, 2004.
Izetbegovic. Alia, *The Muslim Revolution,* Belgrade, 1970.
Kepel, Gilles, *La Revanche de Dieu,* Paris.
Khadduri, Majid, *War and Peace in Islam.*
Mawdoodi, Abu al-'Ala' al-, *Nationalism in India,* Malihabad, 1948.
(The) Qur'an.
Terzic, Slavenko (ed), *Islam, the Balkans and the Great Powers (XIV-XX Centuries),* the Serbian Academy of Science, Volume 14, Belgrade, 1997.

Articles

"10% of Austrians are biased against Muslims," *Khaleej Times Online,* 20 May 2006. http://www.khaleejtimes.com/DisplayArticleNew.asp?xfi le=data/theworld/2006/May/theworld_May727.xml&section=theworld&col.
Abu Gheith, Suleiman, "In the Shadow of the Lances," see Memri, 12 June 2002.
Abul Einein, Tamer, "Preacher Denied Entry, Swiss Muslims Furious," *Islam On-Line*, 19 September 2005, http://www.islamonline.net/English/News/2005-09/19/article04.shtml.
"AEL: Every Dutch Soldier's Death Is a Victory," *Expatica*—25 October 2004.
http://www.expatica.com/source/site_article.asp?subchannel_id=1&story_id=13222&name=AEL%3A+every+Dutch+soldier%27s+death+is+a+victory+

Ali Khan, Ghazanfar, "Products of Danish Dairy Company Return to Super-market Shelves" *Arab News* (Saudi Arabia) 4 April 2006.

Almond, Peter, "Beware: The New Goths Are Coming," *The Sunday Times*—11 June 2006.

Apter-Klinghoffer, Judith, SliwaNews@aol.com, Daily report dated 4 May 2006.

Batakovuc, Dusan,"La Bosnie-Herzegovine: le System des Alliances," in Terzic, op. cit. pp 335- 343.

Belien, Paul, "Brussels Prosecutes Aramaic Priest and Fugitive for Islamopho-bia," http://www.brusselsjournal.com/node/936, 27 March 2006.

Belien, Paul, "Dutch Worry about Radical Muslims in the Military," *The Brussels Journal*, 2 May 2006.

Berlinski, Claire, "Menace in Europe: Why the Continent's Crisis Is America's, Too," Interviewed about Europe, Muslim integration, instapundit.com/ar-chives/028869.php

Binyon, Michael, "Prince Pitches for Religious Tolerance," *The Times*, 5 May 2006.

Bled, Jean-Paul, "La Question de Bosnie-Hercegovine dans La Revue Des Deux Mondes," *Revue des Deux Mondes*, Paris, 1876, Vol II, No 1, pp. 237-254.

Browne, Anthony and Suna Erdem, "Education Clash Hold Up EU Talks," *The Times,* 8 April 2006.

"Brussels Commune Fundamentalist Recruiting Ground Says Journalist," *Expatica*—14 March 2005 http://www.expatica.com/source/site_article. asp?subchannel_id=24&story_id=17996&name=Brussels+commune+% 27extremistMuslim+recruiting+ground%27.

Capper, Scott, "Controversial Muslim Scholar Wins in Court," *Swissinfo*—20 May 2005.

Cardia, Carlo, *Avvenire,* 16 March, 2006. Translated and Cited by Joseph D'Hippolito, *FrontPageMagazine.com* 6 April 2006.

Cesari, Jocelyne, MSANews 6 June 2000.

Conge, George, "Most Dutch Say Islam Incompatible with Western Society," *Jerusalem Post*, 19 June 2006.

"Controversial Imam Threatens to Return to Gaza," *Copenhagen* Pos, 18 May 2006.

Cox, James, *USA Today,* 28 September 2001.

D'Hippolito, Joseph, "How Will Rome Face Mecca?" *FrontPage Magazine. com,* 6 April, 2006.

"Dutch Parliament OKs Anti-Terror Measures," *USA Today*, 23 May 2006, http://www.usatoday.com/news/world/2006-05-23-dutch-terror_x.htm.

"European Imams Stress Social Integration," *Deutsche Welle*—4 April 2006. http://www.dw-world.de/dw/article/0,2144,1965132,00.html.

Evans-Pritchard, Ambrose, "EU 'Covered Up' Attacks on Jews by Young Mus-lims" *Daily Telegraph*, 1 April 2004.

Ewing, Adam, "British Police in Gothenburg 'Terror' Raid," *The Local*—Swe-den's news in English, 30 May 2006.

Fighel, Yoni, "Swiss authorities thwart plot to down El Al passenger plane" *Institute of Counter-Terrorism* (ICT), 20 May 2006. in bulletin of the *Institute of Counter-Terrorism*, May 20, 2006. op. cit.

"FM Bot Explains Dialogue Model to Muslim World," *NIS News Bulletin—Netherlands National News Agency ANP,* DOHA, 17 February 2006.

Ford, Richard, "Curb on sham weddings ruled illegal" *The Times* 11 April 2006.

Fuletic, Duro, "Consequences of a Possible Creation of Greater Albania," *Review of International Affairs*, Vol. L, No. 1085-6, October-November, 1999, p. 23.

Gerstenfeld, Manfred, "The Muhammed Cartoon Controversy, Israel and the Jews: A Case Study," *Post-Holocaust and Anti-Semitism Series,* 43, 2 April 2006, by The Jerusalem Center for Public Affairs.

Ginat, Gitit, "Freedom Fighter," www.haarez.com, 18 May 2006.

"Govt Advisors: Embrace Islam, Tackle Allies," *NIS News Bulletin—Netherlands National News Agency ANP,* The Hague, 12 April 2006.

Guitta, Olivier, "For Jews, Belgium is no better than France," *The American Thinker* 6 July 2004, http://americanthinker.com/articles.php?article_id=3655.

Haines, Lester, "Swiss cuff Islamic hate message duo: Geneva university computer jihad," *The Register,* 31 October 2005. http://www.theregister.co.uk/2005/10/31/hate_message_duo.

"Hamas minister thanks Sweden for visa" *The Local*—Sweden's News in English, 6 May 2006, http://www.thelocal.se/article.php?ID=3738&date=20060506&PHPSESSID=04d908160f98e39972b6afe9e01248b5.

Heneghan, Tom, "Vienna imam says yes to Europe, no to 'Euro-Islam,'" *Reuters,* 12 Apr 2006.

Higgins, Andrew, "Taking Leave: Islamist Threats to Dutch Politician Bring Chill at Home: Ms. Hirsi Ali Quits Parliament, Plans to Resettle in U.S. after Losing Safe House," *Wall Street Journal*, 17 May 2006.

Holm, Ulla, "The Danish Ugly Duckling and the Mohammed Cartoons," *DIIS Brief,* Dansk Institut for Internationale Studier, Copenhagen, February 2006.

"IAF Participation a Deal Breaker," *Jerusalem Post,* 26 April 2006; see also Jerusalem Post Lead Article of 30 April 2006.

"Imam Gives Up European Dream: Western Democracy Has Failed to Give Equal Rights to Muslims, says the Controversial Imam, Abu Laban, as He Announces Plans to Leave Denmark," *Copenhagen Post,* 11 May 2006.

"In a New Biography, Denmark's Queen Margrethe II Says Should be Challenged," *Copenhagen Post Online*, 14 April 2005, http://www.cphpost.dk/get/87253.html.

"Islamic Leader Criticizes Austrian Interior Minister for Suggesting Muslims Don't Integrate," *AP Online,* 15 May 2006. http://www.khaleejtimes.com/DisplayArticleNew.asp?col=&section=theworld&xfi le=data/theworld/2006/May/theworld_

Israeli, Raphael, "The Charter of Allah: The Platform of the Islamic Resistance Movement," in R. Israeli, *Fundamentalist Islam and Israel*, University Press of America, Lanham and NY, 1993.

Israeli, Raphael, "Islamikaze and their significance," in *Terrorism and Political Violence*, Vol. 9, No. 3 (Autumn 1997), p. 112-113.

Israeli, Raphael, "Identity and State-building: Educating Palestinian Children after Oslo," *Journal of Terrorism and Political Violence,* Spring 2002.

Jacques, Philippe, "The Challenge Is to Adapt Our Societies to Islam," Cafe Babel—*The European Magazine*, 16 December 2004 (Translated from the French by Veronica Newington).

"Jihadists' Return Worries Europe" *Agence France Press*, cited by *Washington Times*, 18 May 2006.

Kaplan, Lee, "Islamism's Legal Manipulations," *FrontPageMagazine.com*, 9 May 2000.

Kiefer, Peter and Elisabetta Povoledo, "Illegal Immigrants Become Focus of the Election Campaign in Italy," *New York Times*, 28 March 2006.

Kriege, Hilary Leila, "Holland Moves to Ban Holocaust Denial," *Jerusalem Post,* 10 June 2006.

Lappin, Yaakov, http://www.ynetnews.com/articles/0,7340,L-3135697,00. html, 1 September 2005, This site is accompanied by videos showing men training with explosives threatening Sweden with "suffering in the name of Allah."

Lewis, Bernard, "The Roots of Muslim Rage," *Atlantic Monthly,* September 1990.

Lewis, Bernard, "How Did the Infidels Win?", *National Post,* 1 June 2002.

Majer, Hans, "The Functioning of a Multi-ethnic and Multi-religious State: the Ottoman Empire," in Slavenko Terzic (ed), *Islam, the Balkans and the Great Powers (XIV-XX Centuries),* the Serbian Academy of Science, Volume 14, Belgrade, 1997, pp. 61 ff.

Marcus, Itamar, "Islam's Mandatory War against Jews and Israel in Palestinian Authority Religious Teaching," *Studies on Palestinian Culture and Society,* Study No 4, 2 July 2001.

Masood, Ehsan, "Interview with Tariq Ramadan," *Prospect Magazine*—Issue 124, July 2006.

Matboli, Ahmad Al-, "Austrian Muslims Concerned at New Immigration Law," *Islam OnLine*, 15 May 2005 http://www.islamonline.net/English/News/2005-05/15/article02.shtml.

McLean, Renwick, "Imams in Spain say Muslims and Jews Must Confront Extremism," *The New York Times,* 26 March 2006.

Moore, Molly, "With End of French School Year Comes Threat of Deportation" *Washington Post*, 15 June 2006.

Moore, Molly, "Dutch Convert to Islam: Veiled and Viewed as a Traitor: a Woman's Experience Illustrates Europe's Struggle with Its Identity," *Washington Post,* 19 March 2006.

Musharbash, Yassin, and Anna Reimann. "Crisis in Denmark," *Spiegel Online*—1 February 2006. http://www.spiegel.de/international/0,1518,398624,00. html.

"Muslim Council: No Support for Special Laws," *The Local*—29 April 2006 http://www.thelocal.se/article.php?ID=3688&date=20060429.

"Muslim Teacher Fired for Violating Geneva Laws," *Swissinfo*—19 December 2002 http://www.swissinfo.org/eng/swissinfo.html?siteSect=105&sid=1527150.

"Muslims in Holland" *Spiegel Online*—21 April 2006. http://www.spiegel.de/international/0,1518,412355,00.html.

Naughton, Philippe, "Spanish court quashes 9/11 conviction," *Times Online*—1 June 2006.

Papacella, Daniele, (translation: Vanessa Mock), "Muslim Councillor Calls for Dialogue with Islam" *Swissinfo* – 25 April 2004. http://www.swissinfo.org/eng/search/detail/Muslim_councillor_calls_for_dialogue_with_Islam.html?siteSect=881&sid=4889542&cKey=1082887270000.

Patterns of Global Terrorism, The U.S. Department of State, April 1998.

Pipes, Daniel, "Fighting Militant Islam, without Bias," *City Journal*, Autumn 2001. http://www.city-journal.org/htm/41/fi ghtingmilitant.html.

Pipes, Daniel, "The Vatican Confronts Islam," *FrontPageMagazine.com*, 5 July 2006.

Poole, Patrick, "Britain's Tariq TV," *FrontPageMagazine.com* 25 May 2006.

Popovic, Alexander, "La Politique Titiste envers les Religions et ses Consequences," in M. Bodzemir, *Islam, et Laicite: Approches Globales et Regionales*, Paris 1996, pp. 98-102.

"Post subject: The List of Musulman Demands to Swedish Political Parties," *Divine Salamis BBS: The discussion board for the Divine Salamis community 29 April 2006*. http://www.divine-salamis.com/phpBB/viewtopic.php?t=1447.

"'PvdA Director' To Make Film on Gay Islam Leaders," *NIS News Bulletin Netherlands National News Agency ANP* AMSTERDAM, 22 February 2006.

"Radicalisation Increases at Dutch Mosques," *NIS News Bulletin—Netherlands National News Agency ANP*, The Hague, 8 June 2006.

Raved, Ahiya, "Ex-Mossad chief warns of Muslim European cities and of World War Three," in his address to the Board of Trustees to the Technion in Haifa, Israel, 4 June 2006. http://www.ynetnews.com/articles/0,7340,L-3258745,00.html.

Rennie, David, "Artists try not to offend Muslims as satire festival treads softly," *Daily Telegraph*, 10 March 2006.

Reuter, Jens, "From Religious Community to Nation: the Ethnogenesis of the-Bosnian Muslims," in Terzic (ed.) op. cit. pp. 617-623.

Rodríguez, Sebastian Vilar, a circulated article on Internet, end of 2005 and beginning of 2006.

Rolfe, Pamela, "29 Indicted for Roles In Madrid Bombings: Judge Says Al-Qaeda Inspired Local Cell," *The Washington Post*, 12 April 2006.

Rotella, Sebastian, "Swiss Spy in a War of Words: An Ex-informant Who Became a Muslim Says His Handlers Wanted Him to Frame an Islamic Scholar. Officials Say He's on a Personal Vendetta." *LA Times*—22 May 2006. http://www.latimes.com/news/printedition/front/la-fg-mole22may22,1,1426054,full.story?coll=laheadlinesfrontpage&ctrack=1&cset=true34. *Ibid.*

Sadeh, Sharon, "The London Bridge Is Collapsing," *Haaretz*, 30 September 2005.

Sanandaji, Nima, "Sweden's Unholy Alliance," *FrontPageMagazine.com*, 19 May 2006.

Sanandaji, Nima, "Sweden's Immigration Nightmare," *FrontPageMagazine.com*, 2 June 2006.

Sawi, Hassan Fattah and Nada al-, "Possible Crack in the Boycott of Danish Goods," *New York Times*, 5 April 2006.

"Separate Laws for Muslims' Idea Slammed," *The Local*—Sweden's News in English, 28 April 2006.

Sharon, Moshe, "*Hudna* and *Sulh* in Islam" (Hebrew), *Nativ*, Summer 2002.

Spencer, Robert, "Jihad in Switzerland,"cited by AP, 23 August 2004.

Spencer, Robert, "Swiss Seize Five Suspected Extremists," cited by AP, 5 March 2005.

"State to Pay Imams' Wages," *Expatica*—16 December 2004 http://www.ex-patica.com/source/site_article.asp?channel_id=3&storyid=15137

Stavrou, David, "Swedish Company Labels Golan Wines," *Jerusalem Post*, 6 June 2006.

Sullivan, Kevin, "British Slow to Recognize Threat of Terrorism: London Bombings Couldn't Have Been Prevented, Report Says," *Washington Post*, 11 May 2006.

"Sweden's anti-peace policy," Lead Article, *Jerusalem Post*, 30 April 2006.

"Swedish PM Defends Decision to Grant Visa to Hamas Minister," www.haaretz.com, 5 May 2006.

"Talking of Immigrants: America's Debate on Immigration May be Painful, but Europe's Is Dysfunctional" *Economist*, 1 June 2006.

"Terror Attacks Thwarted," *Sky News*, 6 April 2006.

"Terror Cell 'Plotted Airliner Attack',"—*Guardian*, 9 June 2006,

"Terror in America," *MEMRI*, Dispatch 18 (Hebrew), no date.

"The Clash of Civilizations Is Currently on Hold," *Copenhagen Post On-line*—20

"The Future Saints," in Vesna Hadzivukovic and others (eds), *Chronicle of Announced Death*, 1993. p. 46. April 2006, http://www.cphpost.dk/get/95174.html.

"Thousands March in Brussels in Memory of Teen," *Reuters*, 23 April 2006 http://news.yahoo.com/s/nm/20060423/wl_nm/belgium_march_dc_1.

Todorov, Vrban, "The Federalist Idea as a Means for Preserving the Integrity of the Ottoman Empire," in S. Terzic, op. cit. pp. 293-296.

"Top Italian Spy Arrested over CIA Kidnap Plot," *Daily Telegraph*, 5 July 2006.

"Turkey: 56 Mayors Face Trial," *New York Times*—20 June 2006.

Twiston -Davies, Bess, *The Times*—22 April 2006.

Warrick, Joby, "U.S. Silence Impeding Swiss in Nuclear Case: Expert Says Calls Have Been Ignored," *Washington Post* 26 May 2006.

Weigel, George, "Europe's Two Culture Wars," *Commentary*, May 2006.

Wildman, Sarah, "Europe Rethinks Its 'Safe Haven' Status," *The Christian Science Monitor*, 24 May 2006 http://www.csmonitor.com/2006/0524/p07s02-woeu.html.

Winter, Leon de, interviewed by *Spiegel Online*, "The Dutch Are Not Afraid of Islam,"—2 February 2006. URL: http://www.spiegel.de/international/0,1518,398708,00.html.

Woolcock, Nicola and Sean O'Neill, "Once a Friendly Christian, He Now Backs the Bombers: Two Faces, Two Converts—Two Muslim Extremists in Britain," *The Times*, 24 April 2006.

Woolcock, Nicola and Dominic Kennedy, "What the Neo-Nazi Fanatic Did Next: Switched to Islam, Two Faces, two Converts—Two Muslim Extremists in Britain," *The Times*, 24 April 2006.

Zakariya, Yahia Abu, *IslamOnline*.net—8 November 2003, http://www.islamonline.net/English/News/2003-11/08/article08.shtml.

Zawahiri, Ayman al-, *al-Mujahidin* see Memri, 12 June 2002.

Index

Verhofstadt, Prime Minister Guy, 90
Vienna, 1, 11, 14, 26, 136, 139-140, 143,
    198
    Conference of European Imams in,
        139, 141
    Islamic Academy, 139
    Mosque, 139
    Muslim cemetery, 142
    Ringstrasse, 14, 136
Virginia, 101
Visigoth, Ostrogoth, Huns, 34
Voivodina, 23

Wahhabi, 4, 41, 89, 111, 114, 175
Wall Street Journal, 52
War, 8, 12, 48, 119, 134, 160
    Afghanistan, (see Afghanistan), 9
    Civil, 69
    Cold, 9, 121
    Culture, 57, 72
    Gulf, (see Gulf), 77
    Iran-Iraq, 65, 225
    Iraq, (see Iraq)
    Ridda (Apostasy), 116
    Sinai /Suez, 204
    World War I, 1, 201
    World War II, 12, 15, 46, 51, 54, 57,
        63, 66-67, 79, 80, 82, 87, 137, 190,
        202, 209
World War III, 28
Washington (DC), 11, 41, 52, 81, 104
    Georgetown University, 140
    Post, 26 125
    terror against, 101
Weekly Standard, 58
Weigel, George, 56-57
Weitzel, Victor, 92

Weltwoche, 131
West, 1, 3, 6-10, 12-14, 19, 34, 37, 43,
    119-121, 128-129
    anti, 2, 5, 20, 34, 45-46, 62, 148, 231
    civilization, 32, 37-39, 46, 127, 129,
        160, 188, 219
    democracies, 16-17, 47, 51
    immigration to, 17, 19, 47
    pro, 4
West Bank, 16, 39, 148, 230, 242
    and Gaza, 178
Wiesel, Elie, 91
Wilders, MP Geert, 71, 73, 76, 81-82, 86
Winkler, Beate, 26
Winter, Leon de, 73-74

Yale University, 220
Yarkas, Imad Eddin (Abu Dahdah), 101
Yemen, 52, 133
Yugoslavia, 14, 153, 171, 198, 201-202,
    210

Zagreb, 201, 213
Zapatero, Prime Minister Jose Luis, 56,
    96-97
Zarqawi, abu Mus'ab, 29, 43, 171
Zawahiri, Ayman, 161
Zimbabwe, 23
Zionism, 91, 246
    anti, 3, 44-45, 50, 92, 128, 162, 208,
        243
    conspiracy, 128
    Pro, 128-129
Zougam, Jamal, 96-97
Zoroastrian, 11, 36
Zurich, 108, 130